The American Revolution

BY
CINDY BARDEN

COPYRIGHT © 2001 Mark Twain Media, Inc.

ISBN 1-58037-176-0

Printing No. CD-1397

Mark Twain Media, Inc., Publishers
Distributed by Carson-Dellosa Publishing Company, Inc.

Table of Contents

About the American History Series

Welcome to *The American Revolution,* one of the books in the Mark Twain Media, Inc., American History series for students in grades four to seven.

The activity books in this series are designed as stand-alone material for classrooms and home-schoolers or as supplemental material to enhance your history curriculum. Students can be encouraged to use the books as independent study units to improve their understanding of historical events and people.

Each book provides challenging activities that enable students to explore history, geography, and social studies topics. The activities provide research opportunities and promote critical reading, thinking, and writing skills. As students follow the exploits of famous patriots and statesmen and learn about the people who influenced history, they will draw conclusions; write opinions; compare and contrast historical events, people, and places; analyze cause and effect; and improve mapping skills. Students will also have the opportunity to apply what they learn to their own lives through reflection and creative writing.

Students can further increase their knowledge and understanding of historical events by using reference sources at the library and on the Internet. Students may need assistance to learn how to use search engines and discover appropriate websites.

Titles of books for additional reading appropriate to the subject matter at this grade level are included in each book.

Although many of the questions are open-ended, an answer key is included at the back of the book for questions with specific answers.

Share a journey through history with your children as you explore the books in the Mark Twain Media, Inc., American History series:

Discovering and Exploring the Americas
Life in the Colonies
The American Revolution
The Lewis and Clark Expedition
The Westward Movement
The California Gold Rush
The Oregon and Sante Fe Trails
Slavery in the United States
The American Civil War
Abraham Lincoln and His Times
The Reconstruction Era
Industrialization in America
The Roaring Twenties and Great Depression
World War II and the Post-War Years
America in the 1960s and 1970s
America in the 1980s and 1990s

Time Line of *The American Revolution*

1733 • Molasses Act imposed taxes on molasses, rum, and sugar.

1754 • French and Indian War began.

1760 • Bray School for African-American children opened in Williamsburg.
 • George III became king of England.

1763 • Treaty of Paris ended French and Indian War.
 • Proclamation of 1763 forbade colonists to settle west of the Appalachian Mountains.

1764 • Sugar Act taxed colonists on lumber, molasses, rum, and other foods.
 • Currency Act prevented colonies from issuing their own money and devaluated colonial scrip.

1765 • Quartering Act required colonists to provide barracks and supplies for British troops.
 • Stamp Act required colonists to buy government stamps for documents, etc.

1766 • Stamp Act repealed.
 • Declaratory Act gave Parliament the right to tax colonists.

1767 • Townshend Duties taxed colonists on glass, paper, and tea.

1769 • Patrick Henry delivered "Give me liberty ..." speech.
 • Stamp Act Congress pledged not to pay taxes unless approved by colonial legislatures.

1770 • Boston Massacre.
 • Townshend Acts repealed, except tax on tea.

1773 • Tea Act gave British East India Company a monopoly on tea trade in the colonies.
 • Boston Tea Party.

1774 • Intolerable Acts closed the port of Boston and decreased powers of local authority.
 • General Gage and troops arrived in Boston.
 • First Continental Congress met in Philadelphia.

1775 • **April 19:** Battle at Lexington and Concord.
 • **May 10:** Second Continental Congress met.
 • **June 10:** George Washington named commander in chief of Continental Army.
 • **June 12:** Battle at Breed's Hill.

1776 • **July 4:** Declaration of Independence approved.
 • **August 1:** British defeated at Charleston.
 • **August 27–29:** British defeated Washington in Battle of Long Island.
 • **September 6:** First submarine, the *Turtle,* failed to sink Admiral Howe's flagship.
 • **September 22:** Nathan Hale hanged as a spy.
 • **October 28:** Battle of White Plains.
 • **November 16:** British forces captured Fort Washington.

1776 • **December 19:** Thomas Paine published *The Crisis.*
· • **December 25–26:** Washington crossed the Delaware River and attacked the British at Trenton, New Jersey.

1777 • **January 3:** Washington drove the British from Princeton, New Jersey.
· • **June 14:** Congress authorized a United States flag.
· • **July:** The Vermont Constitution abolished slavery.
· • **July 6:** British recaptured Fort Ticonderoga.
· • **September 9–11:** Battle of Brandywine: British forced Washington's army back towards Philadelphia.
· • **September 26:** British captured Philadelphia.
· • **October 4–5:** British won Battle of Germantown.
· • **October 17:** Americans defeated British at Saratoga.
· • **November 15:** Continental Congress approved the Articles of Confederation.
· • **December 17:** Washington's army went into winter quarters at Valley Forge.

1778 • **June 27–28:** Battle of Monmouth.
· • **July 20:** American forces captured fort at Vincennes, Indiana.
· • **August 8:** Battle at Newport, Rhode Island.
· • **September 14:** Benjamin Franklin was appointed Ambassador to France.
· • **December 29:** British captured Savannah, Georgia.

1779 • **January 29:** British captured Augusta, Georgia.
· • **June 1:** British captured forts at Stony Point and Verplanck, New York.
· • **September 23:** John Paul Jones captured British warship, *Serapis.*
· • **September 27:** Congress appointed John Adams to negotiate peace with England.
· • **October 17:** Washington led troops to winter quarters in Morristown, New Jersey.

1780 • **May 12:** Charleston surrendered to the British.
· • **June 23:** British defeated at Battle of Springfield, New Jersey.
· • **September 8:** British forces began invading South Carolina.
· • **September 23–25:** Benedict Arnold revealed as a traitor.
· • **October 7:** American militia won at King's Mountain, North Carolina.

1781 • **March 1:** Articles of Confederation ratified by all states.
· • **March 16:** British won the Battle of Guilford Courthouse.
· • **May 9:** British surrendered Pensacola, Florida, to Spanish.
· • **September 8:** American forces defeated at Eutaw Springs, South Carolina.
· • **October 19:** British surrendered at Yorktown.

1782 • **January:** Loyalists began leaving for Canada or England.
· • **April 12:** Peace talks between Great Britain and the United States began.
· • **October 8:** The United States and the Netherlands signed treaty of commerce and friendship.
· • **November 30:** Preliminary peace treaty signed between the United States and Great Britain.

1783 • **September 1:** Treaty of Paris signed.

3

Name: _____ Date: _____

George III Becomes King

Until George III became king of England in 1760, the colonists had been largely ignored by the king and Parliament of England, mostly because they had been too busy taking care of other matters.

British laws had regulated the government of the colonies from the beginning. For the most part, however, England felt the colonies existed mainly for one purpose—to provide economic benefits for the mother country through trade.

The colonists could send raw materials only to England and only on British ships. They were also expected to buy goods only from England, sent on British ships. Goods imported from or exported to other countries were heavily taxed.

The colonists rarely objected at first, because the prices of goods from England were usually less than the cost of the same goods from other countries. Although they lived far away, the colonists considered themselves subjects of England and loyal to the king.

In 1760, a new king took over the throne of England. King George III, who ruled Great Britain for 60 years, played an important role in the American Revolution.

1. How old was George the III when he became king of England? _____

2. Do you think the colonists would have agreed that they existed only for the benefit of the mother country? Why or why not?

   _____

   _____

   _____

   _____

3. Use a dictionary to define *import*. _____

   _____

4. Use a dictionary to define *export*. _____

   _____

5. Why do you think England taxed goods imported from or exported to other countries?

   _____

   _____

   _____

   _____

Name: _____ Date: _____

What Caused the Revolutionary War?

In 1763, Great Britain finally ended a period of wars with various European powers that had gone on for over 70 years. The last of those wars was the French and Indian War (1754–1763) in North America.

Although the British Empire was at the height of its power, the country was deeply in debt and needed money to repay loans and rebuild the royal treasury.

Since the people in England were already paying high taxes, King George III and the British Parliament decided to raise money by taxing the American colonists. After all, they reasoned, it had cost money for the British government to defend the colonies from the French and Indians, so it was only right that they pay their fair share.

The taxes made many of the colonists very angry because they had no representatives in Parliament to vote against the taxes or speak for the interests of the colonists. That's what Patrick Henry meant when he said, "Taxation without representation is tyranny."

It would have been difficult for anyone to represent the colonies in Parliament at that time, even if it had been allowed, because of the distance and time it took for messages to travel back and forth by ship. If a representative in England had sent news about a proposed law or tax to the colonies, it would have taken about two months for the news to arrive. Then it would have taken another two months for the colonists to send a reply after they made a decision. By that time, the situation could have changed completely.

1. Do you think King George III had good reasons for deciding to raise money by taxing the colonists? Why or why not?

   _____

   _____

   _____

   _____

2. Use a dictionary to define *tyranny.* _____

   _____

   _____

3. List methods of communication and travel we have today that weren't available to the colonists.

   _____

   _____

4. Use the Internet or other resources to find out how long it takes to travel by plane from New York to England today.

   _____

Name: _____   Date: _____

Expansion of the British Empire

Following the French and Indian War, England acquired much territory in the New World. All of North America north of Spanish-controlled Florida and as far west as the Mississippi River now belonged to England. This included land in Canada formerly controlled by France.

1. The area controlled by Great Britain prior to 1763 is shown on the map. Color in the area Great Britain controlled after the French and Indian War.

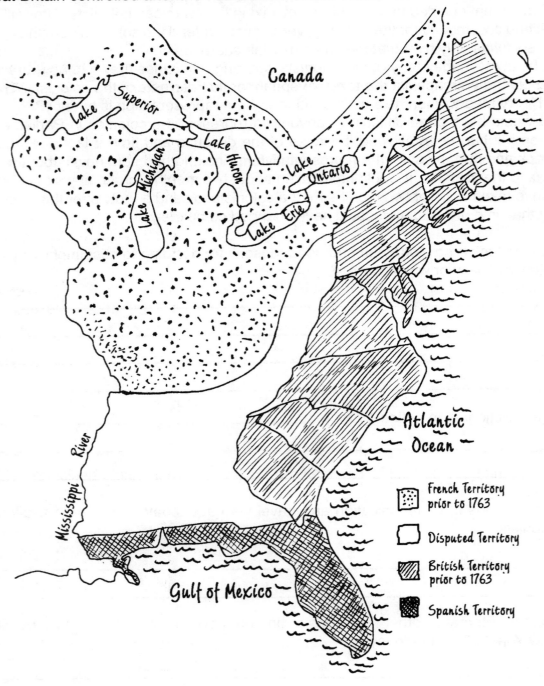

Name: _____ Date: _____

Colonists Forbidden to Move West

The French and Indian War lasted from 1756 until 1763. The combined efforts of British troops and American colonists had defeated the French and their allies. As a result, France was forced to give up almost all of her territory in North America.

With French control broken, colonists expected to expand their settlements to the "West." At that time, the West meant the area from the Appalachian Mountains to the Mississippi River.

Those hopes were dashed when England passed the Proclamation of 1763 forbidding any settlements west of the Appalachian Mountains.

England had made promises to several tribes to keep colonists east of the Appalachians. There had also been an uprising in 1763 led by the Ottawa Chief Pontiac during which many settlers' cabins were burned and people were killed. England feared if more settlers moved west, this would cause further uprisings. It would also force England to maintain a large army to keep the peace.

The Proclamation of 1763 angered many colonists who had lived in that area for more than 20 years. Some had been forced to flee during the uprising, but most planned to return to their homes. Thousands of other immigrants planned to move to the new territory once the war ended. Since the colonists had fought with the British against France and they were part of the British Empire, they considered the territory theirs also.

For the most part, the colonists simply ignored the Proclamation of 1763 and continued to move west. Led by Daniel Boone and other frontiersmen, settlers moved into western Pennsylvania, Kentucky, Tennessee, Ohio, Indiana, and Illinois.

1. Why do you think colonists considered the area from the Appalachians to the Mississippi River the West?

_____

_____

2. Do you think restricting settlement in the West was a reasonable decision? Why or why not?

_____

_____

3. Do you think the colonists had a legitimate complaint about the Proclamation of 1763? Why or why not?

_____

_____

Name: _____ Date: _____

Poor Richard's Almanack

Benjamin Franklin published his famous almanac from the time he was 26 in 1733 until he was 52 years old. Read each of these sayings from *Poor Richard's Almanack*. Explain what you think each one means.

1. People who are wrapped up in themselves make small packages.

   _____

   _____

2. To lengthen thy life, lessen thy meals.

   _____

   _____

3. Little strokes fell big oaks.

   _____

   _____

4. Never confuse motion with action.

   _____

   _____

5. Energy and persistence conquer all things.

   _____

   _____

6. Fish and visitors smell in three days.

   _____

   _____

7. Haste makes waste.

   _____

   _____

8. An empty bag cannot stand upright.

   _____

   _____

Write some words of wisdom of your own in the same style used by Benjamin Franklin.

_____

_____

_____

Name: _____   Date: _____

Taxes on Sugar and Molasses

The Sugar Act, passed by Parliament on April 5, 1764, imposed a tax on all molasses and sugar imported by the colonies from the French and Spanish West Indies.

A similar tax, called the Molasses Act, had been passed in 1733, but it had been mostly ignored. The colonists refused to pay the tax and simply smuggled the goods into the country. The British government didn't try very hard to enforce the law, either.

However, this time the British were determined to enforce the Sugar Act. They sent inspectors to search warehouses and even private residences. The colonists resented paying the taxes and the invasion of their privacy.

The British also offered rewards to citizens who reported anyone smuggling these products. When a smuggler was arrested, the judge who found him guilty also received a reward.

1. Use reference sources: What is molasses?

   _____

   _____

2. If you had been a colonist, how would you have felt if someone had searched your home?

   _____

   _____

   _____

3. Under the circumstances described above, do you think someone accused of smuggling would receive a fair trial? Why or why not?

   _____

   _____

   _____

   _____

   _____

4. Write a slogan on the sign at the right that the colonists might have used to express their feelings about the Sugar Act.

Name: _____ Date: _____

Two New Laws Affect the Colonies

As businesses grew in the colonies, the barter system that had worked before wasn't as effective any more. People needed money.

Several of the colonies began printing their own money, called colonial scrip. British bankers didn't like this, because that meant they might lose control of the American economy.

The Currency Act of 1764 prohibited the colonies from issuing their own money. It also required colonists to use only British money. When colonists exchanged colonial scrip for British goods or money, their money was worth only half as much.

In essence, this doubled the value of British money and cut the price of goods in half for the British, but had the opposite effect on the colonists. They had to pay double for products.

Unlike most of the other laws Parliament passed, this one wasn't designed to raise money through taxes. It was designed to control the American economy.

Another law designed to control the colonists was the Quartering Act of 1765.

1. Use reference sources. What is the barter system? _____

   _____

   _____

2. Give an example of how you could use the barter system today. _____

   _____

   _____

3. If you suddenly found that everything you wanted to buy now cost twice as much as before, how would you feel?

   _____

   _____

4. What did the Quartering Act require colonists to do? _____

   _____

   _____

5. Why did Parliament pass the Quartering Act? _____

   _____

6. How did the colonists react to this new law? _____

   _____

Name: _____ Date: _____

Stamps Required

It was common in England to raise money by requiring people to buy government stamps for all official documents. On March 22, 1765, a similar law went into effect in the colonies. The Stamp Act required colonists to pay for a government stamp on all newspapers, pamphlets, playing cards, dice, documents, and legal papers, including marriage licenses.

This tax was imposed to raise money to pay part of the cost for wages and expenses of the 10,000 British soldiers stationed to defend the frontiers against Native American attacks.

Again, colonists protested that Parliament didn't have the right to tax them because they had no members in Parliament to represent them, a right guaranteed by the British Constitution. Patrick Henry gave a fiery speech. The Virginia House of Burgesses declared the Stamp Act illegal and passed resolutions saying England had no right to tax people in Virginia.

In October 1765, delegates from nine colonies met in New York. The group, known as the Stamp Act Congress, pledged to resist paying any taxes not approved by their colonial legislatures. Many merchants also promised to stop importing British goods. Colonists organized groups like the Sons of Liberty whose members had strong feelings against unjust taxes.

Angry crowds met the Stamp Masters when they arrived from England to enforce the law. People rioted, destroyed offices, burned the stamps, and forced many Stamp Masters to resign or leave town.

The Stamp Act caused so much dissension that it was repealed a year later. However, Parliament passed a Declaratory Act, which gave them the right to pass laws in the colonies.

1. Do you think it was unreasonable to expect the colonists to pay part of the cost for the British troops? Why or why not?

   _____

   _____

   _____

   _____

   _____

2. Many colonists felt they were justified in using violence. Do you agree or disagree? Why?

   _____

   _____

   _____

   _____

   _____

Name: _____ Date: _____

Rules of Civility & Decent Behaviour in Company and Conversation

    Children in the colonies learned to read and write by copying from other sources—over and over. As they wrote, they were expected to learn.

    When George Washington was a boy, there were over 100 "Rules of Civility & Decent Behaviour In Company and Conversation" to be written and learned. Notice that the spelling, capitalization, and punctuation used was much different.

Rewrite each rule using modern words and grammar on another sheet of paper. Use a dictionary if you need help with a word.

Example: Be not apt to relate News if you know not the truth thereof. <u>Don't spread gossip.</u>

1. Being Set at meat Scratch not neither Spit Cough or blow your Nose except there's a Necessity for it.

2. In the Presence of Others Sing not to yourself with a humming Noise, nor Drum with your Fingers or Feet.

3. If You Cough, Sneeze, Sigh, or Yawn, do it not Loud but Privately.

4. Speak not in your Yawning, but put Your handkercheif or Hand before your face and turn aside.

5. Spit not in the Fire, nor Stoop low before it.

6. Be not hasty to beleive flying Reports to the Disparagement of any.

7. While you are talking, Point not with your Finger at him of Whom you Discourse nor Approach too near him to whom you talk especially to his face.

8. Be not Curious to Know the Affairs of Others neither approach those that Speak in Private.

9. Speak not Evil of the absent for it is unjust.

10. Put not your meat to your Mouth with your Knife in your hand neither Spit forth the Stones of any fruit Pye upon a Dish nor Cast anything under the table.

Name: _____   Date: _____

The Rebels Unite

Many groups formed to protest the laws and taxes imposed by King George III and Parliament. Some were merely discussion groups. Others were more active.

Sam Adams was one of the first prominent men in Boston to openly favor separation from Great Britain. He formed a secret radical group known as the Sons of Liberty. Men in other colonies formed similar organizations. They set up Committees of Correspondence to communicate with each other.

After England passed the Stamp Act, Adams recruited more members for the Sons of Liberty and led them in attacks on stamp distributors, customs agents, and other officials loyal to Great Britain.

Minutemen, groups of local militia who promised to be ready at a minute's notice, secretly prepared to fight the British. They gathered weapons and ammunition and trained as soldiers. When they received Paul Revere's warning, the Minutemen gathered at Lexington to meet the British troops.

Samuel Adams

1. Use a dictionary to define *correspondence*.

_____

_____

_____

_____

_____

_____

2. Use a dictionary to define *militia*.

_____

_____

_____

_____

_____

_____

3. Use reference sources to learn more about the Sons of Liberty or the Minutemen. On your own paper discuss the men who joined the organizations, their goals, and activities.

Name: _____ Date: _____

More Taxes in 1767

Passed on June 29, 1767, the Townshend Duties were taxes on glass, lead, paint, paper, and tea shipped to the colonies. A board of customs commissioners (tax collectors) was sent to Boston.

Mobs in Boston and other towns threatened and harassed tax collectors, who wrote urgent letters to London asking for protection. The colonists also began to boycott British goods.

The colonists hoped that by boycotting British goods, English merchants would lose so much money that they would complain to Parliament and persuade them to lift the taxes.

General Gage sent troops to Boston in 1768 to protect the customs officials. This caused further problems, more anger, and retaliation on the part of the colonists.

The British soldiers wore red coats as part of their uniforms. People who resented the presence of the soldiers called them "Redcoats" and "Lobsterbacks," using those terms to make fun of the soldiers.

Again the British backed down and repealed all of the Townshend Duties on March 5, 1770, except for the tax on tea. On the same day that the Townshend Duties were repealed in England, a mob in Boston attacked British troops. The soldiers killed five people. Colonists called this event the "Boston Massacre."

The one good thing that resulted from the Boston Massacre was that British troops were withdrawn from Boston.

1. Use a dictionary to define *boycott*.

   _____

   _____

2. Do you think the boycott was good reasoning on the colonists' part? Why or why not?

   _____

   _____

3. Why do you think the colonists used the term "Lobsterbacks" for the soldiers?

   _____

   _____

4. Use a dictionary to define *massacre*.

   _____

   _____

5. Do you think what happened in Boston was really a massacre? Why or why not?

   _____

   _____

Name: _____ Date: _____

Revolutionary Women's Organizations

Sarah Franklin Bache

In 1774, a group of 51 women in Edenton, North Carolina, led by Penelope Barker signed the Edenton Proclamation, stating they had a duty to become involved in political issues affecting the colonies. They announced they would not buy tea or English-made clothing. The British believed this was an insult to England.

In 1770, Esther Reed began a nationwide drive to raise funds for soldiers. She published a broadside titled "The Sentiments of an American Woman" explaining why women should become involved.

In Philadelphia, 36 women formed a group called the Association to collect money from other women in the city for soldiers. They raised over $300,000 and served as an example for similar groups in at least seven other colonies.

When Reed approached General Washington, he told her it would be better to provide clothing for the soldiers than to give them money that they might spend foolishly.

When Esther Reed died, Sarah Franklin Bache took charge. Using her home as headquarters, volunteers made nearly 2,200 shirts. Each was signed by the woman who made it.

Women formed groups known as the Daughters of Liberty. They met to discuss the political situation and plan ways they could assist in opposing the British. They also contributed their skills at sewing, knitting, and weaving cloth.

When a 4,000-pound lead statue of King George was pulled down by Patriots in New York, a group of women broke the statue into small pieces, melted the lead, and made more than 40,000 musket balls.

1. Why do you think the British felt the Edenton Proclamation was an insult?

   _____

   _____

2. Boycotts by colonial women proved very effective. Why do you think boycotts supported by both men and women would be a good way to prove to the British how strongly they felt about taxes?

   _____

   _____

3. Use reference sources. Explain what a broadside was. _____

   _____

4. Do you think Washington was correct? Why or why not? _____

   _____

5. Why was sewing and making clothing an important contribution? _____

   _____

15

Name: _____ Date: _____

Would You Like a Cup of Tea?

The British East India Company controlled the tea trade between India, Great Britain, and her colonies. By 1773, this company had a surplus of over 18 million pounds of tea. The tax on tea and the boycotts of British products by colonists had hurt the company.

On May 10, 1773, Parliament passed the Tea Act. Rather than raising the tax on tea, it actually lowered it. By lowering the price, it was hoped that the colonists would buy more tea. The law also permitted the British East India Company to sell tea directly to the colonies through its own agents.

It would seem that any law that lowered taxes would be welcomed by the colonists, but that wasn't the case. The first to protest were colonial merchants who had been making money importing tea (sometimes legally, sometimes by smuggling). Other merchants joined the protest. They feared that if Parliament could grant a monopoly on tea to one company, it might grant monopolies on other products also, putting them out of business.

Merchants stirred up the colonial radicals by claiming this was simply another sneaky way for England to tax the colonists. As a result, crowds rioted in protest. In Annapolis, one tea ship was burned. Other ships carrying tea were forced to leave without unloading.

1. Use reference sources to learn more about the British East India Company, when it began, why it had a surplus of tea, and why it was able to influence Parliament to change laws.

_____

_____

_____

_____

_____

2. Do you think it's right for a government to favor a large company by giving it special rights or privileges? Why or why not?

_____

_____

3. Use a dictionary to define *monopoly.* _____

_____

4. Do you think the colonial merchants had a good reason for protesting the Tea Act? Why or why not?

_____

_____

_____

Name: _____ Date: _____

The Boston Tea Party

When three British ships anchored in Boston Harbor and re-fused to leave without unloading, several thousand colonists com-plained to the governor, but he refused to listen. In protest of the Tea Tax, about 150 colonists disguised as Native Americans dumped 340 chests of tea into Boston Harbor on the night of December 16, 1773.

After the Boston Tea Party, people began singing this verse:

Rally, Mohawks! Bring out your axes
And tell King George we'll pay no more taxes!

1. Why do you think this incident was called a "tea party"?

   _____

2. If you had lived in Boston then, would you have participated in the Boston Tea Party? Why or why not?

   _____

   _____

3. A report of the infamous tea party arrived in London on January 27, 1774. Why did it take so long for the news to arrive?

   _____

4. If you had been the king of England, what do you think your response to this news would have been?

   _____

   _____

   Most states have sales taxes. In addition, some counties and cities have additional sales tax.

5. How much is the sales tax where you live? _____

6. Find out the price of a pound of tea at a local store. (Prices will vary depending on the type of tea.) Cost of one pound of tea: _____

7. Calculate the sales tax you would pay on the tea. _____

8. The tax on tea that led to the Boston Tea Party amounted to three cents a pound. How does that compare with the tax on tea you would pay?

   _____

Did You Know? There was another "tea party" in the colonies. At the Yorktown Tea Party on November 7, 1774, two half-chests of tea were thrown into the York River.

      17

Name: _____ Date: _____

Tidbits of Trivia

- One popular variety of green asparagus was named after Martha Washington.

- The Marquis de Lafayette, the colonists' ally during the Revolutionary War, named his only son George Washington Lafayette.

- George Washington never lived in the White House. It wasn't built yet.

- George Washington had two ice cream freezers at his home in Mount Vernon.

- One of Benjamin Franklin's many inventions was a glass harmonica. He made the first one in 1761, using 42 hand-blown glass bowls placed on a rotating spindle that the player rubs with his or her fingers. It is so difficult to play that less then 50 people in the world know how.

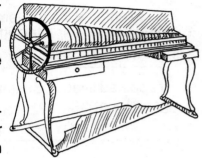

- During the 1700s, people who spent the night at inns when traveling slept in beds with straw mattresses. It wasn't unusual for travelers to be asked to share their beds with strangers when there was a shortage of beds.

- During the Revolutionary War, more inhabitants of the colonies fought for the British than for the Continental Army. Only 16 percent of able-bodied men in the colonies fought in the Continental Army.

- Thomas Jefferson was upset by the changes made in the original version of the Declaration of Independence. For years after, he sent copies of both versions to friends asking their opinions of which they liked better.

- George Washington, Thomas Jefferson, and John Adams enjoyed collecting and playing marbles, a popular game for both children and adults.

- The British paid Hessian soldiers about 25 cents a day to fight against the colonists in the Revolutionary War.

Use reference sources to find two other interesting tidbits of Revolutionary War trivia.

_____

_____

_____

_____

_____

_____

Name: _____ Date: _____

The Intolerable Acts

In retaliation for the Boston Tea Party, Parliament passed what the colonists called the Intolerable Acts.

The Intolerable Acts closed the port of Boston to all shipping. This was to remain in effect until the colonists paid for the dumped tea.

The Intolerable Acts also decreased the powers of the local authority, the Massachusetts Assembly, and increased the power of royal officials. Only one town meeting would be allowed per year.

To enforce the Intolerable Acts, the British sent General Thomas Gage and regiments of soldiers to Boston. A new Quartering Act allowed the British commander to house his troops wherever he wished, even in private homes against the will of the owners.

General Thomas Gage

Although these laws mostly affected those living in Boston, people throughout the colonies protested the Intolerable Acts.

The assemblies (local ruling governments) from various colonies sent protests to England, in the hope that Parliament would repeal the laws. Again England reacted harshly. More than half the colonial assemblies were suspended.

1. Use a dictionary to define *retaliation*. _____

    _____

2. Use a dictionary to define *intolerable*. _____

    _____

3. Do you think passing the Intolerable Acts was a reasonable response to the Boston Tea Party? Why or why not?

    _____

    _____

4. What do you think British leaders hoped to accomplish by allowing people in Massachusetts only one town meeting per year?

    _____

    _____

5. How would you have felt if you had been a colonist and were told that from now on five British soldiers would be living in your home?

    _____

    _____

6. Why do you think people who didn't live in Boston objected to these laws?

    _____

    _____

Name: _____   Date: _____

The First Continental Congress Meets

In protest of the Intolerable Acts, the First Continental Congress met in Philadelphia in September, 1774. Twelve of the thirteen colonies sent representatives.

Although the idea of freedom from British rule and taxes was a very attractive prospect, winning a war against the mightiest country in the world seemed almost hopeless.

Some members of the Congress wanted to break all ties with England. Other members wanted peace with England and tried to persuade the king to repeal the Intolerable Acts. Some members tried to find a compromise that both England and the colonies could agree upon.

After weeks of debate, members of the First Continental Congress agreed to stop all trade with England. If England used force against Massachusetts, they would all resist. They resolved to meet again in May, 1775, if the situation did not improve.

While the First Continental Congress met and debated the issues, colonists in Massachusetts began arming themselves, forming militia groups, and storing gunpowder and weapons. Clashes between colonists and British troops became more frequent.

General Gage, the royal governor of Massachusetts sent to enforce the Intolerable Acts, sent reports to England explaining that the situation was getting much worse. He suggested temporarily suspending the Intolerable Acts and requested an additional 20,000 troops.

Leaders in England thought his reports were exaggerated. They felt he had more than enough troops to put down a few rebels in Boston. The king refused to suspend the Intolerable Acts. If New England was in a state of rebellion, "... blows must decide whether they are to be subject to this country or independent," he stated.

1. Use reference sources. Which colony did not send representatives to the First Continental Congress and why?

   _____

   _____

   _____

2. Which method would you have chosen: rebellion, peace, or compromise? Explain your reasons.

   _____

   _____

   _____

3. What do you think King George III meant by those words?

   _____

   _____

   _____

   _____

Name: _____ Date: _____

A Declaration of War—and of Independence

War or peace? Debates raged for weeks at the Second Continental Congress. Finally, on June 7, 1776, Richard Henry Lee of Virginia proposed this resolution:

"The United Colonies are, and of right ought to be, free and independent states."

The Congress appointed a committee of five men to write a declaration based on Lee's proposal. Fill in the chart with information about the men they selected.

Committee Member	Age	Colony	Occupation
Benjamin Franklin	70		Printer, inventor, scientist, diplomat
Thomas Jefferson			Lawyer, inventor
John Adams		Massachusetts	
Roger Sherman	29		
Robert Livingston		New York	

Each member of the committee expressed his ideas of what should be included in the document, but the actual writing was left to Thomas Jefferson, a task that took 17 days.

For three days, members of the Continental Congress discussed the document Jefferson had written. Changes were made. One paragraph in the original that was deleted from the final version had to do with the abolition of slavery. Finally, on July 4, 1776, they voted to adopt the Declaration of Independence.

The Continental Congress decided to have an official copy printed in ornamental script on parchment. This was the copy that was signed by 56 members of the Congress on August 2, 1776.

When Benjamin Franklin signed his name, he stated, "We must all hang together, or surely we shall all hang separately."

Copies of the Declaration of Independence were printed in Philadelphia and sent to all the colonies. When read out loud in Philadelphia, John Adams reported, "The bells rang all day and almost all night."

1. Why do you think this document was called the "birth certificate of a new nation"?

   _____

   _____

   _____

2. What do you think Franklin meant by his statement?

   _____

   _____

   _____

Name: _____ Date: _____

Meet Benjamin Franklin

Born in Boston in 1706, Benjamin Franklin had 16 brothers and sisters. At the age of 10, after only two years of formal schooling, Franklin began working for his father, a soap and candle maker. Benjamin hated the job. When he was 15, his father apprenticed Benjamin to his older brother, James, a printer.

Using the pen name Silence Dogwood, Franklin secretly submitted a series of satirical essays poking fun at hypocrites and advocating equal rights for women and freedom of speech. Although the articles were praised by readers, James was furious when he found out Benjamin had written them.

Before he completed his apprenticeship, Franklin ran away to New York. Finding no printers there, he continued on to Philadelphia. During the next few years, Franklin traveled to London, worked for several printers, and clerked in a store in Philadelphia. At the age of 23, he purchased his own printing shop and began the *Pennsylvania Gazette.* A few years later, he started writing *Poor Richard's Almanack,* a highly successful "best seller."

When the newly-formed country needed an ambassador to France to earn support for the revolution, they chose Benjamin Franklin, a man many considered a genius.

Among his many other accomplishments, Ben Franklin ...

- ... started the first subscription library.
- ... organized the first volunteer fire department.
- ... initiated a street-paving project for Philadelphia.
- ... discovered that lightning was a form of electricity.
- ... invented bifocals, an odometer, the Franklin stove, the rocking chair, and crop insurance.
- ... proposed a system of daylight saving time.
- ... helped write the Declaration of Independence.

Franklin even influenced fashion. After he published instructions on how to make lightning rods, women in Europe began wearing lightning rods on their hats, with a ground wire trailing behind.

When Franklin died, he was mourned around the world. Comte de Mirabeau, a French nobleman, called him "a mighty genius" who freed men from their fears of "thunderbolts and tyrants."

1. Use a dictionary to define *apprentice.* _____

_____

_____

2. Use reference sources to learn more about Benjamin Franklin. On another sheet of paper, write a report about one aspect of Franklin's life: writer and printer, scientist, inventor, politician, or diplomat.

Name: _____ Date: _____

What Would They Have Said?

Work with a partner. Take turns writing a dialogue that might have taken place "off the record" during the Second Continental Congress between a person who wanted to declare war and colonial independence immediately and another who hoped to avoid war and make peace with England.

Person 1: _____

_____

Person 2: _____

_____

Person 1: _____

_____

Person 2: _____

_____

Person 1: _____

_____

Person 2: _____

_____

Person 1: _____

_____

Person 2: _____

_____

Person 1: _____

_____

Person 2: _____

_____

Name: _____ Date: _____

The Thirteen Original Colonies

Label the 13 colonies that became the first 13 states of the United States of America.

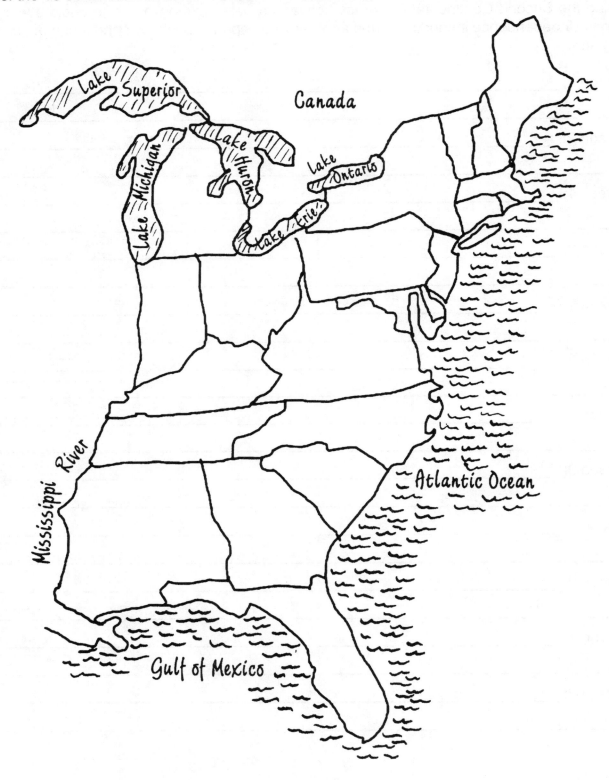

Name: _____ Date: _____

Meet Thomas Jefferson

Use reference sources to answer these questions and learn more about Thomas Jefferson.

1. When and where was Thomas Jefferson born?

   _____

2. Besides English, Thomas Jefferson could read, write, and speak four languages. What were they?

   _____

3. What instrument did Jefferson play?

   _____

Thomas Jefferson was a diplomat, writer, politician, musician, architect, and inventor. He became the third President of the United States.

4. Jefferson designed his mansion, built near Charlottesville, Virginia. What was his home called?

   _____

5. On January 1, 1772, Jefferson married a young widow. What was her name?

   _____

6. How many children did Jefferson and his wife have? _____

7. How long were Jefferson and his wife married? _____

8. Did Thomas Jefferson take part in the Boston Tea Party? _____

9. Thomas Jefferson is credited with inventing several items. Name two of his inventions.

   _____

10. To what position did George Washington appoint Jefferson while he was president?

    _____

11. What European country did Jefferson visit as a diplomat in 1785?

    _____

12. In the presidential election of 1796, Jefferson ran against a Federalist opponent. His opponent won, and Jefferson became vice president. Who was elected president?

    _____

13. What was unusual about the election of 1800?

    _____

    _____

14. Write two other facts you learned about Thomas Jefferson.

    _____

    _____

    _____

Name: _____   Date: _____

Time Line Activities

Use the time line on pages 2 and 3 to answer these questions.

Check the item in each group that came first.

1. ____ The French and Indian War ended.
   ____ George III became king of England.

2. ____ Patrick Henry gave his famous "Give me liberty" speech.
   ____ Great Britain passed the Stamp Act.

3. ____ Boston Massacre
   ____ Boston Tea Party

4. ____ George Washington named commander in chief.
   ____ Battles fought at Lexington and Concord.

5. ____ Declaration of Independence approved.
   ____ Articles of Confederation approved.

6. ____ The submarine, the *Turtle,* failed its mission.
   ____ John Paul Jones captured the British warship *Serapis.*

7. ____ Townshend Acts repealed.
   ____ Stamp Act repealed.

8. ____ British captured Philadelphia.
   ____ Americans won battle at Saratoga.

Use information from the time line to fill in the blanks.

9. When were the Intolerable Acts passed? _____

10. What act by Parliament forbade settlements west of the Appalachian Mountains?

_____

11. What British company was given a monopoly on the tea trade in 1773?

_____

12. Where were the winter quarters for General George Washington and the Continental Army in 1779?

_____

13. Who was hanged as a traitor in 1776? _____

14. Who did the Continental Congress appoint to negotiate peace with Great Britain in 1779?

_____

15. Which river did George Washington and his troop cross to attack the British at Trenton, New Jersey, in 1776?

_____

Name: _____ Date: _____

The Colonies Unite

Eight days after the Second Continental Congress approved the Declaration of Independence, John Dickinson presented a proposal for unifying the colonies. This proposal included provisions for a strong central government that would control the western lands, have the power to levy taxes, and allow equal representation for each state.

Dickinson's proposal was not acceptable to most representatives. They feared a central government could become too strong and powerful. If that happened, they would be no better off than they were under British rule.

Changes to the document, which became the Articles of Confederation, gave each state as much independence as possible and limited the functions of the federal government. As modified, the Articles of Confederation provided for a loose alliance of states with limited powers in a central government.

- The federal government would consist of a Congress in which each state had one vote.
- Congress would have the power to set up a postal department, to request donations from the states to cover costs, to raise armed forces, and to control the western territories.
- With consent from 9 of the 13 states, Congress could also coin money, borrow money, declare war, and sign treaties and alliances with other countries.
- Any amendments to the Articles of Confederation required the approval of all 13 states.

1. What do you think would have happened if the 13 colonies had tried to fight Great Britain individually?

   _____

   _____

2. Do you think the representatives had good reasons for their fears? Why or why not?

   _____

   _____

3. Which provision in the Articles of Confederation do you think was the weakest? Explain your answer.

   _____

   _____

4. Which provision do you think was the strongest? Explain your answer.

   _____

   _____

Name: _____ Date: _____

Problems With the Articles of Confederation

Even with the changes, it took until March 1, 1781, for all of the states to ratify the Articles of Confederation. There were several reasons for the delay.

• Many states were preoccupied with the Revolutionary War.

• Several states quarreled over boundary lines with each other.

• Each state already had its own courts, tariff laws, and trade agreements and didn't want to be forced to change.

• Smaller states wanted equal representation with larger ones.

• Larger states feared they would have to pay more than their share to support the federal government.

• The states disagreed about control over the western territories.

Besides not establishing a strong central government, there were several other weaknesses in the Articles of Confederation.

Although the Articles of Confederation were weak, they did help hold the new nation together until a stronger document, the United States Constitution, was written in 1787 and approved in 1789.

Use a dictionary to define these words.

1. confederation: _____

2. levy: _____

3. ratify: _____

4. judicial: _____

Comment on each of these weaknesses.

5. There was no provision for a leader of the federal government.

_____

_____

6. There was no federal judicial branch of government.

_____

_____

7. Congress could not levy any taxes even to pay soldiers or repay debts.

_____

_____

Name: _____ Date: _____

Be a History Detective

Many of the stories told about George Washington exaggerated the truth or were completely fictional. Be a history detective. Use reference sources to search for the truth about George Washington. Write FACT or FICTION on the line before each statement.

1. _____ When Washington was a child, he chopped down one of his father's favorite cherry trees. When questioned, he said, "I cannot tell a lie," and admitted he had done the deed.

2. _____ George Washington wanted a third term as president, but lost the election to John Adams.

During his life, many people believed George Washington was a great hero and patriot. After he died, people continued to tell stories of his greatness.

3. _____ Not only was George Washington the father of our country, he was also the father of a large family. He and his wife Martha had seven daughters and four sons.

4. _____ Not everyone admired Washington. Alexander Hamilton once wrote that Washington had "a heart of stone."

5. _____ George Washington wore a white, powdered wig because he was completely bald and didn't want anyone to know.

6. _____ George Washington once wrote: "O how I wish I had never seen the Continental Army! I would have done better to retire to the back country and live in a wigwam."

7. _____ During his second term as president, Washington was blasted in some newspapers and called "George I, Perpetual Dictator of the United States."

8. _____ George Washington owned slaves.

9. _____ George Washington was actually a large, imposing man as pictured in portraits done during his lifetime.

10. _____ During a campaign for political office in 1758, Washington supplied potential voters with large quantities of rum, wine, and beer.

Name: _____ Date: _____

Fact or Opinion?

A fact is a statement that can be verified as true.
> Fact: The Revolutionary War began in 1775.

An opinion is a statement that cannot be verified as true.
> Opinion: The colonists had the right to start the Revolutionary War.

Write F for fact or O for opinion on the line by each statement.

1. ____ George Washington was the first President of the United States.

2. ____ George Washington was the best president.

3. ____ The Boston Tea Party was justified.

4. ____ The Boston Tea Party was not justified.

5. ____ Benjamin Franklin invented many useful items.

6. ____ Benjamin Franklin was the smartest man in Philadelphia.

7. ____ The government in England did not treat the colonists fairly.

8. ____ The first battles of the Revolutionary War were fought at Lexington and Concord.

9. ____ Taxes on goods imported from England were unfair.

10. ____ The British government had the right to tax colonists.

11. ____ The British government did not have the right to tax colonists.

12. ____ Fifty-six men signed the Declaration of Independence.

13. ____ All the men who signed the Declaration of Independence were very brave.

14. ____ Taxes imposed on the colonists by Great Britain were one of the causes of the Revolutionary War.

15. ____ Paul Revere was a great hero of the Revolutionary War.

Name: _____ Date: _____

The Adams Family

Samuel Adams

Cousins John and Samuel Adams were both prominent political leaders during the Revolutionary War period. One became the President of the United States. The other founded the Sons of Liberty. But which was which? Use reference sources to find the answers. Write John, Sam, or both on the line before each statement.

John Adams

1. _____ He was the older of the two.

2. _____ He was sent to France as a diplomat in 1777.

3. _____ He was the first American diplomat to England after the Revolutionary War.

4. _____ He was governor of Massachusetts from 1789 to 1793.

5. _____ He was the second President of the United States.

6. _____ He died on the 50th anniversary of the Declaration of Independence.

7. _____ He founded the Sons of Liberty.

8. _____ He was a delegate to the Second Continental Congress.

9. _____ He attended Harvard College and became a lawyer.

10. _____ He was elected tax collector in 1756, a position he held for eight years.

11. _____ His son was elected President of the United States.

12. _____ He was born in Boston.

13. _____ He signed the Declaration of Independence.

14. _____ His marriage to Abigail Smith lasted 54 years.

Name: _____   Date: _____

What About the Founding Mothers?

> Female opinions are of no consequence in public matters.
>
> — printed in the *Pennsylvania Packet,* a colonial newspaper

History speaks of the founding fathers of our country. But what about the founding mothers? Didn't women make any contributions to history during the Revolutionary War? Weren't any women brave or patriotic?

During the eighteenth century, women received little formal education, had no property rights, couldn't vote, and were not considered citizens. Men felt politics was too difficult and dangerous for women. They thought women should be satisfied to stay at home; however, women didn't always agree.

Women usually had many children. Between cooking, baking, spinning, making clothing, churning butter, chopping firewood, tending animals, and other chores, they had little free time. Although running a home was more than a full-time job, many women wanted to become more involved in the decisions that affected their lives and the lives of their families.

Although her work was published anonymously, the writings of Mercy Otis Warren were widely read by colonists. She attacked British policies and representatives through articles, essays, and poems. Her two satirical plays, ridiculing the British for their corruption and inept administration, were published in a radical Boston newspaper.

When Timothy Thayer filled out enlistment papers in 1782, his true identity was discovered, and he was sent home in disgrace. Timothy's real name was Deborah Sampson. Deborah later became a colonial soldier and was wounded in battle. Her fellow soldiers knew her only as Robert Shurtleff. Another woman, known as Samuel Gay, was promoted to sergeant before she was discovered and dismissed. How many other women secretly became soldiers is unknown.

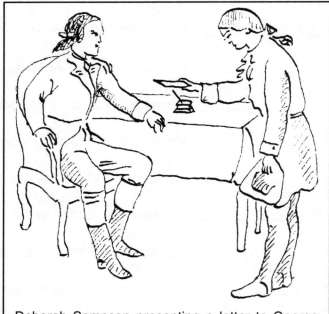

Deborah Sampson presenting a letter to George Washington.

1. Use reference sources to learn more about other women who played an important role in history at this time. On another sheet of paper, describe contributions made by three women.

Name: _____ Date: _____

A Flag of Freedom

The official flag of the United States adopted by the Continental Congress on June 14, 1777, had 13 red and white stripes and a circle of 13 white stars on a field of blue.

Not all soldiers in the Continental Army carried the new American flag into battle, however. Some carried regimental flags or state flags. At the beginning of the war, ships carried a yellow flag with a brown snake and the words: DON'T TREAD ON ME.

Design your own colonial flag on another sheet of paper. Explain what each of the colors, symbols, and words on your flag represent.

The colors represent: _____

_____

_____

_____

_____

_____

The symbols represent: _____

_____

_____

_____

_____

_____

The meaning of the words used: _____

_____

_____

_____

_____

_____

Name: _____   Date: _____

The War Rages On

The War of Independence was a costly and lengthy one for both the Americans and Great Britain. Beginning with the battles at Lexington and Concord in April, 1775, the war continued until the surrender at Yorktown in October 1781. It was another two years before Great Britain and the United States finally signed a peace treaty.

The Continental Army, under the direction of General Washington, achieved many victories against the British troops. They also suffered many defeats. Battles were fought on land and at sea, as far north as Quebec and Montreal in Canada, and as far south as Pensacola, Florida.

Use reference sources to learn more about one of the Revolutionary War battles. On another sheet of paper, write a newspaper article about the battle. In your article, answer these questions:

Who commanded the British army in that battle?

Who commanded the American army in that battle?

When was this battle fought?

Where was this battle fought?

Why was this battle fought?

Why was this battle important?

What did both sides hope to accomplish?

Who won the battle?

How did this battle affect the outcome of the Revolutionary War?

Some battles fought during the Revolutionary War were:

Long Island	Monmouth
White Plains	Augusta
Fort Washington	Charleston
Trenton	Springfield
Princeton	King's Mountain
Fort Ticonderoga	Guilford Courthouse
Brandywine	Charlottesville
Germantown	Chesapeake Bay
Saratoga	Eutaw Springs
Savannah	Yorktown

Name: _____ Date: _____

The *Turtle* Goes to War

Did you know that the first military submarine was invented and used during the Revolutionary War? The *Turtle,* a one-person vessel invented by David Bushnell, was designed to be used against British ships blockading New York Harbor in 1776.

Earlier attempts had been made to build submarines, but the *Turtle* was the first to dive, surface, and be used in naval combat. Only seven and a half feet long and six feet wide, this egg-shaped craft was constructed of oak and banded with iron. Riding in it must have seemed like being submerged in a barrel.

Besides being very small, the *Turtle* had a few problems. The submarine had only one means of propulsion. To move it under water, the operator had to vigorously crank a hand-turned propeller. Air supply on the *Turtle* was also a problem—it had none. The operator had to bring it to the surface every 30 minutes.

When a valve was opened to admit seawater into a ballast tank, the *Turtle* submerged. It rose when the tank was emptied by a hand pump. Lead ballast kept the submarine upright.

For weapons, the sub carried a gunpowder bomb with a time fuse. The *Turtle's* mission was to make an underwater approach to an enemy ship. Then the operator had to attach the bomb to the ship's hull using a screw device operated from within the craft. The other part of the plan involved leaving before the bomb exploded.

Sergeant Ezra Lee of the Continental Army made the one and only attempt to use the *Turtle* in battle. Lee was able to float the *Turtle* against the hull of the British flagship *HMS Eagle,* but he was unable to attach the explosive device because its hull was copper-plated. Lee and the *Turtle* escaped.

1. Use a dictionary to define *blockade.*

   _____

   _____

   _____

2. Use a dictionary to define *ballast.*

   _____

   _____

   _____

3. On another sheet of paper, draw a satirical cartoon of the battle between the *Turtle* and the *Eagle.*

Name: _____ Date: _____

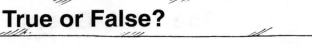

True or False?

Circle T for true or F for false.

1. T F Paul Revere warned the militia in Concord that British troops were on their way.

2. T F The Stamp Act required colonists to use British postage stamps when mailing letters.

3. T F Many members of British royalty were invited to attend the Boston Tea Party.

4. T F The Revolutionary War began when shots were fired at Lexington, Massachusetts, on April 19, 1775.

5. T F Thousands of people were killed by British troops during the Boston Massacre.

6. T F George III was the king of England at the time of the American Revolution.

7. T F Florida was one of the 13 original colonies.

8. T F The Tea Act of 1773 gave the British East India Company a monopoly on the tea trade in the colonies.

9. T F People in Boston were the only ones to protest the Tea Act of 1773.

10. T F "Paul Revere's Ride" was written by Henry Wadsworth Longfellow almost 100 years after the event.

11. T F When the First Continental Congress met in Philadelphia in September 1774, all 13 colonies were represented.

12. T F One of the men who signed the Declaration of Independence had once been the captain of a slave ship.

13. T F The *Turtle* was able to carry out its mission and sink the British warship *HMS Eagle*.

14. List three causes of the Revolutionary War.

_____

_____

_____

_____

Name: _____ Date: _____

In Search of Foreign Aid

Declaring independence from Great Britain was a big step, but winning a war against this most powerful country was a near impossibility the colonists could not hope to achieve without outside help.

Members of the Second Continental Congress asked 70-year-old Benjamin Franklin to travel to France to request supplies, money, and soldiers from the French king, Louis XIV. They thought France might be willing because of what had happened in 1763 following the French and Indian War.

France had already secretly sent some war materials before Franklin arrived in December 1776. Although the French wanted to see England defeated by the colonists, they were reluctant to openly form an alliance with the new country in what might be a losing cause. If the colonists didn't win, England would probably start another war with France in retaliation.

In December 1777, when Franklin learned about the American victory at Saratoga, he repeated his requests. France agreed to sign an alliance, but only if Spain would, too. Spain refused because it feared their colonies in Central and South America might also decide to revolt.

In spite of Spain's refusal, Franklin convinced France to sign an alliance on February 6, 1778. Historians agree that without the soldiers and millions in cash and goods sent by France, the Americans would have lost the war.

1. Why did the Second Continental Congress believe France might join them against England?

    _____

    _____

2. If you had been the ambassador, what other reasons would you have given the French to persuade them to help the colonies?

    _____

    _____

3. Do you think the French had good reasons for not forming an alliance? Why or why not?

    _____

    _____

4. Use reference sources to learn more about the alliance with France. Give details of one example showing how French assistance helped the colonists win the war.

    _____

    _____

    _____

    _____

Name: _____ Date: _____

Surrender at Last

Although he had no orders to do so, Lieutenant General Charles Cornwallis moved his troops north from North Carolina to link up with British forces in Virginia in the summer of 1781. He planned to launch a full-scale offensive against the Continental Army. The British troops drove the Americans, led by the Marquis de Lafayette, out of Virginia.

General Sir Henry Clinton, the commander of British troops in North America, disapproved of this unauthorized action. He sent Cornwallis to establish a defensive position on Chesapeake Bay to fortify the towns of Gloucester and Yorktown.

General Charles Cornwallis

Lafayette sent word about the British position and preparations to General Washington at West Point, New York. When Washington learned that their French ally, Admiral de Grasse, was sailing to the Chesapeake Bay area with 29 warships, he set off for Virginia on August 21 with about 7,000 men. They arrived at Williamsburg a month later.

By the time Washington arrived, de Grasse had driven off the British fleet and blocked Chesapeake Bay, preventing British troops from escaping by sea. De Grasse also provided French troops to reinforce Washington's army.

When the American and French troops arrived at Yorktown on September 28 with a combined force of 16,000, they laid siege to the town. Realizing the hopelessness of his position, Cornwallis requested a truce on October 17 and signed articles of surrender two days later. When they learned of the surrender, 7,000 British reinforcements, on their way to Yorktown, returned to New York.

Use a dictionary to define these words.

1. fortify: _____

2. offensive: _____

3. defensive: _____

4. ally: _____

5. siege: _____

6. It is about 462 miles from West Point to Williamsburg. It took Washington and his troops a month to travel that distance. Averaging 55 miles an hour, how long would it take to drive that far today?

_____

7. If they traveled for 30 days, how many miles a day, on the average, did they march?

_____

Name: _____ Date: _____

Revolutionary Words

Match the words with their definitions.

____ 1. boycott   A. A statement of intent

____ 2. intolerable   B. A heavy substance used to achieve stability

____ 3. representative   C. Returning blow for blow in anger

____ 4. tyranny   D. Take away; remove

____ 5. massacre   E. Something that cannot be taken away

____ 6. blockade   F. Unjust, cruel, or excessive use of power

____ 7. monopoly   G. To refuse to buy or send goods to or from a specific source

____ 8. declaration   H. A person who betrays a trust or is disloyal

____ 9. retaliation   I. A person who loves his/her native country and will do all that is possible for it

____ 10. ballast   J. Colonists who wanted to retain ties with England

____ 11. unalienable   K. Slaughter of defenseless people

____ 12. revoke   L. Completely unacceptable

____ 13. Patriot   M. A slang term for British soldiers

____ 14. traitor   N. Someone who acts on behalf of someone else's best interests

____ 15. Loyalist   O. Something that prevents goods from leaving or entering an area

____ 16. Redcoats   P. Exclusive control of the supply of a product or service

17. Select any two of the words listed above. Write a sentence using both words.

_____

_____

_____

Name: _____   Date: _____

Negotiating a Peace Treaty

The surrender at Yorktown by General Cornwallis on October 19, 1781, was the last major battle of the Revolutionary War, but the Treaty of Paris, which officially ended the war, was not signed until September 3, 1783.

The most important question to the United States was how much territory they would gain. England agreed to give up all claims in North America as far west as the Mississippi River, except for Canada. (Some colonists also wanted to control Canada to prevent "future difficulties.")

The French were upset when a preliminary treaty was signed in November 1782 because they had not been included in the negotiations. The United States agreed not to accept the treaty until terms could be reached that would be acceptable not only to France, but also to Spain and the Netherlands (unofficial allies with the colonists).

1. What do you think they meant by "future difficulties"?

    _____

    _____

2. Use a dictionary to define *negotiations.* _____

    _____

3. Why do you think these countries wanted to be included in negotiations?

    _____

    _____

Claims to North America before the Revolutionary War

Territory controlled by Spain
Territory controlled by Britain

Claims to North America after the Treaty of Paris

Territory controlled by England
Territory controlled by the US
Territory controlled by Spain

Name: _____   Date: _____

Other Provisions of the Treaty of Paris

In addition to the agreement giving the United States control of more territory, Great Britain also promised to ...

... respect American independence and recognize the former colonies as a free and independent United States of America;

... allow American fishing rights off the Great Banks of Newfoundland and Nova Scotia;

... relinquish all claims to government, property, and territorial rights in the former colonies;

... evacuate all British troops;

... return the colony of Florida to Spain;

... return Senegal to France.

The United States agreed to restore the rights and property of Loyalists and allow free movement on the Mississippi River to France, Spain, Great Britain, and the Netherlands.

New York remained the last stronghold of Loyalist support. Beginning in January 1782, thousands of British supporters left the area. Some moved to England; others settled further north in Canada. By December 1873, the last of the British troops had also departed.

The Continental Congress ratified the treaty on January 14, 1784.

1. What is your opinion of the terms of the Treaty of Paris?

   _____

   _____

   _____

   _____

2. Why do you think many Loyalists decided to move after the war, even though the Treaty of Paris promised to restore their rights and properties?

   _____

   _____

   _____

Name: _____ Date: _____

Plan an Interview

You are a reporter for a Philadelphia newspaper in 1775. Your assignment is to interview some-one who is in favor of breaking all ties with England.

Write 12 questions you might ask that person during an interview.

1. _____

   _____

2. _____

   _____

3. _____

   _____

4. _____

   _____

5. _____

   _____

6. _____

   _____

7. _____

   _____

8. _____

   _____

9. _____

   _____

10. _____

    _____

11. _____

    _____

12. _____

    _____

Name: _____ Date: _____

Writing the Constitution

After the Revolutionary War, the 13 colonies realized they needed something stronger than the Articles of Confederation to hold them together as a united nation. However, exactly what they needed was a matter of much debate. Only five states sent delegates to the first Constitutional Convention held in Annapolis, Maryland, in 1786.

All states except Rhode Island sent delegates to the second meeting of the Convention, which was held in Philadelphia the following year. However, it took the delegates four months of debates, arguments, and discussions before they finally made compromises and agreed. On September 17, 1787, 39 delegates signed the final document.

For the Constitution to become official, at least 9 of the 13 states needed to approve it. Although it became effective in July 1788, the last state to ratify the Constitution (Rhode Island), did not do so until May 29, 1790.

The Preamble to the Constitution of the United States is the introduction to the document stating the purpose of the Constitution.

We the People of the United States, in order to form a more perfect Union, establish Justice, ensure domestic Tranquility, provide for the common defense, promote the general Welfare, and secure the Blessings of Liberty, to ourselves and our Posterity, do ordain and establish this Constitution for the United States of America.

The rest of the Constitution is divided into Articles—sections regarding the legislative, judicial, and executive branches of the government, the rights and duties of states and citizens, provisions for new states to enter the union, and describing how the document can be amended.

Use reference sources to answer questions 1–5 about the Constitution. Write your answers on another sheet of paper.

1. Who was nicknamed the "Father of the Constitution"?

2. Who was chairman of the Constitutional Convention?

3. Did Benjamin Franklin advocate abolishing slavery in the Constitution?

4. What was the Virginia Plan proposed by Edmund Randolph?

5. What was the New Jersey Plan proposed by William Paterson?

6. Rewrite the preamble in your own words.

Name: _____   Date: _____

The Bill of Rights

The Constitution was barely a year old when government leaders decided that several guarantees of individual rights needed to be added.

James Madison and other members of the Constitutional Convention proposed 12 changes. Ten of these changes, called the Bill of Rights, were approved and became a permanent part of the Constitution on December 15, 1791.

The Bill of Rights:

1st Amendment: Guarantees freedom of speech, press, religion, and assembly (the right to meet peacefully).

2nd Amendment: Protects the right of citizens to bear arms.

3rd and 4th Amendments: Assures the right to privacy and forbids illegal searches of homes.

5th, 6th, 7th, and 8th Amendments: Protects people accused of crimes and provides for trial by a jury.

9th and 10th Amendments: Forbids Congress from passing laws that would change the protection guaranteed in the first eight amendments.

When the Bill of Rights was passed, these rights did not apply to everyone in the United States. Women, slaves, and American Indians had no legal rights.

Since the Constitution and Bill of Rights were approved and accepted as law by the United States, 17 additional amendments have been added.

1. Use reference sources to learn about one of the later amendments to the Constitution. Summarize the amendment in your own words and explain when and why it was passed.

   _____

   _____

   _____

   _____

   _____

   _____

   _____

   _____

Name: _____ Date: _____

A Battle of Words

Challenge a partner to a revolutionary battle—a battle of words, that is. Use the letters in the words **Revolutionary War** to make new words.

Rules:
1. Words must be three or more letters.
2. Proper nouns can be used.
3. Letters may be used in your words only as many times as they appear in the words **Revolutionary War**. (You could make a word with three "r's" like error, but not one with two "e's" like weave.)

Letters to use:

a	a	e	i	l	n	o	o
r	r	r	t	u	v	w	y

Write your words on the lines. The one with the most words wins the battle.

_____ _____ _____ _____

_____ _____ _____ _____

_____ _____ _____ _____

_____ _____ _____ _____

_____ _____ _____ _____

_____ _____ _____ _____

_____ _____ _____ _____

_____ _____ _____ _____

_____ _____ _____ _____

_____ _____ _____ _____

_____ _____ _____ _____

Number of words made: _____

Name: _____   Date: _____

Revolutionary Word Search

Find and circle the 44 words hidden in the puzzle. Words may be printed forward, backward, vertically, horizontally, and diagonally.

```
F Y U R X S T H G I R F O L L I B A A K K T Q K
E T D I Z M S P W S E Y Q N W O T K R O Y H J N
E R S L P R A T E N O I T U L O V E R C L I E Z
F A O A J T E T B S T A M P A C T D H O I R C A
A P Q Q R F A P S I G N L W O P K D S N B T N U
H A M I N T F Z R T S A B T B S K D I G E E A S
P E O N S O R R A E W E N L T G S G T R R E R H
T T F O Q T I X F C S N L S O J Z Q I E T N F Y
S J B T A V E T O T Y E I F I C W K R S Y A M T
I T P S G S I L U U L L N X I D K Y B S O R D Q
P B W O V C O P L T A N D T E R K A Y Z A C T L
H I I B B N M M R Y I E K C A K B B D L Z T O D
I N V U I A T U O F N T L A K T K V A E Q A R N
L D K E K G T L F G I A S R L L I T E L S X I O
A E S I H E I T L L R Y W N O T N O J W M A E T
D P Q S H G W A L A A E I Y O E N B N X X T S G
E E U T B R N S T E X G A T N C D A Y C X I C N
L N N P Z D T I T N V N G I H H R W I I G O G I
P D I O X A O R A K K O T K O N O P L T Z N G X
H E T D O N E V N E Y N T L I W C V S W I I L E
I N E C I A A X E R O S J E U I N V P D D L S L
A C D L S L Q S Z C Y F A P K C O N V E N E I F
E E Z O V R E B E L O D A S S L C F F P V Z G M
R M N V Q N H T R U O F Y L U J H I C R X U S V
```

BATTLE	DECLARATION	PATRIOTS	TAXATION
BILL OF RIGHTS	ENGLAND	PHILADELPHIA	TAXES
BLOCKADE	FLAG	REBEL	TEA PARTY
BOSTON	FRANCE	REDCOATS	THE TURTLE
BRITISH	INDEPENDENCE	REPRESENTATION	THIRTEEN
COLONIES	JULY FOURTH	REVOLUTION	TORIES
CONCORD	LEXINGTON	RIFLES	TREASON
CONGRESS	LIBERTY	RIGHTS	UNITED
CONSTITUTION	LOYALISTS	SIGN	VOTE
CONTINENTAL ARMY	MILITIA	STAMP ACT	YANKEES
CONVENE	NAVAL	STATES	YORKTOWN

Report on a Patriot

Learn more about a person who was important during the Revolutionary War era. Select one of the people listed below or another person who played a role in the Revolutionary War. Use the Internet and other reference sources to write a three- to five-page report. Add illustrations.

Mercy Otis Warren

Thomas Paine

Abigail Adams
John Adams
Samuel Adams
Ethan Allen
Benedict Arnold
Crispus Attucks
Sarah Franklin Bache
Penelope Barker
David Bushnell
George Rogers Clark
Lydia Darragh
John Dickinson
Benjamin Franklin
Mary Katherine Goddard
Nathanael Greene
Nathan Hale
Alexander Hamilton
John Hancock
Patrick Henry
Stephen Hopkins
John Jay
Thomas Jefferson
John Paul Jones
Marquis de Lafayette
Charles Lee
James Monroe
Francis Marion
Thomas Paine
Mary Hays (Molly Pitcher)
Esther Reed
Paul Revere
Betsy Ross
Deborah Sampson
Mercy Otis Warren
George Washington
Martha Washington
Anthony Wayne
Phillis Wheatley

Anthony Wayne

Phillis Wheatley

Suggested Reading

Cornerstones of Freedom Series
The Bonhomme Richard
The Boston Tea Party
The Constitution
The Declaration of Independence
Lexington and Concord
The Liberty Bell
The Surrender at Yorktown
Valley Forge

The Women of '76 by Sally Smith Booth

If You Were There in 1776 by Barbara Brenner

Come All You Brave Soldiers: Blacks in the Revolutionary War by Clinton Cox

The World Turned Upside Down: George Washington and the Battle of Yorktown by Richard Ferrie

Can't You Make Them Behave, King George? by Jean Fritz

Where Was Patrick Henry on the 29th of May? by Jean Fritz

King George III: English Monarch by Graham Gaines

Why America is Free by Kenneth Hamburger, Joseph Rischer, and Steven Gravlin

The Winter of Red Snow: The Revolutionary War Diary of Abigail Jane Stewart by Kristiana Gregory

African Americans and the Revolutionary War by Judith Harper

The Revolutionary War (A True Book) by Brendan January

The Boston Tea Party by Walter Olesky

A Nation is Born: Rebellion and Independence in America, 1700–1820 by Richard Steins

The Importance of Benjamin Franklin by Gail B. Stewart

The Liberty Bell by Jon Wilson

Those Remarkable Women of the American Revolution by Karen Zeinert

Answer Key

George III Becomes King (page 4)
1. 22
3. to bring in goods from another country
4. to send goods to another country

What Caused the Revolutionary War? (page 5)
2. oppressive and unjust government; very cruel and unjust use of power or authority

Expansion of the British Empire (page 6)
1. All the territory north of Florida and West to the Mississippi River should be shaded.

Taxes on Sugar and Molasses (page 9)
1. a thick, usually dark brown syrup produced during the refining of sugar or from sorghum

Two New Laws Affect the Colonies (page 10)
1. trading goods and services without using money
4. The Quartering Act of 1765 required colonists to provide barracks and supplies including bedding, firewood, cooking utensils, food, and cider for British troops stationed in the area.
5. Parliament passed the Quartering Act to help defray the cost of maintaining troops in the colonies.
6. In most colonies, the local legislatures refused to comply with the law.

The Rebels Unite (page 13)
1. communication by exchange of letters
2. any army composed of citizens rather than professional soldiers, called up in time of emergency

More Taxes in 1767 (page 14)
1. to refuse to buy or send goods to or from a specific source
4. the indiscriminate, merciless killing of a number of human beings

Revolutionary Women's Organizations (page 15)
3. a large sheet of paper printed on one side, as with a political message

Would You Like a Cup of Tea? (page 16)
3. exclusive control of a commodity or service in a given market

The Intolerable Acts (page 19)
1. the act of returning an injury, wrong, etc., for an injury, wrong, etc.
2. unbearable; too severe, painful, cruel, etc., to be endured

The First Continental Congress Meets (page 20)
1. Georgia did not send representatives because it feared it might need help from British troops putting down a Native American uprising.

What Happened at Lexington and Concord? (page 24)
3. a disorderly flight or retreat, as of defeated troops

Singing "Yankee Doodle" (page 25)
1. a meticulously well-dressed man

A Declaration of War—and of Independence (page 29)
Benjamin Franklin   70   Penn. Printer, inventor, scientist, diplomat
Thomas Jefferson   33   Virginia Lawyer, inventor
John Adams   40   Mass. Lawyer, teacher
Roger Sherman   29   Conn. Lawyer, judge
Robert Livingston   55   New York Lawyer

Meet Benjamin Franklin (page 30)
1. a person under legal agreement to work a specified length of time for a master craftsman in a craft or trade in return for instruction

The Thirteen Original Colonies (page 32)
Colonies labeled should be New Hampshire, Massachusetts, Rhode Island, Connecticut, New York, Pennsylvania, New Jersey, Delaware, Maryland, Virginia, North Carolina, South Carolina, and Georgia.

Meet Thomas Jefferson (page 33)
1. 1743 in Goochland, Virginia
2. Greek, Latin, French, and Italian
3. Violin
4. Monticello
5. Martha Wayles Skelton
6. Six
7. About 10 years; she died in 1782.
8. No
9. Possible answers: dumb waiter, swivel chair, lamp heater, improved plow
10. Secretary of State
11. France
12. John Adams
13. After a tie in the Electoral College and 36 ballots by the House of Representatives, Jefferson became president and Aaron Burr, vice president.
14. Answers will vary.

Time Line Activities (page 34)
1. George III became king of England.
2. Britain passed the Stamp Act.
3. Boston Massacre
4. Battles fought at Lexington and Concord
5. Declaration of Independence approved
6. The submarine, the *Turtle,* failed its mission.
7. Stamp Act repealed
8. British captured Philadelphia.
9. 1774
10. Proclamation of 1763
11. British East India Company
12. Morristown, New Jersey
13. Nathan Hale
14. John Adams
15. Delaware River

The Declaration of Independence (page 35)

2. that may not be taken away or transferred
3. having some quality or characteristic

The Signers of the Declaration of Independence (page 36)

1. John Adams and Thomas Jefferson
2. John Hancock
3. Benjamin Rush
4. Samuel Chase
5. Button Gwinnett
6. Benjamin Harrison
7. William Whipple

Problems With the Articles of Confederation (page 40)

1. independent nations or states, joined in a league or confederacy, whose central authority is usually confined to common defense and limited political cooperation
2. an imposing and collecting of a tax or other payment
3. to approve or confirm; especially to give official sanction to
4. of judges, law courts, or their functions

Be a History Detective (page 41)

1. Fiction: This story was first published by Mason Weems in *The Life of Washington* published shortly after the president's death.
2. Fiction. He retired and refused to run for a third term.
3. Fiction. George and Martha had no children together. Martha, who was a widow when she married George, had two children from her first marriage.
4. Fact.
5. Fiction. He had light brown hair that he usually kept powdered. Although it was fashionable for men to wear wigs, Washington rarely did.
6. Fact.
7. Fact.
8. Fact.

9. Fact. He was six feet, three inches tall, and weighed about 200 pounds. The average man at that time was about nine inches shorter.
10. Fact. This was a common practice at that time.

Fact or Opinion? (page 42)

1. F	6. O	11. O
2. O	7. O	12. F
3. O	8. F	13. O
4. O	9. O	14. F
5. F	10. O	15. O

The Adams Family (page 43)

1. Sam	6. John	11. John
2. John	7. Sam	12. Sam
3. John	8. Both	13. Both
4. Sam	9. John	14. John
5. John	10. Sam	

The *Turtle* Goes to War (page 47)

1. a shutting off of a port or region of a belligerent state by the troops or ships of the enemy in order to prevent passage in or out in time of war
2. anything heavy carried in a ship, aircraft, or vehicle to give stability

True or False? (page 48)

1. F	6. T	10. T
2. F	7. F	11. F
3. F	8. T	12. T
4. T	9. F	13. F
5. F		

In Search of Foreign Aid (page 49)

1. England won the French and Indian War and forced France to give up almost all claims to land in North America.

Surrender at Last (page 50)

1. to strengthen against attack, as by building or furnishing with forts, walls, etc.
2. attacking, aggressive; of or for attack
3. defending; of or for defense
4. a country, person, or group joined with another or others for a common purpose

5. the encirclement of a fortified place by an opposing armed force intending to take it, usually by blockade and bombardment
6. Driving from West Point to Williamsburg would take slightly less than eight and a half hours at an average of 55 miles per hour.
7. They averaged 15.4 miles per day

Revolutionary Words (page 51)

1. G	7. P	12. D
2. L	8. A	13. I
3. N	9. C	14. H
4. F	10. B	15. J
5. K	11. E	16. M
6. O		

Negotiating a Peace Treaty (page 52)

2. a conferring, discussing, or bargaining to reach agreement

Writing the Constitution (page 55)

1. James Madison
2. George Washington
3. No
4. The Virginia Plan stated that representation in the federal government should be based on population.
5. The New Jersey Plan stated that each state should have an equal number of representatives in the federal government.

Revolutionary Word Search (page 58)

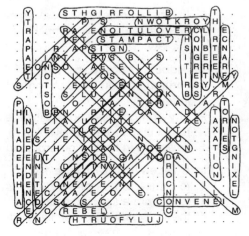

SOME PHYSICAL CONSTANTS

Speed of Light	c	3.00×10^8 m/s
Gravitational Constant	G	6.67×10^{-11} N·m^2/kg^2
Coulomb Constant	k	8.99×10^9 N·m^2/C^2
Planck's Constant	h	6.63×10^{-34} J·s
Boltzmann's Constant	k_B	1.38×10^{-23} J/K
Elementary charge	e	1.60×10^{-19} C
Electron Mass	m_e	9.11×10^{-31} kg
Proton Mass	m_p	1.67×10^{-27} kg
Neutron Mass	m_n	1.68×10^{-27} kg

COMMONLY-USED PHYSICAL DATA:

Gravitational Field Strength g	9.80 m/s^2
Density of Water	1000.0 kg/m^3 = 1 g/cm^3 *
Density of Air	1.2 kg/m^3 *

* at normal pressure, 20°C

STANDARD METRIC PREFIXES
For Powers of Ten

Power	Prefix	Symbol
10^{18}	exa	E
10^{15}	peta	P
10^{12}	tera	T
10^9	giga	G
10^6	mega	M
10^3	kilo	k
10^{-2}	centi	c
10^{-3}	milli	m
10^{-6}	micro	μ
10^{-9}	nano	n
10^{-12}	pico	p
10^{-15}	femto	f
10^{-18}	atto	a

USEFUL CONVERSION FACTORS (IN SI UNITS)

1 meter = 1 m = 100 cm = 39.4 inches = 3.28 ft
1 mile = 1 mi = 1609 m = 1.609 km = 5280 ft
1 inch = 2.54 cm
1 light-year = 1 ly = 9.46 Pm = 0.946×10^{16} m

1 hour = 1 h = 60 min = 3600 s
1 day = 1 d = 24 h = 86.4 ks = 86,400 s
1 year = 1 y = 365.25 d = 31.6 Ms = 3.16×10^7 s

1 J = 1 kg·m^2/s^2 = 0.239 cal
1 kWh = 3.6 MJ

1.0 radian = 1 rad = 57.3° = 0.1592 revolution

1 m/s = 2.24 mi/h
1 mi/h = 1.61 km/h
1 ft^3 = 0.02832 m^3
1 gallon = 1 gal = 3.79×10^{-3} m^3 ≈ 3.8 kg H$_2$O

1 N = 1 kg·m/s^2 = 1 J/m = 0.225 lb
1 lb = 4.45 N
weight of 1-kg object near earth = 9.8 N = 2.2 lbs

1 W = 1 J/s
1 horsepower = 1 hp = 746 W

1 revolution = 360° = 2π radians = 6.28 radians

USEFUL CONVERSION FACTORS INVOLVING SR UNITS

1 s = 3.0×10^8 m, 1 μs = 300 m,   1 ns = 0.30 m ≈ 1 ft
1 min = 18,000,000 km, 1 h = 1.08 Tm = 1,080,000,000 km, 1 day = 2.59×10^{13} m = 25,900,000,000 km
1 kg (energy) = 9.0×10^{16} J,   1 kg (momentum) = 3.0×10^8 kg·m/s
1 eV (energy) = 1.60×10^{-19} J = 1.78×10^{-36} kg

USEFUL ASTRONOMICAL DATA

1 AU = mean distance from earth to sun = 1.50×10^{11} m

	Mass	Radius	Mean Orbital Radius	Orbital Period	Eccentricity
Sun	1.99×10^{30} kg	696,000 km	- - -	- - -	- - -
Moon	7.36×10^{22} kg	1740 km	384,000 km = 1.28 s	27.3 days	0.055
Earth	5.98×10^{24} kg $\equiv M_E$	6380 km	1.000 AU = 8.0 min	1.000 y	0.017
Mars	0.107 M_E	3370 km	1.524 AU = 12.7 min	1.88 y	0.093
Jupiter	318 M_E	69,900 km	5.203 AU = 43.4 min	11.9 y	0.048
Saturn	95.1 M_E	58,500 km	9.539 AU = 1.32 h	29.5 y	0.056
Uranus	14.5 M_E	23,300 km	19.182 AU = 2.66 h	84.0 y	0.047
Neptune	17.2 M_E	22,100 km	30.058 AU = 4.17 h	165 y	0.009
Pluto/Charon	0.0025 M_E	3500/1800 km	39.785 AU = 5.53 h	248 y	0.254

(Based mostly on data in D. Halliday, R. Resnick, *Fundamentals of Physics,* 3/e, New York:Wiley, p. A6.)

SYMBOLS AND THEIR MEANINGS

$=$	is equal to
$\neq$	is not equal to
$\approx$	is approximately equal to
$>$	is greater than
$<$	is less than
$>>$	is much greater than
$<<$	is much less than
$\equiv$	is defined to be
$\propto$	is proportional to
$\Rightarrow$	implies or therefore
$\Leftrightarrow$	if and only if (implies both ways)
∞	infinity
$\cdot$	indicates a dot product of vectors OR a product of units OR ordinary multiplication
$\times$	indicates cross product OR multiplication by a power of 10
i.e.	*id est* "that is"
e.g.	*exempli gratia* "for example"
etc.	*etcetera* "and so on"
Q.E.D.	*quod erat demonstrandum* "which was to be demonstrated"
$\lvert x \rvert$	absolute value of x
mag()	magnitude of a vector
$\int$	indicates an integral
Σ	indicates a sum
$'$	(attached to the right side of a variable, called a "prime") indicates that variable is being measured in the Other Frame
$\alpha,\ \theta,\ \phi$	angles
$\vec{\beta}$	velocity of a reference frame
γ	the useful quantity $[1 - \beta^2]^{1/2}$
Δ	(as prefix) a largish change in the variable whose symbol follows
λ	wavelength
$\Delta\sigma$	spacetime separation between two events
$\Delta\tau$	proper time between two events
$\vec{a}$	acceleration
a	arbitrary scalar constant OR magnitude of $\vec{a}$
$\mathbf{A}$	arbitrary four-vector
b	arbitrary scalar constant
c	the speed of light (in SI units)
d	(as a prefix) a tiny change in the variablewhose symbol follows
Δd	the distance between two points in space
d	distance
eV	(not italic) electron volt, a unit of energy
E	relativistic energy $= P_t$
$\vec{F}$	force
$f(x)$	a function of x
g	gravitational field strength
$\vec{g}$	gravitational field vector
G	the universal gravitational constant
GMT	Greenwich Mean Time
h	height OR the Planck constant

h	(not italic) hour (or light-hour)
i	(as a subscript) means *initial* OR represents an index in a sum
J	(not italic) joule, a unit of energy
K	relativistic kinetic energy $= E - m$
KE	(not italic) kinetic energy
L	length
L_R	rest length
m	mass
M	mass (usually of a system or large object)
MeV	10^6 eV
min	minute (or light-minute)
n	an arbitrary or unknown integer
N	number of particles in a system
N	(not italic) newton, a unit of force
0	(as a subscript) means "initial"
O	the origin (or origin event) of a reference frame
$\vec{p}$	ordinary newtonian momentum
p	relativistic 3-momentum $= [P_x^2 + P_y^2 + P_z^2]^{1/2}$
$\mathbf{P}$	four-momentum (components: P_t, P_x, P_y, P_z)
PE	(not italic) potential energy
$\vec{r}$	a position vector
r	a radius OR a separation OR mag($\vec{r}$)
R	a radius (often the fixed outer radius of some object OR a radius distinct from r)
$d\mathbf{R}$	a displacement four-vector
Δs	the spacetime interval between two events
s	(not italic) second, the SI unit of time and the SR unit of time and distance
S	a slope
SI	refers to the SI unit system
SR	(not italic) refers to the SR unit system, which is the same as the SI system except that distances are measured in seconds
t	coordinate time
Δt	coordinate time between two events
u	an arbitary constant
$\vec{v}$	velocity
v	speed $\equiv$ mag($\vec{v}$)
W	watt, the SI unit of power
x, y, z	position coordinates
x, y, z, t	(as a subscript) indicates a component of a vector or four-vector quantity
$x\text{-},\ y\text{-},\ z\text{-}$	(as a prefix) indicates a component of a vector quantity
y	(not italic) year (or light-year)

SIX IDEAS THAT SHAPED **PHYSICS**

Unit R: The Laws of Physics Are
Frame-Independent

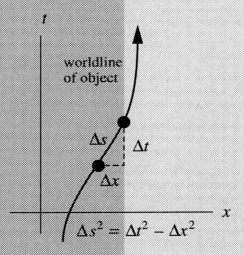

worldline
of object

Δs
Δt
Δx

t

x

$\Delta s^2 = \Delta t^2 - \Delta x^2$

Thomas A. Moore
Pomona College

WCB
McGraw-Hill

Boston   Burr Ridge, IL   Dubuque, IA   Madison, WI   New York   San Francisco   St. Louis
Bangkok   Bogotá   Caracas   Lisbon   London   Madrid
Mexico City   Milan   New Delhi   Seoul   Singapore   Sydney   Taipei   Toronto

WCB/McGraw-Hill
A Division of the McGraw-Hill Companies

SIX IDEAS THAT SHAPED PHYSICS/
UNIT R: THE LAWS OF PHYSICS ARE FRAME-INDEPENDENT

 This book is printed on recycled, acid-free paper containing 10% postconsumer waste.

2 3 4 5 6 7 8 9 0 QPD/QPD 9 0 9 8

ISBN 0-07-043058-6

Vice president and editorial director: *Kevin T. Kane*
Publisher: *James M. Smith*
Sponsoring editor: *John Paul Lenney*
Developmental editor: *Donata Dettbarn*
Marketing manager: *Lisa L. Gottschalk*
Project managers: *Larry Goldberg, Sheila Frank*
Production supervisor: *Mary E. Haas*
Cover designer: *Jonathan Alpert/SCRATCHworks Creative*
Compositor: *Thomas A. Moore*
Typeface: *9/10 Times Roman*
Printer: *Quebecor Printing Book Group/Dubuque*

Cover photo: © Corel

Library of Congress Catalog Card Number: 97-62248

www.mhhe.com

For My Parents, Stanley and Elizabeth,
who taught me the joy of wondering.

CONTENTS

PREFACE

1. INTRODUCTION

This volume is one of six that together comprise the PRELIMINARY EDITION of the text materials for *Six Ideas That Shaped Physics,* a fundamentally new approach to the two- or three-semester calculus-based introductory physics course. This course is still very much a work in progress. We are publishing these volumes in preliminary form so that we can broaden the base of institutions using the course and gather the feedback that we need to better polish both the course and its supporting texts for a formal first edition in a few years. Though we have worked very hard to remove as many of the errors and rough edges as possible for this edition, we would greatly appreciate your help in reporting any errors that remain and offering your suggestions for improvement. I will tell you how you can contact us in a section near the end of this preface.

Much of this preface discusses features and issues that are common to all six volumes of the *Six Ideas* course. For comments about this specific unit and how it relates to the others, see section 7.

Six Ideas That Shaped Physics was created in response to a call for innovative curricula offered by the Introductory University Physics Project (IUPP), which subsequently supported its early development. IUPP officially tested very early versions of the course at University of Minnesota during 1991/92 and at Amherst and Smith Colleges during 1992/93. In its present form, the course represents the culmination of over eight years of development, testing, and evaluation at Pomona College, Smith College, Amherst College, St. Lawrence University, Beloit College, Hope College, UC-Davis, and other institutions.

We designed this course to be consistent with the three basic principles articulated by the IUPP steering committee in its call for model curricula:

1. **The pace of the course should be reduced** so that a broader range of students can achieve an acceptable level of competence and satisfaction.
2. **There should be more 20th-century physics** to better show students what physics is like at the present.
3. **The course should use one or more "story lines"** to help organize the ideas and motivate student interest.

The design of *Six Ideas* was also strongly driven by two other principles:

4. **The course should seek to embrace the best of what educational research has taught us** about conceptual and structural problems with the standard course.
5. **The course should stake out a middle ground** between the standard introductory course and exciting but radical courses that require substantial investments in infrastructure and/or training. This course should be useful in fairly standard environments and should be relatively easy for teachers to understand and adopt.

In its present form, *Six Ideas* course consists of a set of six textbooks (one for each "idea"), a detailed instructor's guide, and a few computer programs that support the course in crucial places. The texts have a variety of innovative features that are designed to (1) make them more clear and readable, (2) teach you *explicitly* about the processes of constructing models and solving complex problems, (3) confront well-known conceptual problems head-on, and (4) support the instructor in innovative uses of class time. The instructor's manual is much

Opening comments about this preliminary edition

The course's roots in the Introductory University Physics Project

The three basic principles of the IUPP project

My additional working principles

A summary of the course's distinctive features

more detailed than is normal, offering detailed suggestions (based on many teacher-years of experience with the course at a variety of institutions) about how to structure the course and adapt it to various calendars and constituencies. The instructor's manual also offers a complete description of effective approaches to class time that emphasize active and collaborative learning over lecture (and yet can still be used in fairly large classes), supporting this with day-by-day lesson plans that make this approach much easier to understand and adopt.

In the remainder of this preface, I will look in more detail at the structure and content of the course and briefly explore *why* we have designed the various features of the course the way that we have.

2. GENERAL PHILOSOPHY OF THE COURSE

Problems with the traditional intro course

The current standard introductory physics course has a number of problems that have been documented in recent years. (1) There is so much material to "cover" in the standard course that students do not have time to develop a deep understanding of any part, and instructors do not have time to use classroom techniques that would help students really learn. (2) Even with all this material, the standard course, focused as it is on *classical* physics, does not show what physics is like *today*, and thus presents a skewed picture of the discipline to the 32 out of 33 students who will never take another physics course. (3) Most importantly, the standard introductory course generally fails to *teach physics*. Studies have shown that even students who earn high grades in a standard introductory physics course often cannot

1. apply basic physical principles to realistic situations,
2. solve realistic problems,
3. perceive or resolve contradictions involving their preconceptions, or
4. organize the ideas of physics hierarchically.

What students in such courses *do* effectively learn is how to solve highly contrived and patterned homework problems (either by searching for analogous examples in the text and then copying them without much understanding, or by doing a random search through the text for a formula that has the right variables.) The high pace of the standard course usually drives students to adopt these kinds of non-thinking behaviors even if they don't want to.

The goal: to help students become competent in using the skills listed above

The goal of *Six Ideas* is to help students achieve a meaningful level of competence in each of the four thinking skills listed above. We have rethought and restructured the course from the ground up so that students are goaded toward (and then rewarded for) behaviors that help them develop these skills. We have designed texts, exams, homework assignments, and activity-based class sessions to reinforce each other in keeping students focused on these goals.

The focus is more on skills than on specific content

While (mostly for practical reasons) the course does span the most important fields of physics, the emphasis is *not* particularly on "covering" material or providing background vocabulary for future study, but more on developing problem-solving, thinking, and modeling skills. Facts and formulas evaporate quickly (particularly for those 32 out of 33 that will take no more physics) but if we can develop students' abilities to think like a physicist in a variety of contexts, we have given them something they can use throughout their lives.

3. TOPICS EXPLORED IN THE COURSE

The six-unit structure

Six Ideas That Shaped Physics is divided into six units (normally offered three per semester). The purpose of each unit is to explore in depth a single idea that has changed the course of physics during the past three centuries. The list below describes each unit's letter name, its length (1 d = one day ≡ one 50-minute class session), the idea, and the corresponding area of physics.

First Semester (37 class days excluding test days):
Unit *C* (14 d) *Conservation Laws Constrain Interactions* (conservation laws)
Unit *N* (14 d) *The Laws of Physics are Universal* (forces and motion)
Unit *R* (9 d) *Physics is Frame-Independent* (special relativity)

Second Semester (42 class days excluding test days):
Unit *E* (17 d) *Electromagnetic Fields are Dynamic* (electrodynamics)
Unit *Q* (16 d) *Particles Behave Like Waves* (basic quantum physics)
Unit *T* (9 d) *Some Processes are Irreversible* (statistical physics)

(Note that the spring semester is assumed to be longer than fall semester. This is typically the case at Pomona and many other institutions, but one can adjust the length of the second semester to as few as 35 days by omitting parts of unit *Q*.)

Dividing the course into such units has a number of advantages. The core idea in each unit provides students with motivation and a sense of direction, and helps keep everyone focused. But the most important reason for this structure is that it makes clear to students that some ideas and principles in physics are more important than others, a theme emphasized throughout the course.

The non-standard order of presentation has evolved in response to our observations in early trials. **[1]** Conservation laws are presented first not only because they really are more fundamental than the particular theories of mechanics considered later but also because we have consistently observed that students understand them better and can use them more flexibly than they can Newton's laws. It makes sense to have students *start* by studying very powerful and broadly applicable laws that they can also understand: this builds their confidence while developing thinking skills needed for understanding newtonian mechanics. This also delays the need for calculus. **[2]** Special relativity, which fits naturally into the first semester's focus on mechanics and conservation laws, also ends that semester with something both contemporary and compelling (student evaluations consistently rate this section very highly). **[3]** We found in previous trials that ending the second semester with the intellectually demanding material in unit *Q* was not wise: ending the course with Unit *T* (which is less demanding) and thus more practical during the end-of-year rush.

Comments about the non-standard order

The suggested order also offers a variety of options for adapting the course to other calendars and paces. One can teach these units in three 10-week quarters of two units each: note that the shortest units (*R* and *T*) are naturally paired with longest units (*E* and *Q* respectively) when the units are divided this way. While the first four units essentially provide a core curriculum that is difficult to change substantially, omitting either Unit *Q* or Unit *T* (or both) can create a gentler pace without loss of continuity (since Unit *C* includes some basic thermal physics, a version of the course omitting unit *T* still spans much of what is in a standard introductory course). We have also designed unit *Q* so that several of its major sections can be omitted if necessary.

Options for adapting to a different calendar

Many of these volumes can also stand alone in an appropriate context. Units *C* and *N* are tightly interwoven, but with some care and in the appropriate context, these could be used separately. Unit *R* only requires a basic knowledge of mechanics. In addition to a typical background in mechanics, units *E* and *Q* require only a few very basic results from relativity, and Unit *T* requires only a very basic understanding of energy quantization. Other orders are also possible: while the first four units form a core curriculum that works best in the designed order, units *Q* and *T* might be exchanged, placed between volumes of the core sequence, or one or the other can be omitted.

Using the volumes alone or in different orders

Superficially, the course might seem to involve quite a bit *more* material than a standard introductory physics course, since substantial amounts of time are devoted to relativity and quantum physics. However, we have made substantial cuts in the material presented in the all sections of the course compared to a standard course. We made these cuts in two different ways.

The pace was reduced by cutting whole topics...

First, we have omitted entire topics, such as fluid mechanics, most of rotational mechanics, almost everything about sound, many electrical engineering topics, geometric optics, polarization, and so on. These cuts will no doubt be intolerable to some, but *something* has to go, and these topics did not fit as well as others into this particular course framework.

... and by streamlining the presentation of the rest

Our second approach was to simplify and streamline the presentation of topics we *do* discuss. A typical chapter in a standard textbook is crammed with a variety of interesting but tangential issues, applications, and other miscellaneous factons. The core idea of each *Six Ideas* unit provides an excellent filter for reducing the number density of factons: virtually everything that is not *essential* for developing that core idea has been eliminated. This greatly reduces the "conceptual noise" that students encounter, which helps them focus on learning the really important ideas.

Because of the conversational writing style adopted for the text, the total page count of the *Six Ideas* texts is actually similar to a standard text (about 1100 pages), but if you compare typical chapters discussing the same general material, you will find that the *density* of concepts in the *Six Ideas* text is much lower, leading to what I hope will be a more gentle perceived pace.

Choosing an appropriate pace

Even so, this text is *not* a "dumbed-down" version of a standard text. Instead of making the text dumber, I have tried very hard to challenge (and hopefully enable) students to become *smarter*. The design pace of this course (one chapter per day) is pretty challenging considering the sophistication of the material, and really represents a maximum pace for fairly well-prepared students at reasonably selective colleges and universities. However, I believe that the materials *can* be used at a much broader range of institutions and contexts at a lower pace (two chapters per three sessions, say, or one chapter per 75-minute class session). This means either cutting material or taking three semesters instead of two, but it can be done. The instructor's manual discusses how cuts might be made.

Part of the point of arranging the text in a "chapter-per-day" format is to bee clear about how the pace should be *limited*. Course designs that require covering *more* than one chapter per day should be strictly avoided: if there are too few days to cover the chapters at the design pace, than chapters will *have* to be cut.

4. FEATURES OF THE TEXT

The texts are designed to serve as students' primary source of new information

Studies have suggested that lectures are neither the most efficient nor most effective way to present expository material. One of my most important goals was to develop a text that could essentially replace the lecture as the primary *source* of information, freeing up class time for activities that help students *practice* using those ideas. I also wanted to create a text that not only presents the topics but goads students to develop model-building and problem-solving skills, helps them organize ideas hierarchically, encourages them to think qualitatively as well as quantitatively, and supports active learning both inside and outside of class.

A list of some of the texts' important features

In its current form, the text has a variety of features designed to address these needs, (many of which have evolved in response to early trials):

1. **The writing style is expansive and conversational**, making the text more suitable to be the primary way students learn new information.
2. **Each chapter corresponds to one (50-minute) class session**, which helps guide instructors in maintaining an appropriate pace.
3. **Each chapter begins with a unit map and an overview** that helps students see how the chapter fits into the general flow of the unit.
4. **Each chapter ends with a summary** that presents the most important ideas and arguments in a hierarchical outline format.
5. **Each chapter has a glossary** that summarizes technical terms, helping students realize that certain words have special meanings in physics.

6. **The book uses "user-friendly" notation and terminology** to help students keep ideas clear and avoid misleading connotations.

7. **Exercises embedded in the text** (with provided answers) help students actively engage the material as they prepare for class (providing an active alternative to examples).

8. **Wide outside margins** provide students with space for taking notes.

9. **Frequent *Physics Skills* and *Math Skills* sections** explicitly explore and summarize generally-applicable thinking skills.

10. **Problem-solving frameworks** (influenced by work by Alan van Heuvelan) help students learn good problem-solving habits.

11. **Two-minute problems** provide a tested and successful way to actively involve students during class and get feedback on how they are doing.

12. **Homework problems** are generally more qualitative than standard problems, and are organized according to the general thinking skills required.

5. ACTIVE LEARNING IN AND OUT OF CLASS

The *Six Ideas* texts are designed to support active learning both inside and outside the classroom setting. A properly designed course using these texts can provide to students a rich set of active-learning experiences.

The *two-minute exercises* at the end of each chapter make it easy to devote at least part of each class session to active learning. These mostly conceptual questions do not generally require much (if any) calculation, but locating the correct answer does require careful thinking, a solid understanding of the material, and (often) an ability to apply concepts to realistic situations to answer correctly. Many explicitly test for typical student misconceptions, providing an opportunity to expose and correct these well-known stumbling blocks.

Active learning using two-minute exercises

I often begin a class session by asking students to work in groups of two or three to find answers for a list of roughly three two-minute problems from the chapter that was assigned reading for that class session. After students have worked on these problems for some time, I ask them to show me their answers for each question in turn. The students hold up the back of the book facing me and point to the letter that they think is the correct answer. This gives me instant feedback on how well the students are doing, and provides me with both grist for further discussion and a sense where the students need the most help. On the other hand, students cannot see each others' answers easily, making them less likely to fear embarrassment (and I work very hard to be supportive).

Once everyone gets the hang of the process, it is easy to adapt other activities to this format. When I do a demonstration, I often make it more active by posing questions about what will happen, and asking students to respond using the letters. This helps everyone think more deeply about what the demonstration really shows and gets the students more invested in the outcome (and more impressed when the demonstration shows something unexpected).

Active demonstrations

The in-text exercises and homework problems provide opportunities for active learning *outside* of class. The exercises challenge students to test their understanding of the material as they read it, helping them actively process the material and giving them instant feedback. They also provide a way to get students through derivations in a way that actively involves them in the process and yet "hides" the details so that the structure of the derivation is clearer. Finally, such exercises provide an active alternative to traditional examples: instead of simply displaying the example, the exercises encourage students to work through it.

The exercises support active reading

The homework problems at the end of each chapter are organized into four types. *Basic* problems are closest to the type of problems found in standard texts: they are primarily for practicing the application of a single formula or concept in a straightforward manner and/or are closely analogous to examples in the text. *Synthetic* problems generally involve more realistic situations, require

The types of homework problems

students to apply *several* concepts and/or formulas at once, involve creating or applying models, and/ or require more sophisticated reasoning. ***Rich-Context*** problems are synthetic problems generally cast in a narrative framework where either too much or too little information is given and/or a non-numerical question is posed (that nonetheless requires numerical work to answer). ***Advanced*** problems usually explore subtle theoretical issues or mathematical derivations beyond the level of the class: they are designed to challenge the very best students and/or remind instructors about how to handle subtle issues.

Collaborative recitation sessions

The rich-context problems are especially designed for collaborative work. Work by Heller and Hollenbaugh has shown that students solving standard problems rarely collaborate even when "working together", but that a well-written rich-context problem by its very open-ended nature calls forth a discussion of physical concepts, requiring students to work together to create useful models. I typically assign one such problem per week that students can work in a "recitation" section where can they work the problem in collaborative groups (instead of being lectured to by a TA).

The goal of the course is that the majority of students should ultimately be able to solve problems at the level of the *synthetic* problems in the book. Many of the rich-context problems are too difficult for individual students to solve easily, and the advanced problems are meant to be beyond the level of the class.

The way that a course is structured can determine its success

In early trials of *Six Ideas*, we learned that whether a course succeeds or fails depends very much the details of how the course is *structured*. This text is designed to more easily support a productive course structure, but careful work on the course design is still essential. For example, a "traditional" approach to assigning and grading homework can lead students to be frustrated (rather than challenged) by the richer-than-average homework problems in this text. Course structures can also either encourage or discourage students from getting the most out of class by preparing ahead of time. Exams can support or undermine the goals of the course. The instructor's manual explores these issues in much more depth and offers detailed guidance (based on our experience) about how design a course that gets the most out of what these books have to offer.

6.   USE OF COMPUTERS

Using computers

The course, unlike some recent reform efforts, is *not* founded to a significant degree on the use of computers. Even so, a *few* computer programs are deployed in a few crucial places to support a particular line of argument in the text, and unit *T* in particular comes across significantly better when supported by a relatively small amount of computer work.

The most current versions of the computer programs supporting this course can be downloaded from my web-site or we will send them to you on request (see the contact information in section 8 below).

7.   NOTES ABOUT UNIT *R*

Why spend so much time on special relativity?

Unit *R* is a relatively short unit that focuses on developing the theory of special relativity as a logical consequence of the principle of relativity. Typically, little time in a traditional introductory physics course is spent exploring relativity, and as a result, few students understand or appreciate the beauties it has to offer. The experience of those of us who have used preliminary versions of this text is that if between two and four weeks of class time are devoted to the study of relativity using the approach outlined in this unit, students at almost any level can develop a robust and satisfying understanding of the logic and meaning of relativity, and many will become genuinely excited about really being able to *understand* such a well-known but counterintuitive topic in physics (the intensity of this excitement actually surprised some of our early users).

There is also perhaps no better or more accessible example in all of physics illustrating how carefully thinking through consequences can uncover unexpected truths beyond the realm of daily experience. Therefore, studying special relativity can provide students with a glimpse of both the process and the rewards of theoretical physics, and also help them take an important first step into the world of contemporary physics, where reaching beyond the level of our daily experience requires an increasing reliance on logical reasoning and abstract models.

This text therefore emphasizes the logical structure of relativity, clearly showing how well-known and bizarre relativistic effects such as length contraction and time dilation are the *inevitable* consequences of the principle of relativity. If students come away from this unit feeling that the universe not only *is* in fact as described by relativity, but indeed almost *has* to be, then this unit has been successful. I urge instructors to tailor their efforts toward this goal.

This text emphasizes relativity's logical structure

This unit should follow a treatment of newtonian mechanics that includes non-relativistic kinematics, Newton's second law, conservation of momentum and energy, and some study of reference frames. This book can be used as a supplement to a traditional introductory text any time after these topics are covered. In a *Six Ideas* course, this unit should definitely follow units C and N.

How this unit is related to the other units

On the other hand, I think that it is good to go against history and schedule unit R before unit E for several reasons. First, knowing some relativity can actually make certain aspects of electricity and magnetism simpler, and unit E takes some advantage of the relativistic perspective in general and the ideas in chapter R8 in particular (see the preface to unit E for a fuller description of exactly how it depends on unit R). Second, I think that it is good for students to get a taste of some exciting contemporary physics between the many weeks of classical physics represented by units C, N, and E. This is especially true if this is the last unit in the first semester: ending the first semester with unit R means that many students will leave the course excited and intrigued about physics and (perhaps) more eager to continue their studies in the second semester.

Unit Q uses relativity only in a couple of places, once in chapter Q5 (where the relativistic de Broglie equation is mentioned) and then in the section on nuclear physics (where the relationship between mass and energy is needed). These ideas could be summarized for students if one really wanted to study unit Q before unit R for some reason. Unit T does not draw on relativity at all.

The shortest possible treatment of relativity using this book would be to omit chapters R5 and R8 through R10. This would yield a six-session introduction to basic relativistic kinematics (with no dynamics or $E = mc^2$). Adding chapter R5 and/or R8 would provide a richer introduction to pure kinematics.

How to make cuts if absolutely necessary

The shortest introduction that includes dynamics would be to omit chapters R5, R7, and R8, and add a single class session devoted to sections R5.2 through R5.5 and section R8.5 (and possibly R8.2 if there is time). This would get everything that is essential for units E and Q within eight class sessions.

However, students find the material in chapters R5 and R7 some of the most interesting in the book, and R7 is also the chapter where they really test their understanding of relativistic kinematics in the context of tough paradoxes. Therefore, I really recommend doing the whole unit if you have time.

The appendix on the Doppler shift can be covered (if desired) any time after section R5.3, and can either displace some of the latter sections of chapter R5, some of the middle sections of chapter R8, or be added to chapter R7 (which, though challenging, involves fewer new ideas than the other chapters).

8. HOW TO COMMUNICATE SUGGESTIONS

As I said at the beginning of this preface, this is a preliminary edition that represents a snapshot of work in progress. I would greatly appreciate your helping me make this a better text by telling me about errors and offering suggestions for improvement (words of support will be gratefully accepted too!). I will also try to answer your questions about the text, particularly if you are an instructor trying to use the text in a course.

Please help me make this a better text!

The *Six Ideas* bulletin board

McGraw-Hill has set up an electronic bulletin board devoted to this text. This is the primary place where you can converse with me and/or other users of the text. Please post your comments, suggestions, criticisms, encouragement, error reports, and questions on this bulletin board. I will check it often and respond to whatever is posted there. The URL for this bulletin board is:

`http://mhhe.com/physsci/physical/moore`

The *Six Ideas* web site

Before you send in an error or ask a question, please check the error postings and/or FAQ list on my *Six Ideas* web site. The URL for this site is:

`http://pages.pomona.edu/~tmoore/sixideas.html`

Visiting this site will also allow you to read the latest information about the *Six Ideas* course and texts on this site, download the latest versions of the supporting computer software, and visit related sites. You can also reach me via e-mail at `tmoore@pomona.edu`.

How to get other volumes or ancillary materials

Please refer questions about obtaining copies of the texts and/or ancillary materials to your WCB/McGraw-Hill representative or as directed on the *Six Ideas* web-site.

9. APPRECIATION

Thanks!

A project of this magnitude cannot be accomplished alone. I would first like to thank the others who served on the IUPP development team for this project: Edwin Taylor, Dan Schroeder, Randy Knight, John Mallinckrodt, Alma Zook, Bob Hilborn and Don Holcomb. I'd like to thank John Rigden and other members of the IUPP steering committee for their support of the project in its early stages, which came ultimately from an NSF grant and the special efforts of Duncan McBride. Early users of the text, including Bill Titus, Richard Noer, Woods Halley, Paul Ellis, Doreen Weinberger, Nalini Easwar, Brian Watson, Jon Eggert, Catherine Mader, Paul De Young, Alma Zook, and Dave Dobson have offered invaluable feedback and encouragement. I'd also like to thank Alan Macdonald, Roseanne Di Stefano, Ruth Chabay, Bruce Sherwood, and Tony French for ideas, support, and useful suggestions. Thanks also to Robs Muir for helping with several of the indexes. My editors Jim Smith, Denise Schanck, Jack Shira, Karen Allanson, Lloyd Black, and JP Lenney, as well as Donata Dettbarn, David Dietz, Larry Goldberg, Sheila Frank, Jonathan Alpert, Zanae Roderigo, Mary Haas, Janice Hancock, Lisa Gottschalk, and Debra Drish, have all worked very hard to make this text happen, and I deeply appreciate their efforts. I'd like to thank reviewers Edwin Carlson, David Dobson, Irene Nunes, Miles Dressler, O. Romulo Ochoa, Qichang Su, Brian Watson, and Laurent Hodges for taking the time to do a careful reading of various units and offering valuable suggestions. Thanks to Connie Wilson, Hilda Dinolfo, and special student assistants Michael Wanke, Paul Feng, and Mara Harrell, Jennifer Lauer, Tony Galuhn, Eric Pan, and all the Physics 51 mentors for supporting (in various ways) the development and teaching of this course at Pomona College. Thanks also to my Physics 51 students, and especially Win Yin, Peter Leth, Eddie Abarca, Boyer Naito, Arvin Tseng, Rebecca Washenfelder, Mary Donovan, Austin Ferris, Laura Siegfried, and Miriam Krause, who have offered many suggestions and have together found many hundreds of typos and other errors. This particular volume is based on my earlier stand-alone relativity text, *A Traveler's Guide to Spacetime* (McGraw-Hill, 1995), and I would like to thank again those named in the preface to that volume. Finally, very special thanks to my wife Joyce and to my daughters Brittany and Allison, who contributed with their support and patience during this long and demanding project. Heartfelt thanks to all!

Thomas A. Moore
Claremont, California
November 23, 1997

THE PRINCIPLE OF RELATIVITY

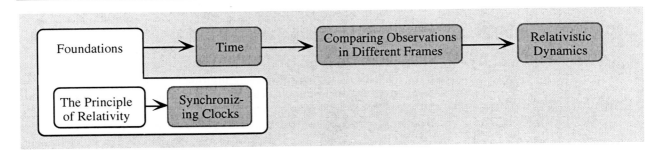

Something old,
Something new...

Traditional wedding poem

R1.1 OVERVIEW

In the last two units, we have been exploring different aspects of the newtonian model of mechanics. Successful as this model is, Albert Einstein argued in 1905 (and many experiments have shown since) that it is not *quite* right: the physics of objects moving at speeds close to that of light are better explained by a different model of mechanics that physicists call the *special theory of relativity*. Our purpose in this unit is to explore this theory.

This chapter lays the foundations for that exploration by describing the "great idea" on which the theory is founded and linking this founding principle to previous material. Here is an overview of the sections in the chapter.

R1.2   *INTRODUCTION TO THE PRINCIPLE* describes in everyday language what we call the *principle of relativity*, the core idea that lies at the heart of relativity theory. This section also provides an overview of the structure of the unit as a whole.

R1.3   *EVENTS AND SPACETIME COORDINATES* introduces the concepts of *event* and *spacetime coordinates*, ideas that will help us clearly describe the consequences of relativity theory.

R1.4   *REFERENCE FRAMES* reviews and extends the concept of a reference frame (which we first encountered in Unit *C*).

R1.5   *INERTIAL REFERENCE FRAMES* reviews the concept of an inertial reference frame (first introduced in Unit *N*) and proves that inertial frames *must* move relative to each other at constant velocities.

R1.6   *THE FINAL PRINCIPLE OF RELATIVITY* presents a refined version of the principle of relativity using ideas developed so far.

R1.7   *NEWTONIAN RELATIVITY* discusses the newtonian concept of time and reviews how (assuming this model of time) newtonian mechanics obeys its own version of the principle of relativity.

R1.2   INTRODUCTION TO THE PRINCIPLE

Everyday experiences with the principle of relativity

If you have ever traveled on a jet airplane, you know that while the plane may be flying through the air at 550 mi/h, things inside the plane cabin behave pretty much as they would if the plane were sitting at the loading dock. A cup dropped from rest in the cabin, for example, will fall straight to the floor (even though the plane moves forward many hundreds of feet with respect to the earth in the time that it takes the cup to reach the floor). A ball thrown up in the air by a child in the seat in front of you falls straight back into the child's lap (instead of being swept back towards you at hundreds of miles per hour). Your watch, the attendants' microwave oven, and the plane's instruments behave just as they would if they were at rest on the ground.

Indeed, imagine that you were confined to a small, windowless, and sound-proofed room in the plane during a stretch of exceptionally smooth flying. Is there any physical experiment that you could perform entirely within the room (that is, that would not depend on any information coming from beyond the walls of the room) that would indicate whether or how fast the plane is moving?

The answer to this question appears to be "no." No one has ever found a convincing physical experiment that yields a different result in a laboratory moving at a constant velocity than it does when the laboratory is at rest. The designers of the plane's electronic instruments do not have to use different laws of electromagnetism to predict the behavior of those instruments when the plane is in flight than they do when the plane is at rest. Scientists working to enhance the performance of the *Voyager 2* space probe tested out various techniques on an identical model of the probe at rest on earth, confident that if the techniques worked for the earth-based model, they would work for the actual probe, even though the actual probe was moving relative to the earth at nearly 72,000 km/h. Astrophysicists are able to explain and understand the behavior of distant galaxies and quasars using physical laws developed in earth-based laboratories, even though such galaxies and quasars move with respect to the earth at substantial fractions of the speed of light.

An informal statement of the principle of relativity

In short, all available evidence suggests that we can make the following general statement about the way that the universe is constructed:

> *The laws of physics are the same inside a laboratory moving at a constant velocity as they are in a laboratory at rest.*

This is an unpolished statement of what we will call the **principle of relativity**. This simple idea, based on common, everyday experience, is the foundation of Einstein's **special theory of relativity**. All of that theory's exciting and mind-bending predictions about space and time follow as *logical consequences* of the principle of relativity! Indeed, the remainder of this book is little more than a step-by-step unfolding of the rich implications of this statement.

Historical notes

The principle of relativity is both a very new and a very old idea. It was not first stated by Einstein (as one might expect) but by Galileo Galilei in his book *Dialog Concerning the Two Chief World Systems* (1632). (Galileo's vivid and entertaining description of the principle of relativity is a wonderful example of a style of discourse that has, unfortunately, become archaic.) In the nearly three centuries that passed between Galileo's statement and Einstein's first paper on special relativity in 1905, the principle of relativity as it applied to the laws of *mechanics* was widely understood and used (in fact, it was generally considered to be a consequence of the particular nature of Newton's laws).

What Einstein did was to assert the applicability of the principle of relativity to *all* of the laws of physics, and most particularly to the laws of electromagnetism (which had just been developed and thus were completely unknown to Galileo). Thus Einstein did not *invent* the principle of relativity, rather, his main contribution was to reinterpret it as being *fundamental* (more fundamental

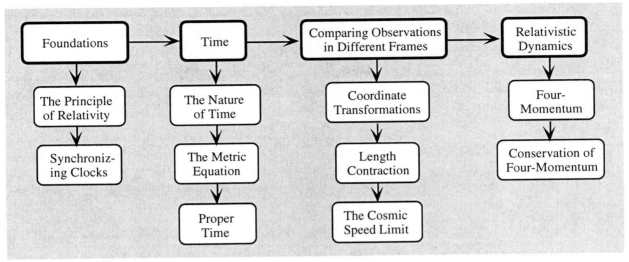

Figure R1.1: A map of Unit *R*.

than Newton's laws or even than the ideas about time that up to that point had been considered obvious and inescapable), and to explore insightfully its implications regarding the nature of light, time, and space.

Overview of the unit

Our task in this text is to work out the rich and unexpected consequences of this principle. Figure R1.1 illustrates how we will proceed to do this in the remaining chapters of this unit. This unit is divided into four subunits that appear as boxes with thick outlines at the top of the diagram: the chapters falling within each subunit are listed in a vertical string below each subunit box.

The first subunit deals with the foundations of relativity theory: we will discuss the principle of relativity and the newtonian approach to defining time in the first chapter, and Einstein's approach to defining time and how it is linked to the principle of relativity in the second. The second subunit explores the implications of the principle of relativity regarding the nature of time, with special emphasis on the *metric equation*, an equation that links space and time into a geometric unity that we call *spacetime*. The third subunit examines how the metric equation and the principle of relativity together determine how observers in different reference frames will interpret the same physical events, how *disagreements* between such observers lead to the phenomenon of length contraction, and how making sure that all observers *agree* about certain crucial things implies that nothing can go faster than light. The final subunit explores how we have to redefine energy and momentum somewhat to make conservation of energy and conservation of momentum consistent with the principle of relativity.

Our focus in *this* chapter is the principle of relativity itself, and on developing an understanding of its meaning in the context of newtonian physics before we proceed to explore the changes that Einstein proposes. It is important before we proceed with this program, however, to understand two important things about the principle of relativity: (1) it is a *postulate*, and (2) it needs to be more precisely stated before we can extract any of its logical implications.

The principle of relativity is a *postulate*

The principle of relativity is one of those core physical assumptions (like Newton's second law or the law of conservation of energy) that have to be accepted on faith: it cannot be *proven* experimentally or logically derived from more basic ideas (for example, it is not possible even in principle to test *every* physical law in every laboratory moving at a constant velocity). The value of such a postulate rests entirely on its ability to provide the foundation for a model of physics that successfully explains and illuminates experimental results.

The principle of relativity has weathered nearly a century of intense critical examination. No contradiction of the principle or its consequences has ever been conclusively demonstrated. Moreover, the principle of relativity has a variety of unusual and unexpected implications that have been verified (to an extraordinary degree of accuracy) to occur exactly as predicted. Therefore, while it cannot be *proven*, it has not yet been *disproven*, and physicists find it to be something that can be confidently believed. The principle of relativity, simple as it is, is a very rich and powerful idea, and one that the physics community has found to be not only helpful but *crucial* in the understanding of much of modern physics.

Our informal statement of the principle has problems

Turning to the other problem, the principle of relativity as we have just stated it suffers from certain problems of both abstraction and ambiguity. For example, what do we *mean* by "the laws of physics are the same"? What exactly do we mean by "a laboratory at rest"? How can we tell if a laboratory is "at rest" or not? If we intend to explore the logical consequences of any idea, it is essential to state the idea in such a way that its meaning is clear and unambiguous.

Our task in the remaining sections of this chapter is to resolve these problems. We will first replace the ambiguous phrases "laboratory," "at rest," and "constant velocity" with a single phrase involving more clearly defined terms. In the final sections, we will explore what we really mean by "the laws of physics are the same" in such laboratories. In so doing, we will provide a firm foundation for exploring the implications of the principle of relativity.

R1.3 EVENTS AND SPACETIME COORDINATES

Our task: specify what we really mean by "laboratory"

The principle of relativity, as we have stated it so far, asserts that the laws of physics are the same in a laboratory moving at a constant velocity as they are in a laboratory at rest. A "laboratory" in this context is presumably a place where one performs experiments that test the laws of physics. How can we more carefully define what we mean by this term?

The most fundamental physical laws describe how particles interact with each other and how they move in response to such interactions. Thus, perhaps the most basic need of a physicist seeking to specify and test the laws of physics is a means of mathematically describing the *motion* of a particle in space.

As we develop the theory of relativity, we need to be *very* careful about describing exactly *how* we will measure the motion of particles (hidden assumptions about the measurement process have plagued thinkers both before and after Einstein). In what follows, I will describe how we can measure the motion of a particle in terms of simple and well-defined concepts that are based on a minimum of supporting assumptions.

Definition of *event*

The first of these concepts is described by the technical term *event*. An **event** is any physical occurrence that can be considered to happen at a definite place in space and at a definite instant in time. The explosion of a small firecracker at a particular location in space and at a definite instant in time is a vivid example of an event. The collision of two particles or the decay of a single particle at a certain place and time also defines an event. Even the simple passage of a particle through a given mathematical point in space can also be treated as if it were an event (simply imagine that the particle sets off a firecracker at that point as it passes by).

Because an event occurs at a specific point in space and at a specific instant of time, we can quantify when and where the event occurs by four numbers: three that specify the location of the event in some three-dimensional spatial coordinate system, and one number that specifies what time the event occurred. We call these four numbers the **spacetime coordinates** of the event.

We can describe motion in terms of events

Note that the exact values of the spacetime coordinates of an event depend on certain arbitrary choices, such as the origin and orientation of the spatial coordinate axes and what time is considered to be $t = 0$. Once these choices are made and consistently used, however, specifying the coordinates of physical events provides a useful method of mathematically describing motion.

Specifically, we can quantify the motion of a particle by treating it as a *series* of events. We can visualize this process in the following manner. Imagine an airplane moving along the *x* axis of some coordinate system. The airplane carries a blinking strobe light. Each blink of the strobe is an event in the sense that we are using the word here: it occurs at a definite place in space and at a definite instant of time. We can describe the motion of the plane by plotting a graph of the position coordinate of each "blink event" vs. the time coordinate of the same, as illustrated in Figure R1.2. If we decrease the time between blink events, we get an even more detailed picture of the plane's motion. We can in fact describe the plane's motion to whatever accuracy we need by listing the spacetime coordinates of a sufficiently large number of blink events distributed along its path.

The preceding example is a specific illustration of a general idea: the motion of any particle can be mathematically described to arbitrary accuracy by specifying the spacetime coordinates of a sufficiently large number of events suitably distributed along its path. Studying the motion of particles is the most basic way to discover and test the laws of physics. Therefore, *the most fundamental task of a "laboratory"* (as a place in which the laws of physics are to be tested) *is to provide a means of measuring the spacetime coordinates of events.*

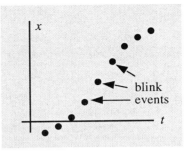

Figure R1.2: We can sketch out a graph of an object's motion (position vs. time) by plotting the "blink events" that occur along the object's path.

R1.4 REFERENCE FRAMES

We have already discussed in Chapter C3 how we can quantify the *spatial* coordinates of an object (and thus presumably an event) using a cubical lattice of measuring sticks (or something equivalent). In our past discussions of reference frames, however, we did not really face the issue of how one might measure the *time* of an event: we simply *assumed* that this could be done in some simple and obvious way.

In order to proceed with our discussion of relativity, we now need to face this issue squarely. In what follows, we will extend the cubical-lattice model of a reference frame to include a mechanism for measuring time in such a way that we can clearly distinguish the approaches to time implicit in newtonian mechanics and special relativity.

The trick is to take our cubical lattice and imagine that we attach a clock to every lattice intersection (see Figure R1.3). We can then define the *time* coordinate of an event like a firecracker explosion to be the time displayed on the lattice clock nearest the event (relative to some specified time $t = 0$) and the event's

The operational definition of spacetime coordinates

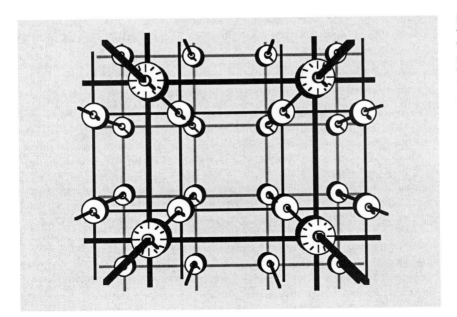

Figure R1.3: A reference frame visualized as a cubical lattice with a clock at every lattice intersection. This figure (and indeed the whole approach in this section) is adapted from E. F. Taylor and J. A. Wheeler's seminal text *Spacetime Physics*, San Francisco: Freeman, 1/e (1966), pp. 17-18.

three *spatial* coordinates to be the lattice coordinates of that nearest clock, specified in the usual way by stating the distances along the lattice directions that one has to travel (from some specified spatial origin) to the clock. We can determine these four numbers to whatever precision we want by sufficiently decreasing the lattice spacing and the time between ticks of the clock.

Why is it important to have a clock at *every* lattice intersection? The point is to make sure that there is a clock essentially *at* the location of any event to be measured. If we attempt to read the time of an event using a clock located a substantial distance away, we need to make assumptions about how long it took the information that the event had occurred to *reach* that distant clock. For example, if we read the time when the *sound* from an event reaches the distant clock, we should correct that value by subtracting the time that it takes sound to travel from the event to the clock, but to do this we have to know the speed of sound in our lattice. We can avoid this kind of complexity if we require that an event's time coordinate is measured by a clock that is essentially *present* at the event.

Note that if we must have all of these clocks, it is also essential that they all be *synchronized* in some meaningful and self-consistent manner. If these clocks were not carefully synchronized, adjacent clocks might differ wildly and thus give one a totally incoherent picture of when a particle moving through the lattice passes various lattice points. What we *mean* exactly when we say that a set of lattice clocks are synchronized is actually precisely where Newton's and Einstein's models diverge. We will discuss this issue later: for now, it is sufficient to recognize that we do have to synchronize the clocks *somehow*.

Once we have specified a synchronization method, the clock-lattice image just described represents a complete definition of a *procedure* that we can use (in principle) to determine the spacetime coordinates of an event. This amounts to an **operational definition** of spacetime coordinates: an *operational definition* of a physical quantity defines that quantity by describing how the quantity may be *measured*. Operational definitions provide a useful way of anchoring slippery human words to physical reality by linking them to specific, repeatable procedures rather than to vague comparisons or analogies.

The procedure just described represents an admittedly idealized method for determining the spacetime coordinates of an event. The actual methods employed by physicists may well differ from this description, but these methods should be *equivalent* to what is described above: the clock-lattice method defines a standard against which actual methods can to be compared. It is such a simple and direct method that it is inconceivable that any actual technique could yield different results and still be considered correct and meaningful.

Technical terms involving reference frames

With this in mind, we define the following technical words to aid us in future discussions:

A **reference frame** is defined to be a rigid cubical lattice of appropriately synchronized clocks *or its functional equivalent*.

The **spacetime coordinates** of an event in a given reference frame are defined to be an ordered set of four numbers, the first specifying the *time* of the event as registered by the nearest clock in the lattice, followed by three that specify the spatial coordinates of that clock in the lattice. For example, in a frame oriented in the usual way on the earth's surface, a firecracker explosion whose spacetime coordinates are [3 s, −3 m, 6 m, −1 m] thus happened 3 m west, 6 m north, and 1 m below the frame's spatial origin, and 3 s after whatever event defines $t = 0$.

An **observer** is defined to be a (possibly hypothetical) person who interprets measurements made in a reference frame (for example, the person who interprets the spacetime coordinates collected by a central computer collecting information from all the lattice clocks).

Note that the act of "observing" in the context of the last definition is an act of interpretation of measurements generated by the reference frame apparatus, and may have little or nothing to do with what that observer sees with his or her own eyes. When we say that "an observer in such-and-such reference frame observes such-and-such", we are actually referring to *conclusions* that the observer draws from measurements taken in that reference frame lattice.

R1.5 INERTIAL REFERENCE FRAMES

While exploring relativity theory, we will often speak of a reference frame in connection with some object. For example, one might refer to "the reference frame of the surface of the earth" or "the reference frame of the cabin of the plane" or "the reference frame of the particle." In these cases, we are being asked to imagine a clock-lattice (or equivalent) fixed to the object in question. Sometimes the actual frame is referred to only obliquely, as in the phrase "an observer in the plane cabin finds ..." Since *observer* in this text refers to someone who is using a reference frame to determine the coordinates of events, this phrase presumes the existence of a reference frame attached to the cabin of the plane.

We can in principle attach a frame to any object

A reference frame may be moving or at rest, accelerating, or even rotating about some axis. The beauty of the definition of spacetime coordinates given above is that measurements of the coordinates of events (and thus measurements of the motion of objects) can be carried out in a reference frame no matter how it is moving (provided only that the clocks in the frame can be synchronized in some meaningful manner).

However, not all reference frames are equally useful for doing physics. We saw in chapter N10 that we can divide reference frames into two general classes: **inertial frames** and **noninertial frames**. An *inertial frame* is one in which an isolated object is always and everywhere observed to move at a constant velocity (as required by Newton's first law); in a *non-inertial frame* such an object is observed to move with a nonconstant velocity in at least some situations.

Distinguishing inertial from noninertial frames

We can operationally distinguish inertial from noninertial frames using a **first-law detector**. Figure R1.4 shows a simple first-law detector. Electrically actuated "fingers" hold an electrically uncharged and non-magnetic ball at rest in the center of an evacuated spherical container. When the ball is released, it should remain at rest by Newton's first law; if it does not, the frame to which the detector container is attached is noninertial. (If we want to operate this detector in a gravitational field, we have to figure out a way to cancel the gravitational force on the ball without inhibiting its freedom to move, but in principle this can be done.) If we attach such a first-law detector to the clock at each lattice location in our reference frame and *none* of these detectors register a violation of Newton's first law, then we can say with confidence that our frame is inertial.

This definition of an inertial frame is simple enough to apply to realistic examples. For example, while a gravity-compensated detector as shown in Figure R1.4 would register no violation of the first law if it is attached to a plane at

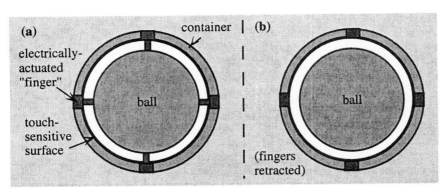

Figure R1.4: (a) A cross-sectional view of a floating-ball first law detector. Electrically actuated "fingers" hold the ball initially at rest in the spherical container. **(b)** After the fingers are retracted, the ball should continue to float at rest in the container, as long as the frame to which the container is attached is inertial.

rest, we know without actually trying it that if the plane begins to accelerate for takeoff, the detector's floating ball will be deflected toward the rear of the plane by the same (fictitious) force that presses us back into our chairs. Similarly, we might expect that detectors in a reference frame floating in deep space (far from any massive objects) would register no violation of Newton's first law, yet we know that detector balls in a similar frame that is rotating around its center will be deflected outward by the (fictitious) centrifugal force in that noninertial frame.

Inertial frames move with constant velocities relative to each other

The following statement is an important and useful consequence of the definition of an inertial reference frame:

> *Any* inertial reference frame will be observed to move at a *constant velocity* relative to *any other* inertial reference frame. Conversely, a rigid, nonrotating reference frame that moves at a constant velocity with respect to any other inertial reference frame must *itself* be inertial.

We first discussed this issue in chapter N10, but the *methods* that we used there unfortunately make certain assumptions about the nature of time that turn out to be inconsistent with the principle of relativity (as we will see). We can, however, prove that the statement above follows *directly* from the definition of an inertial reference frame without having to make any assumptions about the nature of time. Here is an argument for the first part of the statement above; the proof of the converse statement is left as an exercise.

Consider two inertial reference frames (see Figure R1.5), which we will call the **Home Frame** and **Other Frame** respectively. ("Home Frame" and "Other Frame" are phrases that I will use in this text as *names* of inertial reference frames, which I will emphasize by the capitalization.) Since these are *inertial* reference frames, observers will measure an isolated object to move with a constant velocity in either frame *by definition*. Imagine a specific isolated object that happens to be at *rest* relative to the Other Frame. Since such an isolated object must move at a constant velocity in the Other Frame if the frame is inertial, if it is initially at rest, it will have to *remain* at rest in that frame. Now let us observe the same object from the Home Frame. Since the object is isolated and the Home Frame is also inertial, the object must move at a constant velocity relative to that frame as well. But since that object is at rest with respect to the Other Frame, this means that the whole Other Frame must be observed to move relative to the Home Frame at the same constant velocity as the object! Therefore, the Other Frame will be observed to move at a constant velocity relative to the Home Frame, consistent with the statement above.

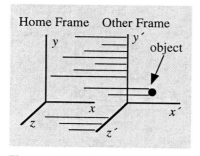

Figure R1.5: An isolated object at rest in the other frame must move at a constant velocity with respect to the Home Frame, so the whole Other Frame must move at the same constant velocity relative to the Home Frame.

Exercise R1X.1: Using a similar approach, prove the converse part of the statement above (that is, that a rigid reference frame that moves at a constant velocity with respect to any other inertial reference frame must *itself* be inertial).

R1.6 THE FINAL PRINCIPLE OF RELATIVITY

"Rest" has no physical meaning in relativity

Our first informal statement of the principle of relativity stated that "the laws of physics are the same in a laboratory moving at a constant velocity as they are in a laboratory at rest." We have subsequently developed the idea of a *reference frame* to express the essence of what we mean by a *laboratory*. However, how can we physically distinguish a reference frame "moving at a constant velocity" from one "at rest?"

The short answer is that we cannot! The principle of relativity specifically states that a reference frame moving at a constant velocity is *physically equivalent* to a frame "at rest." Therefore, there can be no physical basis for distinguishing a laboratory at rest from another frame moving at a constant velocity. Imagine that you and I are in spaceships coasting at a constant velocity in deep space. You will consider yourself to be at rest, while I am moving by you at a constant velocity. I, on the other hand, will consider myself to be at rest, while *you* are moving by me at a constant velocity. According to the principle of relativity, there is no physical experiment that can resolve our argument about who is "really" at rest. We could, of course, agree to *choose* one or the other of us to be at rest, but this choice is completely arbitrary. Therefore, if the principle of relativity is true, there is no basis for assigning an absolute velocity to any reference frame: only the *relative* velocity between two frames is a physically meaningful concept.

On the other hand, it is plausible that what we *really* mean by a reference frame "at rest" is an *inertial frame*. Moreover, we have just seen that a reference frame moving at a constant velocity relative to it must *also* be an inertial frame. Therefore, we can remove both the vague word "laboratory" and the ambiguity of the concepts "at rest" and "moving at a constant velocity" in our original statement of the principle of relativity by restating it as follows.

THE PRINCIPLE OF RELATIVITY
The laws of physics are the same in all inertial reference frames.

Our final statement of the principle of relativity

This is our final polished statement of the principle of relativity. It replaces the fuzzy and ambiguous ideas in our original statement with the sharply and operationally-defined idea of an inertial reference frame. What this principle essentially claims is that if Newton's *first* law (which describes what happens to an isolated object) is the same in two given reference frames, then *all* the laws of physics are the same in both frames. (Note that the "great idea" of this unit that appears on the front cover is a compressed version of this statement.)

But what *exactly* do we mean when we say that "the laws of physics are the same" in two frames? In the next section, we will discuss the newtonian assumption about how we can synchronize clocks in an inertial reference frame. We will then use this as a framework to explore what the principle of relativity means in newtonian mechanics.

R1.7 NEWTONIAN RELATIVITY

Imagine that we have an inertial frame floating in deep space, ready to use. We would like to use this frame to measure the coordinates of events happening in it so as to test the laws of physics. But an important problem remains to be solved: how do we synchronize its clocks?

"The solution is easy," says a newtonian physicist. "Everyone knows that time is absolute and flows equably without regard to anything external. *Any* good clock will therefore measure the flow of this absolute time. Therefore, we can simply designate one clock to be a master clock, carry it around to each of the lattice-clocks, and synchronize each lattice clock to the master. Since the master clock and the lattice clocks all measure the flow of immutable absolute time, the motion of the master clock as it is carried from place to place in the lattice is irrelevant. Once a lattice clock is set to agree with the master clock, it will certainly remain in agreement with it, since both clocks measure the flow of absolute time. Indeed, if the master clocks in two different reference frames are in agreement at any given event, then all of the clocks in the two frames will always agree. It doesn't matter whether the frames are in motion with respect to each other; it doesn't even matter if they are inertial or not. This follows from the self-evident absolute nature of time."

The newtonian approach to clock synchronization

This picture of the nature of time is straightforward and believable. It reflects the intuitive picture of time that most of us already hold. But what are its consequences?

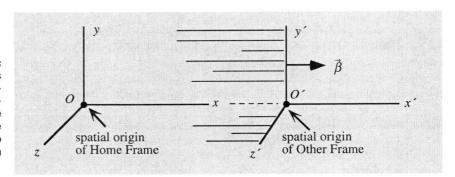

Figure R1.6: A schematic drawing of two reference frames in standard orientation. The spatial origins of the frames coincided at $t = t' = 0$ just a little while ago. (You should imagine the frame lattices intermeshing so that events can be recorded in both frames.)

Again consider two inertial frames that we will call the Home Frame and the Other Frame. We will often (but not always) imagine ourselves to be in the Home Frame (so that this frame appears to *us* to be at rest). The Other Frame will move at a *constant* velocity $\vec{\beta}$ with respect to the Home Frame according to the proof given in section R1.5. (I will consistently use the Greek letter β to represent the relative velocity of frames, standing for the "boost" in velocity that one needs to go from being at rest in one frame to being at rest in the other.)

Standard orientation for inertial reference frames

These frames might in principle have any relative orientation, but it is conventional when working with relativity theory to use our freedom to choose the orientations to put the two frames in **standard orientation**, where the Home Frame's x, y, and z axes point in the same directions as the corresponding axes in the Other Frame. We conventionally distinguish the Home Frame and Other Frame axes by referring to the Home Frame axes as x, y, and z and the Other Frame axes as x', y', and z' (the mark is called a *prime*). It also is conventional to define the origin event (the event that defines $t = 0$ in both frames) to be the instant that the spatial origin of one frame passes the origin of the other. Finally, we conventionally choose the common x axis so that the Other Frame moves in the $+x$ direction with respect to the Home Frame (implying that the Home Frame moves in the $-x$ direction with respect to the Other Frame). Signs in many equations in this text depend on this conventional choice, so it is wise to consistently follow it. Figure R1.6 illustrates two frames in standard orientation.

Consequences of the newtonian view of time

Now consider an object moving in space that periodically emits blinks of light. Let the spatial position of a certain blink event as measured in the Home Frame be represented by the vector $\vec{r}(t)$ and the same measured in the Other Frame by $\vec{r}'(t)$ (we conventionally write symbols for quantities observed in the Other Frame with an attached prime). Since according to our assumption time is universal and absolute, observers in both frames should agree at what time this blink event occurs: $t = t'$. The position of the spatial origin of the Other Frame in the Home Frame at that time is simply $\vec{\beta}t$, since the Other Frame moves at a constant velocity $\vec{\beta}$ with respect to the Home Frame, and we conventionally take both frame's origins to coincide at $t = 0$. The relationship between the object's position vectors in the two frames at the time of the blink is (as shown in Figure R1.7) given by $\vec{r}(t) = \vec{r}'(t') + \vec{\beta}t$, or

$$\vec{r}'(t') = \vec{r}(t) - \vec{\beta}t \qquad (\text{R1.1})$$

For frames in standard orientation, $\vec{\beta}$ points in the $+x$ direction, meaning that we can write equation R1.1 in component form as follows:

The galilean transformation equations

$$t' = t \qquad \text{(reminding us that time is absolute)} \qquad (\text{R1.2a})$$
$$x' = x - \beta t \qquad (\text{R1.2b})$$
$$y' = y \qquad (\text{R1.2c})$$
$$z' = z \qquad (\text{R1.2d})$$

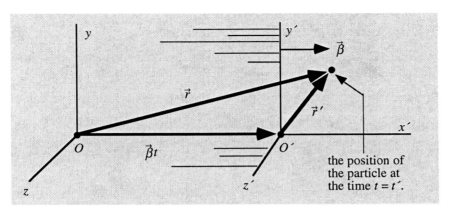

the position of
the particle at
the time $t = t'$.

Figure R1.7: The relationship between $\vec{r}$ and $\vec{r}\,'$ for two inertial reference frames (assuming that time is universal and absolute).

Physicists call these four equations the **galilean transformation equations**. These equations allow us to find the position of the object at a given time t' in the Other Frame if we know its position at time $t = t'$ in the Home Frame (*assuming*, of course, that time is universal and absolute).

If we take the time derivative of both sides of each of the last three equations, we get

$$v_x' = v_x - \beta \qquad \text{(R1.3a)}$$

$$v_y' = v_y \qquad \text{(R1.3b)}$$

$$v_z' = v_z \qquad \text{(R1.3c)}$$

The galilean *velocity* transformation equations

(Note that since $t'= t$, it really doesn't matter that we are taking a derivative with respect to t' on the left side and a derivative with respect to t on the right.) These equations tell us how to find the velocity of an object in the Other Frame given its velocity in the Home Frame: we call these equations the **galilean velocity transformation equations**.

If we take the time derivative again, we get

$$a_x' = a_x \qquad \text{(R1.4a)}$$

$$a_y' = a_y \qquad \text{(R1.4b)}$$

$$a_z' = a_z \qquad \text{(R1.4c)}$$

An object's acceleration is the same in all inertial reference frames

Equations 1.4 tell us that *observers in both inertial frames agree about an object's acceleration at a given time*, even though they may well disagree about the object's position and velocity components at that time!

Now we are in a position to discuss more fully what we might mean by "the laws of physics are the same" in every inertial reference frame in the newtonian context at least. Consider the following example. A child on an airplane throws a ball vertically into the air and catches it again. As measured in the plane cabin (which we will take to be the Other Frame), the ball appears to travel vertically along the y axis. Now imagine that you watch this process from a nearby mountain-top as the plane passes by. Instead of observing the ball travel vertically up and down, *you* will instead observe the ball to follow a shallow parabolic trajectory, because in your frame (which we will take to be the Home Frame), the ball, plane, and child all have a considerable horizontal velocity (see Figure R1.8).

An illustration of how the laws of physics can be the same in different frames

The motion of the ball in these two reference frames looks very different: it looks entirely vertical in the plane's cabin but parabolic (almost horizontal!) in your frame. Even so, you and an observer on the plane would *agree* that (1) the ball has a certain mass m (which you and the observer could each measure with your own balances) and thus should experience a gravitational force of magnitude

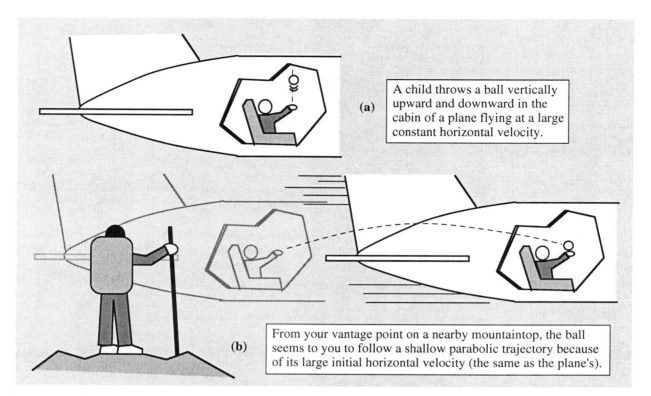

(a) A child throws a ball vertically upward and downward in the cabin of a plane flying at a large constant horizontal velocity.

(b) From your vantage point on a nearby mountaintop, the ball seems to you to follow a shallow parabolic trajectory because of its large initial horizontal velocity (the same as the plane's).

Figure R1.8: An example illustrating the application of the principle of relativity in newtonian physics. Newton's second law describes the motion of the ball in both frames.

mg acting on it, (2) this force must be the net force on the object while it is in flight (since nothing else is in contact with the ball, ignoring air friction), and (3) the ball has the same acceleration in your respective reference frames (see equation R1.4). Since you agree on the value of m, the magnitude and direction of the net force on the ball, and the acceleration that the ball experiences, you will *both* agree that Newton's second law

$$\vec{F}_{net} = m\vec{a} \quad \text{(with } \vec{F}_{net} = m\vec{g} \text{ here)} \tag{R1.5}$$

accurately predicts the ball's motion, even if you disagree about the initial velocity of the ball and thus the exact character of its subsequent motion (that is, whether it is vertical or parabolic).

In a similar fashion, you might imagine observing a game of pool in the plane cabin. You on the mountain-top and your friend on the plane will totally disagree about the initial and final velocities of the balls in any given collision (since you will observe them to have a large horizontal component of velocity that your friend does not observe). Even so, you both will find that the total momentum of the balls before a given collision is equal to the total momentum of the balls afterwards, consistent with the law of conservation of momentum (see Problems R1S.6 through R1S.8).

This is what it means to say that the "laws of physics are the same" in different inertial frames. Observers in different inertial frames may disagree about the values of various quantities (particularly positions and velocities) but each observer will agree that if one takes the mathematical equation describing a physical law (like Newton's second law) and plug in the values measured in that observer's frame, one will always find that the equation is satisfied. In other words, the same basic equations will be found to describe the laws of physics in all inertial reference frames.

SUMMARY

I. INTRODUCTION TO THE PRINCIPLE
  A. An informal statement of the principle of relativity: *The laws of physics are the same inside a laboratory moving at a constant velocity as they are in a laboratory at rest.*
    1. This is supported by everyday experience and experimental results
    2. The theory of relativity is little more than an exploration of the logical consequences of taking this as a fundamental hypothesis
  B. Subunits of Unit *R*
    1. *Foundations* (a basic exploration of principle of relativity)
    2. *Time* (an unfolding of the nature of time implied by the principle)
    3. *Comparing Observations in Different Frames*
    4. *Relativistic Dynamics* (consequences for the laws of mechanics)
  C. The informal statement of the principle is:
    1. a *postulate* (but well-supported by experimental evidence)
    2. somewhat vague and ambiguous as stated

II. REFERENCE FRAMES
  A. Our general task: specify more clearly what we mean by "laboratory"
  B. Important basic concepts and technical terms
    1. *event*: something that happens at a well-defined place and time (we can describe motion in terms of a sequence of events)
    2. *reference frame*: a cubical lattice of an appropriate size with a clock at every intersection (or something functionally equivalent)
      a. this insures that there is a clock *present* at any event
      b. clocks have to be synchronized somehow
    3. *spacetime coordinates*: an ordered set of four numbers specifying *when* an event occurs (according to nearest clock) and *where* it occurs (lattice location of that nearest clock)
    4. *observer*: person who uses a reference frame to interpret events
  C. *Inertial* reference frames:
    1. *Definition:* an isolated object is *always* and *everywhere* observed to move at a constant velocity in an inertial frame
    2. *Implication:* the relative velocity of two inertial frames is constant
  D. Steps toward a final statement of the principle of relativity:
    1. The real meaning of "laboratory moving at a constant velocity" and "laboratory at rest": both are *inertial reference frames*
    2. The principle of relativity itself implies that there can be no physical way to distinguish "rest" from "constant velocity": only the relative velocity *between* frames is physically meaningful.
  E. Final polished statement of the principle of relativity: *The laws of physics are the same in all inertial reference frames.*

III. NEWTONIAN RELATIVITY
  A. Our task: understand what we mean by "laws of physics are the same..."
  B. The newtonian assumption about time is that: *Time is universal and absolute, independent of motion or frame.* We can thus synchronize clocks in a frame by carrying around a clock.
  C. Discussing this idea's consequences is simpler if we consider two inertial frames with relative constant velocity $\vec{\beta}$ in *standard orientation:*
    1. the axes of both frames point in the same direction in space
    2. the Other Frame moves in +*x* direction relative to Home Frame
  D. Consequences of the newtonian assumption about time:
    1. *galilean transformation:* $t' = t,\quad \vec{r}' = \vec{r} + \vec{\beta}t$ (R1.2)
    2. *galilean velocity transformation:* $\vec{v}' = \vec{v} - \vec{\beta}$ (R1.3)
    3. accelerations are equal in both frames: $\vec{a}' = \vec{a}$ (R1.4)
  E. The last implies that Newton's second law is the same in both frames

GLOSSARY

the principle of relativity: the statement that *the laws of physics are the same in all inertial reference frames.* This principle is the foundation of the special theory of relativity, which is little more than an unfolding of the logical consequences of this statement.

the special theory of relativity: the model of mechanics that follows from the principle of relativity. This theory is a special case of the *general theory of relativity*, which also handles noninertial reference frames and is our currently-accepted theory of gravitation.

event: a physical occurrence or process that happens at a well-defined position in space and instant of time.

reference frame: is defined to be a rigid cubical lattice with appropriately synchronized clocks at every lattice location (or its functional equivalent).

spacetime coordinates (of a given event in a given reference frame): an ordered set of four numbers, the first specifying the *time* of the event as registered by the nearest clock in the reference frame lattice, followed by three that specify the spatial coordinates of that clock in the lattice. [Note that these coordinates depend not only on one's choice of reference frame but on one's choice of origin for the spatial axes and origin of time.]

observer: a (possibly hypothetical) person who interprets measurements made in a reference frame.

inertial reference frame: a reference frame in which an isolated object is always and everywhere observed to move with a constant velocity.

noninertial reference frame: a reference frame in which an isolated object is observed at least at some place and some time to move with a nonconstant velocity.

first-law detector: a device that continually examines the trajectories of isolated objects in its vicinity for evidence of nonconstant velocities.

Home Frame and **Other Frame:** convenient names for any pair of inertial reference frames we are comparing.

standard orientation (for two inertial frames): We say that a Home Frame and Other Frame are in standard orientation with respect to each other (1) if their coordinate axes point in the same directions in space, (2) if their relative velocity is directed along their common x axis, and (3) if the Other Frame moves in the $+x$ direction relative to the Home Frame.

galilean transformation equations: the four equations $t' = t$, $x' = x - \beta t$, $y' = y$, and $z' = z$ that specify the spacetime coordinates $[t', x', y', z']$ of an event in the Other Frame in terms of the coordinates $[t, x, y, z]$ of the same event in the Home Frame. These equations are true (1) if the frames are in standard orientation, and (2) if the newtonian assumption that time is universal and absolute is true.

galilean transformation equations: the equations $v'_x = v_x - \beta$, $v'_y = v_y$, $v'_z = v_z$ that specify the velocity components $[v'_x, v'_y, v'_z]$ of an object in the Other Frame in terms of the object's velocity components $[v_x, v_y, v_z]$ in the Home Frame. These equations are true if (1) the frames are in standard orientation, and (2) if the newtonian assumption that time is universal and absolute is true.

TWO-MINUTE PROBLEMS

R1T.1 Which of the following are (at least nearly) inertial reference frames and which are not? (Respond T if the frame is inertial, F if it is non-inertial. *Both* answers might be right in some cases: this could be an opportunity to discuss the issues involved.)
(a) a nonrotating frame floating in deep space
(b) a rotating frame floating in deep space
(c) a nonrotating frame attached to the sun
(d) a frame attached to the surface of the earth
(e) a frame attached to a car moving at a constant velocity
(f) a frame attached to a roller-coaster car

R1T.2 Which of the following physical occurrences fit the physical definition of an "event"?
A. the collision of two point particles
B. a point particle passing a given point in space
C. a firecracker explosion
D. a party at your dorm
E. a hurricane
F. A, B, and C
T. *any* of the above could be an event, depending on the scale and precision of our reference frame.

R1T.3 Since the laws of physics are the same in every inertial reference frame, there is no meaningful physical distinction between an inertial frame at rest and one moving at a constant velocity (T or F).

R1T.4 Since the laws of physics are the same in every reference frame, an object must have the same kinetic energy in all inertial reference frames (T or F).

R1T.5 Since the laws of physics are the same in every inertial reference frame, an interaction between objects must be observed to conserve energy in every inertial reference frame (T or F).

R1T.6 Since the laws of physics are the same in every inertial reference frame, if you perform identical experiments in two different inertial frames, you should get *exactly* the same results (T or F).

R1T.7 Imagine two boats. One travels 3.4 m/s eastward relative to the earth and the other 5.0 m/s eastward relative to the earth. We set up a reference frame on each boat with the x axis pointing eastward. Which boat would we conventionally select to be the Home Frame?
A. the faster boat is the Home Frame
B. the slower boat is the Home Frame
C. we are free to choose either boat to be the Home Frame

R1T.8 Imagine you are in a train traveling at half the speed of light relative to the earth. Assuming that photons emitted by the train's headlight travel at the speed of light relative to you, they would (according to the galilean velocity transformation) travel at 1.5 times the speed of light relative to the earth (T or F).

HOMEWORK PROBLEMS

BASIC SKILLS

R1B.1 A train moving with a speed of 55 m/s passes through a railway station at time $t = t' = 0$. Fifteen seconds later a firecracker explodes on the track 1.0 km away from the train station in the direction that the train is moving. Find the coordinates of this event in both the station frame (consider this to be the Home Frame) and the train frame. Assume that the train's direction of motion relative to the station defines the x direction in both frames.

R1B.2 Imagine that we define the rear end of a train 120 m long to define the origin $x' = 0$ in the train frame, and we define a certain track signal light to define the origin $x = 0$ in the track frame. Imagine that the rear end of the train passes this sign at $t = t' = 0$ as the train moves in the $+x$ direction at a constant speed of 25 m/s. Twelve seconds later, the engineer turns on the train's headlight.
(a) Where does this event occur in the train frame?
(b) Where does this event occur in the track frame?
(Please explain your response in both cases.)

R1B.3 Imagine that boat A is moving relative to the water with a velocity of 6 m/s due east and boat B is moving with a velocity of 12 m/s due west. Assume that observers on both boats use reference frames where the x direction points east. What is the velocity of boat A relative to boat B? (*Hint*: Draw a picture! What is the Home Frame attached to here? What is the Other Frame attached to?)

R1B.4 Imagine that in an effort to attract more passengers, Amtrak trains now offer free bowling in a specially constructed "bowling alley" car. Imagine that such a train is traveling at a constant speed of 35 m/s relative to the ground. A bowling ball is hurled by a passenger on the train in the same direction as the train is traveling. The ball is measured in the ground frame to have a speed of 42 m/s. What is its speed in the frame of the train according to the galilean velocity transformation? [*Hints*: Draw a picture. How should you define the $+x$ direction? Which frame is the Home Frame? Which is the Other Frame?]

R1B.5 Consider the situation described in the last problem, except assume that we know that the ball's velocity is 8 m/s in the train frame. What will be its speed relative to the ground?

SYNTHETIC

R1S.1 Read Galileo's 1632 presentation of the principle of relativity (if your professor does not make a copy available, you can find the core of Galileo's argument quoted in E. F. Taylor and J. A. Wheeler, *Spacetime Physics*, 2/e, San Francisco: Freeman, 1992, pp. 55-55). In a short paragraph, compare and contrast his presentation of the principle with the presentation in section R1.2. What for Galileo corresponds to a "laboratory moving at a constant velocity"? What for Galileo corresponds to the phrase "the laws of physics are the same" in such laboratories?

R1S.2 Imagine that Frames R Us, Inc. is constructing an economy reference frame whose price will be below every other frame on the market. Placing a clock at every point in the frame lattice is too expensive, so they decide to place *one* clock at the origin. At all other positions, they simply place a flag that springs up when an object goes by. The flag has the lattice location printed on it, so an observer

sitting at the origin can assign spacetime coordinates to every event by noting *when* he or she sees the flag spring up (according to the clock at the origin) and noting the spatial coordinates indicated by the flag. Why *doesn't* this method yield the same spacetime coordinates as having a clock at every location would? Pinpoint the *assumption* that the engineers at Frames R Us are making that is incorrect. (See problem R1R.2 for a further exploration of the problems with this reference frame.)

R1S.3 Consider a pellet-gun first-law detector like the one shown in Figure R1.4a. If the box is 20 cm across and the pellets are fired with a speed of 2.5 m/s, about how far will a pellet be deflected if the box accelerates at 0.1 m/s^2 perpendicular to the pellets' initial direction of motion?

R1S.4 Two firecrackers explode simultaneously 125 m apart along a railroad track, which we can take to define the x axis of an inertial reference frame (the Home Frame). A train (which defines the Other Frame) moves at a constant 25 m/s in the $+x$ direction relative to the track frame.
(a) According to the galilean transformation equations, do the firecrackers explode at the same time?
(b) How far apart are the explosions as measured in the train frame? (*Hint*: if $x_2 - x_1 = 125$ m, what is $x_2' - x_1'$?)
(c) Assume that instead of being simultaneous, the firecracker farthest ahead in the $+x$ direction explodes 3.0 s before the other. Now how far apart would the explosions be as measured in the train frame?

R1S.5 In a certain particle accelerator experiment, two subatomic particles A and B are observed to fly away in opposite directions from a particle decay. Particle A is observed to travel with a speed of $0.6c$ relative to the laboratory and Particle B is observed to travel with a speed of $0.9c$, where c is the speed of light (3.0×10^8 m/s) According to the galilean velocity transformation equations, what speed would particle B be measured to have in an inertial frame attached to particle A? (*Hints*: For simplicity's sake, let's agree to take the direction of motion of particle to define the $+x$ direction in both the laboratory frame and particle A's frame. If this is so, which frame should we choose to be the Home Frame in this problem? Which should we choose to be the Other Frame?)

R1S.6 Some people are playing a game of shuffleboard on an ocean cruiser moving down the Hudson at a constant speed of 17 m/s in the $+x$ direction relative to the shore. During one shot, a puck (which has a mass $m = 750$ g and is traveling at 10 m/s in the $-x'$ direction in the boat frame) hits a puck having the same mass at rest. After the collision, the first puck comes to rest and the other puck travels at 10 m/s in the $-x'$ direction in the boat frame. (Assume that the ground frame's x axis points in the same direction as the boat frame's x' axis.)
(a) Show that the total momentum of the two-puck system is conserved in the boat frame.
(b) Imagine that someone sitting on a bridge under which the boat is passing takes a video of this important game. What velocity will each puck be measured to have relative to the shore? Show that in spite of the fact that the puck's x-velocities have signs and magnitudes that are *different* from those measured on the boat, the total momentum of the two-puck system is still conserved in the shore frame.

R1S.7 A person in an elevator drops a ball of mass m from rest from a height h above the elevator floor. The elevator is moving at a constant speed β downward with respect to its enclosing building.

(a) How far will the ball fall in the building frame before it hits the floor? [*Hint*: $> h$!]

(b) What is the ball's initial vertical velocity in the building frame? [*Hint*: not 0!]

(c) Use the law of conservation of energy in the building frame to compute the ball's final speed (as measured in that frame) just before it hits the elevator floor.

(d) Use the galilean velocity transformation equations and the result of part (c) to find the ball's final speed in the elevator frame.

(e) Use the result of part (d) to show that the law of conservation of energy apparently holds in the elevator frame (assuming that it holds in the building frame).

R1S.8 Imagine two inertial reference frames in standard orientation, where the Other Frame moving with a speed β in the $+x$ direction relative to the Home Frame. Imagine that an observer in the Home Frame observes the following collision: an object with mass m_1 and velocity $\vec{v}_1$ hits an object with mass m_2 traveling with velocity $\vec{v}_2$. After the collision, the objects move off with velocities $\vec{v}_3$ and $\vec{v}_4$ respectively. Do *not* assume that all or even *any* of these velocities are in the x direction. Assume though, that total momentum is measured to be conserved in the Home Frame, that is, that:

$$m_1\vec{v}_1 + m_2\vec{v}_2 \ = \ m_1\vec{v}_3 + m_1\vec{v}_4 \quad \text{(assume this!)} \quad \text{(R1.6)}$$

Using this equation and the galilean transformation equations, show that if the newtonian view of time is correct,

then the total momentum of the two objects will also be conserved in the Other Frame

$$m_1\vec{v}_1' + m_2\vec{v}_2' \ = \ m_1\vec{v}_3' + m_1\vec{v}_4' \quad \text{(prove this!)} \quad \text{(R1.7)}$$

even though the velocities measured in the two frames are very different.

RICH-CONTEXT

R1R.1 Design a first-law detector that does *not* use a pellet gun as the basic active element. Your detector should primarily test Newton's first law and not some other law of physics (though it is fine if other laws of physics are involved in addition to the first law). Preferably, your detector should be reasonably practical and (if at all possible) usable in a gravitational field. (*Note*: there are *many* possible solutions to this problem. Be creative!)

R1R.2 Consider the economy reference frame described in problem R1S.2. Prove that an object that actually moves at a constant velocity close to that of light will be observed in the economy frame to move faster as it approaches the origin and slower as it departs. Describe what happens if the object moves *faster* than light.

ADVANCED

R1A.1 A totally symmetrical way to orient a pair of reference frames is so their $+x$ directions point in the direction that the other frame is moving. How is this different than "standard" orientation (draw a picture)? How would the galilean position and velocity transformation equations be different if we were to use this convention?

ANSWERS TO EXERCISES

R1X.1 Imagine that the Home Frame is an inertial frame. Consider a set of isolated objects arrayed around the Home Frame that happen to be initially at rest in that frame. Since their velocity with respect to the inertial Home Frame has to be constant, these objects will *remain* at rest relative to the Home Frame. Now, if the Home Frame moves at a constant velocity relative to the Other Frame (and the latter is rigid and nonrotating so that all parts of the Other frame move with a constant velocity relative to the Home Frame and vice versa), then our set of isolated objects must also move with a constant velocity relative to the Other Frame. Since these isolated objects are observed to move with a constant velocity everywhere in the Other Frame, it must be an inertial frame as well.

SYNCHRONIZING CLOCKS

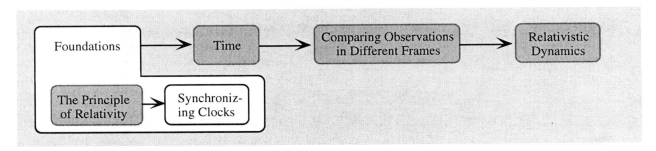

Absolute, true, and mathematical time, of itself, and from its nature, flows equably without relation to anything external...

Isaac Newton

Newton, forgive me; you found the only way which, in your age, was just about possible for a man of highest thought and creative power. The concepts that you created are even today still guiding our thinking in physics, although we now know that they will have to be replaced by others further removed from the sphere of immediate experience, if we aim at a more profound understanding of relationships.

Albert Einstein

R2.1 OVERVIEW

In the last chapter, we saw that if the newtonian view of time as universal and absolute is correct, then Newton's first and second laws of mechanics are consistent with the principle of relativity. In this chapter, we will see that if this view of time is correct, then the laws of electromagnetism are not consistent with the principle of relativity. If we take both the laws of electromagnetism and the principle of relativity to be correct, then we need to *change* our view of time. Here is an overview of the sections in this chapter.

R2.2 *THE PROBLEM OF ELECTROMAGNETIC WAVES* discusses why the laws of electromagnetism cannot be consistent with both the principle of relativity and the newtonian view of time.

R2.3 *RELATIVISTIC CLOCK SYNCHRONIZATION* shows how we can synchronize clocks in inertial frames in such a way that the laws of electromagnetism *do* become consistent with the principle.

R2.4 *THE SR SYSTEM OF UNITS* explores how we can simplify both our recipe for synchronization by measuring distance in units of time.

R2.5 *SPACETIME DIAGRAMS* introduces a useful tool for visualizing the relationships between events and the trajectories of particles.

R2.6 *SPACETIME DIAGRAMS AS MOVIES* shows how we can convert such diagrams into a motion picture of the events and particles depicted.

R2.7 *THE RADAR METHOD* presents an approach to determining the spacetime coordinates of events that is different from (but equivalent to) the clock-lattice approach.

R2.2 THE PROBLEM OF ELECTROMAGNETIC WAVES

Review of newtonian approach to relativity

To Newton and his followers, time was self-evidently universal and absolute, flowing "equably without relation to anything external". This makes time a *frame-independent* quantity: every observer in every reference frame (inertial or not!) should be able to agree on what time it is. This assumption about time was considered "self-evident" because it is consistent with our immediate experience about the way that time works.

We saw in the last chapter that this assumption implies directly that if an object is measured to have a velocity in one inertial reference frame (the Home Frame), its velocity measured in another inertial frame (the Other Frame) is given by the vector equation

$$\vec{v}' = \vec{v} - \vec{\beta} \qquad\qquad (R2.1)$$

where $\vec{\beta}$ is the velocity of the Other Frame with respect to the Home Frame: this is the vector equivalent of the galilean velocity transformation equations (equations R1.3). This equation is a direct consequence of the definition of an inertial reference frame and the assumption that time is frame-independent.

Maxwell's equation and light waves

In 1873, James Clerk Maxwell published a set of equations (now called **Maxwell's equations**) that summarized the laws of electromagnetism in compact and elegant form. These equations (which we will study in depth in the latter part of Unit *E*) were the culmination of decades of intensive and ingenious research by a number of physicists into the connection between the phenomena of electricity and magnetism, and they represent one of the greatest achievements of 19th century physics.

Among the many fascinating consequences of these equations was the prediction that traveling waves could be set up in an electromagnetic field, much like ripples could be produced on the surface of a lake. The speed at which such waves would travel is *completely determined* by various universal constants appearing in the equations, constants whose values were fixed by experiments involving electrical and magnetic phenomena and were fairly well known in 1873. The predicted speed of such electromagnetic waves turns out to be about 3.00×10^8 m/s. Light was already known to have wavelike properties (as the result of research work done in the early 19th century by Thomas Young and Augustin-Jean Fresnel) and to travel roughly this speed (as measured by Ole Rømer in 1675 and Jean-Bernard Leon Foucault in 1846). On the basis of this information, Maxwell concluded that light consisted of such electromagnetic waves. This assertion was supported by later experiments confirming that the value of the speed of light was indeed indistinguishable from the value predicted on the basis of the constants in Maxwell's equations, and particularly by the work of Heinrich Hertz, who was able to directly generate low-frequency electromagnetic waves (that is, radio waves) and demonstrate that they had the properties predicted by Maxwell's equations.

The ether hypothesis

In short, Maxwell's equations of electromagnetism predicted that light waves must travel at a specific speed $c = 3.00 \times 10^8$ m/s. The question is, relative to what? The consensus in the physics community at the time (one that Maxwell shared) was that electromagnetic waves were oscillations of a hypothetical medium called the **ether**, just as sound waves are oscillations in air and water waves are oscillations in the surface of a body of water. Physicists therefore generally assumed that light waves would travel at the predicted speed c relative to this ether, and therefore would be measured to have speed c in a reference frame at rest with respect to the ether.

In all other inertial reference frames, however, light waves must be observed to travel at a speed different from c. To see this, imagine a spaceship flying away from a space station at a speed β. A blinker on the space station emits a

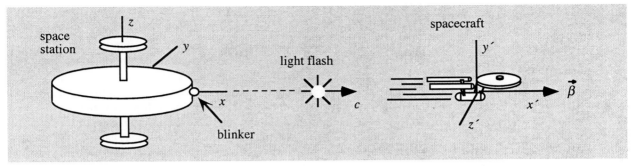

Figure R2.1: A light flash chasing a departing spaceship.

pulse of light waves toward the departing spacecraft (see Figure R2.1). Let's imagine that the space station is at rest with respect to the ether and treat this as the Home Frame. Observers on the space station will then measure the emitted pulse of light to move away from the blinker at a speed of c. How rapidly would the pulse of light waves from the blinker be observed to travel in a frame fixed to the spaceship?

The answer, according to the galilean velocity transformation equations, is as follows. By construction, both the flash and the spacecraft move in the $+x$ direction. The x component of the galilean velocity transformation equation (equation R2.1) thus reads in this case:

$$v'_{\text{light},x} = v_{\text{light},x} - \beta = c - \beta \qquad (R2.2)$$

This means that the speed of the light flash, as measured in the frame of the spacecraft (that is the Other Frame), is $c - \beta$. This makes sense: if the spacecraft happened to travel at the speed of light (so that $\beta = c$), the flash should *intuitively* appear to be motionless in the frame of the spacecraft and thus never catch up with it, in agreement with equation R2.2. In any frame moving with respect to the ether, then, light waves would be measured to have a speed $\neq c$.

But this means that Maxwell's equations strictly apply only in a *certain* inertial reference frame (the frame at rest with respect to the ether), since they state that light waves move with a *specific* speed c. Presumably some small modifications would have to be made to these equations to make them work in frames *not* at rest with respect to the ether.

Now, the ether concept proved to be problematic from the beginning. This ether had to fill all space and permeate all objects, and yet be virtually undetectable. It had to have virtually zero density and viscosity, because it was not observed to significantly impede any object's motion. On the other hand, it had to be extraordinarily "stiff" with regard to oscillations because generally the speed of waves in a medium increase with the stiffness of the medium, and c is very large (for comparison, mechanical waves traveling through *solid rock* have speeds of only 6000 m/s).

In 1887, American physicists Albert Michelson and Edward Morley performed a sensitive experiment designed to prove the existence of this seemingly indiscernible "ether". If this ether filled all space, the Earth must (as a result of its orbital motion around the Sun) be moving through the ether at a speed comparable to its orbital speed of about 30 km/s. This "ether wind" would have the effect of making the speed of light depend on the direction of its travel: a light wave moving against the ether wind would move more slowly than a wave moving across the wind. Michelson and Morley therefore constructed a very sensitive experiment that compared the speed of two beams of light sent in perpendicular directions in a very clever way. The presence of an ether wind would manifest itself in a slight difference between the speeds of light in these two directions.

Physicists fail to detect the ether

To the surprise of everyone involved, it turned out that there was no discernible difference in the speeds of the two light waves. The experiment was repeated with different orientations of the apparatus, at different times of the year (just in case the earth happened to be at rest with respect to the ether at the time of the first experiment), and by other physicists. In all cases, the result was that the speed of light was apparently a fixed value independent of the earth's motion.

(In an experiment performed in the 1930s, R. J. Kennedy and E. M. Thorndike showed that although the relative speed of the earth's reference frame in July and its frame in January is roughly 60 km/s, the numerical value of the speed of light differed by less than 2 m/s during this time span. This affirms the constant value of the speed of light with a fractional uncertainty of less than 10^{-8}.)

The Michelson-Morley result (and other corroborating results) caused a ruckus in the physics community, as physicists strove to explain away these results while saving the basic ether concept. Many explanations were offered (some involving bizarre effects of the ether wind on measurement devices), but none provided a satisfactory explanation of all known experimental data.

Einstein's proposed solution to the problem

In 1905, Albert Einstein published a short paper on the subject in the European journal *Annalen der Physik* that changed the direction of physics. In that paper, Einstein proposed that since it seemed to be impossible to demonstrate the existence of the ether, the concept of the ether should be rejected and that we simply accept the idea that light is able to move in a vacuum. But since the vacuum of empty space provides no anchor defining a special frame where the speed of light is c (what would such a frame be attached to?), if we accept that the speed of light in a vacuum is c, then we must accept that this speed is c in *every* inertial reference frame, in direct contradiction to equation R2.2! The assumption that *the speed of light is a frame-independent quantity* is necessary, Einstein argued, to make Maxwell's equations consistent with the principle of relativity, since Maxwell's equations are laws of physics that predict a specific and well-defined value for the speed of light.

The frame-independence of the speed of light goes deeply against our intuition. How can a pulse of light waves be measured to move at a speed c in the frame of the space station of our previous example and *also* in the frame of the spacecraft, when the two frames are not at rest with respect to each other? Einstein's bold idea, while neatly sidestepping the experimental difficulties associated with the ether idea, seemed impossible to most of his contemporaries.

However, there are really only three possibilities: either the principle of relativity is wrong, Maxwell's equations are wrong, or the galilean velocity transformation equations are wrong. By accepting the ether concept, physicists before Einstein had opted to accept the idea that Maxwell's equations would have to be modified in frames moving with respect to the ether, thus keeping the galilean velocity transformation and implicitly rejecting the full principle of relativity. Even as evidence against the ether hypothesis became firm and incontrovertible, rejection of the galilean velocity transformation, so solidly based on simple and obvious ideas, seemed absurd.

On the other hand, what Einstein suggested did have a certain simplicity and elegance. Throw away the ether idea, he said. It is an unhelpful, *ad hoc* hypothesis with no experimental backing. Throw away the awkward and bizarre theories that arose to explain our inability to detect the ether. Embrace instead the beautiful simplicity of the principle of relativity and Maxwell's equations. The speed of light then is the same in all inertial reference frames as a matter of course, and the null results of experiments like the Michelson-Morely experiment are trivially explained.

The cost? *The galilean transformation equations must be wrong.* But what could possibly be wrong with their derivation? It is the idea of universal and absolute time that is wrong, argued Einstein. Let's look at what the principle of relativity requires of time...

R2.3 RELATIVISTIC CLOCK SYNCHRONIZATION

Our basic problem is that the concept of universal and absolute time seems to be at odds with having the principle of relativity apply to Maxwell's equations, yet experimental results support the idea that the principle of relativity *does* apply to Maxwell's equations. If time is not "universal and absolute", how can we even define what time means?

The solution, as Einstein was the first to see, is that we must define what we mean by "time" *operationally* within each inertial frame by specifying a concrete and specific procedure for synchronizing that frame's clocks that is consistent with both the principle of relativity and the laws of electromagnetism.

But how can we synchronize clocks in such a manner? Here is a simple method. Maxwell's equations imply that light moves through a vacuum at a certain fixed speed c. The principle of relativity requires that this speed be the same in every inertial reference frame, as we discussed in the previous chapter. Therefore, *any* synchronization method consistent with the principle of relativity will lead to light being found to have the speed c in any inertial reference frame.

Einstein's method of clock synchronization

Since the speed of light has to be c in every inertial frame anyway, let us in fact synchronize the clocks in our inertial reference frame by *assuming* that light always has the same speed of c! How do we do this? Imagine that we have a master clock at the spatial origin of our reference frame. At exactly $t = 0$, we send a light flash from that clock that ripples out to the other clocks in the frame. Since light is assumed to travel at a speed of $c = 299,792,458$ m/s, this flash will reach a lattice clock exactly 1.0 meter from the master clock at exactly $t = (1.0 \text{ m})/(299,792,458 \text{ m/s}) = 3.33564095 \times 10^{-9}$ s $= 3.33564095$ ns. Therefore, if we set this clock to read 3.33564095 ns exactly as the light flash passes, we know that it is synchronized with the master clock. The process is similar for all of the other clocks in the lattice.

So here is a first draft of a description of Einstein's approach to synchronize the clocks in an inertial reference frame:

A light flash is emitted by clock A in an inertial frame at time t_A (as read on clock A) and received by clock B in the same frame at time t_B (as read on clock B). These clocks are defined to be **synchronized** if $c(t_B - t_A)$ is equal to the distance between the clocks. That is, the clocks are synchronized if they measure the speed of a light signal traveling between them to be c.

Exercise R2X.1: Imagine that we have a clock on the earth and a clock on the moon. How can we tell if these clocks are synchronized according to this definition? Imagine that we send a flash of light from the earth clock toward the moon at exactly noon, as registered by the earth clock. What time will the clock on the moon read when it receives the flash if the two clocks are synchronized? (The distance between the earth and the moon is 384,000,000 m.)

"Now, wait a minute!" I hear you cry. "Isn't all this a bit circular? You claim that Maxwell's equations predict that light will be measured to have the same speed c in every inertial reference frame. But then you go setting up the clocks so that this result is *assured*. Is this fair?"

Note we are *assuming* that Maxwell's equations obey the principle of relativity

This *is* fair. We are not trying here to *prove* that Maxwell's equations obey the principle of relativity, we are *assuming* that they do, so that we can determine the consequences of this assumption. To make this clear in his original paper, Einstein actually stated the frame-independence of the speed of light as a separate postulate, *emphasizing* that it is an assumption. The point is that if the principle of relativity is true, the speed of light will be measured to have the speed c no matter *what* valid synchronization method we use, so why not use a method based on that fact?

Moreover, there *are* other valid ways of synchronizing the clocks in a given inertial reference frame, ways that make no assumptions whatsoever about the frame-independence of the speed of light.[*] If such a method were used to synchronize clocks in an inertial frame, such a frame could be used to verify *independently* that the speed of light is indeed frame-independent. Theorists have shown that these alternative methods yield the same consequences as one gets assuming the frame-independence of the speed of light. These methods are, however, also more complex and abstract: the definition of synchronization in terms of light is much more vivid and easy to use in practice.

R2.4 THE SR SYSTEM OF UNITS

In ordinary SI units, the speed of light c is equal to 299,792,458 m/s, a somewhat ungainly quantity. The definition of clock synchronization given in the last section means that we will often need to calculate how long it would take light to cover a certain distance or how far light will travel in a certain time. You can perhaps see how messy such calculations will be.

Definition of the "second" of distance

For this reason (and many others) it will be convenient when studying relativity theory to measure distance not in the conventional unit of meters but in a new unit called a *light-second* or just *second* for short. A **light-second** is defined to be the distance that light travels in one second of time. Since 1983, the meter has in fact been officially *defined* by international agreement as the distance that light travels in 1/299,792,458 second. Therefore there are exactly 299,792,458 meters in 1 light-second *by definition*.

Advantages of using this unit of distance

We can, of course, measure distance in any units that we please: there is nothing magically significant about the meter. Choosing to measure distance in light-seconds has some important advantages. In the first place, light travels exactly one second of distance in one second of time by definition. This allows us to talk about clock synchronization much more easily. For example, if clock A and clock B are 7.3 light-seconds apart in an inertial reference frame and a light flash leaves clock A when it reads $t_A = 4.3$ seconds, the flash should arrive at clock B at a time $t_B = (4.3 + 7.3)$ s = 11.6 s if the two clocks are correctly synchronized, since light travels exactly 1 light-second in 1 second of time by definition. You can see that there are no ungainly unit calculations to perform if we measure distance this way.

Indeed, agreeing to measure distance in seconds allows us to state the definition of clock synchronization in an inertial frame in a particularly nice and concise manner (this will be our *final* draft of this description):

Two clocks in an inertial reference frame are defined to be synchronized if the time interval (in seconds) registered by the clocks for a light flash to travel between them is equal to their separation (in light–seconds).

In spite of the tangible advantages that measuring distance in seconds yields when it comes to talking about synchronization, this is not the most important reason for choosing to do so. In the course of working with relativity theory, we will uncover a deep relationship between time intervals and distance intervals,

---

[*]One of the simplest is described by Alan Macdonald, *Am. J. Phys.*, **51**(9), 1983. Macdonald's method is as follows. Assume that clocks A and B emit flashes of light toward each other at $t = 0$ (as read on each clock's *own* face). If the readings of the two clocks also agree when they receive the light signal from the other clock, they are synchronized. This method only assumes that the light flashes take the same time to travel between the clocks in each direction (that is, there is no preferred direction for light travel): it does *not* assume light has any frame-independent speed. Achin Sen [*Am. J. Phys.*, **62**(2), 1994] presents a particularly nice example of an approach that side-steps the synchronization issue, showing mathematically that the results of relativity follow directly from the principle of relativity. Sen's article also contains an excellent list of references.

akin to the relationship between distances measured north and distances measured east on a plane. One would not think of measuring northward distances in feet, say, and eastward distances in meters: that would obscure the fundamental similarity and relationship of these measurements. Similarly, measuring time intervals in seconds while measuring distance intervals in meters obscures the fundamental similarity in these measurements that will be illuminated by relativity theory. Choosing to measure time in the same units as distance will make this beautiful symmetry of nature more apparent.

The standard unit system used by scientists studying ordinary phenomena is the *Système International,* or SI, unit system. In this system, the units for mechanical quantities (such as velocity, momentum, force, energy, angular momentum, pressure, and so on) are based on three fundamental units: the *meter*, the *second*, and the *kilogram*. In this text, however, we will use a slightly modified version of the SI unit system (let's call it the *Système Relativistique,* or SR unit system) where distance is measured in *seconds* (that is, light–seconds) instead of in meters (with the other basic units being the same).

The SR unit system

As discussed in chapter C2 of unit C, the standard method of converting any quantity from one kind of unit to another is the method of *conversion factors*. One first writes down an equation stating the basic relationship between the units in question: 1 mile = 1.609 km, for example. We then rewrite this in the form of a ratio equal to one: 1 = (1 mi / 1.609 km) or 1 = (1.609 km / 1 mi). Since multiplying by one doesn't change a quantity, you can multiply the original quantity by whichever ratio leads you to the correct final units upon cancellation of any units that appear in both the numerator and denominator.   For example, to determine how many miles there are in 25 km, you simply multiply the 25 km by the first of the two ratios described above, as follows:

$$25 \text{ km} = 25 \text{ km} \cdot 1 = 25 \text{ km} \left(\frac{1 \text{ mi}}{1.609 \text{ km}} \right) = \frac{25}{1.609} \text{ mi} \approx 16 \text{ mi} \qquad \text{(R2.3)}$$

The factors used to convert from SI distance units to SR distance units are based on the fundamental definition of the light-second: 299,792,458 m $\equiv$ 1 s. Thus the basic conversion factors that we need are 1 = (1 s / 299,792,458 m) or 1 = (299,792,458 m / 1 s). For example, a distance of 25 km can be converted into a distance in (light)seconds as follows:

$$25 \text{ km} = 25 \text{ km} \cdot 1 \cdot 1 = 25 \text{ km} \left(\frac{1000 \text{ m}}{1 \text{ km}} \right) \left(\frac{1 \text{ s}}{2.998 \times 10^8 \text{ m}} \right)$$

$$\approx 8.3 \times 10^{-5} \text{ s} = 83 \text{ μs} \qquad \text{(R2.4)}$$

meaning that 25 km is equivalent to the distance that light travels in 83 millionths of a second.

The light-second is a rather large unit of distance (the moon is only about 1.3 light-seconds away from the earth!). A light-nanosecond $\equiv 10^{-9}$ light-second (= 0.2998 m $\approx$ 1 ft) is a more appropriate unit on the human scale. On the astronomical scale, the light-year $\approx 3.16 \times 10^7$ s $\approx 0.95 \times 10^{15}$ m is the appropriate (and commonly used) distance unit. The dimensions of the solar system are conveniently measured in light-hours (it is about 10 light-hours in diameter). All of these units represent extensions of the basic unit of the light-second.

In the SR unit system, the light-second is considered to be *equivalent* to the second of time and both units are simply referred to as *seconds*. This means that these units can be canceled if one appears in the numerator of an expression and the other in the denominator. For example, in the SI system, velocity has units of meters/second, but in the SR system, it has units of seconds/second = unitless(!). Thus an object that travels 0.5 light-seconds in 1.0 second has a speed in the SR system of (0.5 s / 1.0 s) = 0.5 (no units!). The bare number

Velocity is unitless in the SR unit system

representing a speed in this case actually represents a comparison of the particle's speed to the speed of light, since light covers 1.0 second of distance in 1.0 second of time by definition. Thus a particle traveling at a speed of 0.5 (in SR units) is traveling at half the speed of light.

Natural SR units for other physical quantities

In a similar manner, one can find the natural units for any physical quantity in the SR system. For example, the kinetic energy of a particle has the same units as mass·(speed)^2. In the SI system, these units would be kg·m^2/s^2. Thus the natural unit of energy in the SI system is the joule, defined to be 1 kg·m^2/s^2. In the SR system, mass·(speed)^2 has units of kg·s^2/s^2 = kg. Thus the natural SR unit for energy is the kilogram (the same as the unit of mass!). How much energy is represented by a SR kilogram of energy? We can determine this by using the standard conversion factor to convert the SR distance unit of seconds to the SI distance unit of meters:

$$1 \text{ kg (energy)} = 1 \text{ kg} \frac{s^2}{s^2} \left(\frac{2.998 \times 10^8 \text{ m}}{1 \text{ s}} \right)^2 \left(\frac{1 \text{ J}}{1 \text{ kg} \cdot \text{m}^2/\text{s}^2} \right) = 8.988 \times 10^{16} \text{ J} \quad (R2.5)$$

This unit is roughly equal to the yearly energy output of ten full-sized electrical power plants!

Exercise R2X.2: What is the natural unit for momentum in the SR system?

In general, what we need to do to convert from SR units to SI units is to multiply the SR quantity by whatever power of the conversion factor 1 = (299,792,458 m / 1 s) yields the correct power of meters in the units of the final result. Similarly, to convert from SI units to SR units, we simply multiply the SI quantity by whatever power of this factor causes the units of meters to disappear. (See Appendix A for a complete discussion of how to convert units and equations from one unit system to the other.)

R2.5 SPACETIME DIAGRAMS

The clock synchronization method described at the beginning of this chapter completes the description of how to build and operate an inertial reference frame. We now know how to assign spacetime coordinates to any event occurring within that inertial frame in a manner consistent with the principle of relativity.

Problems in relativity theory often involve studying how physical events relate to one another. The coordinates of events can be conveniently depicted using a special kind of graph called a **spacetime diagram**. Throughout the unit, we will find spacetime diagrams to be indispensable in helping us express and understand the relationships between events.

How to draw events on a spacetime diagram

Consider an event A whose spacetime coordinates are measured in some inertial frame to be t_A, x_A, y_A, z_A. To simplify our discussion somewhat, assume that $y_A = z_A = 0$ (that is, the event occurs somewhere along the x axis of the frame). Now imagine drawing a pair of coordinate axes on a sheet of paper. Label the vertical axis with a t and the horizontal axis with an x: it is conventional to take the t axis to be vertical in spacetime diagrams. Choose an appropriate scale for each of these axes. Now you can represent when and where event A occurs by plotting the event as a point on the diagram (in the usual manner that you would use in plotting a point on a graph) as shown in Figure R2.2. Any event that occurs along the x axis in space can be plotted as a point on such a diagram in a similar manner.

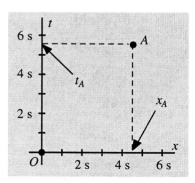

Figure R2.2: How to plot an event A on a spacetime diagram. In this particular case, event A has a time coordinate $t_A \approx 5.4$ s and an x coordinate $x_A \approx 4.5$ s.

Note that the point marked O on Figure R2.2 also represents an event. This event occurs at time $t = 0$ and at position $x = 0$. We call this event the **origin event** of the diagram.

If we need to draw a spacetime diagram of an event A that occurs in space somewhere in the xy plane (i.e. which has $z_A = 0$ but nonzero t_A, x_A, y_A), we must add another axis to the spacetime diagram (as shown in Figure R2.3). The resulting diagram is somewhat less satisfactory and more difficult to draw because we are trying to represent a three-dimensional graph on a two-dimensional sheet of paper. A spacetime diagram showing events with *three* nonzero spatial components is impossible to draw, as that would involve trying to represent a four-dimensional graph on a two-dimensional sheet of paper. A four-dimensional graph is hard to visualize at all, much less draw! Fortunately, diagrams with one or two spatial dimensions will be sufficient for most purposes.

In chapter R1 we visualized describing the motion of an object by imagining the object to carry a strobe light that blinks at regular intervals. If we can specify when and where each of these blink events occurs (by specifying its spacetime coordinates), we can get a pretty good idea of how the object is moving. If the time interval between these "blink events" is reduced, we get an even clearer picture of the object's motion. In the limit that the interval between blink events goes to zero, the object's motion can be described in unlimited detail by a list of such events. Thus the motion of any object can be described in terms of a connected *sequence* of events. We call the set of all events occurring along the path of a particle the particle's **worldline**.

On a spacetime diagram, an event is represented by a point. Therefore a worldline is represented on a spacetime diagram by an infinite set of infinitesimally separated points, which is a *curve*. This curve is nothing more than a graph of the position of the particle vs. time (except that the time axis is conventionally taken to be vertical on a spacetime diagram). Figure R2.4 illustrates worldlines for several examples of objects moving in the x direction.

Note that because the time axis is taken to be vertical, the slope of the curve on a spacetime diagram representing the worldline of an object traveling at a constant velocity in the x direction is not its x-velocity v_x (as one might expect) but [rise/run] $= \Delta t/\Delta x = 1/v_x$! Thus the slope of the curve representing the worldline of an object at rest is infinity and *decreases* as v_x increases. The worldline of an object traveling at a constant x velocity has a constant slope.

Occasionally we need to draw a spacetime diagram of the worldline of an object moving in two spatial dimensions. The spacetime diagram in such a case is necessarily three-dimensional, which is hard to draw on two-dimensional paper. Figure R2.5 shows an example of such a spacetime diagram.

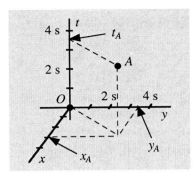

Figure R2.3: Plotting an event A that has nonzero x and y coordinates (but zero z coordinate).

Worldlines

A worldline's slope is the *inverse* of its particle's *x*-velocity

Figure R2.4: A sequence of spacetime diagrams illustrating various important things to know about worldlines.

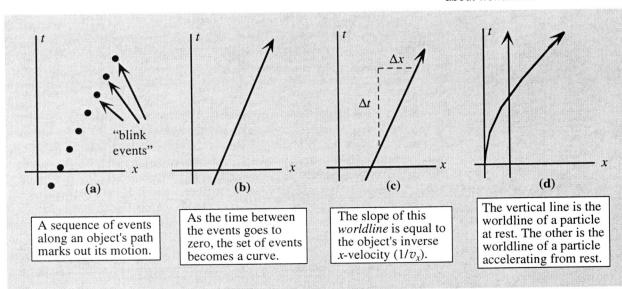

(a) — A sequence of events along an object's path marks out its motion.

(b) — As the time between the events goes to zero, the set of events becomes a curve.

(c) — The slope of this *worldline* is equal to the object's inverse x-velocity ($1/v_x$).

(d) — The vertical line is the worldline of a particle at rest. The other is the worldline of a particle accelerating from rest.

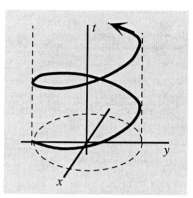

Figure R2.5: The worldline of a particle traveling in a circular path in the xy plane.

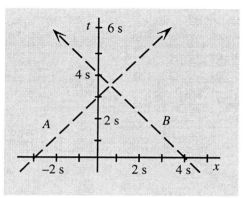

Figure R2.6: Light-flash worldlines on a spacetime diagram. Worldline *A* represents a light flash moving in the +x direction. Worldline *B* represents a flash traveling in the opposite direction.

Light-flash worldlines have slopes of ±1

In drawing spacetime diagrams it is also convenient and conventional to use the same-sized scale on both axes. If this is done, the worldline of a flash (that is, a very short pulse) of light always has a slope of either 1 (if the flash is moving in the +x direction) or –1 (if the flash is moving in the –x direction), since light travels 1.0 second of distance in 1.0 second by definition in every inertial reference frame. It is also conventional to draw the worldline of a flash of light with a dashed line instead of a solid line (see Figure R2.6).

Exercise R2X.3: On Figure R2.6, draw the worldline of a particle moving in the –x direction through the origin event with a speed of 0.2 (1 light-sec per 5 s).

Exercise R2X.4 Assume that the worldline of the center of the earth in Figure R2.6 coincides with the vertical *t* axis. If at $t = 0$, the moon lies in the +x direction relative to the earth, draw its worldline as well (the earth is 384,000 km from earth). The moon actually orbits the earth once a month. Are you going to be able to see the curvature of the moon's worldline on this diagram? Explain.

R2.6 SPACETIME DIAGRAM AS MOVIES

It is easy to get confused about what a spacetime diagram really represents. For example, in the spacetime diagram shown in Figure R2.6, it is easy to forget that the light flashes shown are moving in only one dimension (along the *x* axis), not in two. The velocity vectors of the light flashes shown above point opposite to each other, not perpendicular to each other.

Making a movie viewer for a spacetime diagram

There is a technique that you can use to make the meaning of any spacetime diagram clear and vivid: turn it into a movie! Here's how. Take a 3×5 index card and cut a slit about 1/16 of an inch wide and about 4 inches long using a knife or a razor blade. This slit represents the spatial *x* axis at a given instant of time. Now place the slit over the *x* axis of the spacetime diagram. What you can see through the slit shows you what is happening along the spatial *x* axis at time $t = 0$. Now slowly move the slit up the diagram, keeping it horizontal: you will see through the slit what is happening along the spatial *x* axis at successively later times. You can watch the objects whose worldlines are shown on the diagram move to the left or right as the slit exposes different parts of their worldlines. Events drawn as dots on the diagram will show up as flashes as you move the slit past them. What you see through the slit as you move it up the diagram is essentially a movie of what happens along the *x* axis as time passes. Figure R2.7 illustrates the process.

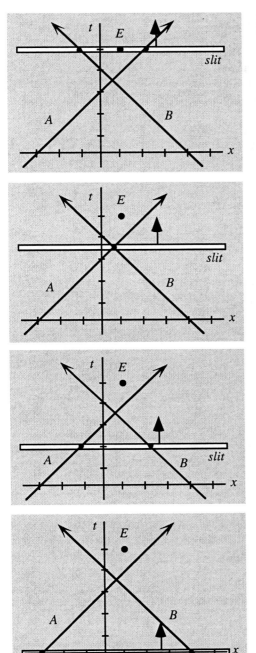

READ THIS FIGURE FROM THE BOTTOM UP!

Figure R2.7d: Now the light flashes have passed each other and are moving away from each other. You can also see through the slit the momentary flash representing the firecracker explosion (event *E*).

Figure R2.7c: At this instant, the light flashes pass through each other at a position of about *x* = + 1 m.

Figure R2.7b: As time passes (and you move the slit up the diagram) the dots representing the light flashes approach each other.

Figure R2.7a: The spacetime diagram is basically the same as Figure R2.6 with a firecracker explosion (Event *E*) thrown in to make things more interesting. At time *t* = 0, the light flashes are represented by black dots that you can see through the slit at *x* = − 3 m and *x* = + 4 m.

If you employ this technique, you cannot fail to interpret a spacetime diagram correctly. After a bit of practice with the card, you will be able to convert diagrams to movies in your head.

R2.7 THE RADAR METHOD

If we are willing to confine our attention to events occurring only along the x axis (and thus to objects moving only along that axis), it is possible to determine the spacetime coordinates of an event with a single master clock and some light flashes: we don't need to construct a lattice at all! The method is analogous to locating an airplane using radar.

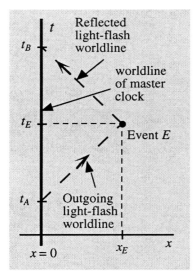

Figure R2.8: At time t_A, the master clock at rest at x = 0 in the Home Frame sends out a flash of light, which reflects from something at event E and returns to the master clock at time t_B.

Imagine that at the spatial origin of our reference frame (that is, at $x = 0$), we have a master clock that periodically sends flashes of light in the $\pm x$ directions. Imagine that a certain flash emitted by the master clock at t_A happens to illuminate an event E of interest that occurs somewhere down the x axis. The reflected light from the event travels back along the x axis to the master clock, which registers the reception of the reflected flash at time t_B (see the spacetime diagram of Figure R2.8).

The values of the emission and reception times t_A and t_B are sufficient to determine both the location and the time that event E occurred! Consider first how we can determine the location. The light-flash's round trip time is $t_B - t_A$. Since in this time the light covered the distance from $x = 0$ to event E and back, and since the light flash travels 1 second of distance in 1 second of time by definition, the distance to event E (in seconds) must be half of the round trip time (in seconds). The x coordinate of event E is thus

$$x_E = \pm \tfrac{1}{2}(t_B - t_A) \qquad \text{(R2.6a)}$$

We determine the sign of x_E by noting whether the reflected flash comes from the $-x$ or $+x$ direction. (In this case, the reflected flash comes from the $+x$ direction, so we would select the positive sign.)

We can determine the time coordinate t_E of the event as follows. Since the light flash traveled the same distance to the event as back from the event, and since the speed of light is a constant, the event must have occurred exactly halfway between times t_A and t_B. The midpoint in time between times t_A and t_B can be found by computing the average, so

$$t_E = \tfrac{1}{2}(t_B + t_A) \qquad \text{(R2.6b)}$$

The radar method yields the same result as the clock-lattice method.

Equations R2.6 represent a method of determining the spacetime coordinates of an event that does *not* require the use of a complete lattice of synchronized clocks, but you should be able to convince yourself that *this method produces exactly the same coordinate values that you would get from a clock-lattice*. For example, imagine that you actually had a lattice clock at x_E (the location of event E). The distance between that clock and the master clock at the origin must be equal to half the time that it would take a flash of light to go from one clock to the other and back, since light travels a second of distance in a second of time by definition. The lattice clock at x_E at the time of event E must read t_A + (the light travel time between the two clocks) $= t_A + \tfrac{1}{2}(t_B - t_A) = \tfrac{1}{2}(t_B + t_A)$, since two clocks are only defined to be synchronized if they measure a light flash to travel between them at the speed of light (1 s of distance in 1 s of time).

Using the radar method to determine spacetime coordinates is therefore equivalent to using a lattice of synchronized clocks. In some cases in this text, we will find it clearer or more convenient to use one method, and in some cases the other. The important thing to realize is that *either* the radar method or the clock-lattice method provides specific, well-defined, and equivalent ways of assigning time coordinates to events, and both methods are based on the assumption that the speed of light is a frame-independent constant. These methods essentially define what time means in special relativity, and thus will provide the foundation for most of the arguments in the remainder of the text. *Make sure that you understand both of these methods thoroughly.*

Adapting the method for three spatial directions

The radar method is actually used to track the trajectories of aircraft (the impracticality of using a clock-lattice to do the same is obvious!) We can precisely locate an object in three spatial dimensions if we not only record the time that the outgoing pulse is sent and the time that the reflected pulse was received but also the *direction* from which the reflected pulse was received. The analysis is more complicated (see Problem R2S.6), but the basic method is the same.

SUMMARY

I. THE PROBLEM OF ELECTROMAGNETIC WAVES
    A. Newtonian assumption that time is absolute $\Rightarrow \vec{v}\,' = \vec{v} - \vec{\beta}$ (R2.1)
    B. Maxwell's equations predict electromagnetic waves which Maxwell identified as being light and completely determine their speed c
    C. What is c measured with respect to? The ether hypothesis:
        1. waves move at speed c relative to a medium called the *ether*
        2. so speed of light $\neq c$ in frames moving with respect to ether
    D. The physics community fails to detect the ether (most famous of many experiments is Michelson/Morley experiment, which failed to detect the ether wind that earth's orbital motion must cause)
    E. Einstein's proposed solution: *there is no ether*. Consequences:
        1. Maxwell's equations specify c relative to *vacuum*
        2. We cannot define a unique reference frame attached to the vacuum
        3. only solution: speed of light must be c in *all* inertial frames
            (i.e. Maxwell's equations are consistent with principle of relativity)

II. RELATIVISTIC CLOCK SYNCHRONIZATION
    A. This solution contradicts Eqn. R2.1 and thus newtonian idea of time
    B. Einstein's synchronization method: *clocks in a frame are synchronized if they measure light-flashes traveling between them to have speed c.*
        1. this method *assumes* that c is a universal constant
        2. which *has* to be true if principle of relativity is true!

III. SR SYSTEM OF UNITS
    A. SR = *Système Relativistique* (pun on SI = *Système International*)
    B. Replace SI distance unit of meters with SR distance unit of seconds
        1. 1 (light-)second of distance = distance light travels in 1 s
        2. by international convention, this is now $\equiv$ 299,792,458 m
        3. Note that speed of light is 1 second/second = 1 by definition
    C. Natural units of various physical quantities in this unit system
        1. velocity is *unitless* (value = fraction of speed of light)
        2. energy is naturally measured in kg (1 kg = 8.988×10^{16} J), etc.
    D. Conversion between SR and SI units (see Appendix A also)
        1. SI to SR: multiply quantity by power of 1 = (3.00×10^8 m / 1 s) that makes units of meters all go away
        2. SR to SI: do same until you get appropriate power of meters

IV. SPACETIME DIAGRAMS
    A. Important visual aid for displaying relationships between events
    B. Basic characteristics and conventions
        1. spacetime diagram is a graph of time coordinate versus position
        2. t axis is conventionally drawn vertical, x axis horizontal
        3. both axes are conventionally given the same scale
    C. Implications
        1. *events* in spacetime $\rightarrow$ points on diagram
        2. worldline = connected sequence of events $\rightarrow$ curve on diagram
        3. slope of worldline curve on diagram = $\Delta t / \Delta x = 1/v_x$
        4. light-flash worldlines (conventionally dashed) have slope ± 1
    D. View diagram through an upward-moving horizontal slit to display a movie of what happens along x axis as time passes

IV. RADAR METHOD
    A. Alternative to clock-lattice approach uses *one* clock and light flashes
    B. Process for determining spacetime coordinates of event E on x axis:
        1. send flash of light from master clock at time t_A
        2. if master clock receives the reflection from event E at time t_B, then
            $x_E = \frac{1}{2}(t_B - t_A)$, $t_E = \frac{1}{2}(t_B + t_A)$
    C. Results are equivalent to those from light-synchronized clock-lattice

GLOSSARY

Maxwell's Equations: a set of equations that summarize the laws of electromagnetism. These equations predict the existence of electromagnetic waves that travel with a certain completely determined speed c. (If these waves have the appropriate wavelength we perceive them as light.)

ether: a hypothetical substance that was thought at the turn of the century to be provide the medium that light waves moved through. The ether was also thought to define the reference frame where the speed of light had the value c predicted by Maxwell's equations.

synchronization (according to Einstein): two clocks in an inertial reference frame are *synchronized* if the time interval registered by the clocks for a light flash to travel between them is equal to their separation divided by c (that is, if the speed of a light flash moving between them is measured by them to have the speed c).

second (of distance): the distance that light travels in one second of time (also known as a *light-second*). By international convention, 1 s (of distance) = 299,792,458 m.

SR unit system: the same unit system as the SI unit system, except that we measure distance in seconds instead of meters. In this unit system, velocity is unitless and mass, momentum, and energy are all measured in kg [We can convert quantities in one unit system to the other by multiplying or dividing by an appropriate power of the conversion factor $1 = (3.00 \times 10^8 \text{ m} / 1 \text{ s})$.]

spacetime diagram: a graph where we plot the time coordinates of events versus their position coordinates. Spacetime diagrams are very helpful for displaying the relationships between events. An event in spacetime is plotted as a point in space.

worldline: the continuous set of events that represents a particle's passage through space and time. On a spacetime diagram, a worldline is represented by a line or curve.

radar method: a method of assigning spacetime coordinates to events using a single clock and light-flashes rather than a clock-lattice synchronized according to the Einstein method. (Both methods are equivalent, but sometimes one is more useful than the other for explaining something.)

TWO-MINUTE PROBLEMS

R2T.1 Imagine that in the distant future there is a space station on the planet Neptune. While you (on earth) are watching a video transmission from the planet Neptune, which at the time is known to be 5.0 light-hours from earth, you notice that a clock on the wall behind the person speaking in the video reads 12:10 p.m. You note that your watch reads exactly the same time. Is the station clock synchronized with your watch?
A.   Yes it is   B.   No it isn't
C.   The problem doesn't give enough information to tell

R2T.2 Imagine that you receive a message from a starbase that is 13 light-years from earth. The message is dated July 15, 2127. What year does your calendar indicate at the time of reception if your calendar and the station's calendar are correctly synchronized?
A.   2127   B.   2114   C.   2140   D.   other (specify)

R2T.3 The speed of a typical car on the freeway expressed in SR units is most nearly
A. 10^{-7} C. 10^{-8} E. 10^{-4}
B. 10^{-10} D. 10^{-6} F.   other (specify)
T.   None of these answers is right: we have to state units!

R2T.4 The spacetime diagram in Figure R2.9 shows the worldlines of various objects. Which object has the largest speed at time $t = 1$ s?

R2T.5 The spacetime diagram in Figure R2.9 shows the worldlines of various objects. Which object has the largest speed at time $t = 4$ s?

R2T.6 The spacetime diagram in Figure R2.9 shows the worldlines of various objects. Which worldline cannot possibly be correct? (Explain why.)

R2T.7 In Figure R2.9, the object whose worldline is labeled B is moving along the x axis (T or F).

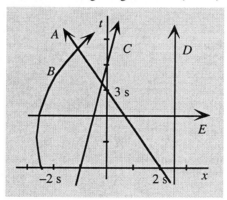

Figure R2.9

R2T.8 A light-flash leaves a master clock at $x = 0$ at time $t = -12$ s is reflected from an object a certain distance in the $-x$ direction from the origin, and then returns to the origin at $t = +8$ s. From this information, we can infer that the spacetime coordinates of the reflection event are $[t, x] =$
A.   [4 s, 20 s]   D.   [2 s, –10 s]
B.   [–4 s, –20 s]   E.   [–2 s, –10 s]
C.   [10 s, –2 s]   F.   other (specify)

HOMEWORK PROBLEMS

BASIC SKILLS

R2B.1 (Practice with SR units.)
(a) What is the diameter of the earth in seconds?

(b) A sign on the highway reads "Speed Limit 6×10^{-8}", meaning speed in SR units. Translate this to mi/h.
(c) Argue that the unit of acceleration in the SR is s^{-1}. What is 1 s^{-1} expressed as a multiple of g?

R2B.2 (Practice with SR units.)
(a) A sign on a hiking trail reads "Viewpoint: 5.5 μs." About how long would it take you to walk to this viewpoint at typical walking speed of 1 m/s?
(b) Section R1.2 mentions that the *Voyager 2* spacecraft achieved speeds in excess of 72,000 km/h. What is this speed in SR units?
(c) In the SI unit system, power is measured in watts (where $1\ W = 1\ J/s = 1\ kg \cdot m^2/s^3$). Argue that the natural units of power in the SR system are kg/s. Let's define 1 SR-watt = 1 SRW $\equiv$ 1 kg/s. A large electrical power plant produces energy at a rate of about 10^9 W. What is this in SRW?

R2B.3 Argue that in the SR unit system, mass, momentum, and kinetic energy all are measured in kilograms. Imagine a truck with a mass of 25 metric tons (25,000 kg) barreling down a highway at a speed of 59 mi/h. What is the truck's momentum in kilograms? What is its kinetic energy in kilograms?

R2B.4 For each of the worldlines shown in the spacetime diagram below, describe in words what the particles are doing, giving numerical values for velocities when possible. For example, you might say "Particle *A* is traveling in the +*x* direction with a constant speed of 1/3."

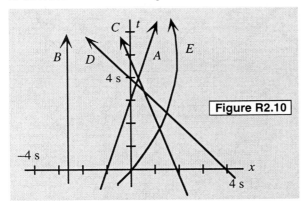

Figure R2.10

R2B.5 Imagine that you send out a light flash at *t* = 3.0 s as registered by your clock, and receive a return reflection showing your kid brother making a silly face at *t* = 11.0 s as registered by your clock. At what time did your brother actually make this silly face? How far is your brother away from you (express in seconds and kilometers)? Is this far enough away that he can't really be a nuisance?

R2B.6 Say that you send out a radar pulse at *t* = –22 h as registered by your clock and receive a return reflection from an alien spacecraft at *t* = +12 h, as registered by your clock. Is the spaceship inside or outside the solar system? When did the spaceship reflect the radar pulse?

SYNTHETIC

R2S.1 A firecracker explodes 30 km away from an observer sitting next to a certain clock *A*. The light from the firecracker explosion reaches the observer at exactly *t* = 0, according to clock *A*. Imagine that the flash of the firecracker explosion illuminates the face of another clock *B* which is sitting next to the firecracker. What time would clock B register at the moment of illumination, if it is correctly synchronized with clock A? Express your answer in milliseconds.

R2S.2 Imagine that you are in an inertial frame in empty space with a clock, a telescope, and a powerful strobe light. A friend is sitting in the same frame a very large (unknown) distance from your clock. At precisely 12:00:00 noon according to your clock, you set off the strobe lamp. Precisely 30.0 seconds later, you see in your telescope the face of your friend's clock illuminated by your strobe flash. How far away is your friend away from you (in seconds)? What should you see on the face of your friend's clock if that clock is synchronized with yours? Describe your reasoning in a few short sentences.

R2S.3 The spacetime diagram shown in the drawing below shows the worldline of a rocket as it leaves the earth, travels for a certain amount of time, comes to rest, and then explodes.
(a) The rocket leaves the earth; the rocket comes to rest in deep space; the rocket explodes. What are the coordinates of each of these three events?
(b) What is the constant speed of the rocket relative to the earth before it comes to rest.
(c) A light signal from the earth reaches the rocket just as it explodes. Indicate on the diagram exactly where and when this light signal was emitted.

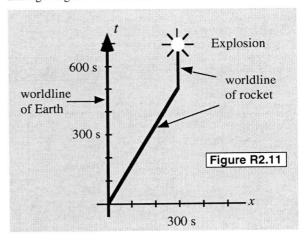

Figure R2.11

R2S.4 A rocket is launched from the moon and travels away from it at a speed of 2/5. Call the event of the rocket's launching event *A*. After 125 s as measured in the reference frame of the moon, the rocket explodes: call this event *B*. The light from the explosion travels back to the moon: call its reception event *C*. Let the moon be located at *x* = 0 in its own reference frame and let event *A* define *t* = 0. Assume that the rocket moves along the +*x* direction.
(a) Draw a spacetime diagram of the situation, drawing and labeling the worldlines of the moon, the rocket, and the worldline of the light-flash emitted by the explosion and received on the moon.
(b) Draw and label the events *A*, *B*, and *C* as points at the appropriate places on the diagram. Write down the *t* and *x* coordinates of these events.

R2S.5 Imagine that a spaceship in deep space is approaching a space station at a constant speed of *v* = 3/4. Let the space station define the position *x* = 0 in its own reference frame. At time *t* = 0, the spaceship is 16.0 light-hours away from the station. At that time and place (call this event *A*), the spaceship sends a laser pulse of light toward the station, signaling its intention to dock. The station receives the signal at its position of $x = 0$ (call this event B), and after a pause of 0.5 h, emits another laser pulse signaling permission to dock (call this event C). The spaceship receives this pulse (call this event D) and immediately begins to decelerate at a constant rate. It arrives at rest at the space station (call this event E) 6.0 h after Event D, according to clocks in the station.

(a) Carefully construct a spacetime diagram showing the processes described above. On your diagram, you should show the worldlines of the space station, the approaching spaceship and the two light pulses, as well as indicating the time and place (in the station's frame) of events A through E by labeling the corresponding points on the spacetime diagram. In particular, exactly when and where does event D occur? Event E? Write down the coordinates of these events in the station frame. Scale your axes using the hour as the basic time and distance unit, and give your answers in hours.

(b) Compute the magnitude of the average acceleration of the spaceship between events D and E in natural SR units (s^{-1}) and in g's $(1\ g \equiv 9.8\ \text{m/s}^2)$. Note that a shockproof watch can typically tolerate an acceleration of about $50g$.

R2S.6 An air-traffic control radar installation receives a radar pulse reflected from a certain jet plane 280 μs after the pulse was sent. The signal comes from a direction that is 35° north of west and 5.5° up from horizontal. If the sending of the outgoing pulse defines $t = 0$, an in a frame fixed to the earth's surface and oriented in the usual way with the installation at the spatial origin of the frame, what are the spacetime coordinates $[t, x, y, z]$ of the plane at the instant it reflects the pulse?

R2S.7 (*Seeing* is not the same as *observing*!) Imagine that a bullet-train running at a *very* high speed passes two track-side signs (A and B) as shown in the aerial view in diagram below. Let event A be the passing of the front end of the train by sign A and event B be the passing of the rear end of the train by sign B. An observer is located at the cross marked by an "O" in the diagram. This observer *sees* (that is, receives light with her eyes) event A to occur at time $t = 0$, and sees event B to occur at time $t = 25$ ns. When does she *observe* these events to occur? That is, what would a clock present at sign A read at event A, and what would a clock present at sign B read at event B if these clocks were correctly synchronized with the clock at O? In what way is the diagram above misleading about the implied time relationship between events A and B? [*Hint:* Remember that the clocks at signs A and B must be syn-

chronized with the clock at O in such a way that they would read the speed of a light-signal traveling between them and O to be 1 second/second. Knowing this, the distance between O and A, and the time that light from event A reached O, can you *infer* when event A must have happened?]

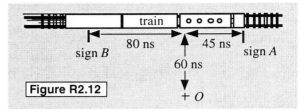

Figure R2.12

RICH-CONTEXT

R2R.1 Imagine that an advanced alien race, bent on keeping humans from escaping the solar system into the galaxy, places an opaque spherical force-field around the solar system. The force field is 6 light-hours in diameter, is centered on the sun, and is formed in a single instant of time as measured by synchronized clocks in an inertial frame attached to the sun. That instant corresponds to 9 p.m. on a certain night in your time zone. When does the opaque sphere appear to start blocking light from the stars from your vantage point on earth (8 light-minutes from the sun)? Does the opaque sphere appear all at once? If not, how long does it take for the sphere to appear, and what does it look like as it appears? Describe things as completely as you can. (Inspired by the novel *Quarantine* by Greg Egan.)

R2R.2 Two radar pulses sent from the earth at 6:00 a.m. and 8:00 a.m. one day bounce off an alien spaceship and are detected on earth at 3:00 p.m. and 4:00 p.m. (but you aren't sure which reflected pulse corresponds to which emitted pulse). Is the spaceship moving toward earth or away? If its speed is constant (but less than c), when will it (or did it) pass by the earth? (*Hint:* Draw a space-time diagram.)

ADVANCED

R2A.1 A meter stick moves at a speed of 0.5 (SR units) along a line parallel to its length that passes within 1 m of a camera. The camera shutter opens for an incredibly brief instant just as the meter stick's center passes closest to the camera. Explain why the marks on the meter stick do not look equally spaced in the resulting picture, and describe what they look like. (Ignore length contraction.)

ANSWERS TO EXERCISES

R2X.1 About 1.28 s after noon.

R2X.2 In SI units, the units of momentum are kg·m/s, so in SR units, the units of momentum are kg·s/s or simply kg, just like energy.

R2X.3 and R2X.4 With the added worldlines, Figure R2.6 looks as shown in Figure R2.13. Note that the particle worldline discussed in Exercise R2X.3 has a slope of -5 on the diagram, since it moves 1 s of distance in the $-x$ direction per 5 seconds of time. Since the moon is 1.28 s of distance from the earth, we should draw its worldline 1.28 s from the t axis. In six seconds of time, the moon is not going to move appreciably on this diagram, so its worldline will be essentially straight and vertical.

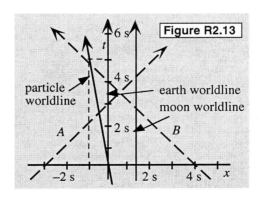

THE NATURE OF TIME

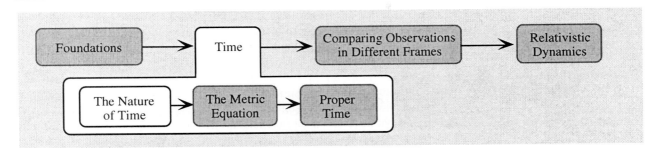

Philosophy is written in this great book (by which I mean the universe) which stands always open to our view, but it cannot be understood unless one first learns how to comprehend the language and interpret the symbols in which it is written, and its symbols are triangles, circles and other geometric figures, without which it is not humanly possible to comprehend even one word of it; without these, one wanders in a dark labyrinth.

Galileo Galilei

R3.1 OVERVIEW

In the last chapter we developed a method of synchronizing clocks consistent with the principle of relativity and discovered how to use spacetime diagrams to depict the coordinates of events and the motion of particles in a vivid and accessible way. We now have the tools to unwrap the package that the Principle represents and discover the surprises and beauties within.

What is the nature of time, now that we have unhooked ourselves from the notion of a universal and absolute time? We have defined a *procedure* to measure the time coordinate of an event. Does this mean that time is simply a human mental construct, or does there remain something real and universal about time that doesn't depend on how we build reference frames? In the next three chapters we will explore the meaning of time in the context of relativity theory.

In this chapter, we will lay the qualitative foundations for our understanding of time. Here is an overview of the sections in this chapter.

R3.2 *THREE KINDS OF TIME* discusses how relativistic definition of time implies that there are three distinct ways to measure the time between two events: *coordinate time*, *proper time*, and *spacetime interval*.

R3.3 *COORDINATE TIME IS FRAME-DEPENDENT* argues using the definition of synchronization that the numerical value of the coordinate time between two events depends on the frame one uses to measure it.

R3.4 *THE SAME RESULT FROM THE RADAR METHOD* shows that we will arrive at the same conclusion if we use the radar method instead of a synchronized clock-lattice to determine coordinates.

R3.5 *THE GEOMETRIC ANALOGY* presents an analogy for understanding the nature of time based on plane geometry. (We will draw on this very important analogy throughout this unit.)

R3.6 *PROPER TIME AND THE SPACETIME INTERVAL* introduces these kinds of time with the help of the geometric analogy.

R3.2 THREE KINDS OF TIME

A firecracker explodes. Some time later and somewhere else, another fire-cracker explodes. How much time passes between these two events? How can we measure that time interval?

There is only one kind of newtonian time

In a newtonian universe, such questions would be easy to answer. We might measure the time between the events with a pair of synchronized clocks, one present at each event. We might instead measure the time between the events with a single clock that travels in such a way that it arrives at each event's location just as it happens. Since all clocks in a newtonian universe register the same univer-sal, absolute time, these methods (and any of a number of other valid methods) will yield the same result. It is unimportant what method we actually use.

There are three kinds of time in relativity theory

In the last chapter, however, we argued that in *our* universe, universal and absolute time does not exist, and the problem of measuring the time interval between two events is thus somewhat more problematic. In this chapter, we will discover that there are *three* fundamentally different ways to measure the time interval between two events in the theory of special relativity, and that these different methods yield different results, even if applied to the same two events!

Because it is important in the real universe to distinguish between the various methods used to measure the time interval between two events, we will refer to the time interval determined by each method with a special technical name: we speak of the **coordinate time**, the **proper time**, and the **space-time interval** between the events. Our purpose in this chapter is to describe and understand these distinct ways of measuring time and begin the process of uncovering the quantitative relationships between them.

R3.3 COORDINATE TIME IS FRAME-DEPENDENT

Once the clocks in an inertial reference frame have been satisfactorily syn-chronized, we can use them to measure the time coordinates of various events that occur in that frame. In particular, we can measure the time between two events A and B in our reference frame by subtracting the time read by the clock nearest event A when it happened from the time read by the clock nearest event B when it happened: $\Delta t_{BA} \equiv t_B - t_A$. Note that this method of measuring the time difference between two events requires the use of two synchronized clocks in an established inertial reference frame. Such a measurement therefore cannot be per-formed in the absence of an inertial frame.

In short, we define the **coordinate time** between two events as follows:

The definition of *coordinate time* between events

We call the time measured between two events either by a pair of synchron-ized clocks at rest in a given inertial reference frame (one clock present at each event) or by a single clock at rest in that inertial frame (if both events happen to occur at that clock in that frame) the *coordinate time* between the events in that frame. We use the symbol Δt to represent the coordinate time between two events.

The coordinate time be-tween events depends on your choice of frame

Now, imagine that the observer in some inertial reference frame (let's call this frame the Other Frame: we'll talk about a Home Frame in a bit) sets out to synchronize its clocks. In particular, let us focus on two clocks in that frame that lie on the x axis an equal distance to the left and right of the master clock at $x' = 0$. At $t' = 0$, the observer causes the center clock to emit two flashes of light, one traveling in the $+x'$ direction and the other in the $-x'$ direction. Let's call the emission of these flashes from $x' = 0$ at $t' = 0$ the origin event O.

Now, since both of the other clocks are the *same distance* from the center clock and since the speed of light is 1 (light-)second/second in every inertial reference frame, the left-hand clock will receive the left-going light flash (call the event of reception event A) at the *same* time that the right-hand clock receives

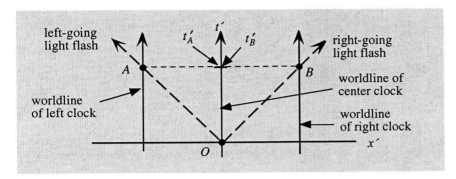

Figure R3.1: The synchronization of two clocks equally spaced from a center clock, as observed in the Other Frame. If the right and left clocks are set to agree at events *A* and *B*, they will be synchronized with each other.

the right-going flash (event *B*). By the definition of synchronization, both clocks should thus be set to read the *same* time at events *A* and *B* (a time in seconds equal to their common distance from the center clock).

The spacetime diagram in Figure R3.1 illustrates this process. Note that since all three clocks are at rest in this frame, their worldlines on the spacetime diagram are vertical. Moreover, since the speed of light is 1 s/s in this (and every other inertial) frame, the worldlines of the light flashes will have slopes of ±1 on the spacetime diagram (that is, they make a 45° angle with each axis) as long as the axes have the same scale. On this diagram it is clear that events *A* and *B* really do occur at the same time in the Other Frame.

Now consider a second inertial reference frame (the Home Frame) within which the Other Frame is observed to move in the +*x* direction at a speed β. Let us look at the same events from the vantage point of the Home Frame. For convenience, let us take the event of the emission of the flashes to be the origin event in this frame also (so event *O* occurs at $t = x = 0$ in the Home Frame).

The observer in the Home Frame will agree that the right and left clocks in the Other Frame are always equidistant from the center clock in the Other Frame. Moreover, at $t = 0$, when the center clock passes the point $x = 0$ in the Home Frame as it emits its flashes, the right and left clocks are equidistant from the emission event. But as the light flashes are moving to the outer clocks, the observer in the Home Frame observes the left clock to move up the *x* axis *toward* the flash coming toward it and the right clock to move up the *x* axis *away* from the flash coming toward it. As a result, the left-going light flash has less distance to travel to meet the left clock than the right-going flash does to meet the right clock. Since the speed of light is 1 in the Home Frame as well as the Other Frame, this means that the left clock receives its flash first. *Therefore, event A is observed to occur BEFORE event B in the Home Frame.*

Figure R3.2 shows a spacetime diagram of the process as observed in the Home Frame. In drawing the worldlines of the clocks in question, it is important to note that the clocks are *not* at rest in the Home Frame. Their worldlines on a Home Frame spacetime diagram will be equally spaced lines with slopes of $1/\beta$, indicating that the clocks are moving to the right at a speed β. The light flashes

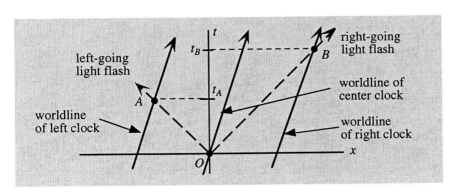

Figure R3.2: The same events as observed in the Home Frame. In this frame, event *B* is measured to occur *after* event *A*.

have a speed of 1 s/s in the Home Frame (and every other frame) so their world-lines have to be drawn with a slope of ±1 on the spacetime diagram.

In summary, the coordinate time between events A and B as measured in the Other Frame is $\Delta t' = 0$ (by construction in this case), but the coordinate time between these events as measured in the Home Frame is $\Delta t \neq 0$. We see that the coordinate times between the *same two events* measured in different reference frames are *not* generally equal. Thus we say that the coordinate time differences are **relative** (that is, they depend on one's choice of inertial reference frame).

Why? If each observer synchronizes the clocks in his or her own reference frame according to our definition, *each will conclude that the clocks in the other's frame are not synchronized.* Notice that the Other Frame observer has set the right and left clocks to read the same time at events A and B. Yet these events do *not* occur at the same time in the Home Frame. Therefore the observer in the Home Frame will claim that the clocks in the Other Frame are not synchronized. (Of course, the observer in the Other Frame will make the same claim about the clocks in the Home Frame.) The definition of synchronization that we are using makes perfect sense *within* any inertial reference frame, but it does not allow us to synchronize clocks in *different* inertial frames. In fact, the definition *requires* that observers in different inertial frames measure *different* time intervals between the same two events, as we have just seen.

In general, two observers in different frames will also disagree about the *spatial* coordinate separation between the events. Consider two events C and D that both occur at the center clock in the Other Frame, but at different times. Since the center clock defines the location $x' = 0$ in the Other Frame, the events have the same x' coordinate in that frame, so $\Delta x' = 0$. But in the Home Frame, the center clock is measured to move in the time between the events, and so the two events do *not* occur at the same place: $\Delta x \neq 0$ (see Figure R3.3.)

Spatial coordinate differences are relative also

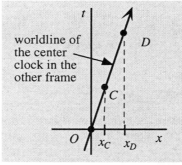

worldline of the center clock in the other frame

Figure R3.3: Events C and D both occur at the same place in the Other Frame ($\Delta x' = 0$) but not in the Home Frame ($\Delta x = 0$). (This diagram is drawn by an observer in the Home Frame.)

Exercise R3X.1: Note that the frame-dependence of the *spatial* coordinate difference between two events has nothing to do with clock synchronization or relativity: this would be true even if time were universal and absolute. Show using the galilean transformation equations that if the separation between two events in the Other Frame is $\Delta x' = 0$ but $\Delta t' \neq 0$, then the separation between these events in the Home Frame is *not* zero ($\Delta x \neq 0$).

R3.4 THE SAME RESULT FROM THE RADAR METHOD

The reason why observers in different inertial frames disagree about whether the clocks in a given frame are synchronized is that *synchronization is defined so that light flashes are measured to have a speed of 1 in every inertial frame*: the frame-dependence of coordinate time differences is a logical consequence of this assertion. This can be illustrated by considering the radar method of assigning spacetime coordinates: though the radar method does not involve the use of synchronized clocks, it does depend on the assumption that the speed of light is the same in every inertial frame. Does the radar method also imply that the coordinate time difference between two events is frame-dependent?

Figure R3.4 shows that it does. Figure R3.4a shows the observer in the Other Frame using the radar method to determine the space and time coordinates of the event C. The observer in that frame will conclude that event C and event D occur at the same time, where D is the event of the master clock at $x' = 0$ registering $t_D' = \frac{1}{2}(t_A' + t_B')$, that is, at the instant of time halfway between the emission of the radar pulse at t_A and its reception at t_B. According to the radar method, then, the coordinate time between events C and D is $\Delta t' = 0$. [Radar and visible light are both electromagnetic waves (with different frequencies), so both will move at a speed of 1 (light-)second / second = 1.]

Radar method yields the same conclusion

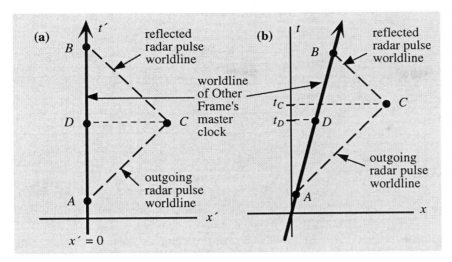

Figure R3.4: (a) In the Other Frame, events *C* and *D* are defined to be simultaneous if *D* occurs at the master clock at a time halfway between the emission event *A* and the reception event *B*. The coordinate time difference between events *C* and *D* in the Other Frame is thus $\Delta t' = 0$.
(b) In the Home Frame, the Other Frame's master clock moves to the right as time passes, so its worldline is slanted. On the other hand, radar pulse worldlines still have slope ± 1 as shown. This means that an observer in the Home Frame will conclude that event *C* happens after event *D*, so the coordinate time difference between the events is $\Delta t \neq 0$.

When the same sequence of events is viewed from the Home Frame, though, a different conclusion emerges (see Figure R3.4b). According to observers in the Home Frame, the Other Frame's master clock is moving along the *x* axis with some speed β, so in a spacetime diagram based on measurements taken in the Home Frame, the worldline of that clock will appear as a slanted line (with slope $1/\beta$) instead of being vertical. Radar pulse worldlines, on the other hand, still have slopes of ± 1, just as they did in the Other Frame spacetime diagram. The inevitable result (as you can see from the diagram) is that observers in the Home Frame are forced to conclude that event *C* occurs *after* event *D* does, and thus that the time difference between events *C* and *D* in the Home Frame is $\Delta t \neq 0$.

The point is that the relativity of coordinate time interval between events is a direct consequence of the fact that we are *defining* coordinate time by assuming that the speed of light is 1 in every inertial reference frame. Remember, though, that we *must* make this assumption if the laws of electromagnetism are to be consistent with the principle of relativity!

Frame-dependence of coordinate time follows from principle of relativity

R3.5 THE GEOMETRIC ANALOGY

You may find it troubling that coordinate differences between events are not absolute but are instead frame-dependent. This is particularly true of the time coordinate separation: it is not easy to let go of the newtonian notion of absolute time! The fact is, though, that *we have no trouble at all with these ideas when they appear in a related but more familiar guise.*

Consider Askew, a hypothetical town somewhere in the western U. S. (the residents wish its precise location to remain secret). Most towns in rural America have streets that run directly north/south or east/west. The surveyor who laid out the streets of Askew in 1882, however, *tried* to calibrate his compass against the North Star the night before, but in fact had forgotten exactly where it was (it was a long time since he had this stuff in high school after all), and ended up choosing a star that turned out to be 28° east of the true North Star. Therefore, all of the streets of Askew are twisted 28° from the standard directions.

Now, if we would like to assign *x* and *y* coordinates to points of interest in this town (or any town), we have to set up a Cartesian coordinate system. It is conventional to orient coordinate axes on a plot of land so that the *y* axis points north and the *x* axis points east (see Figure R3.5a). This is usually convenient as well, since the streets will be parallel to the coordinate axes. There is no reason why this *has* to be done, though, and in Askew's case, it is actually more convenient to use a coordinate system oriented 28° to the east (Figure R3.5b). Note that City Hall is the origin of both coordinate systems.

An illustration of alternative coordinate systems in plane geometry

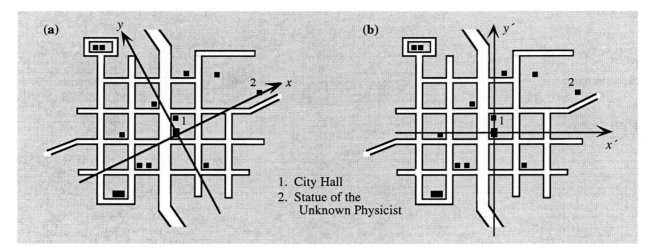

1. City Hall
2. Statue of the
   Unknown Physicist

Figure R3.5: (a) A standard northward-oriented cartesian coordinate system superimposed on the town of Askew. **(b)** A more convenient coordinate system oriented 28° clockwise.

We are not surprised by frame-dependence of coordinates in this case!

We can of course use any coordinate system we like to quantify the position of points of interest in the town: coordinate systems are an arbitrary human artifact that we impose for our convenience on the physical reality of the town. However, the coordinates we actually *get* for various points certainly *do* depend on the coordinate system used. For example, the coordinate differences between City Hall and the Statue of the Unknown Physicist in Memorial Park, might be $\Delta y = 0$, $\Delta x = 852.0$ m in the standard coordinate system, but $\Delta y' = 399.9$ m, $\Delta x' = 752.3$ m in the conveniently oriented coordinate system.

Is it surprising that the results are different? Do the differences in the results cause us to suspect that one or the other coordinate system has been set up incorrectly? Hardly! We can accept the fact that both coordinate systems are perfectly correct and legal. We already *know and expect* that differently oriented coordinate systems on a plane will yield different coordinate measurements. This causes no discomfort: we understand that this is the way that things are.

In an entirely analogous way, we have carefully and unambiguously defined a procedure for setting up an inertial reference frame and synchronizing its clocks. This definition happens to imply that spacetime coordinate measurements in different frames yield different results. This should be no more troubling to us than the fact that Askew residents who use different sets of coordinate axes will assign different coordinates to various points in town. *Coordinates have meaning only in the context of the coordinate system or inertial frame that we use to observe them.*

The only reason that the relativity of time coordinate differences is a difficult idea is that we don't have *common experience* with inertial reference frames moving with high enough relative speeds to display the difference. The frames that we typically experience in daily life have relative speeds below 300 m/s, or about one millionth of the speed of light. If for some reason we could only construct cartesian coordinate systems on the surface of the earth that differed in orientation by no more than a millionth of a radian, then we might think of cartesian coordinate differences as being "universal and absolute" as well!

So, to summarize, the coordinate differences between points on a plane (or events in spacetime) are "relative" because coordinate systems (or inertial reference frames) are human artifacts that we *impose* on the land (or spacetime) to help us quantify that physical reality by assigning coordinate numbers to points on the plane (or events in spacetime). Because we are free to set up coordinate systems (or reference frames) in different ways, the coordinate differences between two points (or events) reflect not only something about their real physical separation, but also something about the artificial choice of coordinate system (or reference frame) that we have made.

So, is it true then that *everything* is relative? Is there nothing that we can measure about the physical separation of the points (or events) that is absolute (that is, independent of reference frame)?

There *is* in fact a coordinate-independent quantity that describes the separations of two points on a plot of land: the *distance* between those two points. For example, the distance between City Hall and the Statue of the Unknown Physicist in Askew is $\Delta d = [\Delta x^2 + \Delta y^2]^{1/2} = [(852.0 \text{ m})^2 + 0]^{1/2} = 852.0 \text{ m}$ in the standard (north-oriented) coordinate system and $\Delta d' = [(\Delta x')^2 + (\Delta y')^2]^{1/2} = [(399.9 \text{ m})^2 + (752.3 \text{ m})^2]^{1/2} = 852.0 \text{ m}$ in the convenient coordinate system. It doesn't matter what coordinate system you use to calculate the distance: you always will get the same answer.

Distance and pathlength, on the other hand, are coordinate-*independent*

The distance between two points on a plot of ground thus reflects something that is deeply real about the nature of the plot of ground itself, without reference to the human coordinate systems imposed on it. This independence from coordinate systems arises because there is in fact a method of determining the distance between two points *without* using a coordinate system at all: simply lay a tape measure between the points! Since this method yields a certain definite result for the distance, calculations of this distance in *any* coordinate system should yield the same result if they are valid.

Of course, there are many ways that one could lay a tape measure between City Hall and the Statue of the Unknown Physicist. One could lay the tape measure along a straight path between the two points: this would measure the distance "as the crow flies", which is what is usually meant by the phrase "the distance between two points". But there are other possibilities. One might, for example, lay the tape measure two blocks down Elm Street from City Hall, then one block over along Grove Avenue, then up Maple Street, and so on. This would measure a different kind of distance between the two points that we might call a *pathlength*.

Both the straight-line distance and the more general pathlength between two points can be measured directly with a tape measure, and thus are quantities independent of any coordinate system. But the distance and the pathlength between two points may not be the same. In general, the pathlength between two points will depend on the path chosen, and will always be greater than (or at best equal to) the straight-line distance.

To summarize, we have at our disposal three totally different ways to quantify the separation of two points on a plane. We can measure the *coordinate separations* between the points using a coordinate system. (The results will depend on one's choice of coordinate system.) We can measure the *pathlength* between the points with a tape measure laid along a specified path. (The result here will depend on the path chosen, but is independent of coordinate system.) Or we can measure the *distance* between the points with a tape measure laid along the unique path defined by the straight line line between the points. Because in this last case the path of the tape is unique, the distance between two points is a unique number that quantifies in a very basic way the separation of the points in space.

The three kinds of spatial separation

R3.6 PROPER TIME AND THE SPACETIME INTERVAL

Consider two events. Label them *A* and *B*. Is there any way that we can measure the time between events *A* and *B without* using a reference frame, analogous to the way that we can measure the pathlength between two points on the plane without using a coordinate system?

We can avoid the use of a reference frame lattice if we measure the time interval between these events with a clock that is *present* at both events. In a manner analogous to laying a tape measure between two points so that it passes

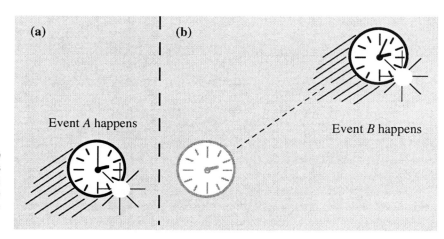

Figure R3.6: Measuring the *proper time* between two events with a clock present at both events. (Events *A* and *B* here are represented by firecracker explosions.)

(a)

Event *A* happens

(b)

Event *B* happens

close by each point, we can send a clock between the events along just the right path so that it is very close to each event as it occurs (see Figure R3.6).

A tape measure stretched between two points marks off the distance between those points and presents a scale that can be laid right next to the two points for easy and unambiguous reading. In an entirely similar manner, a clock that travels between two events marks off the time between those events and presents its face at each event for easy and unambiguous reading. Since the clock's face is right there at each event, *everyone* looking at the clock will agree as to its reading as each event happens. The quantity measured by this clock is therefore **frame independent**: it is measuring something basic about the *absolute* physical relationship between the events.

We call a time interval measured this way a *proper time*:

Definition of the *proper time* between two events

> The time between two events measured by any clock present at both events is a **proper time** $\Delta\tau$ between those events. The numerical value of a proper time measured by a given clock between two given events is an absolute, *frame-independent* quantity.

(Note that *proper* is a misleading adjective here. In English, this word has fairly recently come to mean almost exclusively "appropriate," or "correct in moral or manners." But the meaning intended here is more accurately "proprietary," that is, the time between the events measured specially by the *particular* clock in question. *Path time* might be a more appropriate term.)

Proper time depends on clock worldline

There is, however, one thing that the proper time between two events *might* well depend on other than the events themselves. It might depend on the *worldline* that the clock follows in traveling from one event to the other, just as a pathlength measured by a tape measure depends on the path along which it is laid (see Figure R3.7). We will see in the next chapter that the path dependence of proper time is a straightforward consequence of the principle of relativity: for now it is enough to understand that this path-dependence is a *possibility* suggested by the geometric analogy.

In an experiment performed in 1971 by J. C. Haefele and R. E. Keating (see *Science*, **117**, 168, July 14, 1972), a pair of very accurate atomic clocks were synchronized, and then one was put on a jet plane and sent around the world, while the other remained in the laboratory. These clocks were both present at the same two events (the event of the departure of the plane clock from the laboratory and the event of its return): both thus measured proper times between these events. But the worldlines followed by each of these clocks were very different: one clock's worldline was simply a straight line at constant position (in the reference frame of the surface of the earth), while the other's worldline went around the world. When these initially synchronized clocks were again brought together, it was found that they disagreed by several hundred nanosec-

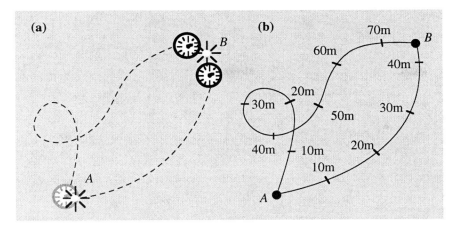

Figure R3.7: The proper time measured between two events may depend on exactly how the measuring clock travels between those events **(a)**, just as the pathlength between two points depends on the path along which it is measured **(b)**.

onds (a difference that is in fact consistent with the quantitative prediction based on the theories of special and general relativity). The point is that it is not merely *possible* that the time that a clock measures depends on the nature of its worldline: it is an established experimental *fact*.

When measuring distances on a plane, we distinguish between the *path-length* between two points measured along a certain path and the *distance* between the points: the distance is measured along the special path that is the unique straight line between the two points. Because the straight-line path is unique, the distance between two points along a straight line is a unique number reflecting something definite about the separation of those points in space.

Consider an **inertial clock** present at both events (a clock is *inertial* if an attached first law detector registers no violation of Newton's first law). Such a clock follows a unique and well-defined worldline through spacetime between two events. Observed in an inertial frame, a clock would travel between the events in a straight line at a constant velocity. Such a worldline defines a unique path in space, and since there is only one value of a constant velocity that will be just right to get the clock from one event to the other, the clock's velocity along that worldline is also uniquely specified.

The **spacetime interval** between two events is defined to be the proper time measured by an *inertial* clock present at both events. This quantity is a unique, frame-independent number that depends on the separation of the events in space and time and nothing else. We conventionally use the symbol Δs to represent the spacetime interval between two events.

It is important to note that the definitions of *coordinate time, proper time,* and the *spacetime interval* between two events overlap in certain special cases. The definition above makes it clear that the spacetime interval between two events is a special case of a proper time between two events, just as the distance between two points is a special case of the more general concept of pathlength between two points. An inertial clock present at both events also measures the *coordinate time* between those events in the clock's own reference frame, since the time interval measured between two events by a clock or clocks at rest in any inertial reference frame is a coordinate time by definition. So the spacetime interval between two events is a special case of a proper time *and* a special case of a coordinate time (see Figure R3.8).

Tables R3.1 and R3.2 summarize and organize the ideas presented in this chapter. In the next chapter, we will explore the relationship between the coordinate time and the spacetime interval between two events with the help of an equation called the *metric equation*. In the following chapter, we will use the metric equation to link coordinate time to proper time.

What is the analogue of distance?

Definition of the *spacetime interval* between events

Spacetime interval is a proper time and also a coordinate time

Figure R3.8: Let points in the left circle represent the set of all possible coordinate times that observers in inertial frames moving at various different velocities might measure between two given events. Let points in the right circle represent the set of all possible proper times measured between the same events by clocks present at both events but moving between the events along various different worldlines. The single point in common between these sets is the spacetime interval Δs between the events.

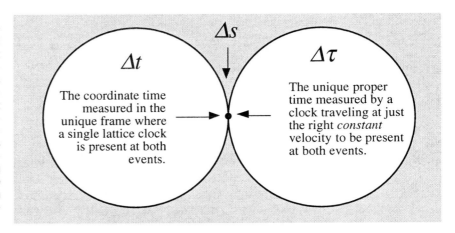

$$\Delta s$$

Δt

The coordinate time measured in the unique frame where a single lattice clock is present at both events.

$\Delta \tau$

The unique proper time measured by a clock traveling at just the right *constant* velocity to be present at both events.

TABLE R3.1:   THREE KINDS OF TIME

	Coordinate time	Proper time	Spacetime Interval
Definition	The time between two events measured in an inertial reference frame by a *pair of synchronized* clocks, one present at each event. (If both events happen to occur at the same place, a single clock suffices.)*	The time between two events as measured by a single clock present at both events. (Its value depends on the worldline that the clock follows in getting from one event to the other.)	The time between two events as measured by an inertial clock present at both events. (Because an inertial clock follows a unique worldline between the events, the spacetime interval's value is unique for a given pair of events.)
Conventional symbol	Δt	$\Delta \tau$	Δs
Is value frame-independent?	No	Yes	Yes
Geometric analogy	Spatial coordinate differences	Pathlength	Distance

*Note: Alternatively, the coordinate time difference between two events might be inferred from measurements of the spacetime coordinates of these events using the radar method.

TABLE R3.2:   THE GEOMETRIC ANALOGY

Plane geometry	Spacetime geometry
Map	Spacetime diagram
Points	Events
Paths or curves	Worldlines
Coordinate systems	Inertial reference frames
Relative rotation of coordinate systems	Relative velocity of inertial reference frames
Differences between spatial coordinate values	Differences between spacetime coordinate values
Pathlength along a path	Proper time along a worldline
Distance between two points	Spacetime interval between two events

SUMMARY

I. THREE KINDS OF TIME
    A. The *coordinate time* Δt between two events
        1. *Definition:* Time inferred from the difference in event times registered by a *pair* of synchronized clocks in an inertial frame, where one clock is present at each event. (If the events occur at the same place in the frame, a single clock suffices.)
        2. The coordinate time between events is *frame-dependent:*
            a. The light-flash synchronization scheme presented in the last chapter is self-consistent *within* a given inertial reference frame
            b. But observers think clocks in *other* frames are *not* synchronized. Since determining coordinate time involves comparing the values registered by a pair of synchronized clocks, its value depends on whose synchronized clocks one uses!
    B. The *proper time* (read *proprietary* time) $\Delta\tau$ between two events
        1. *Definition:* time interval measured between the events by a *single* clock that moves in such a way as to be *present* at both events.
        2. The proper time between events is *frame-independent* (since we are not comparing readings on different synchronized clocks, there can be no disagreement about what such a clock registers)
        3. The proper time depends on clock's worldline between the events
            a. analogous to pathlength between points depending on path
            b. this is an experimental fact (Haefele and Keating experiment)
    C. The *spacetime interval* Δs between two events
        1. *Definition:* time interval measured between the events by a single *inertial* clock that is physically present at both events. (A clock is *inertial* if an attached first law detector registers no violation of Newton's first law.) This implies that:
            a. Δs is a special case of proper time (it is proper time measured by a *special* clock present at both events)
            b. Δs is also special case of *coordinate time* (since clock defines an inertial frame where events occur at the same place)
        2. The spacetime interval is *frame-independent*
        3. The path followed by such a clock between two events is unique (straight line in space with constant velocity in any inertial frame)
            a. Thus value of Δs is unique for a given pair of events.
            b. Since it is also frame-independent, this quantity specifies something important and absolute about the two events

II. THE GEOMETRIC ANALOGY
    A. The geometry of spacetime is analogous to the geometry of a plane
    B. List of analogous elements:
        1. map of space $\leftrightarrow$ spacetime diagram
        2. points in space $\leftrightarrow$ events in spacetime
        3. paths or curves in space $\leftrightarrow$ worldlines in spacetime
        4. coordinate systems $\leftrightarrow$ inertial reference frames
        5. relative orientation of $\leftrightarrow$ relative velocity of inertial
            coordinate systems   reference frames
        6. space coordinate differences $\leftrightarrow$ space, time coordinate differences
        7. pathlength along a path $\leftrightarrow$ proper time along a worldline
        8. distance $\leftrightarrow$ spacetime interval
    C. Relativity of coordinate differences and path-dependence of pathlength obvious in plane geometry: helps us understand same in spacetime
    D. Analogy between *distance* and *spacetime interval* is *very* important:
        1. both are *frame-independent* quantities
        2. both are measured along a straight-line path/worldline
        3. both are *unique* values for given pair of points/events

GLOSSARY

coordinate time Δt: the time interval between two events as measured in an inertial reference frame by computing the difference between the time coordinates of the events registered by two synchronized clocks in the frame (one present at each event). If the two events happen to occur at the same place in the frame, then *one* clock suffices to measure the coordinate time.

frame-independent: a quantity whose value does not depend on one's choice of reference frame. For example, an particle's electrical charge q is frame-independent, but its velocity $\vec{v}$ is not. In special relativity, the coordinate time Δt between two events is NOT frame-independent.

proper time $\Delta \tau$: the time interval between two events measured by any clock that is physically present at both events. The value of this quantity is frame-independent

(since one does not use a reference frame to measure it), but does depend on the nature of the worldline that the clock follows between the two events. The proper time between two events is analogous to the *pathlength* between two points in space. (The adjective *proper* here should be thought of as meaning "proprietary," not "correct.")

spacetime interval Δs: the time interval between two events measure by an *inertial* clock that is physically present at both events. The value of this quantity is frame-independent (since one does not use a reference frame to measure it) and since there is only one unique worldline that takes a clock along a straight line from one event to the other at a constant velocity, this quantity has a unique value for a given pair of events. The spacetime interval between two events is analogous to the *distance* between two points in space.

TWO-MINUTE PROBLEMS

R3T.1 Coordinate time would be frame-independent if the newtonian conception of time were true (T or F).

R3T.2 Observers in the Home Frame will conclude that the clocks in an Other Frame moving relative to the Home Frame in the $+x$ direction will be out of synchronization, even if the observers in the Other Frame have carefully synchronized clocks using the Einstein prescription (T or F). Specifically, Home Frame observers will see that for events farther and farther up the common $+x$ axis, the times registered by Other Frame clocks at the event
A. become further and further ahead of
B. become further and further behind of
C. remain the same as
D. have no clear relationship to
the values that Home Frame clocks register for the same events.

R3T.3 A person riding a merry-go-round passes very close to a person standing on the ground once (event A) and then again (event B). Which person's watch measures *proper time* between these two events? (Assume that the ground is

an inertial frame and that the merry-go-round rider moves at a constant speed.)
A. the rider in the merry-go-round
B. the person standing on the ground
C. both
D. neither

R3T.4 In the situation described in the previous problem, which person (if any) measures the *spacetime interval* between the events? (Select from the same answers.)

R3T.5 In the situation described in problem R3T.4, which person (if any) measures coordinate time between the two events in some inertial reference frame? (Select from the same answers.)

R3T.6 A spaceship departs from the solar system (event A) and travels at a constant velocity to a distant star. It then returns at a constant velocity, finally returning to the solar system (event B). A clock on the spaceship registers which of the following kinds of time between these events?
A. proper time   D. A and C
B. coordinate time   E. B and C
C. spacetime interval   F. A, B, and C

HOMEWORK PROBLEMS

BASIC SKILLS

R3B.1 Two firecrackers A and B are placed at $x' = 0$ and $x' = 100$ ns respectively on a train that is moving in the $+x$ direction relative to the ground frame. According to synchronized clocks on the train, both firecrackers explode simultaneously. Which firecracker explodes first according to synchronized clocks on the ground? Explain carefully. (*Hint*: Study Figure R3.2.)

R3B.2 Figure R3.2 implies that an observer in the Home Frame concludes that clocks that have been carefully synchronized in the Other Frame are *not* synchronized in the Home Frame. Would an observer in the Other Frame conclude that clocks that have been carefully synchronized in

the Home Frame are not synchronized in the Other Frame? Justify your response.

R3B.3 Clock P is at rest alongside a racetrack. A jockey on horseback checks her watch against clock P as she passes it during the first lap (call this event A) and then checks her watch again as she passes clock P the second time (call this event B). Which clock (clock P or the watch) measures the spacetime interval between events A and B? Which measures proper time? (Careful!) Do either of the clocks measure coordinate time between the events in ground frame? Discuss.

R3B.4 Alyssa is a passenger on a train moving at a constant velocity relative to the ground. Alyssa synchronizes her watch with the station clock as she passes through the Banning town station, and then compares her watch with the station clock as she passes through the Centerville town station further down the line. Is the time that she measures between the events of passing through these towns a proper time? Is it a coordinate time? Is it the spacetime interval between the events? If one subtracts the Centerville station clock reading from the Banning station clock reading, what kind of time interval between the events does one obtain? Defend your answers carefully. (Treat the ground as an inertial frame, and assume that the Banning and Centerville clocks are synchronized.)

SYNTHETIC

R3S.1 Redraw Figure R3.2 assuming that the newtonian concept of time is true. How does your redrawn diagram differ from the original, and how is this difference related to the behavior of light according to the newtonian and relativistic models?

R3S.2 After reading this chapter, your roommate exclaims "Relativity cannot be right! This chapter claims that events that are simultaneous in one inertial reference frame are not simultaneous in another. Yet it is clear that two events are really simultaneous or really not simultaneous! This is not something that different observers could disagree about, or if they do, one has to be right and the other wrong!" Carefully and politely argue to your roommate that relativity *could* be right even so, and pinpoint the assumption that your roommate makes that could be debated. (*Hint*: You might be able to use the geometric analogy to good effect. Two different surveyors set up differently-oriented coordinate systems on a plot of land. In one system, two rocks both lie along the *x* axis; in the other they do not. Is this a problem?)

R3S.3 Imagine that in the year 2065, you are watching a live broadcast from the space station at the planet Neptune, which is 4.0 light-hours from earth at the time. (Assume that the TV signal from Neptune is sent to earth via a laser light communication system.) At exactly 6:17 p.m. (as registered by the clock on your desk), you see a technician on the TV screen suddenly exclaim, "Hey! We've just detected an alien spacecraft passing by here." Let this be event *A*. Exactly one hour later, the alien spaceship is detected passing by earth: let this be event *B*. Assume that the earth and Neptune stations can be considered parts of the inertial reference frame of the solar system, and assume that the spaceship travels at a constant velocity.
(**a**) During the broadcast, you can see on your TV screen the face of a clock sitting on the technician's desk. What time should you see on this clock face at 6:17 p.m. your time if that clock is synchronized with yours?
(**b**) What is the coordinate time between events *A* and *B* in the solar system frame? Defend your response carefully.
(**c**) What is the speed of the alien spaceship, as measured in the solar system frame?
(**d**) What kind(s) of time would the spaceship's clock measure between events *A* and *B*?

R3S.4 Imagine two clocks, *P* and *Q*. Both clocks leave the spatial origin of the Home Frame at time *t* = 0: call this the origin event *O*. Both clocks move along the +*x* axis, with clock *P* originally traveling at a speed of about 4/5, while *Q* travels at a speed of about 1/5. After a while, however, clock *P* decelerates, comes to rest, and then begins to move back toward the origin. A short time later, clock *P*

collides with the slower clock *Q*, which has been moving with constant speed up the *x* axis during all this. Let the collision of the clocks be event *A*.
(**a**) Draw a qualitatively accurate spacetime diagram of the situation described above, labeling the world-lines of clocks *P* and *Q* and the locations of events *O* and *A*.
(**b**) Assume that clocks *P* and *Q* were both synchronized with the clock at the origin of the Home Frame when they left the origin. Will *P* and *Q* necessarily agree when they collide? Explain.
(**c**) An observer in the Home Frame measures the time between events *O* and *A* with a pair of synchronized clocks (one at the spatial location of event O and one at the spatial location of event *A*). Clocks *P* and *Q* each also register a time between these events. Which clock(s) measure proper time between the events? The spacetime interval between the events? The coordinate time between the events?

R3S.5 A *particle accelerator* is a device that boosts subatomic particles to speeds close to that of light. Such an accelerator is typically shaped like a ring (which may be several kilometers in diameter): the particles are constrained by magnetic fields to travel inside the ring. Imagine such an accelerator having a radius of 2.998 km. Assume that there are two synchronized clocks (*P* and *Q*) located on opposite sides of the ring. A certain particle in the ring is measured to travel from clock *P* to clock *Q* in 34.9 μs, as registered by those clocks. Let event *A* be the particle's departure from clock *P* and event *B* be the particle's arrival at clock *Q*. Assume that the particle contains an internal clock that measures the time between these events, and that the particle travels at a constant speed.
(**a**) What is the speed of the particle in the lab frame?
(**b**) Does the synchronized pair of lab clocks measure the proper time, the coordinate time, or the spacetime interval between events *A* and *B*?
(**c**) Does the particle's internal clock measure the proper time, the coordinate time, or the spacetime interval between events *A* and *B*?

R3S.6 After reading this chapter, your roommate exclaims "I know how to tell a moving frame from one at rest. This chapter clearly shows that after observers in a moving frame carefully try to synchronize clocks in that frame, they are still out of synch with clocks in a frame at rest. Therefore, the frame with the clocks that are out of synch is the moving frame and a frame whose clocks are in synch must be at rest." Is your roommate right? Does this provide a way to distinguish *physically* a frame that is at rest from one that is not? Why or why not?

R3S.7 Imagine that you are looking through a telescope at a distant spaceship that is moving perpendicular to your line of sight at a constant speed that is a significant fraction of the speed of light. Imagine that the spaceship is several kilometers long in its direction of motion and has lights in a row along its length. Imagine that the spaceship's captain blinks these lights every so often, and that all the lights blink at once in the ship's frame. Do the lights all blink at once as you see them? If not, explain why not, and which lights you see blinking first. (*Hint*: Since the spaceship is very distant, it takes essentially the same time for light to travel from all parts of the spaceship to your telescope. So if the lights all blink simultaneously in your reference frame, they will also look to you as if they blink simultaneously. Therefore, differing light travel times from various parts of the ship is *not* the issue here.)

RICH-CONTEXT

R3R.1 A train is moving due east at a large constant speed on a straight track. Imagine that Harry is riding on the train exactly halfway between its ends. Sally is sitting by the tracks only a few feet from the train. Let the event of Harry passing Sally be the origin event O in both frames. At this same instant, both Harry and Sally receive the light from lightning flashes that have struck both ends of the train, leaving scorch marks on both the train and the track. Harry concludes that since he is in the middle of the train and he received the light from the strikes at the same time, the lightning strikes must have occurred at the same time in his reference frame. Is he right? If not, which strike (the one at the front of the train or the one at the rear) really happened first? Can Sally conclude from her seeing the flashes at the same time that the strikes happened at the same time in the ground frame? Why or why not? If not, which strike happened first in her frame? (This problem is adapted from one of Einstein's own illustrations of the implications of the constant speed of light.)

ADVANCED

R3A.1 Consider Figure R3.2. We used that spacetime diagram to argue that clocks synchronized in the Other Frame will *not* be synchronized in the Home Frame. Imagine that the spatial separation between each side clock and the center clock is $L = 12$ ns as measured in the Home Frame, and that the speed of the clocks relative to the Home Frame is $\beta = 0.40$ in SR units. Find the time separation $t_B - t_A$ between events A and B as measured in the Home Frame. [Hints: This is a tricky problem, but it is not as impossible as it looks. Consider the left clock. In the time between $t = 0$ and $t = t_A$, this clock moves a distance βt_A toward the light-flash coming toward it. Thus the total distance that the light flash has to cover in this time interval is $L - \beta t_A$. But since the light flash travels with unit speed in the Home Frame (and every frame), the *time* that it takes to travel to the clock is equal to the distance that it has to travel (in SR units). Write this last sentence as an equation, and then solve the equation for t_A. Repeat for the right-hand clock.]

ANSWERS TO EXERCISES

R3X.1 Consider events C and D with x coordinates x_C and x_D respectively in the Home Frame and x_C' and x_D' respectively in the Other Frame. According to the galilean transformation equations (equations R1.2), we have

$$x_D' - x_C' = (x_D - \beta t_D) - (x_C + \beta t_C)$$

$$= (x_D - x_C) - \beta(t_D - t_C) \qquad (R3.1)$$

If $\Delta x' = x_D' - x_C' = 0$, then

$$0 = (x_D - x_C) - \beta(t_D - t_C)$$

$$\Rightarrow \quad x_D - x_C = \beta(t_D - t_C) \qquad (R3.2)$$

So if $\Delta t' = \Delta t = t_D - t_C \neq 0$, then $\Delta x = x_D - x_C \neq 0$.

THE METRIC EQUATION

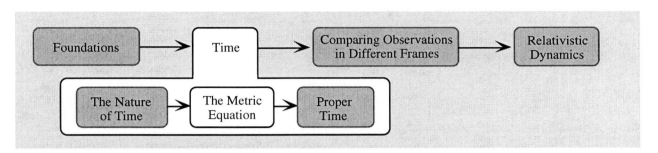

The most incomprehensible thing about the world is that it is comprehensible.

Albert Einstein

R4.1 OVERVIEW

The last chapter provided the conceptual foundations for our discussion of time in the theory of relativity. We saw that there are three fundamentally distinct ways of measuring the time interval between two events, and saw that these techniques can yield different results even for the same pair of events. Time is a complex phenomenon in the theory of relativity!

In this chapter we will reduce some of this complexity by working out a mathematical link between coordinate time and the spacetime interval. This link is the *metric equation*, which is to spacetime what the pythagorean theorem is to plane geometry, and which is the foundation for almost everything that we do in the rest of the unit. Here is an overview of the sections in this chapter.

R4.2 *INTRODUCTION TO THE METRIC EQUATION* reviews ideas from the last chapter and sets the stage for appreciating the metric equation.

R4.3 *DERIVING THE METRIC EQUATION* shows how we can derive the metric equation from the principle of relativity.

R4.4 *ABOUT PERPENDICULAR DISPLACEMENTS* discusses why the principle of relativity requires that observers in different inertial reference frames get the *same* results when measuring displacements perpendicular to the line of relative motion of the frames.

R4.5 *EVIDENCE SUPPORTING THE METRIC EQUATION* looks at some experiments that have tested the implications of the metric equation.

R4.6 *SPACETIME IS NOT EUCLIDEAN* shows that the very helpful analogy between spacetime and plane geometry is not a *perfect* analogy.

R4.7 *MORE ABOUT THE GEOMETRIC ANALOGY* compares and contrasts the metric equation and the pythagorean theorem.

R4.8 *SOME EXAMPLES* provides some examples of how the metric equation can be applied in (semi)realistic situations.

In the following chapter, we will use the metric equation to link proper time to the spacetime interval and coordinate time, thus completing a web of mathematical relationships between these quantities.

R4.2   INTRODUCTION TO THE METRIC EQUATION

Review of the three kinds of time

In the last chapter, we discussed three different ways to measure the time interval between two events. An observer in an inertial reference frame can measure the *coordinate time* Δt between the events by comparing the reading of the clock present at one event with the synchronized clock present at the other event. Since observers in different reference frames will disagree about whether a given pair of clocks is synchronized, the coordinate time Δt measured between the events depends on the reference frame used.

One can avoid this problem by measuring the time between the events by a single clock that moves between the events so that it is present at both. Such a clock measures a *proper* (proprietary) time $\Delta \tau$ between the events. The magnitude of such a proper time, while frame-independent (in the sense that all observers will agree on what a given clock present at both events actually registers between those events), is known experimentally to depend on the worldline traveled by the clock as it moves from one event to the other.

There is, however, one and only one worldline that takes a clock from one event to the other at a *constant velocity*. The proper time between the events measured by an *inertial* clock is thus a unique, frame-independent number that depends on the spacetime separation of the two events and nothing else. This unique proper time is called the *spacetime interval* Δs.

Analogy between space-time interval and distance

We also discussed in the last chapter an analogy that compared these different ways of measuring the time between events in spacetime with different ways of measuring the separation of two points on a plane. The coordinate time corresponds to the north-south (or east-west) coordinate displacement between the points. Since surveyors using different coordinate systems will disagree about the exact direction of "north", the value of the north-south displacement between two points will depend on one's choice of coordinate system. The proper time corresponds to the *pathlength* between the two points measured along a certain path using a tape measure. Since measuring the pathlength does not require determining where "north" is, its value is independent of one's choice of coordinate system, but does depend on the path chosen. The spacetime interval corresponds to the straight-line *distance* between the points. Since there is one and only one straight line between a given pair of points, the pathlength measured along this line is a unique, coordinate-independent number for characterizing the spatial separation of the points.

Analogy between metric equation and the pythagorean theorem

As discussed in section R3.5, we can actually *calculate* the distance Δd between two points on the plane using the coordinate displacements Δx and Δy between the points (as measured in any given coordinate system) and the pythagorean theorem:

$$\Delta d^2 = \Delta x^2 + \Delta y^2 \qquad (R4.1)$$

The amazing thing about this formula is that while the values Δx and Δy between two points depends on one's choice of coordinate system, the distance Δd calculated from these does not.

It turns out that there is an analogous formula that links the coordinate time Δt and spatial displacements Δx, Δy, and Δz between two events measured in any given inertial reference frame with the frame-independent spacetime interval Δs between the events. This equation, which we call the *metric equation*, provides the crucial key needed to escape the "relativity" of inertial reference frames and quantify the separation of the events in *absolute* (frame-independent) terms.

Our purpose in this chapter is to derive the metric equation and describe some of its immediate consequences. In the next chapter we will show how the metric equation can be used to compute proper times along more general worldlines as well.

R4.3 DERIVING THE METRIC EQUATION

The derivation that follows is the very core of the special theory of relativity. The metric equation is the key to understanding all of the unusual and interesting consequences of the theory of relativity. You should make a special effort to understand this argument thoroughly.

What we want to do is compare the time interval Δt between two events measured in some inertial frame (call it the Home Frame) with the time Δs measured by a clock moving at a constant velocity that is present at both events. To make this argument easier, I want to consider a special kind of clock we will call a **light-clock**. An idealized light clock is shown in Figure R4.1. It consists of two mirrors a fixed distance L apart, and a flash of light that bounces back and forth between the mirrors. Each time the flash of light bounces off the bottom mirror, a detector in that mirror sends a signal to an electronic counter. The clock dial thus essentially registers the number of round trips that the light flash has completed. Since the speed of light is *defined* to be 1 second of distance per one second of time in any inertial frame, we should calibrate this clock face to register a time interval of $2L$ (where L is expressed in seconds) for each "tick" of the clock (that is, each time the light flash bounces off the bottom mirror): the clock will then read correct time as long as it is inertial.

Now consider an arbitrarily chosen pair of events A and B. Let the coordinate time interval and spatial separation between these events (as measured in the Home Frame) be Δt and $\Delta d = [\Delta x^2 + \Delta y^2 + \Delta z^2]^{1/2}$ respectively. Also imagine that we have a light clock moving between these events (with its beam-path oriented perpendicular to its direction of motion) at just the right constant velocity to be present at both events. To simplify our argument, let us also imagine that the length L between the light-clock mirrors has just the right value so that Events A and B happen to coincide with successive ticks of the light clock (in principle, we could always adjust L to make this true for two given events).

In the inertial frame of the light clock, both events occur at the clock face, and the clock's light flash completes exactly one round trip. The time interval recorded by this clock between events A and B is thus exactly $2L$. Since this inertial clock is present at both events, it registers the spacetime interval between these events, so $\Delta s = 2L$.

In the Home Frame, the time of each event is registered by the clock nearest the event: since the events occur at different places, we will determine the coordinate time interval between the events by taking readings from a *pair* of clocks. In this frame, the light clock is observed to move the distance Δd in the time interval Δt. This means that the light flash will be observed in the Home Frame to follow the zig-zag path shown in Figure R4.2.

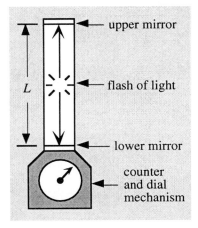

Figure R4.1: Schematic diagram of a light clock. Each "tick" of the light clock represents the passage of a time interval equal to $2L$ (in SR units).

Beginning of the derivation

Figure R4.2: As the light clock moves from event A to event B in the Home Frame, its internal light flash will be observed to follow the zig-zag path shown.

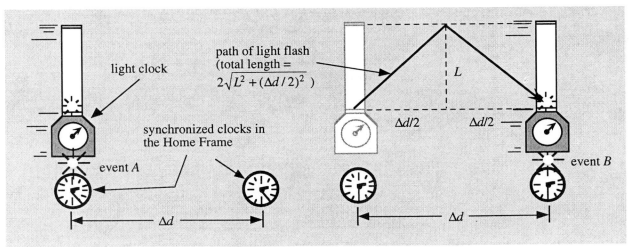

light clock

path of light flash
(total length = $2\sqrt{L^2 + (\Delta d/2)^2}$)

synchronized clocks in the Home Frame

event A

event B

L

$\Delta d/2$ $\Delta d/2$

Δd

Δd

As you can see from Figure R4.2, the total distance that the light flash travels in the Home Frame is (according to the pythagorean theorem)

$$2\sqrt{L^2 + (\Delta d / 2)^2} \;=\; \sqrt{4L^2 + \Delta d^2} \;=\; \sqrt{(2L)^2 + \Delta d^2} \tag{R4.2}$$

Since the synchronized clocks in the Home Frame must (by definition of "synchronization") measure the speed of light to be 1, the coordinate time interval Δt registered on the pair of synchronized clocks in the Home Frame must be equal to the distance that the light flash traveled between the events:

$$\Delta t = \sqrt{(2L)^2 + \Delta d^2} \tag{R4.3}$$

But we saw above that the light clock registers the spacetime interval between the two events to be $\Delta s = 2L$. Plugging this into equation R4.3 and squaring both sides, we get

$$\Delta t^2 \;=\; \Delta s^2 + \Delta d^2 \quad \text{or} \quad \Delta s^2 \;=\; \Delta t^2 - \Delta d^2 \tag{R4.4}$$

Since $\Delta d^2 = \Delta x^2 + \Delta y^2 + \Delta z^2$ (where Δx, Δy, and Δz are the coordinate differences measured between the events in the Home Frame), we have, finally:

The metric equation

$$\boxed{\Delta s^2 \;=\; \Delta t^2 - \Delta x^2 - \Delta y^2 - \Delta z^2} \tag{R4.5}$$

This extremely important equation links the frame-*independent* spacetime interval Δs between any two events to the frame-*dependent* coordinate separations Δt, Δx, Δy, Δz measured between those events *in any arbitrary inertial reference frame*! Note that we have not sacrificed anything by using a light clock in this argument: since the speed of light is defined to be 1 in any inertial frame any decent clock that we construct must agree with what the light clock says. The only real limitation to our argument is that Δt must be greater than Δd for the two events in question so that it is possible for a light flash to travel between the events. (Note that if $\Delta t < \Delta d$, equation R4.5 yields an imaginary value for Δs, an absurd result indicating that the conditions of the proof have been violated.)

Just as the spacetime interval Δs between two events is analogous to the distance Δd between two points on a plane, the formula $\Delta s^2 = \Delta t^2 - \Delta x^2 - \Delta y^2 - \Delta z^2$ is directly analogous to the pythagorean theorem $\Delta d^2 = \Delta x^2 + \Delta y^2 + \Delta z^2$. Note that the pythagorean theorem also relates a coordinate-independent quantity (the distance Δd between two points) with quantities whose values depend on the choice of coordinate system (the coordinate differences Δx, Δy, and Δz). Indeed, the formula for the spacetime interval would be just like a four-dimensional version of the pythagorean theorem if it were not for the minus signs that appear. We will see that these minus signs have a variety of interesting and unusual consequences.

We call equation R4.5 the **metric equation**. It is the link between our human constructed reference frames and the absolute physical reality of the separation between two events in space and time. It is difficult to overemphasize the importance of this equation: virtually all the rest of our study of the theory of relativity will revolve around the implications of this equation.

R4.4   ABOUT PERPENDICULAR DISPLACEMENTS

What if *L* is not the same in both frames?

The previous argument *assumes* that the vertical length L between the light-clock mirrors is the same in both the light-clock frame (where it was used to compute the spacetime interval) and the Home Frame (where it was used to compute the coordinate time). But how do we *know* that this is true? Since coor-

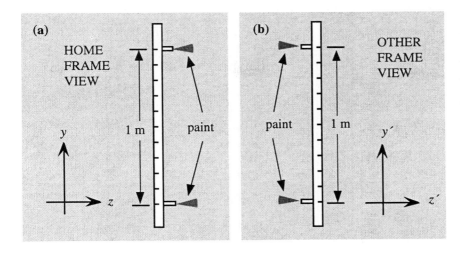

Figure R4.3: (a) The spray paint nozzles on the Home Frame measuring stick are 1.00 m apart in the *y* direction as measured in that frame. They point directly at their counterparts in the Other Frame so that stripes are painted on the Other Frame's measuring stick as it moves by. The *x* axis points directly into the plane of the paper here.

(b) Similarly, the paint nozzles on the Other Frame stick are 1.00 m apart in that frame and are pointed to paint stripes on the Home Frame measuring stick as it moves by.

dinate differences between events are generally frame-dependent, what gives us the right to assume that the displacement between the mirrors has the same value in both frames?

In this section, I will argue that if we have two reference frames in relative motion along a given line, any displacement measured *perpendicular* to that direction of motion will have the same *value* in both reference frames. I will demonstrate that this statement follows directly from the principle of relativity.

The proof presented here will be a proof by contradiction. We will assume that there *is* a contraction (or expansion) effect that applies to perpendicular lengths and show that the existence of such an effect contradicts the principle of relativity. Turned around, this argument will then imply that if the principle of relativity is true, no such effect can exist.

Consider two inertial reference frames (a Home Frame and an Other Frame) in standard orientation, so that the line of relative motion is along the frames' common *x* and *x′* axis. In each frame we set up a measuring stick along the *y* or *y′* direction with spray-paint nozzles set 1.00 m apart (as shown in Figure R4.3). Note in the diagram that the common *x* and *x′* axes (which lie along the line of relative motion of the frames) are perpendicular to the plane of the paper. This means that as the frames move relative to each other, one of the measuring sticks will move into the paper and the other out of the paper. The paint nozzles in each frame are pointed in the direction of the secondary frame's measuring stick, so as the two measuring sticks pass each other, they will spray-paint stripes on each other.

Now imagine that there exists some kind of contraction effect so that an observer in the Home Frame measures the measuring stick at rest in the Other Frame to be vertically contracted. This means that an observer in the Home Frame will measure the distance between the spray-paint nozzles on that stick to be *less* than 1.00 m apart. This in turn means that the stripes painted by these nozzles will be less than a 1.00 m apart in the Home Frame: they will be painted *inside* the nozzles on the measuring stick at rest in the Home Frame. Conversely, the nozzles on the measuring stick at rest in the Home Frame will paint stripes on the stick in the Other Frame which are *outside* the nozzles in that frame (see Figure R4.4a).

Now, the principle of relativity requires that the laws of physics be exactly the same in any inertial reference frame. More specifically, this means that if you perform exactly the same experiment in two inertial reference frames, one should get exactly the same result. There should be *no* way of experimentally distinguishing the two frames. How does this principle apply in this situation?

Proof that distances measured perpendicular to the line of relative motion of two inertial frames will be the *same* in both frames

Figure R4.4: If the contraction effect is real, than the principle of relativity implies that observers in each frame must observe the stick in the other frame to be contracted. **(a)** So an observer in the Home Frame observes the Home Frame stick to paint stripes *outside* the Other Frame's nozzles as the latter moves by (into the plane of the drawing here). **(b)** Similarly, an observer in the Other Frame observes their stick to paint stripes *outside* the nozzles on the Home Frame's stick as the latter moves by (*out* of the plane of the paper here).

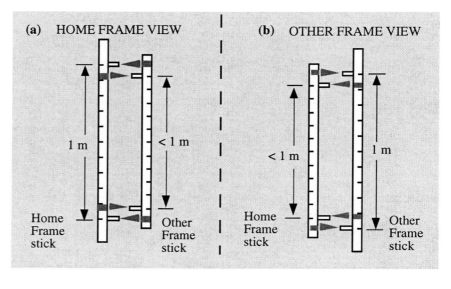

In the Other Frame, it is the Home Frame stick that is moving. Therefore, the principle of relativity requires that if a contraction effect exists, an observer in the Other Frame *must* measure the Home Frame stick to be contracted, just as the Home Frame observer measured the Other Frame stick to be contracted. This in turn means that the stripes painted by the Other Frame stick will be *outside* the Home Frame stick's nozzles, and the stripes painted by the Home Frame stick will be *inside* the Other Frame stick's nozzles, as shown in Figure R4.4b.

Now compare Figures R4.4a and R4.4b: they describe a logical contradiction. In Figure R4.4a, stripes are being painted on the Home Frame stick *inside* its nozzles. In Figure R4.4b, stripes are being painted on the Home Frame stick *outside* its nozzles. These cannot be simultaneously true! The paint marks on the Home Frame stick are permanent and unambiguously visible to all observers in *every* reference frame. They cannot be "inside" the nozzles according to some observers and "outside" to others. So *either* Figure R4.4a or Figure R4.4b can be true, but *not both*. But the principle of relativity *requires* that both be true!

How can we resolve this conundrum? The only way is to reject the hypothesis that got us into this trouble in the first place, that is, the hypothesis that distances measured perpendicular to the line of relative motion of the frames have different values in the two frames. If we assume that there is no contraction (or expansion) effects operating between the frames, then there is no problem with the principle of relativity. As shown in Figure R4.5, both sticks will paint stripes across each other's nozzles. The situation is exactly the same in both frames, and the contradiction disappears.

This argument forces us to conclude:

Any displacement measured perpendicular to the line of relative motion of two inertial frames must have the same value in both frames.

This means that the distance L between the mirrors used in the derivation of the metric equation does in fact have the same value in the light-clock frame as it does in the Home Frame, so our derivation should be correct.

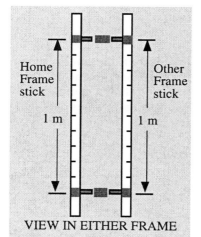

Figure R4.5: If we assume that there is no contraction, the contradiction disappears.

Implication: *L is* the same in both frames in the proof of the metric equation

Exercise R4X.1 We will see in Chapter R7 that a measuring stick *is* observed in a given reference frame to be contracted *parallel* to its direction of motion in that frame. Explain why the argument above *cannot* exclude contractions or expansions parallel to the line of motion. [*Hint*: What kind of stripes would the sticks paint on each other if they move relative to each other in a direction parallel to their lengths?]

R4.5 EVIDENCE SUPPORTING THE METRIC EQUATION

Careful and compelling as the derivation of the metric equation above may be, we as physicists should not simply accept such an equation without some experimental confirmation: physics is a study of the physical world and not simply a collection of pretty logical arguments. We need to support the metric equation with some experimental evidence.

One of the classic experiments testing the validity of the metric equation involves **muons**. A muon is an elementary particle that is a more massive version of the electron (see Chapter C4). Muons are continually generated in the upper atmosphere (at heights of approximately 60 km) by the interaction of cosmic rays with atmospheric gas molecules. Many of these muons stream downward toward the earth with speeds in excess of 0.99 (that is, 99% of c).

Now, muons are unstable, decaying after a short period of time into lighter particles. The half-life of muons at rest in a laboratory is about 1.52 μs, which means that if you have N muons at a certain time, after 1.52 μs you will have $N/2$ left, after another 1.52 μs you will have $N/4$ left, and so on. A batch of muons moving together in a bunch can thus serve as a clock: to determine how much time has passed in the muon frame, all that we need to do is measure the number of undecayed muons in the bunch. You can imagine that each muon contains a built-in clock, and that each time the clock "ticks" the muon has a certain small probability of decaying, a probability such that after 1.52 μs worth of such ticks have passed, half the muons in a bunch will have decayed.

It is possible to build a muon detector that will count the number of muons reaching it from a particular direction and traveling at a particular speed. Imagine building two detectors that only register muons traveling vertically downward at a speed of roughly 0.994 as measured in the earth's reference frame. We place one such detector at the top of a mountain and count the number of muons that it sees per unit time, and another at the foot of the mountain 1907 m (≈ 6.36 μs of distance) lower and count the number of muons that it sees per unit of time.

Let's follow a single muon that happens to go through both detectors. Let event A be the event of this muon passing through the upper detector, and event B be this muon passing through the bottom detector. The distance Δd between these events in the earth's frame of reference is 6.36 μs in SR units. The coordinate time interval between these events measured in the Earth's frame is simply the time required for a muon traveling at a speed of 0.994 to traverse this distance: $\Delta t = \Delta d/v = 6.36$ μs$/0.994 = 6.40$ μs.

Note that since the muon is present at each of these events by definition, and moves between them at a constant velocity of 0.994 downward, the clock inside this muon measures the spacetime interval Δs between the events. If the newtonian conception of time were true, all clocks would measure the same time interval between two events, implying that $\Delta s = \Delta t = 6.40$ μs. This corresponds to $(6.40$ μs$/1.52$ μs$) \approx 4.21$ muon half-lives, so most of the hypothetical muon's co-moving siblings that make it through the top detector would decay before reaching the bottom detector. Specifically, if N muons make it through the top detector, we would expect to see N times $(1/2)^{4.21} \approx N/18.5$ make it to the bottom detector if the newtonian assumption about time is true.

Exercise R4X.2: Check that $(1/2)^{4.21} \approx 1/18.5$.

But if the *metric* equation is true, the spacetime interval between the events would actually be $\Delta s = [\Delta t^2 - \Delta d^2]^{1/2} \approx [(6.40$ μs$)^2 - (6.36$ μs$)^2]^{1/2} \approx 0.714$ μs. This time, which is the time that our muon (and its co-moving siblings) measures between the events, is only $(.714$ μs$/1.52$ μs$) \approx 0.47$ of a muon half-life, meaning that the internal clocks in most of the muons will *not* signal that it is time to decay before they reach the bottom detector. Specifically, if N muons

Properties of muons

Description of a muon experiment that tests the metric equation pass through the upper detector, then you can show that about $N/1.38$ should make it to the bottom detector.

Exercise R4X.3: Verify this last statement.

In summary, the newtonian conception of time leads to the prediction that the ratio of number of muons passing through the upper detector to the number passing through the lower detector should be 18.5, while the metric equation predicts that the same ratio should be 1.38. This is a substantial difference that can be easily measured.

Actual results support the metric equation

This experiment was done in the early 1960's by D.H. Frisch and J.B. Smith (*Am. J. Phys.*, **31**:342, 1963). They reported observing the ratio to be 1.38 (within experimental uncertainties), thus confirming the metric equation (and utterly refuting the newtonian conception of time by a substantial margin).

R4.6 SPACETIME IS *NOT* EUCLIDEAN

We have found the analogy between ordinary euclidean plane geometry and spacetime geometry to be very illuminating, and this basic analogy will remain fruitful as we continue to develop the consequences of the theory of relativity. Nevertheless, it is important at this point to describe some of the important differences between euclidean geometry and spacetime geometry that are a result of the negative signs in the metric equation $\Delta s^2 = \Delta t^2 - \Delta x^2 - \Delta y^2 - \Delta z^2$ that do not appear in the corresponding pythagorean theorem $\Delta d^2 = \Delta y^2 + \Delta x^2$.

Distance between two points on a map of a flat space are proportional to actual distance in space

One important difference concerns the representation of distances on a map and spacetime intervals on a spacetime diagram. If one prepares a scale drawing (e.g. a map) of various points in a town, the distance between any two points on the map is *proportional* to the actual distance between those points in space. That is, distances on the drawing directly correspond to distances in the physical reality being represented. In Figure R4.6a, for example, to determine the distance between City Hall and the Statue of the Unknown Physicist, one need merely measure the distance (in inches) between the two sites on the map shown above and multiply by the conversion factor (1000 m = 1 inch). It doesn't matter how the line between the two sites is oriented or where the sites are located on the drawing: the distance in the physical space being represented by the map is always proportional to the distance measured on that map.

Distance between events on a spacetime diagram is *not* proportional to Δs

However, it is *not* true that the displacement between two points on a spacetime diagram is proportional to the spacetime interval between the corresponding events. In fact, the spacetime interval between two events separated in space can even be zero (see Figure R4.6b)!

Figure R4.6: (a) A scale drawing (map) of Askew (1 in = 1 km). The actual distance between City Hall and the Statue of the Unknown Physicist is 852 m. The distance between City Hall and the particle accelerator ride at Quark Park is also 852 m. The length of both double-arrows on the map is thus 0.852 inch.

(b) Both events B and C are the same distance from event A on the spacetime diagram. The spacetime interval between A and B is 4 s, while the spacetime interval between A and C is *zero* (since $\Delta t = \Delta x$)!

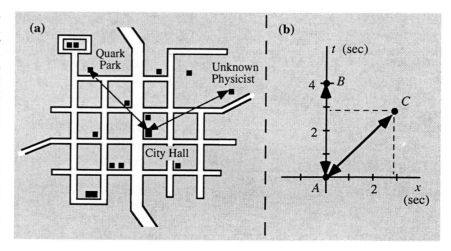

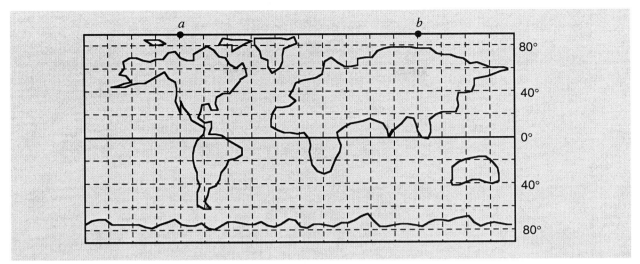

Figure R4.7: A pseudo-Mercator projection map of the world, where the lines of longitude are represented as being equally-spaced straight lines

A spacetime diagram thus may accurately display the spacetime *coordinates* of various events, but the distances between the points representing those events on the diagram are *not* proportional to the actual spacetime intervals between those events in spacetime.

Analogy: distances on a flat map of curved earth

This is very strange, and it may seem particularly strange that two events (such as *A* and *C* in Figure R4.6b) can occur at different places and times and yet have zero spacetime interval between them. Nonetheless, there exists a useful analogy with something you may have seen before. Imagine a map of the world where the lines of longitude and latitude are drawn as equally-spaced straight lines (see Figure R4.7). Have you ever noticed how the shapes and sizes of the continents appear very warped near the north and south poles on such maps? For example, look at the continent of Antarctica on the map. It looks huge and seems to be shaped like a strip. But in fact it is not so large, and it has a nearly *circular* shape: its size and shape are quite distorted by the nature of the map. The shapes of Greenland and northern Canada are distorted as well. As a matter of fact, the two points marked *a* and *b* on the map are both at 90° north latitude, that is, at the *north pole*. Thus though these points are separated by a significant distance on the map, the physical distance between these points on the surface of the earth is zero!

Why does this map not accurately represent the distances between points on the earth's surface? The problem is that the surface of the earth as a whole is the surface of a *sphere*, which has a very different geometry than the euclidean geometry of a flat sheet of paper. For example, on a sheet of paper the interior angles of a triangle always add up to 180° and parallel lines never intersect. But on the surface of the earth, the interior angles of a triangle add up to *more* than 180° (consider a triangle with one vertex at the north pole and two vertices at the equator) and initially parallel lines may converge or diverge (consider lines of longitude, which are parallel at the equator!). Because of these fundamental geometric differences between the surface of the earth and the sheet of paper, any flat map of the earth will *necessarily* be a distorted representation: one cannot make a map of the surface of the earth on a flat sheet of paper and have distances on the sheet correspond to actual distances on the earth.

Problem is that the geometry of the earth is not the same as that of map

Similarly, one cannot draw a spacetime diagram in such a way that distances between points on the drawing are proportional to the spacetime intervals between the corresponding events. Like the surface of the earth, spacetime has a different geometry than the flat sheet of paper on which a spacetime diagram is drawn. The negative signs in the metric equation where the corresponding pythagorean relation has positive signs is symptomatic of this difference.

Similarly, geometries of spacetime and spacetime diagram are different

The moral of the story is, don't expect a spacetime diagram to give you *direct* information about the spacetime interval between events, any more than you would expect a flat map of the earth to give you accurate information about distances on the earth's surface. A spacetime diagram visually represents the *coordinates* of events and the worldlines of particles, nothing more. You can always compute the spacetime interval between two events from their coordinates if necessary.

R4.7 MORE ABOUT THE GEOMETRIC ANALOGY

In spite of the issue raised in the previous section, we can further extend the analogy between the geometry of a plane and the geometry of spacetime by exploring the similarities (as well as differences) in how the metric equation describes the geometry of spacetime and how the pythagorean theorem describes the geometry of a plane.

When viewed in different coordinate systems, point B always lies somewhere on a *circle* around point A.

The most important thing about both these equations is that they enable us to calculate an absolute quantity (Δs or Δd) in terms of frame-dependent coordinate differences measured in an arbitrary inertial frame or coordinate system. This similarity is illustrated in Figures R4.8 and R4.9. Figure R4.8 shows the same pair of points on the plane (A and B) that are 5 m apart, plotted in various coordinate systems having different orientations with respect to "north." Note that if

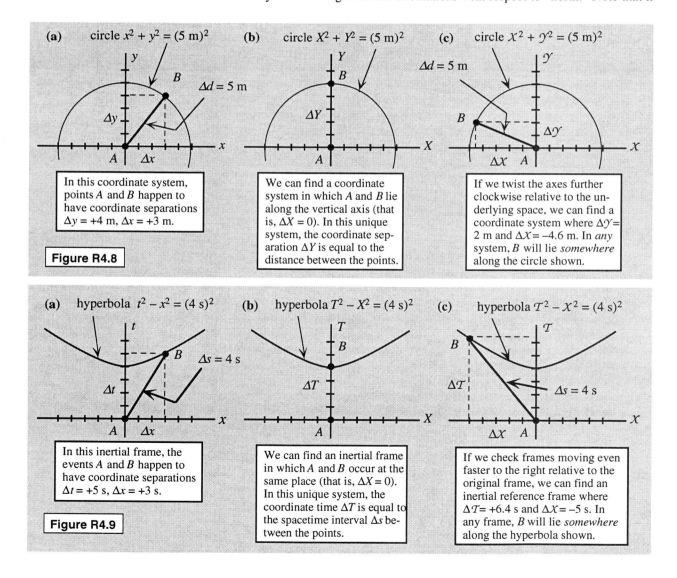

(a) circle $x^2 + y^2 = (5\text{ m})^2$

$\Delta d = 5$ m

In this coordinate system, points A and B happen to have coordinate separations $\Delta y = +4$ m, $\Delta x = +3$ m.

Figure R4.8

(b) circle $X^2 + Y^2 = (5\text{ m})^2$

We can find a coordinate system in which A and B lie along the vertical axis (that is, $\Delta X = 0$). In this unique system, the coordinate separation ΔY is equal to the distance between the points.

(c) circle $\mathcal{X}^2 + \mathcal{Y}^2 = (5\text{ m})^2$

$\Delta d = 5$ m

If we twist the axes further clockwise relative to the underlying space, we can find a coordinate system where $\Delta\mathcal{Y} = 2$ m and $\Delta\mathcal{X} = -4.6$ m. In *any* system, B will lie *somewhere* along the circle shown.

(a) hyperbola $t^2 - x^2 = (4\text{ s})^2$

$\Delta s = 4$ s

In this inertial frame, the events A and B happen to have coordinate separations $\Delta t = +5$ s, $\Delta x = +3$ s.

Figure R4.9

(b) hyperbola $T^2 - X^2 = (4\text{ s})^2$

We can find an inertial frame in which A and B occur at the same place (that is, $\Delta X = 0$). In this unique system, the coordinate time ΔT is equal to the spacetime interval Δs between the points.

(c) hyperbola $\mathcal{T}^2 - \mathcal{X}^2 = (4\text{ s})^2$

$\Delta s = 4$ s

If we check frames moving even faster to the right relative to the original frame, we can find an inertial reference frame where $\Delta\mathcal{T} = +6.4$ s and $\Delta\mathcal{X} = -5$ s. In any frame, B will lie *somewhere* along the hyperbola shown.

we set up the coordinate systems so that point A is at the origin, then point B in each coordinate system lies somewhere on the circle defined by the equation $x^2 + y^2 = \text{constant} = \Delta d^2$, where Δd^2 is the squared distance between the points (since Δd is the distance between the points in all coordinate systems). Note that in these drawings, I have kept the axes of each coordinate system vertical and horizontal, and rotated the space containing the points A and B "underneath" these coordinate axes: please understand that the points A and B are meant to be the *same* physical points in all of the diagrams.

Similarly, Figure R4.9 shows a pair of events (A and B) separated by a spacetime interval of 4 s, plotted on spacetime diagrams drawn by observers in different inertial frames. If we choose the origin event in these frames so that event A occurs at $t = x = 0$, then event B lies somewhere on the curve defined by $t^2 - x^2 = \text{constant} = \Delta s^2$, where Δs^2 is the squared spacetime interval between the events (since Δs has a frame-independent value): such a curve is a *hyperbola*, as shown. (Note that we are assuming that $\Delta y = \Delta z = 0$ for these two events.) Again, remember, that these spacetime diagrams are meant to show how different observers would plot the *same* physical events A and B on their diagrams.

When viewed in different reference frames, event B lies somewhere on a *hyperbola* about event A.

The point is that the set of all points a given distance from the origin on the plane form a circle: the set of all events a given spacetime interval from the origin event in spacetime form a hyperbola. The reason that both curves aren't circles is the negative sign in the metric equation that doesn't appear in the pythagorean relation. But there is a nice one-to-one correspondence between circles in plane geometry and hyperbolae in spacetime geometry.

Note that one consequence of the difference between the metric equation and the pythagorean relation, is that in Figures R4.8, we see that the north-south coordinate separation between a pair of points is always *less* than or equal to the distance between the points (the "hypotenuse" on the diagram): $\Delta y \le \Delta d$. In Figures R4.9, though, we see that the coordinate time Δt between a pair of events is always *greater* than the spacetime interval Δs between them: $\Delta t \ge \Delta s$, even though the "hypotenuse" that represents Δs on the diagram *looks* larger.

Comparing the magnitudes of the distance and spacetime interval with coordinate separations

R4.8 SOME EXAMPLES

EXAMPLE R4.1

Problem: A firecracker explodes. A second firecracker explodes 25 ns away and 52 ns later, as measured in the Home Frame. In another inertial frame (the Other Frame), the two explosions are measured to occur 42 ns apart in space. How long a time passes between the explosions in the Other Frame?

Solution The key in this problem is to recognize that the spacetime interval between the two explosion events is frame-independent. That is, if we calculate it using the metric equation in the Home Frame, we must get the same answer that we would get if we calculated it in the Other Frame. That is:

$$\Delta t^2 - \Delta d^2 = \Delta s^2 = (\Delta t')^2 - (\Delta d')^2 \qquad (R4.6)$$

Solving this equation for the unknown $\Delta t'$, we get:

$$(\Delta t')^2 = \Delta t^2 - \Delta d^2 + (\Delta d')^2 = (52\text{ ns})^2 - (25\text{ ns})^2 + (42\text{ ns})^2 = 3800\text{ ns}^2$$

$$\Delta t' = \sqrt{3800\text{ ns}^2} \approx 62\text{ ns} \qquad (R4.7)$$

Exercise R4X.4: Imagine that two events that are separated by 30 ns of distance in the Home Frame are also simultaneous in that frame. If in the Other Frame, the events are separated by 10 ns of time, what must their spatial separation in the Other Frame be?

EXAMPLE   R4.2

Problem: A certain physics professor fleeing the wrath of a set of irate students covers the length of the physics department hallway (a distance of about 120 ns) in a time of 150 ns as measured in the frame of the earth. Assuming that the professor moves at a constant velocity, how much time does the professor's watch measure during the trip from one end of the hallway to the other?

Solution Part of the trick in many relativity physics problems is to rephrase a word-problem in terms of *events*. In this case, let event A be the professor entering the hallway, and event B be the professor's hasty departure from the other end. In the reference frame of the earth, these events occur a time $\Delta t = 150$ ns apart and a distance $\Delta d = 120$ ns apart. The professor's watch, however, is present at each of the events, so that watch registers the *spacetime interval* between these two events. Therefore, by the metric equation, the professor's watch reads:

$$\Delta s^2 = \Delta t^2 - \Delta d^2 = (150 \text{ ns})^2 - (120 \text{ ns})^2 = 8100 \text{ ns}^2$$

$$\Delta s = \sqrt{8100 \text{ ns}^2} = 90 \text{ ns} \tag{R4.8}$$

**EXAMPLE   R4.3:
(A First Glance at the
Twin Paradox)**

Problem: A spaceship departs from our solar system and travels at a constant speed to the star Alpha Centauri 4.3 light-years away, then instantaneously turns around (never mind about the impossible accelerations involved) and returns to the solar system at the same constant speed. Assume that the trip takes 13 years as measured by clocks here on earth. How long does the trip take as measured by clocks on the spaceship?

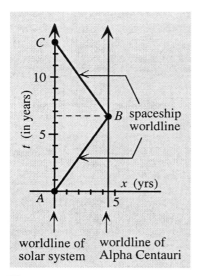

Figure R4.10: Spacetime diagram of a trip to Alpha Centauri and back.

Solution Again, we need to translate the word problem into a problem about measuring the time between events. Let event A represent the ship's departure from the starbase, Event B its arrival at Alpha Centauri, and *E*vent C its return to the solar system (see Figure R4.10). A clock in the spaceship does *not* measure the spacetime interval between events A (departure from the solar system) and C (return to the solar system) even though the clock is present at both events. This is because the clock is accelerated when the spaceship turns around, and so is not inertial. To find the total elapsed time registered on the ship clock, we can, however, consider each leg of the trip separately. The ship's clock *does* measure the spacetime interval between events A and B, and also measures the spacetime interval between events B and C, as it is inertial during each individual leg of the trip and is present at the events in question. The total time registered by the ship's clock is thus the sum of the spacetime intervals between A and B and between B and C.

We can use the metric equation to compute these spacetime intervals from the coordinate differences for these events measured in the earth's frame. Events A and B occur $\Delta t = 6.5$ y apart in time and $\Delta d = 4.3$ y apart in space. The spacetime interval between these events is

$$\Delta s_{AB} = \sqrt{(6.5 \text{ y})^2 - (4.3 \text{ y})^2} \approx 4.9 \text{ y} \tag{R4.9}$$

The spacetime interval between events B and C is the same. The total elapsed time for the trip as measured by a clock on the ship is thus $2(4.9 \text{ y}) = 9.8$ years, which is somewhat shorter than the time of 13 y measured by clocks on earth.

Note that the line on the diagram connecting points A and B looks *longer* than 6.5 y, but the spacetime interval that this line represents is actually shorter than 6.5 yrs. This is an illustration of the issue discussed in section R4.6.

Exercise R4X.5: If spaceship clocks measure only 2 y for this round trip, how long did it take according to clocks on the earth?

SUMMARY

I. THE METRIC EQUATION
   A. Design for a *light clock*
      1. A flash of light bounces between two mirrors a distance L apart
      2. A display mechanism counts the bounces
      3. In its own frame, then, each cycle of the clock takes a time $2L$
   B. Derivation of the metric equation:
      1. Imagine a light clock moves at a constant velocity in the Home Frame (with beam-path perpendicular to line of motion).
      2. Consider endpoints of single cycle of light-flash to be two events
      3. This clock is present at both events and is inertial $\Rightarrow$ measures Δs
      4. But flash follows a zig-zag path in the Home Frame
      5. Since light must move with speed 1 in the Home Frame, Δt between events in Home Frame must be *longer* than $2L$.
   C. Final result is the *metric equation*: the spacetime interval Δs between two events separated by Δt, Δx, Δy, Δz in a given inertial reference frame is given by $\Delta s^2 = \Delta t^2 - \Delta x^2 - \Delta y^2 - \Delta z^2$
      1. links frame-independent Δs with frame-dependent Δt, Δx, Δy, Δz
      2. is for spacetime what pythagorean theorem is to plane geometry

II. ABOUT PERPENDICULAR DISPLACEMENTS
   A. Any displacement measured perpendicular to the line of relative motion of two inertial reference frames must have the same value in both.
   B. Argument for this assertion:
      1. Imagine measuring sticks perpendicular to the line of motion that paint stripes on each other a measured distance apart
      2. Assume that lengths of sticks are *not* the same in both frames.
      3. However, the principle of relativity requires a symmetry between the two inertial frames that contradicts the last assumption.
      4. So the assumption must be false: lengths *are* the same

III. MUON EXPERIMENT SUPPORTING THE METRIC EQUATION
   A. Outline of an experiment performed by D.H. Frisch and J.B. Smith
      1. High-speed muons are formed continually in the upper atmosphere
      2. Experimenters selected muons that move vertically at speed 0.994 and counted them using detectors separated vertically by 1907 m
   B. Analysis of the experiment
      1. Consider a batch of muons flowing from one detector to the other
      2. Since muons are present at both detection events, they measure Δs (A batch of muons decay with halflife of 1.52 μs in own frame, so monitoring their decay is like watching a clock.)
      3. The metric equation predicts $\Delta s = 0.47$ half-lives between events; the newtonian assumption about time predicts $\Delta s = 4.21$ half-lives.
   C. The results support metric equation by a wide margin

IV. MORE ABOUT THE GEOMETRIC ANALOGY
   A. Spacetime is *not* euclidean:
      1. The distance between points on a map $\propto$ to the actual distance between them in space, but the distance between points on spacetime diagram is *not* $\propto$ to the actual spacetime interval between them
      2. This is because geometry of spacetime is not the same as geometry of the paper on which the diagram is drawn (world map analogy)
   B. Circles and hyperbolas
      1. In plane geometry, the set of all points having the same distance from origin form a *circle* around the origin in a map of the plane
      2. In spacetime, the set of all events having the same Δs from the origin event form a *hyperbola* on a spacetime diagram

GLOSSARY

light-clock: an imaginary device that uses a flash of light bouncing back and forth between two mirrors a fixed distance L apart as the reference for measuring time intervals. The time displayed by the clock is determined by counting complete cycles of the bouncing flash: each cycle lasts $2L$ of time (if L is measured in seconds) by definition.

metric equation: the equation $\Delta s^2 = \Delta t^2 - \Delta x^2 - \Delta y^2 - \Delta z^2$ that links the frame independent spacetime interval Δs between two events with the frame *dependent* coordinate sep-

arations Δt, Δx, Δy, Δz measured between those two events in any inertial reference frame. This equation, which is for spacetime what the pythagorean theorem is to plane geometry is one of the most important equations relativity.

muon: an elementary particle of the lepton family that is essentially a massive version of the electron (about 206 times as massive as the electron). Muons are unstable and decay with a half-life of 1.52 μs to an electron and a pair of neutrinos.

TWO-MINUTE PROBLEMS

R4T.1 The spacetime interval Δs between two events is smaller than the coordinate time Δt between those events as measured in any reference frame (T or F).

R4T.2 Two events occur 5.0 s apart in time and 3.0 s apart in space. A clock traveling at a speed of 0.60 can be present at both these events. What time interval will such a clock measure between the events?

A. 8.0 s   C. 5.0 s   E. 2.0 s
B. 5.8 s   D. 4.0 s   F. other (specify)

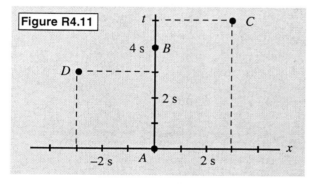

Figure R4.11

R4T.3 The spacetime coordinates of events A and B are shown in this spacetime diagram in Figure R4.11. What is the spacetime interval between these events?

A. 0 s   C. 3 s   E. 5 s
B. 2 s   D. 4 s   F. other (specify)

R4T.4 The spacetime coordinates of events A and C are shown in this spacetime diagram in Figure R4.11. What is the spacetime interval between these events?

A. 0 s   C. 3 s   E. 5 s
B. 2 s   D. 4 s   F. other (specify)

R4T.5 The spacetime coordinates of events A and D are shown in this spacetime diagram in Figure R4.11. What is the spacetime interval between these events?

A. 0 s   C. 3 s   E. 5 s
B. 2 s   D. 4 s   F. other (specify)

R4T.6 Consider the spacetime diagram shown below. Let the spacetime interval between events O and A be Δs_{OA} and let the spacetime interval between events O and B be Δs_{OB}. Which of these two spacetime intervals is larger? (Assume that the y and z coordinates of all of these events are zero.)

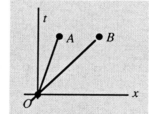

A. $\Delta s_{OA} > \Delta s_{OB}$

B. $\Delta s_{OA} < \Delta s_{OB}$

C. $\Delta s_{OA} = \Delta s_{OB}$

D. there is no way to tell from this diagram.

R4T.7 An inertial clock present at two events always measures a *shorter* time than a pair of synchronized clocks in *any* inertial reference frame would register between the same two events (as long as the events don't occur at the same place in that frame). (T or F.)

HOMEWORK PROBLEMS

BASIC SKILLS

R4B.1 In a certain inertial reference frame, two events are separated in time by $\Delta t = 25$ ns and by $\Delta d = 15$ ns in space. What is the spacetime interval between these events?

R4B.2 In the reference frame of the solar system, two events are separated by 5.0 h of time and 4.0 h of distance. What is the spacetime interval between these events?

R4B.3 In the Home Frame, two events are observed to occur with a spatial separation of 12 ns and a time coordinate separation of 24 ns. (a) An inertial clock travels between these events in such a manner as to be present at both events. What time interval does this clock read between the

events? (b) What is the speed of this clock, as measured in the Home Frame?

R4B.4 An alien spaceship moving at a constant velocity goes from one end of the solar system to the other (a distance of 10.5 hours) in 13.2 hours as measured by clocks on the Earth. What time does a clock on the spaceship read for the passage? [*Hint:* Rephrase in terms of events.]

R4B.5 A spaceship travels from one end of the Milky Way galaxy to the other (a distance about of 100,000 y) at a constant velocity of magnitude $v = 0.999$, as measured in the frame of the galaxy. How much time does a clock in the spaceship register for this trip? [*Hint:* Rephrase this problem in terms of events.]

R4B.6 In the Home Frame, two events are measured to occur 500 ns apart in time and 300 ns apart in space. In an Other Frame, these events are found to occur 400 ns apart in time. What is the spatial separation of these events in the Other Frame?

R4B.7 In the solar system frame, two events are measured to occur 3.0 h apart in time and 1.5 h apart in space. Observers in an alien spaceship measure the two events to be separated by only 0.5 h in space. What is the time separation between the events in the alien's frame?

SYNTHETIC

R4S.1 Imagine that you and a friend are riding in trains that are moving relative to each other at relativistic speeds. As you pass each other, you both measure the time separation and spatial separation of two firecracker explosions that occur on the tracks between you. (You can measure the latter by measuring the distance between the scorch marks that the explosions leave on the side of your train.) You find the firecracker explosions to be separated by 1.0 μs of time and 0.40 μs of distance in your frame. By radio, your friend reports that the explosions were separated by only 0.60 μs of time in your friend's frame? Is this possible? If it is, find the spatial separation of the events in your friend's frame. If not, explain why not.

R4S.2 A muon is created by a cosmic-ray interaction at an altitude of 60 km. Imagine that after its creation, the muon hurtles downward at a speed of 0.998, as measured by an ground-based observer. After the muon's "internal clock" registers 2.0 μs (which is a bit longer than the average life of a muon), the muon decays. (a) If the muon's internal clock were to measure the same time between its birth and death as clocks on the ground do (i.e. Special Relativity is not true and time is universal and absolute), about how far would this muon have traveled before it decays? (b) How far will this muon *really* travel before it decays?

R4S.3 In one inertial frame (the Home Frame), two events are observed to occur at the same place, but $\Delta t = 32$ ns apart in time. In another inertial frame (the Other Frame) the same two events are observed to occur 45 ns apart in space. (a) What is the coordinate time interval between the events in the Other Frame? (b) Compute the speed of the Home Frame as measured by observers in the Other Frame. [*Hint*: The events occur at the same place in the Home Frame. So how far does the Home Frame appear to move in the time between the events as seen in the Other Frame? What is the time between the events in the Other Frame?]

R4S.4 A new rapid transit line advertises that they will carry you from Los Angeles to Seattle (a distance of about 3000 km) at such a high rate of speed that your watch only registers half the time for the trip that synchronized clocks in the station read. (a) What is the approximate distance between Los Angeles and Seattle expressed in microseconds? (b) What time interval must the synchronized station clocks register between the train's departure from Los Angeles and its arrival in Seattle if the advertisement is to be true? (c) What is the approximate speed of the train?

R4S.5 The spacetime diagram in Figure R4.12 shows the worldline of a rocket as it leaves the earth, travels for a certain time, comes to a stop, and then explodes. (a) What is the elapsed time between the rocket's departure and explo-sion, as measured by a clock on the rocket? (b) What is the spacetime interval between these two events?

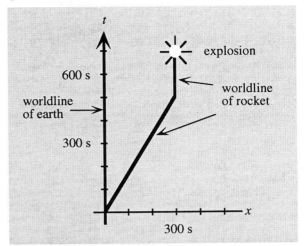

Figure R4.12: Spacetime diagram of the rocket discussed in problem R4S.5.

R4S.6 Imagine that a certain unstable subatomic particle decays with a half-life at rest of about 2.0 μs (that is, if at a certain time you have N such particles at rest, about 2.0 μs later you will have $N/2$ remaining). We can think of a batch of such particles as being a clock that registers the passage of time by the decreasing number of particles in the batch. Now imagine that with the help of a particle accelerator, we manage to produce in the laboratory a beam of these particles traveling at a speed $v = 0.866$ in SR units (as measured in the laboratory frame). This beam passes through a detector A, which counts the number of particles passing through it each second. The beam then travels a distance of about 2.08 km to detector B, which also counts the number of particles passing through it, as shown in Figure R4.13. (a) Let event A be the passing of a given particle through detector A and event B be the passing of the same particle through detector B. How much time will a laboratory observer measure between these events? [*Hint*: you don't need to know anything about relativity to answer this question!] (b) How much time passes between these events as measured by the clock inside the particle, according to relativity theory? If relativity is true, about what fraction of the particles that pass through detector A survive to pass through detector B? (c) According to the newtonian conception of time, the time measured by a particle clock between the events would be the same as the time measured by lab clocks. If this were so, what fraction of the particles passing through detector A survive to detector B?

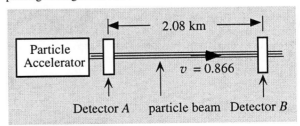

Figure R4.13: Laboratory setup for the particle-decay experiment described in problem R4S.6.

RICH-CONTEXT

R4R.1 In 2095 a message arrives at earth from the growing colony at Tau Ceti (11.3 y from earth). The message asks for help in combating a virus that is making people seriously ill (the message includes a complete description of the viral genome). Using advanced technology available on earth, scientists are quickly able to construct a drug that prevents the virus from reproducing. You have to decide how much of the drug can be sent to Tau Ceti. The space probes available on short notice could either boost 200 g of drug (in a standard enclosure) to a speed of 0.95, 1 kg to a speed of 0.90, 5 kg to a speed of 0.80, or 20 kg to a speed of 0.60 relative to the earth. The only problem is that a sample of the drug in a standard enclosure at rest in the lab is observed to degrade due to internal chemical processes at a rate that will make it useless after 5.0 y. Is it possible to send the drug to Tau Ceti? If so, how much can you send?

ADVANCED

R4A.1 Just as we can describe the relationship between the hypotenuse of a triangle and the coordinate lengths of its sides using the sine and cosine functions, it turns out that we can describe the relationship between the spacetime interval Δs between two events in terms of the coordinate separations Δt and Δx between those events in terms of the hyperbolic sine and cosine functions. The *hyperbolic sine* and *hyperbolic cosine* functions of a quantity θ are defined as follows:

$$\sinh\theta = \tfrac{1}{2}(e^\theta - e^{-\theta}), \quad \cosh\theta = \tfrac{1}{2}(e^\theta + e^{-\theta}) \qquad \text{(R4.10)}$$

(a) Prove that $\cosh^2\theta - \sinh^2\theta = 1$. This means that if the spacetime interval between two events occurring along the spatial x axis is Δs, then the coordinate separations Δt and Δx between these events can be written $\Delta t = \Delta s \cosh\theta$ and $\Delta x = \Delta s \sinh\theta$ for some appropriately chosen value of θ, just as in plane geometry, $\Delta x = \Delta d \cos\theta$ and $\Delta y = \Delta d \sin\theta$ (see Figure R4.14).

(b) Argue that θ in the hyperbolic case is *not* the angle that the line AB makes with the t axis in the spacetime diagram of Figure 4.13b. Argue in fact that as $\theta \to \infty$, the angle that AB makes with the t axis approaches $45°$.

(c) Argue that if v is the speed of an object that goes from event A to event B at a constant velocity, the "angle" θ is in fact $\tanh^{-1}v$.

(d) When $v = 0.80$, $\theta = 1.10$ (if your calculator can do inverse hyperbolic functions, verify this). What are the values of $\cosh\theta$ and $\sinh\theta$ for this value of θ? (Use the definitions of these functions given above if your calculator cannot evaluate hyperbolic functions). When $v = 0.99$, we have $\theta = 2.65$ (again, verify if you can). What are the values of $\cosh\theta$ and $\sinh\theta$ for this value of θ?

(e) Argue that as $\theta \to 0$, $\sinh\theta \to 0$ while $\cosh\theta \to 1$, just like the corresponding trigonometric functions. This also means that $\tanh\theta \to 0$ in this limit. Use this to argue that as $v \to 0$, $\Delta s \to \Delta t$ and $\Delta x \to 0$.

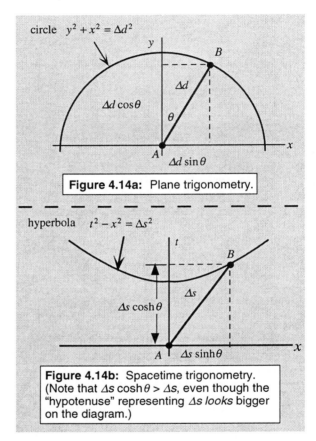

circle $\quad y^2 + x^2 = \Delta d^2$

Figure 4.14a: Plane trigonometry.

hyperbola $\quad t^2 - x^2 = \Delta s^2$

Figure 4.14b: Spacetime trigonometry. (Note that $\Delta s \cosh\theta > \Delta s$, even though the "hypotenuse" representing Δs *looks* bigger on the diagram.)

ANSWERS TO EXERCISES

R4X.1 Measuring sticks placed parallel to the line of relative motion will simply paint stripes down each other's length. There is no way to extract information about the length of a given stick from such stripes.
R4X.2 (Answer is given.)
R4X.3 If N muons travel through the top detector, the number that make it through the bottom detector after 0.47 times a muon halflife have passed will be (by analogy to the calculation above exercise R4.5.1) $N(1/2)^{0.47} = 0.722N$ $= N/1.385$.
R4X.4 In this situation, we have $\Delta t = 0$, $\Delta d = 30$ ns. Since we must have $(\Delta t')^2 - (\Delta d')^2 = \Delta t^2 - \Delta d^2$, and since we are given that $\Delta t' = 10$ ns, we can find the spatial separation $\Delta d'$ between the events in the Other Frame by solving the equation above for $\Delta d'$:

$$\Delta d' = \sqrt{(\Delta t')^2 - \Delta t^2 + \Delta d^2}$$
$$= \sqrt{(10 \text{ ns})^2 - 0 + (30 \text{ ns})^2} = 31.6 \text{ ns} \qquad \text{(R4.11)}$$

R4X.5 If the round trip takes a total proper time of 2.0 y as measured on the ship, then each constant-velocity leg of the trip will take $\Delta\tau = \Delta s = 1.0$ y. Since we know that the distance between the trip's endpoints in the solar system frame is $\Delta d = 4.3$ y, we can find Δt for one leg of the trip by solving the metric equation $\Delta s^2 = \Delta t^2 - \Delta d^2$ for Δt:

$$\Delta t = \sqrt{\Delta s^2 + \Delta d^2} = \sqrt{(1.0 \text{ y})^2 + (4.3 \text{ y})^2} = 4.4 \text{ y} \qquad \text{(R4.12)}$$

This means that the round trip takes about 8.8 y according to observers in the solar system frame, and the speed of the spaceship in that frame is $\Delta d/\Delta t \approx 4.3$ y / 4.4 y ≈ 0.98.

R5

PROPER TIME

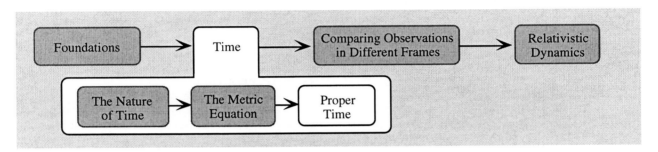

The great discoverers can readily be classed under two types of mentality: those who dig deep and those who range wide. Those who possess the gift of combining depth with breadth are rare indeed. Einstein was one of them.

François le Lionnais

R5.1 OVERVIEW

In the last chapter, we derived the metric equation, which links the spacetime coordinate differences between two events measured in any reference frame with the frame-independent spacetime interval Δs between those events. In this chapter, we will explore how we can use the metric equation to calculate the proper time measured along *any* worldline, not just those that are straight.

R5.2 *A CURVED FOOTPATH* begins the study of curved worldlines by reminding ourselves how we would compute the length of a curved footpath on a flat two-dimensional plane.

R5.3 *CURVED WORLDLINES IN SPACETIME* builds on that analogy to show how we can compute the proper time along a curved worldline.

R5.4 *THE BINOMIAL APPROXIMATION* presents an approximation that is very useful for calculating the difference between the spacetime interval and coordinate time when v is small compared to the speed of light.

R5.5 Δs *IS THE LONGEST POSSIBLE PROPER TIME* proves that the spacetime interval between two events is the *longest* possible proper time that we could measure between the events.

R5.6 *EXPERIMENTAL EVIDENCE* reviews some of the evidence supporting our formula for computing proper time along a curved worldline.

R5.7 *THE TWIN PARADOX* applies the proper time formula to the famous *twin paradox* of relativity, a puzzle that has perplexed people since the theory of relativity was first announced.

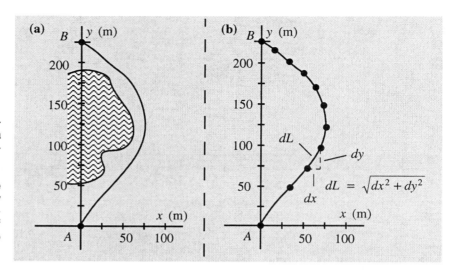

Figure R5.1: (a) Map of a foot-path around a small pond, with a superimposed *xy* coordinate system.

(b) We can find the length of the path by subdividing it into many infinitesimal, almost straight sections, finding the length *dL* of each section, and summing to find the total length *L*.

R5.2   A CURVED FOOTPATH

The metric equation $\Delta s^2 = \Delta t^2 - \Delta x^2 - \Delta y^2 - \Delta z^2$ connects the spacetime coordinate differences between two events measured in some inertial reference frame to the spacetime interval Δs between the same events measured by an inertial clock present at both events. In this section and the next, we will use the metric equation to connect coordinate time in a given inertial frame to the proper time $\Delta \tau$ measured by *any* clock present at both events, inertial or not.

One might think that we would have to use the theory of *general* relativity to properly analyze the behavior of accelerating (noninertial) clocks. In fact, we can quite adequately analyze the behavior of such clocks using only the metric equation if we remember the analogy between the proper time between events in spacetime and the pathlength between two points on a plane.

We compute the length of a curved path by breaking it up into tiny straight pieces

Consider a footpath around a small pond (see Figure R5.1a) by a scale drawing with a superimposed coordinate system. We could measure the length of this path from point *A* to point *B* with a long, flexible tape measure. But once we have set up a coordinate system, we can also *compute* the length of the path in the following manner. Imagine dividing up the path into a large number of infinitesimally small sections, as shown in Figure R5.1b.[*] If we make these sections small enough, each will be approximately straight. In this limit, the pathlength *dL* of a given segment as measured by a flexible tape measure will be almost equal to the straight length computed (using the pythagorean theorem) from the coordinate differences of the segment's endpoints:

$$dL^2 \approx dx^2 + dy^2 \qquad \text{or} \qquad dL = \sqrt{dx^2 + dy^2} \qquad \text{(R5.1)}$$

The total length L_{AB} of the path from *A* to *B* is the sum of all the segment lengths, which in the limit where the segments are truly infinitesimal becomes the integral

$$\Delta L_{AB} = \int_{\text{path}} dL = \int_{\text{path}} \sqrt{dx^2 + dy^2} \qquad \text{(R5.2)}$$

Note that since the length *dL* of each segment is greater than its northward extension *dy*, the total pathlength between points *A* and *B* will be greater than the straight-line northward distance of 225 m between *A* and *B*: we can say quite generally, therefore, that $\Delta L_{AB} \geq \Delta d_{AB}$.

---

[*]The analogy with pathlength presented here follows E. F. Taylor and J. A. Wheeler, *Spacetime Physics*, 1/e, San Francisco, Freeman, 1963, pp. 32–34.

If we think of the path as being specified by giving the x coordinate of each point on the path as a function of y [that is, the path is specified by the function $x(y)$], then we can write the integral above as a single-variable integral over x by pulling a factor of dy out of the square root:

$$\Delta L_{AB} = \int_{y_A}^{y_B} \sqrt{1+(dx/dy)^2}\ dy \qquad (R5.3)$$

Formula for computing the length of a path $x(y)$

[Note that we are considering y to be the independent variable and x to be the dependent variable in the equation above. This reversal of convention is necessary because $y(x)$ is not well-defined for a path shown in Figure R5.1.]

As we have discussed before, though this equation uses the coordinates x and y measured in a given coordinate system, the pathlength itself is an invariant quantity: we'll get the same answer (the answer that a flexible tape measure would give) no matter *what* coordinate system we use.

R5.3 CURVED WORLDLINES IN SPACETIME

The analogy to events in spacetime is direct. Consider the worldline of a particle that travels out from the origin of some inertial reference frame a certain distance along the x axis and then returns. Such a worldline is shown on the spacetime diagram in Figure R5.2a with the coordinate axes of that frame superimposed. Such a worldline describes an *accelerating* particle; we can see from the graph that the particle's x velocity $= dx/dt$ (which is the inverse slope of its worldline on the diagram) changes as time progresses.

The situation in spacetime is directly analogous

A clock traveling with the particle measures the proper time $\Delta\tau_{AB}$ between events A and B along this worldline (by definition of proper time). But once we have measured the worldline of the particle in an inertial reference frame (any inertial frame), we can calculate what this clock will read between events A and B by using the metric equation in a manner analogous to our determination of the pathlength between points A and B in the previous section.

Imagine that we divide the particle's worldline up into many infinitesimal segments, each of which is nearly a straight line on the spacetime diagram (Figure R5.2b). We choose each segment to be short enough so that the particle's velocity is approximately constant as it traverses that segment. If a given segment is short enough so that the particle's velocity is almost constant along it, the proper time $d\tau$ that a clock would measure along that segment will be almost equal to the spacetime interval ds between the events that mark the ends of the segment, since the clock is present at both these events and travels between

We compute $\Delta\tau$ along a worldline by dividing the worldline into many tiny straight segments

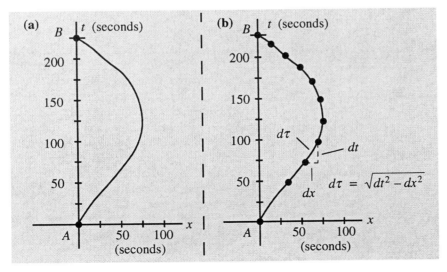

Figure R5.2: (a) A spacetime diagram of the motion of a particle's worldline based on measurements obtained in some inertial reference frame.

(b) We can find the proper time along the worldline by subdividing it into many infinitesimal (almost straight) worldlines, finding the proper time $d\tau$ along each segment and then summing to find the total proper time. Note that because of the minus sign in the metric equation, $d\tau \le dt$ here, even though it *looks* like $d\tau \ge dt$ on the diagram.

them with an *almost* constant velocity. Therefore, by the metric equation:

$$d\tau^2 \approx ds^2 = dt^2 - dx^2 - dy^2 - dz^2 \tag{R5.4}$$

Taking the square root and pulling out a factor of the coordinate time *dt*, we get:

$$d\tau = \sqrt{1 - \left(\frac{dx}{dt}\right)^2 - \left(\frac{dy}{dt}\right)^2 - \left(\frac{dz}{dt}\right)^2} \; dt$$

$$= \sqrt{1 - v_x^2 - v_y^2 - v_z^2} \; dt \quad = \quad \sqrt{1 - v^2} \; dt \tag{R5.5}$$

This equation expresses the infinitesimal proper time $d\tau$ measured by a clock traveling between two *infinitesimally separated* events in terms of the coordinate time *dt* between those events measured in some inertial frame and the clock's instantaneous *speed v* measured in that frame. The clock may be moving along *any* smooth worldline (*v* does not *have* to be constant).

To find the *total* proper time measured between events *A* and *B* by a clock traveling along the worldline, we sum up the proper times measured for each nearly-straight segment of the worldline, which in the limit of truly infinitesimal segments amounts to integrating equation R5.5:

General formula for computing the proper time along a worldline

$$\Delta\tau_{AB} = \int_{\text{wordline}} \sqrt{1 - v^2} \; dt \tag{R5.6}$$

If the speed *v* of the clock is expressed as a function of time $v(t)$, then the integral is simply an ordinary one–variable integral with respect to *t*, which can be evaluated in principle. This equation links the total proper time $\Delta\tau_{AB}$ between two events measured by a clock traveling between events *A* and *B* to the clock's speed as a function of time $v(t)$ as measured in some given (but arbitrary) inertial reference frame. Though we are using an inertial frame to measure *v*, remember that the *result* of equation R5.6 is frame-independent, since the clock in question measures $\Delta\tau_{AB}$ *directly* without reference to any reference frame.

If the *speed v* of the clock happens to be constant, the integral in equation R5.6 can be done very easily:

Formula for the special case where the object's *speed* is constant.

$$\Delta\tau_{AB} = \sqrt{1 - v^2} \int_{\text{wordline}} dt = \sqrt{1 - v^2} \; \Delta t_{AB} \quad \text{if } v = \text{constant} \tag{R5.7}$$

Please note that "constant speed" here does not necessarily imply "constant velocity", as the *direction* of a particle's velocity may change without changing its speed. Thus equation R5.7 can be applied to clocks traveling along straight or curved worldlines, as long as the speed of the clock remains fixed. Equation R5.6 must be used whenever the speed changes.

Any proper time between two events is smaller than the coordinate time between the same events

Note that since $[1-v^2]^{1/2}$ is always ≤ 1, any proper time measured between two events will be *smaller* than (or at most equal to) the coordinate time between those events measured in any inertial frame: $\Delta\tau_{AB} \leq \Delta t_{AB}$ always. However, if the clock's speed is small compared to that of light ($v \ll 1$), that clock will register almost the same time between the events as measured in the inertial frame: $\Delta\tau_{AB} \approx \Delta t_{AB}$. (This is true whether *v* is constant or not.)

Two things to remember

When applying either equation R5.6 or R5.7, it is important to remember two things. First of all, coordinate time Δt and the proper time $\Delta\tau$ represent the time interval between two events measured in two fundamentally different ways (just as the northward displacement Δy and the pathlength ΔL represent two fundamentally different ways of measuring the spatial separation of two points on the earth's surface). The coordinate time between events is measured with a pair of *synchronized clocks* in an inertial frame, while the proper time is measured by a *clock present at both events*. One cannot use these equations to link readings on just any old clocks.

Secondly, the quantities $\Delta\tau$ and Δt appearing on both sides of equation R5.7 always refer to the time between the *same* pair of events measured in these two different ways. Perhaps the most common error made by beginners in applying that equation is implicitly using *different* pairs of events to delimit the time intervals $\Delta\tau$ and Δt. To avoid this, think *carefully* about the events involved!

Note also that equations R5.6 and R5.7 break down if $v > 1$: in such a case, they predict that the time registered by the traveling clock is an *imaginary* number (which is even worse than being a negative number!). Remember that these equations are all based on the metric equation, whose derivation (see Section R4.2) is only valid for pairs of events for which $\Delta t > \Delta d$, that is, events between which it is possible to send a clock traveling with $v < 1$. Therefore, the equations presented so far do not specify what a clock traveling faster than the speed of light would read between two events. We will see later that the principle of relativity in fact implies that it is *impossible* for a clock to travel faster than the speed of light in any reference frame. The failure of these equations for the case where $v > 1$ is our first indication of this basic truth.

The equations for proper time fail when $v > 1$

EXAMPLE R5.1

Problem: Imagine that you are at rest in an inertial frame (the Home Frame) and you are whirling a clock around your head at a constant rate on the end of a string 3.0 m long. A friend compares the reading of the whirling clock as it speeds by with readings from a stationary clock. Find out how long it takes the whirling clock to go once around its circular path if its reading for one cycle is 0.01 percent smaller than the period read by your friend's clock.

Solution The first step is to rephrase the problem in terms of *events*. Let event A be the whirling clock passing by the stationary clock. Let event B be the next such passage event. The whirling clock measures a proper time between these events. The stationary clock measures a *different* proper time between the events (because it is also present at both events). Since the stationary clock is at rest in the Home Frame, the time that it registers is the same as the coordinate time between the events in the Home Frame. The whirling clock, on the other hand, is non-inertial (its velocity is constantly changing direction as it goes around the circle). But since its *speed* is constant, we can use equation R5.7 to find the proper time that it measures between events A and B. We are given that the result is 99.99 percent of the time measured by the stationary clock, so:

$$\Delta\tau_{AB,\ \text{whirl}} = \sqrt{1-v^2}\ \Delta t_{AB} = 0.9999\ \Delta t_{AB} \tag{R5.8}$$

implying that $\sqrt{1-v^2} = 0.9999$ or $1 - v^2 = (0.9999)^2$, implying that:

$$v^2 = 1 - (0.9999)^2 \Rightarrow v = \sqrt{1-(0.9999)^2} \approx 0.014 \tag{R5.9}$$

The radius of the circle in seconds is $(3.0\ \text{m})(1\ \text{s}\ /\ 3.00 \times 10^8\ \text{m}) = 1.0 \times 10^{-8}\ \text{s} = 10$ ns. The coordinate time that a clock traveling at $v = 0.014$ would take to go once around this circle is:

$$\Delta t_{AB} = 2\pi R/v = 2\pi(1.0 \times 10^{-8}\ \text{s})/0.014 \approx 4.40 \times 10^{-6}\ \text{s}. \tag{R5.10}$$

This implies frequency of revolution of $1/\Delta t_{AB} \approx 225{,}000$ Hz. This answer makes it clear that the scenario presented in this problem is completely unrealistic. Yet this speed is what would be necessary to get even a 0.01 percent difference in the rate of the whirling clock relative to a stationary clock. It is a small wonder that we think of time as being universal and absolute!

Exercise R5X.1: If the clock in this situation has a mass of 100 g, estimate the tension force that the string would have to exert on it. Is this realistic?

EXAMPLE R5.2

Problem: Imagine that the speed of a certain spaceship relative to an inertial frame fixed to the sun is given by $v = at$, where $a = 10$ m/s^2. How long does it take the ship to accelerate from rest to a speed of 0.5 (in SR units) relative to the sun, as measured by clocks on the *ship*?

Solution Again, the first step is to rephrase the problem in terms of events. Let event A be the event of the ship starting to accelerate and event B the event of its passing $v = 0.5$ (in SR units). Since the ship is present at both events, its clock measures proper time between them. Since the speed of the ship is *not* constant in this case, we must use equation R5.6 to compute this proper time:

$$\Delta \tau_{AB} = \int_{t_A}^{t_B} \sqrt{1 - v^2} \, dt = \int_{t_A}^{t_B} \sqrt{1 - a^2 t^2} \, dt \qquad (R5.11)$$

In spite of the simple form of the equation $v = at$, this is not a simple integral to evaluate. We can put it in a somewhat simpler form by doing the following. First, note that $t_A = 0$, because if $v = at$, then $t = 0$ when the ship is at rest but beginning to accelerate. Secondly, note that $dv = a \, dt$ in this case, so we can change the variable in the integral from t to v as follows:

$$\Delta \tau_{AB} = \frac{1}{a} \int_0^{t_B} \sqrt{1 - a^2 t^2} \, a \, dt = \frac{1}{a} \int_0^{0.5} \sqrt{1 - v^2} \, dv \qquad (R5.12)$$

This integral now has a simple enough form that we can try looking it up in a table of integrals. My table of integrals says that

$$\int \sqrt{1 - v^2} \, dv = \frac{v\sqrt{1 - v^2}}{2} - \frac{\sin^{-1} v}{2} \qquad (R5.13)$$

Therefore:

$$\Delta \tau_{AB} = \frac{1}{2a} \left[0.5\sqrt{1 - (0.5)^2} - \sin^{-1}(0.5) - 0\sqrt{1 - 0^2} + \sin^{-1} 0 \right]$$

$$= \frac{1}{2a} [0.433 + 0.524 - 0 - 0] = \frac{0.478}{a} \qquad (R5.14)$$

To finish the derivation, we have to know what a is in SR units (since equation R5.6 and everything we have done presumes that we are working in SR units). To change $a = 10$ m/s^2 to SR units, we must convert the unit of meters appearing in this expression to units of seconds:

$$a = 10 \frac{\text{m}}{\text{s}^2} \left(\frac{1 \text{ s}}{3.0 \times 10^8 \text{ m}} \right) = \frac{1}{3.0 \times 10^7 \text{ s}} \qquad (R5.15)$$

Plugging this into equation R5.14, we get that:

$$\Delta \tau_{AB} = 0.478(3.0 \times 10^7 \text{ s}) = 1.43 \times 10^7 \text{ s} \qquad (R5.16)$$

Because integrals in cases where $v \neq$ constant are so difficult, we will generally stick to cases where $v =$ constant in this course. This example is mainly to illustrate how a calculation where $v \neq$ constant can be done: you will not be asked to do anything as difficult as this (outside of the advanced problems at the end of this chapter).

Exercise R5X.2: Show that $\Delta \tau_{AB}$ found in the example above is 0.957 times the time Δt_{AB} measured between the events in the sun's frame.

Exercise R5X.3: Imagine that electrons in a certain particle accelerator ring travel in a circular path at a constant speed of 0.98. What is the time that would be measured by a clock traveling with the electrons for one complete cycle around the ring as a multiple of the time measured by a clock at rest in the lab?

R5.4 THE BINOMIAL APPROXIMATION

The square root that appears in equations R5.6 and R5.7 is rather difficult to evaluate for very small speeds($v \ll 1$). The speeds of objects we encounter on an everyday basis are on the order of $v = 10^{-8}$ in SR units, meaning $v^2 \approx 10^{-16}$. When one tries to evaluate the square root $[1-v^2]^{1/2}$ in such a case, one's calculator usually simply returns just 1.0, since few calculators keep track of enough decimal places to accurately register the subtraction of 10^{-16} from 1. Such an answer is not really helpful. In such cases, however, there is an approximation we can use to help us convert the square root to a more usable form.

It can be shown (see problems R5S.4 and R5A.2) that

$$(1+x)^a \approx 1 + ax, \quad \text{if } |x| \ll 1 \tag{R5.17}$$

Motivation for the binomial approximation

General statement of the binomial approximation

This equation, called the **binomial approximation**, is a very useful approximation with a wide range of applications in physics (memorize it!). In the case that we are considering here, if we identify $x \equiv -v^2$ and $a = 1/2$, we find that

$$\sqrt{1-v^2} \approx 1 + \tfrac{1}{2}(-v^2) = 1 - \tfrac{1}{2}v^2 \tag{R5.18}$$

Exercise R5X.4: Using your calculator, check the accuracy of this approximation for $v = 0.1$, 0.01, and 0.001.

Problem: You and a friend stand at a street corner and synchronize your watches. You leave your friend (call this event A) and walk around the block, traveling at a constant speed of 2 m/s (about 4.5 miles per hour). After a time $\Delta t_{AB} = 550$ s, as measured by your friend's watch, you return (call this event B). How much less than 550 s does your watch register between events A and B?

EXAMPLE R5.3

Solution Take your friend's frame to be inertial; your friend's watch thus measures the coordinate time between A and B in that frame (also the spacetime interval!). In your friend's frame, you have a constant speed of $v = 2$ m/s, or in SR units, $v \approx 6.7 \times 10^{-9}$. This is extremely small compared to 1, so we can employ the binomial approximation. The proper time that you measure between events A and B is therefore given by:

$$\Delta \tau_{AB} = \sqrt{1-v^2}\,\Delta t_{AB} \approx \left(1 - \tfrac{1}{2}v^2\right)\Delta t_{AB} = \Delta t_{AB} - \tfrac{1}{2}v^2\,\Delta t_{AB} \tag{R5.19}$$

The difference between $\Delta \tau_{AB}$ (the time *you* read between events A and B) and Δt_{AB} (the time your friend reads) is thus approximately:

$$-\tfrac{1}{2}v^2\Delta t_{AB} = -\tfrac{1}{2}(6.7 \times 10^{-9})^2(550 \text{ s}) \approx -2.5 \times 10^{-14} \text{ s} \tag{R5.20}$$

meaning that the time that you measure is about 549.999999999999975 s. Clearly, the difference between this and 550 s is not going to be even remotely measurable. The difference between proper time and coordinate time is utterly negligible when the clock measuring proper time moves between the events in question at ordinary velocities. Again, it is no wonder that we all intuitively have the idea that time is universal and absolute!

R5.5 Δs IS THE LONGEST POSSIBLE PROPER TIME

Δτ along a *straight* worldline between two events is
the *longest* possible Δτ
between those events

Analogy to a straight line
being the shortest dis-
tance between two points

Note that equation R5.6 implies that generally the proper time measured by a clock between two events will indeed depend on the worldline that the clock follows between the events: specifically, the proper time depends on the particular way that the speed v of the clock varies with time. This is analogous to the way that the pathlength between two points on a plane depends on the curvature of the path along which it is measured.

In euclidean geometry, the straight-line distance between two points is the shortest possible pathlength between the two points. In this section, we will prove that an *inertial* clock that travels between two events (which thus measures the spacetime interval Δs between them) measures the longest *possible* proper time between those events, longer than any non-inertial clock: $\Delta s \geq \Delta \tau$ *for all possible worldlines between the events.*

How might we prove such a theorem? Consider an arbitrary pair of events, A and B. The time between these events is measured by two clocks that are present at both events. Imagine that clock I follows an inertial worldline between the events, while clock NI follows a non-inertial worldline. Since clock I is inertial, its proper time $\Delta \tau_I$ will be equal (by definition) to the spacetime interval Δs_{AB} between the events. We will take advantage of the fact that we can calculate the proper time for *any* given worldline using *any* inertial reference frame that we please, since the *result* is frame-independent. With this in mind, it is convenient for us to evaluate the proper times for clocks I and NI in that particular inertial frame where clock I is at *rest*. Since that clock is inertial, the frame in which it is at rest will also be inertial: let's call this the Home Frame.

To compute the proper time along *any* path from event A to event B in this frame, we calculate $\int_{t_A}^{t_B} [1 - v^2]^{1/2} \, dt$, where $v(t)$ and the endpoints t_B and t_A are all measured in the Home Frame. For clock I, $[1 - v^2]^{1/2} = 1$, since that clock is at rest in the Home Frame by construction. Since clock NI travels along a *different* worldline by hypothesis, it must at least *sometimes* have $v \neq 0$ in the Home Frame, so that the integrand $[1 - v^2]^{1/2}$ must be *less* than one for at least *part* of the range of integration. So $\Delta s_{AB} = \Delta \tau_I = \int_{t_A}^{t_B} 1 \, dt > \int_{t_A}^{t_B} [1 - v^2]^{1/2} \, dt = \Delta \tau_{NI}$ (note that both integrals have the same endpoints). Since the values of the proper times $\Delta \tau_I$ and $\Delta \tau_{NI}$ are frame-independent, this inequality must be true no matter *what* inertial frame we use to actually calculate $\Delta \tau_I$ and $\Delta \tau_{NI}$. Q.E.D.

Note that in a spacetime diagram based on measurements made in an inertial reference frame, an inertial clock will have a straight worldline (since it moves with constant velocity with respect to any inertial frame) whereas a non-inertial clock will have a curved worldline. The theorem we have just proven thus says that *a straight worldline between any two events on a spacetime diagram is the worldline of greatest proper time between the events.*

That the spacetime interval between two events in spacetime represents the *longest* proper time between those events while the distance between two points on a plane represents the *shortest* pathlength between those points is direct consequence of the negative signs that appear in the metric equation where only positive signs appear in the corresponding Pythagorean relation. This is another of the basic differences between spacetime geometry and the Euclidean geometry of points on a plane. Even so, there remains a similarity in that a straight worldline (or path) leads to an *extreme* value for the proper time (or pathlength).

Equation R5.7 implies that the coordinate time Δt between two events measured in any inertial reference frame is greater than (or at minimum equal to) *any* proper time measured between the points (*including* the spacetime interval Δs between those events). The three kinds of time interval that you can measure between two events thus stand in the strict relation:

$$\Delta t \geq \Delta s \geq \Delta \tau \tag{R5.21}$$

where the first inequality $\Delta t \geq \Delta s$ becomes an equality if the events occur at the *same place* in the inertial reference frame where Δt is measured (so that a single clock in that frame is present at both events) and the second inequality $\Delta s \geq \Delta \tau$ becomes an equality if the clock measuring the proper time follows an *inertial path* between the events (so that the proper time that it measures between the events *is* the spacetime interval between them as well).

Exercise R5.5.1: Alan and Beth operate synchronized clocks at two points on the earth's surface. Clarissa rides a train that travels at a constant speed between these two points: let the event of her departure from Alan's clock be event A and her arrival at Beth's clock be event B. Dave, on the other hand, pilots a plane that takes a complicated three-dimensional path between these two points, but leaves Alan's clock at the same time as Clarissa and arrives at Beth's clock just as Clarissa does. Which registers the *greatest* time interval between the events: the difference between Alan and Beth's clock readings, the difference between Clarissa's initial and final watch readings, or the difference between Dave's initial and final watch readings? Which measures the smallest interval? Explain.

R5.6 EXPERIMENTAL EVIDENCE

Equation R5.6 implies that if two clocks are synchronized at event A and then travel to event B along different worldlines, they will generally *not* be synchronized when they arrive at event B, since the clocks' speeds (as measured in some inertial frame) will not generally be the same as they follow their different worldlines. This prediction severely conflicts with our newtonian intuition about time but is a direct and testable consequence of the principle of relativity.

In one experiment,[*] muons were generated using a particle accelerator and then kept in a circular storage ring around which they traveled at a measured constant speed $v = 0.99942$. Though the muons' speed was constant, their *velocity* was not constant because they were traveling in uniform circular motion. In fact, the worldline of such a muon is quite curved and looks something like that shown in the spacetime diagram in Figure R5.3.

Consider a clock at rest in the laboratory at one point on the storage ring. A pulse of muons passes that clock (call this event A). After going once around the ring, the pulse passes that clock again (call this event B). Both the lab clock and the muons measure proper times between events A and B, since both are present at both events A and B. But the clock and the muons travel along very different worldlines to get there. The clock travels along a straight worldline of constant velocity ($\vec{v} = 0$ in the lab frame) and thus measures the spacetime interval between the events. The muons travel along a curved worldline of constant speed ($v = 0.99942$ in the lab frame) but with ever-changing velocity. Since the *speeds* of both clocks are constant, equation R5.7 can be used in both cases to compute the time measured.

The lab clock case is easy: $v = 0$ for this clock in the lab frame, so that the proper time that it reads between events A and B is simply:

$$\Delta \tau_{AB}[\text{lab}] = \sqrt{1 - 0^2} \, \Delta t_{AB} = \Delta t_{AB} \tag{R5.22}$$

where Δt_{AB} is the *coordinate* time between the events in the lab frame (note that this is also the *spacetime interval* between the events). A clock traveling with a muon, however, reads:

$$\Delta \tau_{AB}[\text{muon}] = \sqrt{1 - (0.99942)^2} \, \Delta t_{AB} \approx (1/29.3)\Delta t_{AB} \tag{R5.23}$$

A muon-decay experiment

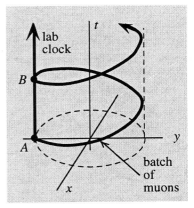

Figure R5.3: The worldlines of a lab clock and a batch of orbiting muons, as drawn by an observer in the lab frame. A clock traveling with the muons would register less time between events A and B than the lab clock does.

---

[*]J. Bailey et al., *Nature*, **268**, 1977.

meaning that a clock traveling with the muon should measure a little more than 1/30 the time between *A* and *B* that the laboratory clock does!

As we have discussed before, the fact that muons decay with a certain fixed half-life makes them effectively little clocks, and measuring the rate at which a batch of muons decays amounts to reading those clocks. If the muon clocks measure 1/30 of the time between events *A* and *B* that an equivalent clock would at rest in the laboratory, then the muons in the storage ring will be seen to decay roughly 30 times slower than they would at rest in the laboratory. Since the half-life of a muon at rest is known to be 1.52 μs, all that remains to be done is to measure the half-life of the muons in the storage ring. This was done: the muons in the storage ring were measured to have a half-life that was 29.3 times longer than their rest half-life (within experimental uncertainties) in complete agreement with equation R5.23. As a point of interest, the acceleration of these muons as measured in the lab frame is about 10^{15} times the acceleration of gravity! Therefore, equation R5.7 (at least) is seen to apply even in cases of extreme acceleration.

Exercise R5X.5: Check that the lab-frame acceleration of the muons in this experiment really is about 10^{15} times the acceleration of gravity (the radius of the muons' circular path was 14.02 m).

An experiment involving a clock flown around the world in a jet plane

In a less extreme experiment performed by J. C. Hafele and R. E. Keating in 1971,[*] a pair of very accurate atomic clocks were synchronized, and then one was put on a jet plane and sent around the world. Upon its return, the jet clock (which followed a noninertial worldline in its trip around the earth) was compared with the inertial clock that remained at rest in the frame of the earth. With suitable corrections for the effects of gravity (predicted by *general* relativity), the results were found to be in complete agreement with equation R5.6.

Exercise R5X.6: Ignoring gravitational effects and the rotation of the earth, estimate the amount by which the two clocks in the previous experiment will disagree if the plane goes around the equator at a constant speed of 300 m/s.

Many other experiments have been performed to check this prediction of the theory of relativity, and all have been in complete agreement with the predictions of equation R5.6. Outrageous as it may seem, the idea that two clocks present at the same two events do not register the same time between those events is a well-established experimental fact.

R5.7 THE TWIN PARADOX

As a result of misinterpreting the meaning of equation R5.7, many people (including competent professors of physics) have been unnecessarily perplexed by apparent paradoxes in the theory of relativity. Physicists call one of the most famous of these the *twin paradox* (or sometimes the *clock paradox*). This problem generated reams of journal articles (as late as into the 1960s) before the inadequacy of the language and concepts commonly used to describe relativity at that time was sufficiently well-understood.

Here is a statement of the apparent paradox. Andrea and Bernard are twins. When they are both 25 years old, Andrea accepts a commission to be an exobiologist on a expedition to Tau Ceti, a star nearly 8 light years away from Earth. So she flies away on a ship that is capable of near-light speeds, leaving her brother Bernard on earth. The years roll by and the world waits. Finally, hurtling out of the emptiness of space, the spacecraft returns.

---

[*]J. C. Hafele and R. E. Keating, Science, **117**, 168, July 14, 1972.

As he waits for his sister to emerge from the newly arrived spacecraft, Bernard (now a distinguished man of 50) muses on the bit of relativity that he remembers from college. "$\Delta \tau_{AB} = \int \sqrt{1 - v^2} \, dt$," he recalls. Since Andrea has been moving with a large speed v for much of the trip, Andrea's clocks should measure much less time for the trip than his clocks register. This includes biological as well as mechanical clocks, and so Bernard expects to see a substantially younger sister emerge from the hatch, still displaying their once common youthful vitality. Bernard chews his lip, wondering what it will be like to have a younger "twin" sister.

Bernard expects Andrea to be younger

Similar thoughts run through Andrea's mind as she prepares to disembark. In Andrea's frame of reference, however, she and the spacecraft were motionless, and it is the earth (and thus Bernard) that has moved backward 8 light years and returned. Andrea (who had the same course in college) thinks that since it is Bernard whose speed v has been $\neq 0$, it will be *Bernard* who will be younger.

Andrea expects Bernard to be younger

The paradox is clear: each expects the other to be younger from their partial recollection of the relativity theory. To this confusion, we can add a third perspective. The principle of relativity states that the laws of physics are the same in every inertial frame. This means that there is no way of making a physical distinction between two inertial frames: if you perform identical experiments within each reference frame, you must get the same results. But isn't the aging process essentially a physical experiment that each person performs in his or her reference frame? If *either* twin is younger than the other, won't that distinguish between the frame of the earth and the frame of the spaceship, contrary to the principle? So perhaps they should have the same age?

Doesn't the principle of relativity imply that they should have the same age?

We have in fact *already* resolved this paradox in this chapter: we simply need to rephrase it in more appropriate language. The first task is to clarify what *events* we are talking about. Let us define event A to be the departure of the ship from earth. Let its arrival back on earth be event B. Both twins are present at both events A and B, so their clocks (including their biological clocks) measure proper time between the events. The question is, which of these twins measures the longer proper time between these events? To find this out, we need to sketch their worldlines as measured in some inertial reference frame.

Solution to the paradox

For our master inertial reference frame, let us choose a frame at rest with respect to the sun. Since the sun is freely falling around a very distant galactic center of mass, this will be an excellent approximation to an inertial frame.

Now let us sketch the twins' worldlines as observed in this frame. Andrea takes off from the earth at event A, which we can take to be the origin event (that is, the event that defines $t = x = 0$ in both frames). Her spacecraft travels slowly at first, but gradually picks up speed as the spacecraft strains toward the speed of light. Finally, after a few years, the spacecraft reaches cruising speed. But long before it reaches Tau Ceti, it must begin to slow down, lest it flash by the star at some outrageous velocity. Finally, it coasts into the star system and lands. The process of acceleration and deceleration repeats on the way home. Event B is the event of her return to Earth. The resulting worldline is drawn on the spacetime diagram of Figure R5.4.

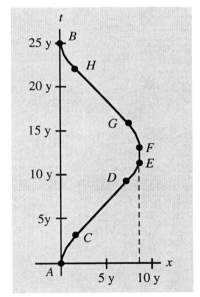

Figure R5.4: The worldline of Andrea's spaceship as drawn by an observer in the frame of reference of the sun.

A: Andrea's departure from earth
C: ship reaches cruising speed
D: ship begins decelerating
E: ship arrives at Tau Ceti
F: ship departure from Tau Ceti
G: ship reaches cruising speed
H: ship begins decelerating
B: ship arrives at earth

On this diagram, the earth's (and thus Bernard's) worldline is a tiny helix winding around the t axis, twisting around it about 25 times in the roughly 25-year duration of the flight. So Bernard does *not* measure coordinate time between events A and B, as his vague argument seems to suggest: rather he measures a *proper time* between those events that is somewhat different than coordinate time. Since Bernard is never more than about 8 light-minutes ($\approx 1.5 \times 10^{-5}$ y) from the sun, though, the squiggles of his little helix are far too tiny to show up on the diagram: his worldline is essentially a straight line up the t axis. Moreover, since Bernard's speed in his worldline (roughly equal to the orbital velocity of the earth) is about 30 km/s $\approx 10^{-4}$ in SR units, the proper time measured by his clocks only differs from that measured by coordinate clocks in the sun's frame by about $(1 - \sqrt{1 - v^2})\Delta t_{AB} \approx +\frac{1}{2}v^2\Delta t_{AB} = (5\times10^{-9})(25 \text{ y}) \approx 4$ s over the time period between events A and B. We see for Bernard that the proper time he measures between events A and B is essentially the same as the time measured in the sun's frame between those events.

But for Andrea, the situation is different. In the sun's frame, Andrea spends quite a bit of time traveling at nearly the speed of light: her average speed in this frame is $(16.0 \text{ ly}/25 \text{ y}) \approx 0.64$. Therefore the factor that appears in the formula for her proper time will be a small number for major portions of the trip. As a result Andrea's clocks (including her body's biological clocks) register much less time between A and B than Bernard's clocks do. Even though 25 years pass on earth, clocks traveling with Andrea will measure a proper time of (approximately) $[1-0.64^2]^{1/2}(25 \text{ y}) \approx 19$ y between her departure and arrival (we would need to do the integral of equation R5.6 more carefully to get a more accurate answer). So it is indeed a young Andrea of about 44 that bounds out of the spacecraft to greet her substantially older twin Bernard.

The core issue: Andrea's frame is *not inertial*

But Andrea's reasoning seems perfectly logical. Why is it wrong? And what of the principle of relativity? The answer to both questions is the same: *Andrea is in a noninertial reference frame*. Every time that the spacecraft engines fire, first-law detectors in *Andrea's* frame register a violation of that law (equivalent detectors in the sun's frame would read nothing). It is *Andrea* who is pressed into her chair as the engines accelerate and decelerate the spacecraft, not Bernard who is sitting at home. Since Andrea's frame is not inertial, the *principle of relativity does not apply to her*. This exposes the error in the argument favoring the *equality* of the twins.

Andrea's mistake is to apply the proper time formula as if her own reference frame were inertial (and thus her clocks measure coordinate time Δt_{AB}). She should compute proper times between events A and B using speeds and times measured in a *real* inertial reference frame, which her frame is clearly not.

Thus there is no paradox! Bernard's *answer* is right (though his *reasoning* is really no better than Andrea's, since he is not in an inertial frame either!) But since Bernard's frame is *nearly* inertial, when he applies the proper time formula to the times measured between event A and B, he gets an answer that is at least *approximately* correct. Andrea *really is* about 6 years younger than Bernard.

A footpath analogy

This situation should be no more paradoxical than the following (more familiar) situation. Imagine that Chris and Dana both set off from a given point A on the surface of the earth. Dana (analogous to Bernard here) takes an approximately straight path from point A to the destination point B, while Chris takes a curved path. Should they be shocked when they arrive at B and find that Chris has walked more miles than Dana? Hardly! Chris might try to claim that it was Dana who departed and then returned and so must have taken the curved path, but this is misleading. The curvature of Chris' path is an absolute physical property of that path, a property that can be displayed in any fixed coordinate system. Chris' personal coordinate system, whose axes change direction every time Chris takes a new turn, is not an appropriate coordinate system for displaying a path's curvature. We don't have trouble accepting the non-equivalence of the distance measured along Chris' curved and Dana's straight footpaths in *this* case: we should not have trouble accepting the non-equivalence of the proper times measured along Andrea's and Bernard's worldlines in the first case.

Exercise R5X.7: Why is the statement that Andrea's proper time is equal to $[1-0.64^2]^{1/2}(25 \text{ y})$ an approximation? Do you think that it is likely to be a bit too high or a bit too low as an estimate?

I. CURVED FOOTPATHS AND CURVED WORLDLINES
   A. The proper time $\Delta\tau_{AB}$ along a curved worldline between events A and B
      1. We compute $\Delta\tau_{AB}$ between two events along a given worldline by
         a. dividing the worldline into a set of tiny straight segments
         b. finding the infinitesimal elapsed proper time along each segment using metric equation: $d\tau = ds = [dt^2 - dx^2 - dy^2 - dz^2]^{1/2}$
         c. and then summing these $d\tau$ to get the total proper time
      2. This is directly analogous to what we would do to find the path-length ΔL_{AB} between two points along a curve lying on a plane
      3. For worldline described by $\vec{r}(t)$ in a given frame, doing this yields

$$\Delta\tau_{AB} = \int_{\text{wordline}} \sqrt{1 - v^2}\ dt \quad \text{(very generally)} \qquad \text{(R5.6)}$$

      4. In the special case that the object's *speed* v is constant, this reads:

$$\Delta\tau_{AB} = \sqrt{1 - v^2}\ \Delta t_{AB} \quad \text{(if } v \text{ is constant)} \qquad \text{(R5.7)}$$

   B. Just as the length of a given curve is independent of the coordinate system we use to calculate it, $\Delta\tau_{AB}$ is a frame-independent quantity.
   C. Two important things to remember about these formulas:
      1. Δt and $\Delta\tau$ are two fundamentally *different* ways of measuring time
      2. Δt_{AB} and $\Delta\tau_{AB}$ in R5.7 are between the *same two events* A and B

II. THE BINOMIAL APPROXIMATION
   A. This approximation states that $(1+x)^a \approx 1 + ax$ when $x \ll 1$ (R5.17)
   B. Therefore $[1 - v^2]^{1/2} \approx 1 - \frac{1}{2}v^2$ when $v \ll 1$ (R5.18)
   C. This makes calculator calculations involving everyday speeds possible

III. THE SPACETIME INTERVAL IS THE LONGEST PROPER TIME
   A. *Theorem:* The proper time measured by a clock traveling between two given events A and B is longest if the clock follows a straight worldline
   B. Outline of proof:
      1. $\Delta\tau$ is a frame-independent number: we can calculate it in any frame.
      2. Let us use a frame where events A and B occur at the *same place*
      3. In this frame, the straight-line worldline connecting these events is a path where $v = 0$ at all times between the events: all *other* paths must have $v \neq 0$ for at least some time between the events
      4. The integral $\Delta\tau = \int [1 - v^2]^{1/2}dt$ will be largest when $v = 0$ always
      5. $\Delta\tau$ is frame independent, so this inequality must apply in *all* frames: $\Delta\tau$ is longest when measured along a straight worldline
   C. The proper time measured along a straight worldline is equal to Δs
   D. Therefore we have the important inequality $\Delta t \geq \Delta s \geq \Delta\tau$ (R5.21)

IV. EXPERIMENTAL SUPPORT
   A. Experiment involving muons in a storage ring (Bailey et al.)
      1. The muons in question follow a circular path at speeds $v \approx c$
      2. Their observed decay rate is much smaller than for muons at rest
   B. Haefele-Keating experiment: a clock sent around the world on a jet plane disagrees with a clock remaining at rest on the ground.

V. THE TWIN PARADOX
   A. The situation: one twin leaves earth and returns; the other stays at home
   B. A statement of the apparent paradox:
      1. A naïve use of R5.6 leads each to think the other will be younger
      2. The principle of relativity seems to imply that neither will be
   C. Resolution of the apparent paradox
      1. The traveling twin's frame is *noninertial*
      2. This means that the twins' situations are not symmetrical at all!
      3. They follow different worldlines, so their proper times *are* different

GLOSSARY

binomial approximation: the very useful approximation that states that $(1+x)^a \approx 1+ax$ if $x \ll 1$.

twin (or clock) paradox: a famous problem that has puzzled students of relativity almost since the theory was first stated. The situation involves a pair of twins, one of which travels to a distant star and back, while the other stays at home. Naïve applications of the the proper time formula lead each twin to think that the other is younger, while a naïve application of the principle of relativity itself seems to imply that the twins should have the same age. The apparent paradox dissolves when we recognize that (at least) the traveling twin is *not* in an inertial reference reference frame. Each of the twins follows his or her own worldline, and thus registers his or her own time between the departure and arrival events.

TWO-MINUTE PROBLEMS

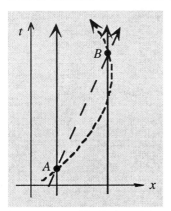

Figure R5.5: This figure is a spacetime diagram showing a pair of events *A* and *B* and the worldlines of various clocks for use in the two-minute problems R5T.1 – R5T.3.

R5T.1 In Figure R5.5, the clock(s) following which worldline(s) measure the spacetime interval between events *A* and *B*?
A. ⎯⎯⎯⎯   D. ⎯⎯⎯⎯ and ⎯ ⎯ ⎯ ⎯ ⎯
B. ⎯ ⎯   E. ⎯ ⎯ and ⎯ ⎯ ⎯ ⎯ ⎯
C. ⎯ ⎯ ⎯ ⎯ ⎯   F.   none of these choices

R5T.2 In Figure R5.5, the clock(s) following which worldline(s) measure the *shortest* time interval between events *A* and *B*?
A. ⎯⎯⎯⎯   D. ⎯⎯⎯⎯ and ⎯ ⎯ ⎯ ⎯ ⎯
B. ⎯ ⎯   E. ⎯ ⎯ and ⎯ ⎯ ⎯ ⎯ ⎯
C. ⎯ ⎯ ⎯ ⎯ ⎯   F.   none of these choices

R5T.3 In Figure R5.5, the clock(s) following which worldline(s) measure the *longest* time interval between events *A* and *B*?
A. ⎯⎯⎯⎯   D. ⎯⎯⎯⎯ and ⎯ ⎯ ⎯ ⎯ ⎯
B. ⎯ ⎯   E. ⎯ ⎯ and ⎯ ⎯ ⎯ ⎯ ⎯
C. ⎯ ⎯ ⎯ ⎯ ⎯   F.   none of these choices

The next four problems refer to the following situation. Two identical atomic clocks initially standing next to each other (call them *P* and *Q*) are carefully synchronized. Clock *Q* is then placed on a jet plane, which then flies around the world at an essentially constant speed of 300 m/s, returning 134,000 s (37.1 h) later. The two clocks are then compared again. Assume for the sake of this problem that the earth's surface defines an inertial reference frame and ignore possible effects of gravity.

R5T.4 Which clock measures the spacetime interval between the synchronization and comparison events?
A. Clock *P*   B. Clock *Q*   C. both   D. neither

R5T.5 Which clock measures coordinate time between the synchronization and comparison events?
A. Clock *P*   B. Clock *Q*   C. both   D. neither

R5T.6 Which clock measures the shorter time interval between the synchronization and comparison events?
A. Clock *P*   B. Clock *Q*   C. measured times are equal

R5T.7 What is the minimum accuracy that the clocks must have to clearly display the relativistic effect?
A. both clocks must be accurate to the nearest 10 ms
B. both clocks must be accurate to the nearest 10 µs
C. both clocks must be accurate to the nearest 10 ns
D. both clocks must be accurate to the nearest 10 ps

The next two problems refer to the following situation. Jennifer bungee-jumps from a bridge (event *A*). Since Jennifer's bungee cord is perfectly elastic, she bounces exactly back up to the bridge and lands on her feet (event *B*). The time between these events is measured by Jennifer's watch, a stopwatch held by Jennifer's friend Rob who is standing on the bridge, and by two passengers (one present at event *A* and one present at event *B*) that are riding on a train traveling across the bridge at the time (the passengers have synchronized watches and later compare readings later).

R5T.8 Who measures the longest time interval between these events?
A. Jennifer   B. Rob   C. the train passengers

R5T.9 Who measures the shortest time interval between these events?
A. Jennifer   B. Rob   C. the train passengers

HOMEWORK PROBLEMS

BASIC SKILLS

R5B.1 Two clocks are synchronized, and then one is put in a high-speed train car that subsequently runs 50 times around a circular track (radius 10.0 km) at a constant speed of 300 m/s. The two clocks are then compared. By how much do the clocks now differ?

R5B.2 Two clocks are synchronized, and then one is put in a race car that subsequently goes 50 times around a circular track (radius 5.0 km) at a constant speed of 60 m/s. The two clocks are then compared. By how much do the clocks now differ?

R5B.3 A spaceship leaves the earth (event *A*), travels to Pluto (which is 5.0 h of distance away at the time) and then returns (event *B*) exactly 11.0 h later. If the spaceship's acceleration time is very short, so that it spends virtually all of its time traveling at a constant speed, estimate the time measured between events *A* and *B* by the ship's clock.

R5B.4 A spaceship leaves the earth (event *A*), travels to Alpha Centauri (which is 4.3 y of distance away) and then returns (event *B*) exactly 9.0 y later. If the spaceship's acceleration time is very short, so that it spends virtually all of its time traveling at a constant speed, estimate the time measured between events *A* and *B* by the ship's clock.

R5B.5 Compare $[1-v^2]^{1/2}$ and $1 - \frac{1}{2}v^2$ for the following values of *v*: 0.5, 0.2, 0.1, 0.05, 0.01, 0.002. Which is the largest of these values for which the difference between the two expressions smaller than 1%? Smaller than 0.01%?

R5B.6 Imagine that a new hyperjet is constructed that can go all the way around the world in 6.235 seconds as measured by clocks at the airport. Assuming that the jet cruises at a constant speed, how long do the pilots' watches register for a complete circumnavigation of the globe? The radius of the earth is about 6380 km.

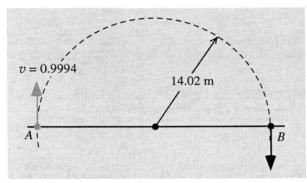

Figure R5.6: A particle in a particle-accelerator ring. The gray point and arrow shows the particle's position and velocity at event A, while the black point and arrow show the same at event B.

R5B.7 The designers of particle accelerators use electromagnetic fields to boost particles to relativistic speeds while at the same time constraining them to move in a circular path inside a donut-shaped evacuated cavity. Imagine a particle traveling in such an accelerator in a circular path of radius 14.02 m at a constant speed of 0.9994 (as measured by laboratory observers). Let event *A* be the particle passing a certain point on its circular path, and let event *B* be the particle passing the point of the circle directly opposite that point, as illustrated in Figure R5.6.
(a) What is the coordinate time Δt and the distance Δd between these events in the laboratory frame? [*Hint*: $\Delta d \neq \pi(14.02\text{m})$! Think about it more carefully!]
(b) What is the spacetime interval Δs between the events?
(c) What is the proper time $\Delta \tau$ between the events, as measured by a clock traveling with the particle? About how many times greater than $\Delta \tau$ is Δt?

SYNTHETIC

R5S.1 A jogger runs exactly 22 times around a 0.5-km track in 48 minutes, as measured by a friend sitting at rest on the side. If the jogger and friend synchronize watches

before the run, how much are they out of synchronization afterward? Is this the reason that many people expect joggers to live longer than people who don't jog? Explain.

R5S.2 The half-life of a muon at rest is 1.52 μs. One can store muons for a much longer time (as measured in the laboratory) by accelerating them to a speed very close to that of light and then keeping them circulating at that speed in an evacuated ring. Assume that you want to design a ring that can keep muons moving so fast that they have a laboratory half-life of 0.25 s (about the time that it takes a person to blink). How fast will the muons have to be moving? If the ring is 14.02 m in diameter, how long will it take a muon to go once around the ring (as measured in the laboratory)? [*Hint*: Define $u = \Delta s/\Delta t$ and use the binomial approximation help you answer the first question.]

R5S.3 Here is a simple way to understand the binomial approximation. Consider $(1+x)^2 = (1+x)(1+x)$. If you multiply this out, you get $(1+x)^2 = 1+2x+x^2$. Now, if $|x| \ll 1$, then $x^2 \ll x$, so we have $(1+x)^2 \approx 1+2x$, just as the binomial approximation states. Apply the same kind of reasoning to $(1+x)^3$ and $(1+x)^4$ and show that the binomial approximation works in these cases too when *x* is small enough so that we can ignore x^2 (and higher power of *x*) compared to *x*. (While this is not a proof, it may help you understand the basic issues involved.)

R5S.4 It is possible to *prove* the binomial approximation more generally as follows. According to the definition of the derivative, we have for any function *f(x)*:

$$\frac{f(x)-f(0)}{x} \approx \left[\frac{df}{dx}\right]_{x=0} \quad \text{(if } x \text{ is very small)} \quad \text{(R5.24)}$$

where $[df/dx]_{x=0}$ tells us to evaluate the derivative at $x = 0$. Now consider the function $f(x) = (1+x)^a$. Apply equation R5.24 and the chain rule to this function to arrive at equation R5.17.

R5S.5 In section R5.6, we proved that the coordinate time, the spacetime interval, and the proper time between a given pair of events stand in the relationship $\Delta t \geq \Delta s \geq \Delta t$, no matter what inertial frame is used to measure Δt and no matter what worldline is followed by the clock measuring $\Delta \tau$. It was asserted there that $\Delta t = \Delta s$ if and only if Δt is measured in a frame where the distance Δd between these events is zero. It was also *asserted* that $\Delta s = \Delta \tau$ if and only if the clock measuring $\Delta \tau$ is inertial. Write a short argument supporting each of these statements (for both directions of the "if and only if").

R5S.6 Imagine that the shuttle astronauts go into near-earth orbit for a period of 14 days and 3.45 hours. About how much less time passed between the departure and arrival of the shuttle according to the astronauts' clocks than passed on the ground? (Assume for the sake of argument that the surface of the earth defines an inertial reference frame.)

R5S.7 Redo the previous problem, except this time assume that the *center* of the earth defines the origin of our reference frame and do *not* ignore the earth's rotation.

R5S.8 Imagine that a person commutes 50 mi to work and back 250 days a year for 35 y. During the commute, the person drives almost entirely on the freeway at an approximately constant speed of 65 mi/h. How much less time has this person's watch registered in 35 y compared to someone who has stayed at home?

RICH-CONTEXT

R5R.1 Consider the Hafele-Keating experiment discussed in section R5.6. In this experiment, two atomic clocks were synchronized, one was put on a jet and flown around the world, then the clocks were compared. Our task in this problem is to make a realistic prediction of the discrepency that we would expect between the clocks. Imagine that the plane starts at a point on the equator and flies around the world at a speed of 290 m/s due east. Note also that general relativity predicts that a clock that is a distance h higher in a gravitational field than a second clock will run *faster* than the lower clock by the factor $1+(g/c^2)h$, where g is the gravitational field strength (9.8 m/s^2). Assume the plane cruises at about 35,000 ft. Using this information, make a prediction about how much the clocks will disagree when they are compared at the end of the experiment (do not ignore the earth's rotation). Describe any assumptions or approximations that you are compelled to make. Also explain why it makes a difference whether the plane flies east as opposed to west.

R5R.2 Because the earth is freely falling around the sun, its center defines a pretty good inertial reference frame. With this in mind, consider the fates of two identical twins, one placed, one living since infancy at the north pole and the other living since infancy on the equator. Imagine that both twins die after exactly the same biological time has passed (as determined by their own bodies). If this is so, about how much longer will the equatorial twin live than the northern twin, if both live for approximately normal time spans? Describe any approximations or assumptions that you have to make.

ADVANCED

R5A.1 Consider an inertial frame at rest with respect to the earth. An alien spaceship is observed to move along the x axis of this frame with $x(t) = [\sin(\omega t + \pi/4) - b]/\omega$, where both x and t are measured in the inertial reference frame, $\omega = (\pi/2)$ radians/h, and $b = \sin(\pi/4)$. Assume also that the earth is located at the origin ($x = 0$) in this frame.
(a) Argue that the ship passes the earth at $t = 0$ and again at $t = 1.0$ h. [*Hint*: The value of ωt is $\pi/2$ at this time.]
(b) Draw a quantitatively accurate spacetime diagram of the spaceship's worldline, labeling the events where and when it passes the earth as events A and B.
(c) Show that the ship's x-velocity is $v_x = \cos(\omega t + \pi/4)$ as measured in the inertial frame attached to the earth. [*Hint*: You don't need to know anything about relativity!]
(d) Find the proper time measured by clocks on the ship between the time the ship passes earth the first time and the time it passes the second time. [*Hint*: $1 - \cos^2 x = \sin^2 x$.]

R5A.2 If you know about Taylor series, you can prove the binomial approximation quite generally. Any continuous function $f(x)$ can be expressed in terms of a Taylor series expansion as follows:

$$f(x) = f(0) + x\frac{df}{dx} + \frac{x^2}{2!}\frac{d^2 f}{dx^2} + \frac{x^3}{3!}\frac{d^3 f}{dx^3} + \dots \qquad (R5.25)$$

Apply this to the function $f(x) = (1+x)^a$ and show that if you drop terms in this power series involving x^2 or higher, you end up with the binomial approximation. Also, show how you would write the approximation if you were to keep terms involving x^2 but drop higher-order terms.

ANSWERS TO EXERCISES

R5X.1 0.59 TN $\approx$ 130 billion pounds. No.
R5X.2 Answer is given. (*Hint*: To accelerate to a speed of $0.5c$ at a rate of 10 m/s^2 takes 1.50×10^7 s.)
R5X.3 The proper time measured by a clock traveling with the electrons between two events marking out a complete cycle is 0.20 times the proper time measured between the same two events by a clock in the lab frame.
R5X.4 See the table below. All results are rounded to nine decimal places.

v	$[1-v^2]^{1/2}$	$1-\frac{1}{2}v^2$
0.1	0.994987437	0.995000000
0.01	0.999949999	0.999950000
0.001	0.999999500	0.999999500

R5.5.1 Alan and Beth measure the longest time interval (since they measure coordinate time) and Dave measures the smallest (since he measures proper time along a curved worldline).
R5X.5 Answer is given: just use $a = v^2/R$.
R5X.6 About 67 ns.
R5X.7 Andrea is not moving at a constant speed, so the use of the constant-speed formula for proper time is not

appropriate, even when one uses the average speed. On the other hand, she spends most of her time traveling at a constant speed, so this will be a reasonable approximation. To see whether this is likely to yield an answer too high or too low, let us consider a specific and fairly extreme case. Imagine that Andrea travels at a speed of 0.96 for 2/3 of the time at is at rest in for the remaining time, as measured in the sun-based frame (that is, we imaging here periods of acceleration to be extremely short). Andrea's average speed in this case is 0.64. If we use this average speed to predict her elapsed time, we get $\Delta\tau \approx [1-0.64^2]^{1/2}\Delta t = 0.768\Delta t$, where Δt is the trip time measured in the sun-based frame. In this case though, we can compute the proper time more accurately by breaking up the path into two segments, one where she is moving at a constant speed of 0.96 and one where she is at rest. Andrea's total elapsed proper time is

$$[1-0.96^2]^{1/2}\tfrac{2}{3}\Delta t + [1]^{1/2}\tfrac{1}{3}\Delta t = 0.52\Delta t \qquad (R5.26)$$

If this example calculation is any indication, using the average speed yields an estimate that is too low.

COORDINATE TRANSFORMATIONS

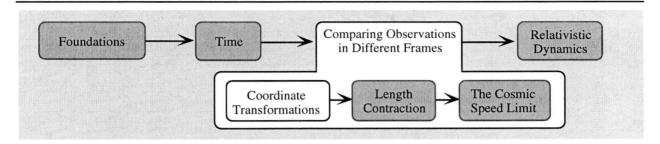

From this hour on, space as such and time as such shall recede into the shadows and only a kind of union of the two retain significance.

H. Minkowski[*]

R6.1 OVERVIEW

In the last two chapters, our task was to learn how to use the metric equation to calculate the frame-independent quantities Δs and $\Delta \tau$ in terms of frame-based coordinate quantities. To delve further into the implications of the principle of relativity, we need to go a step further: we need to find a way of linking an event's coordinates t, x, y, z in one inertial frame with its coordinates t', x', y', z' in another inertial frame. We need to understand such coordinate transformations to describe length contraction (see chapter R7), find the relativistic generalization of the galilean velocity transformation equations and explain why nothing can go faster than the speed of light (see chapter R8), and so on. Understanding how event coordinates in different inertial frames are linked is thus our main task in this chapter. Here is an overview of this chapter's sections.

R6.2 *OVERVIEW OF TWO-OBSERVER DIAGRAMS* provides an overview and motivation for two-observer spacetime diagrams, the main tool that we will use for describing coordinate transformations in this text.

R6.3 *CONVENTIONS* describes some conventions that we will use regarding orientation of frames relative to each other.

R6.4 *DRAWING THE DIAGRAM t´ AXIS* shows how we can construct and calibrate a time axis for the Other Frame on a two-observer diagram.

R6.5 *DRAWING THE DIAGRAM x´ AXIS* shows how we can construct and calibrate a spatial axis for the Other Frame on a two-observer diagram.

R6.6 *READING THE TWO-OBSERVER DIAGRAM* discusses how to use a two-observer diagram to read an event's coordinates in either frame.

R6.7 *THE LORENTZ TRANSFORMATION* uses the two-observer diagram to derive the famous Lorentz transformation equations that mathematically describe the coordinate transformation linking two inertial frames.

R6.8 *TRANSFORMATIONS: VISUAL AND ANALYTICAL* illustrates how two-observer diagrams and the Lorentz transformation equations represent two different but equivalent methods for transforming coordinates.

---

[*]Lorentz, Einstein, et al., *The Principle of Relativity*, New York: Dover, 1952, p. 75.

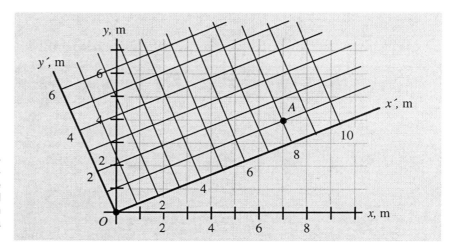

Figure R6.1: A drawing showing two sets of cartesian coordinate axes superimposed on the same plane. We can easily read the coordinates of point *A* in both coordinate systems from such a diagram.

R6.2   OVERVIEW OF TWO-OBSERVER DIAGRAMS

Our task in this chapter is to understand how, given an event's spacetime coordinates *t, x, y, z* in one inertial reference frame, we can find the same event's coordinates *t´, x´, y´, z´* in another inertial reference frame. Physicists call the equations that mathematically describe this coordinate transformation process the **Lorentz transformation equations**.

The derivation of the Lorentz transformation equations is straightforward but somewhat abstract, and that abstraction can blunt one's intuition about what is really going on. Therefore, in this text we will address the same problem using a more visual, intuitive tool called a **two-observer spacetime diagram**. In a two-observer spacetime diagram, we superimpose the coordinate axes for two different observers on the same spacetime diagram. What we will end up with will be analogous to the drawing shown in Figure R6.1, which shows two ordinary cartesian coordinate systems (one rotated with respect to the other) superimposed upon the plane. Once we have set up such a cartesian two-observer diagram, if we know the coordinates of a given point *A* in the *xy* coordinate system ($x_A = 7$ m, $y_A = 4$ m in the case shown), we can plot point *A* relative to point *O*. Then we can just *read* the coordinates of *A* in the *x´y´* coordinate system from the diagram (the coordinates are $x_A´ = 8$ m, $y_A´ = 1$ m in this case). We do not have to use any equations or do any calculations at all!

Setting up such a diagram is straightforward for plane cartesian coordinate systems: it merely involves drawing two sets of perpendicular axes (one rotated with respect to the other), scaling the axes, and drawing coordinate grid lines for each set of axes. Setting up the two sets of coordinate axes representing different inertial frames on a spacetime diagram is a *similar* process, but the peculiarities of spacetime geometry relative to plane geometry lead to some surprising dissimilarities as well. Therefore we need to develop the procedure in a careful step-by-step manner so that we are sure to catch all these dissimilarities.

This is well worth the effort, though, because two-observer diagrams vividly illustrate how different observers see the same events differently in a way that the dry Lorentz transformation equations cannot. The Lorentz transformation equations help us *calculate* how events in one frame will be viewed in another, but two-observer diagrams help us really *understand* what is going on.

R6.3   CONVENTIONS

To make the task of constructing two-observer spacetime diagrams easier, it is convenient to make several assumptions. First, *we assume that the two inertial reference frames are in standard orientation* with respect to each other, as

What is a two-observer spacetime diagram?

Two-observer diagrams are a powerful tool for displaying how different observers see events

Standard orientation

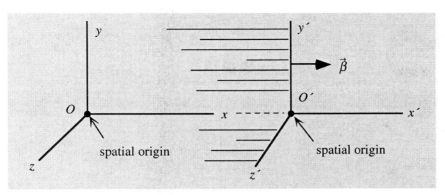

spatial origin   spatial origin

Figure R6.2: Two inertial reference frames in standard orientation. The frames are represented schematically here by bare orthogonal axes. Note that when frames are in standard orientation, the Other Frame is always taken to be the frame moving in the positive direction along the common *x* direction (alternatively, we can say that the Home Frame is the frame moving in the *negative x* direction).

defined in section R1.7. That is, we assume that our frames' corresponding spatial axes point in the same directions in space and the relative motion of the frames is directed along the common *x* direction. Since one can choose whatever orientation desired for the axes of a spatial coordinate system, we do not really lose anything by choosing the frames to have this orientation, and we gain much in simplicity.

Second, *we will work with only those events that occur along the common x and x´ axes of these frames* (that is, those having coordinates $y = y´ = z = z´ = 0$). This is a substantial concession to convenience: we would really like to be able to handle any event, but plotting an event with arbitrary coordinates on a spacetime diagram would require that the diagram have four dimensions, which is impossible to represent on a sheet of paper. We choose therefore to limit our attention to events that can be easily plotted on a two-dimensional spacetime diagram. We will see that many interesting problems can still be treated within this restriction. So until you are told otherwise, you should assume that $y´ = y = z´ = z = 0$ for all events under discussion.

In two-observer diagrams, we can only display events that occur on the *x* axis

The first step in actually drawing a two-observer spacetime diagram is to pick one of the two frames to be the **Home Frame**, and call the other frame the **Other Frame** (easy to remember, right?). Remember that the terms Home Frame and Other Frame are capitalized in this text to emphasize that these phrases are actually *names* of inertial frames.

It is conventional (but not absolutely necessary) to pick the Other Frame to be the frame of the two that moves in the +*x* direction with respect to the Home Frame as shown in Figure R6.2 (alternatively, one can think of the Home Frame as the one that moves in the –*x* direction with respect to the Other Frame): some signs in equations that follow assume we are following this convention. It is also conventional to distinguish each frame's axes and coordinate measurements by using *t*, *x*, *y*, and *z* for Home Frame axes and coordinates and *t´*, *x´*, *y´*, and *z´* for the Other Frame axes and coordinates.

The distinction between the Home and Other frames

Now, our choice of a Home Frame does not *necessarily* mean we are considering that frame to be at rest and the Other Frame to be moving: we still want to reserve the freedom to consider either frame as being at rest. What this choice does imply is simply that we will represent the Home Frame *t* and *x* axes in the *usual* manner in a spacetime diagram: (that is, we will draw its *t* axis as a vertical line and its *x* axis as a horizontal line).

Exercise R6X.1: A train moves due west relative to the ground. If the train moves at a constant velocity, the train and the ground each define an inertial reference frame. If we define the *x* axis to be positive eastward, which would we call the Home Frame and which the Other Frame? Does your answer change if we define the *x* axis to be positive westward?

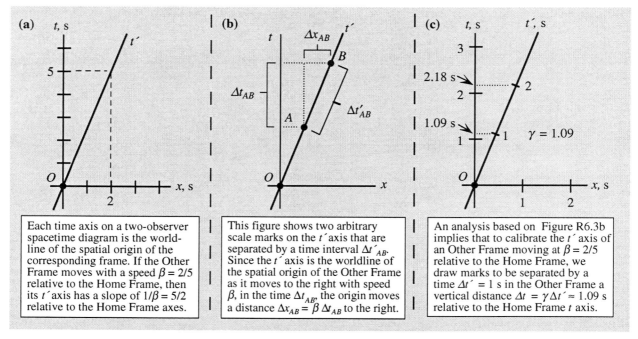

(a) Each time axis on a two-observer spacetime diagram is the world-line of the spatial origin of the corresponding frame. If the Other Frame moves with a speed $\beta = 2/5$ relative to the Home Frame, then its t' axis has a slope of $1/\beta = 5/2$ relative to the Home Frame axes.

(b) This figure shows two arbitrary scale marks on the t' axis that are separated by a time interval $\Delta t'_{AB}$. Since the t' axis is the worldline of the spatial origin of the Other Frame as it moves to the right with speed β, in the time Δt_{AB}, the origin moves a distance $\Delta x_{AB} = \beta \Delta t_{AB}$ to the right.

(c) An analysis based on Figure R6.3b implies that to calibrate the t' axis of an Other Frame moving at $\beta = 2/5$ relative to the Home Frame, we draw marks to be separated by a time $\Delta t' = 1$ s in the Other Frame a vertical distance $\Delta t = \gamma \Delta t' \approx 1.09$ s relative to the Home Frame t axis.

Figure R6.3: Steps in figuring out how to construct the t' axis on a two-observer spacetime diagram.

R6.4   DRAWING THE DIAGRAM t' AXIS

The **time axis** for any frame on a spacetime diagram is by definition the line connecting all events having x coordinate = 0 in that frame. This means that the time axis is the worldline of the clock at the spatial origin of the reference frame (all events happening at the spatial origin of a reference frame have spatial coordinate $x = 0$ by definition). The t axis of the Home Frame is drawn as a vertical line by convention. How should we draw the t' axis of the Other Frame?

The slope of the t' axis

The Other Frame moves with speed β along the $+x$ direction with respect to the Home Frame by hypothesis. This means that as measured in the Home Frame, the Other Frame's spatial origin moves β units in the $+x$ direction every unit of time. The worldline of the Other Frame's origin as plotted on the space-time diagram is thus a straight line of slope $1/\beta$ as shown in Figure R6.3a. Note that this line goes through the origin event O since the spatial origins of both frames coincide at $t = t' = 0$ if the frames are in standard orientation.

An appropriate scale for the t' axis

The next step is to put an appropriate scale on the Other Frame's t' axis. It is (unfortunately) *not* correct to simply mark this axis using the same scale as used for the t and x axes. How can we correctly scale the t' axis?

Consider the marks on the t' axis labeled A and B on Figure R6.3b. Each of these marks corresponds to an event in spacetime: in the Other Frame, these events are separated by the coordinate differences $\Delta t'_{AB} = 1$ sec and $\Delta x'_{AB} = 0$ (since *all* events along the t' axis occur at the spatial origin of the Other Frame by definition). Let Δt_{AB} and Δx_{AB} be the coordinate differences between the same two events as measured in the Home Frame. Since the spacetime interval between these two events is frame-independent, we have

$$\Delta t^2_{AB} - \Delta x^2_{AB} = \Delta s^2_{AB} = (\Delta t'_{AB})^2 - (\Delta x'_{AB})^2 = (\Delta t'_{AB})^2 \qquad \text{(R6.1)}$$

because $\Delta x'_{AB} = 0$ in this case. But we just decided that the slope of the t' axis was $1/\beta$ (where β is the velocity of the Other Frame with respect to the Home Frame). This means that Δt_{AB} and Δx_{AB} must be related as follows:

$$\frac{\Delta x_{AB}}{\Delta t_{AB}} = \beta \qquad \text{or} \qquad \Delta x_{AB} = \beta \Delta t_{AB} \qquad \text{(R6.2)}$$

(Another way to think of this is to remember that the t' axis is the worldline of the spatial origin of the Other Frame, which in the time Δt_{AB} between the events travels a distance $\Delta x_{AB} = \beta \Delta t_{AB}$, since it is moving at speed β by definition.) Plugging equation R6.2 into equation R6.1, we get:

$$(\Delta t'_{AB})^2 = \Delta t^2_{AB} - \Delta x^2_{AB} = \Delta t^2_{AB} - \beta^2 \Delta t^2_{AB} = (1 - \beta^2)\Delta t^2_{AB} \qquad \text{(R6.3)}$$

Solving for Δt_{AB}, we get:

$$\Delta t_{AB} = \frac{\Delta t'_{AB}}{\sqrt{1 - \beta^2}} \qquad \text{(R6.4)}$$

The quantity $1/\sqrt{1 - \beta^2}$ occurs so often in relativity theory that it is given its own special symbol (the Greek letter "gamma"):

$$\gamma \equiv \frac{1}{\sqrt{1 - \beta^2}} \qquad \text{(R6.5)}$$

(Note that γ is a number that is always larger than 1.) Using this definition, equation R6.4 becomes:

$$\Delta t_{AB} = \gamma \Delta t'_{AB} \qquad \text{(R6.6)}$$

The point of all this is that if you want to draw marks on the t' axis of the graph that are separated by some time interval $\Delta t'$, then you must draw these marks so that they have a vertical separation of $\Delta t = \gamma \Delta t'$. To give a concrete example, imagine that your Other Frame moves at a speed of $\beta = 2/5$ and you want to draw marks on the t' axis for that frame that are separated by $\Delta t' = 1$ s. According to equation R6.6, you need to draw these marks so that they have a vertical separation (as measured on the Home Frame t axis) of

$$\Delta t = \gamma \Delta t' = \frac{1\text{ s}}{\sqrt{1 - (2/5)^2}} \approx 1.09 \text{ s} \qquad \text{(R6.7)}$$

as shown in Figure R6.3c.

Exercise R6X.2: Construct and calibrate the t' axis for an Other Frame that moves with a speed of $\beta = 4/5$ with respect to the Home Frame.

R6.5 DRAWING THE DIAGRAM x' AXIS

In the last section we defined the t axis for a given frame to be the line on a spacetime diagram connecting all events that occur at the spatial origin $x = 0$ of that frame (that is, at the same *place* as the origin event). Analogously, we define the **diagram x axis** for a given inertial reference frame to be the line on a spacetime diagram connecting all events that occur at $t = 0$ in that frame (that is, at the same *time* as the origin event). We conventionally draw the Home Frame's diagram x axis as a horizontal line on a spacetime diagram. How should we draw the diagram x' axis for the Other Frame?

(*Note*: In this text, the phrases "diagram x' axis" or "diagram x axis" refer to a line drawn on a *spacetime diagram* that connects all events occurring at zero time. This is to be sharply distinguished from the line in *physical space* that goes through the spatial origin and connects all points with $y = z = 0$. When talking about the latter, I will speak of the "x direction" or the "spatial x-axis".)

Intuitively we might expect to draw the diagram x' axis perpendicular to the t' axis. Unfortunately, drawing the x' axis this way is *not* consistent with the

Definition of the diagram x' axis

The distinction between the diagram x axis and the spatial x axis

Figure R6.4: (a) This diagram shows that the x' axis on a two-observer diagram must tilt upward at an angle. If a flash emitted from the Other Frame origin at time $t' = -T$ is reflected at event B and the return flash is received back at the origin at time $t' = +T$, then event B must have occurred at $t' = 0$, and thus should lie on the x' axis, as shown.

(b) This diagram shows that the x' axis must make the same angle with the x axis as the t' axis makes with the t axis. After we add a new light-flash worldline from the origin event, it is easy to prove that triangles OEC and OEB are identical, which means that $\alpha_1 = \alpha_2$ and thus that $\theta_1 = \theta_2$.

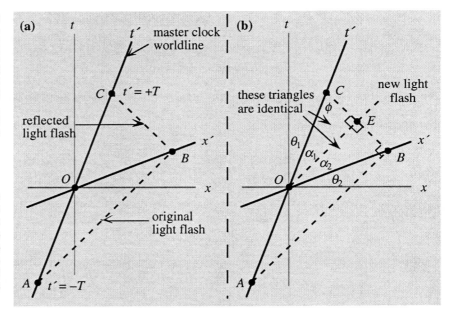

The diagram x' axis must tilt upward

The diagram x' makes the same angle with the x axis as the t' axis makes with the t axis

definition of the diagram x' axis just stated. To figure out the *right* way to draw this axis, we have to consider carefully the implications of the idea that *the diagram x' axis connects events that are simultaneous in the Other Frame.*

We begin by considering a set of events that illustrates the use of the radar method to determine coordinates in the Other Frame. Imagine that at some time $t' = -T$ (where T is some arbitrary number) a light flash is sent from the master clock (located at the spatial origin of the Other Frame) in the $+x$ direction (call the emission of the flash event A). This flash reflects from some event B, and returns to the Other Frame's master clock at time $t' = +T$ (call the reception of the flash by the master clock event C). Since the light flash must take the same time to return to the origin from event B as it took to get there, observers in the Other Frame are forced to conclude that event B *must* have happened at a time halfway between $t_A' = -T$, and $t_C' = +T$, that is, at time $t_B' = 0$. This implies that event B is *simultaneous* with the origin event O.

Let us draw this set of events on a spacetime diagram based on the Home Frame (see Figure R6.4a). Events A, O, and C all occur at $x' = 0$, so they all lie on the t' axis of the spacetime diagram. Since events A and C occur at $t' = -T$ and $t' = +T$, they must be symmetrically spaced along the t' axis on opposite sides of the origin event, as shown. Note that since the speed of light is 1 in every reference frame, these light-flash worldlines must have a slope of ± 1 on this diagram.

Now, by the definition of clock synchronization in the Other Frame, events O and B both occur at time $t' = 0$. The diagram x' axis is defined to be the line connecting all events that occur at time $t' = 0$. Therefore, the diagram x' axis must go through events O and B. This means that *the diagram x' axis must angle upward*, as shown in the diagram.

In fact, by considering the geometric relationships implicit in Figure R6.4a, we can see that *the diagram x' axis makes the same angle with the diagram x axis that the t' axis makes with the t-axis*. The argument is easier if we imagine that the master clock emits a right-going light flash at the origin event O: let event E be this flash meeting the incoming reflected flash. This new light flash is shown in Figure R6.4b. (This new light flash has no physical importance: it just makes the following argument simpler.) Since light flash worldlines always have a slope of ± 1, they all make a 45° angle with respect to the vertical or horizontal directions. This means that if light-flash worldlines cross at all, they always cross at right angles.

Now, I claim that triangles ABC and OEC in Figure R6.4b are *similar* triangles: they are right triangles that share the common angle ϕ. Moreover, the hypotenuse of ABC is *twice* as long as that of OEC, since A and C are symmetrically placed about the event O. This means that the triangle ABC must be exactly twice as large as the triangle OEC, implying that the line BC must also be twice as large as the line EC (remember that if two triangles are similar, the lengths of their corresponding sides are proportional).

But if line BC is twice as large as EC, then the length of line BE must be equal to the length of line EC. This means that triangles OEC and OEB are *identical*, since they are both right triangles and their corresponding legs are equal in length. Therefore, $\alpha_1 = \alpha_2$, which in turn means that $\theta_1 \equiv 45° - \alpha_1$ is equal to $\theta_2 \equiv 45° - \alpha_2$. Thus *the diagram x´ axis makes the same angle with the diagram x axis that the t´ axis makes with the t axis*, as previously asserted.

Another important consequence is that the length of the line OC (which represents the coordinate time interval $\Delta t´ = +T$) is the same as the length of the line OB (which represents the coordinate displacement $\Delta x´ = T$, the distance in the Other Frame that the light signal had to travel to get to event B). This means that *the scale of both axes must be the same*; that is, the spacing of marks on the diagram $x´$ axis will be exactly the same as the spacing of marks on the $t´$ axis!

Exercise R6X.3: Explain why the x coordinate difference between events O and B must be $\Delta x´ = T$.

Note that $\tan \theta_1$ = (run/rise for the $t´$ axis) = 1/(slope of $t´$ axis) = β. Note also that $\tan \theta_2$ = (rise/run for the diagram $x´$ axis) = slope of diagram $x´$ axis. Since we have just seen that $\tan \theta_1 = \tan \theta_2$, we have

The slope of the diagram x´ axis

$$\text{slope of the } x´ \text{ axis} = \beta \qquad (R6.8)$$

So to be consistent with the principle of relativity, we *must* draw the Other Frame diagram $t´$ and $x´$ axes with slopes $1/\beta$ and β respectively.

Exercise R6X.4: Draw and calibrate the $t´$ and $x´$ axes for an Other Frame moving with a speed of $\beta = 4/5$ with respect to the Home Frame.

R6.6   READING THE TWO-OBSERVER DIAGRAM

In summary, what have we discovered? To construct a two-observer space-time diagram, we (1) construct the Home Frame's t axis and diagram x axis perpendicular with each other (with the t axis vertical), (2) draw the diagram $t´$ axis of the Other Frame with slope $1/\beta$ and the diagram $x´$ axis of the Other Frame with slope β, (3) calibrate the Other Frame time axis with marks that are separated vertically by $\Delta t = \gamma \Delta t´$ (where $\Delta t´$ is the time interval between the marks in the Other Frame and $\gamma \equiv \sqrt{1 - \beta^2}$), and (4) calibrate the diagram $x´$ axis with marks separated by the *same* distance as marks on the $t´$ axis (that is, the marks should be separated horizontally by $\Delta x = \gamma \Delta x´$, where $\Delta x'$ is the spatial separation between the marks in the Other Frame).

Summary of how to construct a two-observer spacetime diagram

We can now find the $t´$ and $x´$ coordinates of any event on the diagram as follows. The $t´$ axis is by definition the line on the spacetime diagram connecting all events that occur at $x´ = 0$. The line connecting all events that have coordinate $x´ = 1$ s (or any given value not equal to zero) will be a line *parallel* to the $t´$ axis, because the Other Frame's lattice clock at $x´ = 1$ s moves at the same velocity as the master clock at $x´ = 0$, and the latter's worldline defines the $t´$ axis.

Why we have to find coordinates by drawing lines *parallel* to the axes

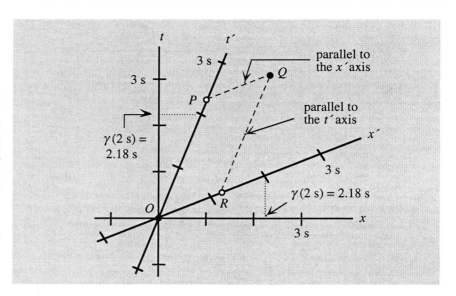

Figure R6.5: Events Q and R occur at the same place in the Other Frame, since all events that occur at the same place in that frame lie along a line parallel to the t' axis. Similarly, events P and Q occur at the same time in the Other Frame. Thus the time of Q is the same as the time of P in that frame (that is, $t'_Q \approx 2.3$ s in this case) and the position of Q is the same as the position of P (that is, $x' \approx 1.2$ s in this case). The relative speed of the frames is $\beta = 2/5$ in the case shown.

Similarly, the line on the diagram connecting all events that have the same t' coordinate must be a line parallel to the diagram x' axis (the line connecting all events having $t' = 0$). Here is an argument for this statement. If the line connecting all events that occur at $t' = 1$ s, for example, were *not* parallel to the line connecting all events that occur at $t' = 0$, then these lines would intersect at some point on the diagram. The event located at the point of intersection would thus occur at both $t' = 1$ s *and* $t' = 0$, which is absurd. Thus a line connecting events having the same t' coordinate *must* be parallel to any other such line.

So if the line connecting all events occurring at the same *time* in the Other Frame is parallel to the diagram x' axis, and the line connecting all events occurring at the same *place* in that frame is parallel to the t' axis, we find the coordinates of an event in the Other Frame by drawing lines through the event that are *parallel* to the diagram t' and x' axes (and *not* perpendicular to them). The places where these lines of constant x' and t' cross the coordinate axes indicate the coordinates of the event in the Other Frame (see Figure R6.5).

Finding the coordinate values by dropping *parallels* instead of perpendiculars may seem strange to you, and will probably take some getting used to. Nonetheless, I hope you see from the argument above that dropping "parallels" is the only way to read the coordinates that makes any sense in this case.

Exercise R6X.5: Use Figure R6.5 to estimate the Other Frame coordinates of an event that occurs at $t = 0$ and $x = +2$ s in the Home Frame.

Exercise R6X.6: Use Figure R6.5 to estimate the Home Frame coordinates of an event that occurs at $t' = 3$ s and $x' = -1$ s in the Other Frame.

Exercise R6X.7: Are events that are simultaneous in one inertial frame generally simultaneous in any other frame? (*Hint*: consider Figure R6.5.)

R6.7 THE LORENTZ TRANSFORMATION

The two-observer spacetime diagram discussed in the preceding sections provides a very powerful visual and intuitive tool for linking the coordinates of an event measured in one inertial reference frame with the coordinates of the same event measured in another inertial frame. Because it is visual in nature, it is much more immediate and less abstract than working with equations. But this tool does give us the quantitative precision that only equations can provide.

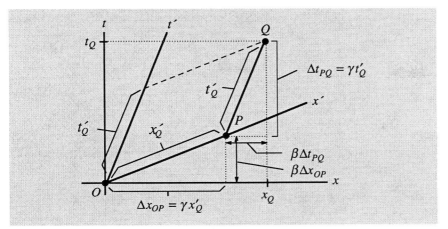

Figure R6.6: Pick an arbitrary event Q. Then choose event P to occur at $t' = 0$ (that is, on the x' axis) and at the same place as Q in the Other Frame. Note that since the line connecting events P and Q is parallel to the t' axis, its slope must be equal to $1/\beta$. Note also that the x' axis has slope β. These slopes, along with the procedure for calibrating axes that we developed in section R6.3 imply the relationships displayed on the diagram.

The purpose of this section is to develop a set of *equations* that link the coordinates of an event measured in the Home Frame with the coordinates of the same event measured in the Other Frame. These equations do *mathematically* exactly what the two-observer diagram does *visually*. Together, these two tools will enable us to discuss relativity problems with both clarity and precision.

Consider an arbitrary event Q, as illustrated in Figure R6.6. Imagine that we know the coordinates t'_Q and x'_Q of this event in the Other Frame. This means that we can locate an event P which occurs at $t' = 0$ (that is, on the diagram x' axis) and at the same *place* as Q in the Other Frame (that is, $x'_Q = x'_P$). Let the time coordinate separation between events P and Q be Δt_{PQ} and the spatial coordinate separation between O and P be Δx_{OP} in the Home Frame. Proper calibration of the Other Frame axes requires that $\Delta t_{PQ} = \gamma t'_Q$ and $\Delta x_{OP} = \gamma x'_Q$. Also, since the line connecting events P and Q is parallel to the t' axis, its slope must be $1/\beta$, implying that the bottom leg of the triangle involving points P and Q has to have length $\beta \Delta t_{PQ}$. Similarly, the slope of the diagram x' axis is β, so the vertical leg of the triangle involving points O and P must have length $\beta \Delta x_{OP}$. All of these relationships are illustrated in Figure R6.6.

Now, you can see from the diagram that:

$$t_Q = \Delta t_{PQ} + \beta \Delta x_{OP} = \gamma t'_Q + \gamma \beta x'_Q \qquad \text{(R6.9a)}$$

$$x_Q = \Delta x_{PQ} + \beta \Delta t_{OP} = \gamma x'_Q + \gamma \beta t'_Q \qquad \text{(R6.9b)}$$

Derivation of the Lorentz transformation equations

Since the event Q is purely arbitrary, we can drop the subscript and simply say that the Home Frame coordinates t and x of any event can be expressed in terms of the Other Frame coordinates t' and x' of the *same* event as follows:

$$t = \gamma(t' + \beta x') \qquad \text{(R6.10a)}$$

$$x = \gamma(\beta t' + x') \qquad \text{(R6.10b)}$$

The inverse Lorentz transformation equations

We call these equations the **inverse Lorentz transformation equations**.

The "just plain" **Lorentz transformation equations** (or LTEs for short), which express the Other Frame coordinates of an event in terms of the Home Frame coordinates, can be easily found by solving equations R6.10 for t' and x'. The results are:

$$t' = \gamma(t - \beta x) \qquad \text{(R6.11a)}$$

$$x' = \gamma(-\beta t + x) \qquad \text{(R6.11b)}$$

The (direct) Lorentz transformation equations

Exercise R6X.8: Verify equations R6.11a,b.

Transformation of the *y* and *z* coordinates

These equations can be easily generalized to handle events having nonzero coordinates *y* and *z*. We learned in section R4.4 that if two inertial frames are in relative motion along a given line, any displacement measured perpendicular to that line has the same value in both frames. Since frames in standard orientation move relative to each other along their common *x* axis, this means that

$$y' = y \qquad (R6.11c)$$

$$z' = z \qquad (R6.11d)$$

Together, all four equations R6.11 represent the relativistic generalization of the galilean transformation equations R1.2.

Often we are not so much interested in the raw coordinates of an event as we are in the coordinate *differences* between two events. Consider a pair of events *A* and *B* separated by coordinate differences $\Delta t \equiv t_B - t_A$, and $\Delta x \equiv x_B - x_A$ in the Home Frame. What are the corresponding coordinate differences $\Delta t' \equiv t'_B - t'_A$ and $\Delta x' \equiv x'_B - x'_A$ measured in the Other Frame? Applying Equation R6.11a to t'_A and t'_B separately, we get:

$$\Delta t' \equiv t'_B - t'_A = \gamma(t_B - \beta x_B) - \gamma(t_A - \beta x_A)$$
$$= \gamma(t_B - \beta x_B - t_A + \beta x_A) = \gamma[(t_B - t_A) - \beta(x_B - x_A)]$$

The Lorentz transformation equations for coordinate *differences*

$$\Rightarrow \quad \Delta t' \equiv \gamma(\Delta t - \beta \Delta x) \qquad (R6.12a)$$

Similarly you can show that

$$\Delta x' \equiv \gamma(-\beta \Delta t + \Delta x) \qquad (R6.12b)$$

$$\Delta y' = \Delta y \qquad (R6.12c)$$

$$\Delta z' = \Delta z \qquad (R6.12d)$$

These are the Lorentz transformation equations for coordinate differences. Note that they have the same form as the ordinary Lorentz transformation equations (equations R6.11): one simply replaces the coordinate quantities with the corresponding coordinate differences.

The inverse Lorentz transformation equations for coordinate differences

The inverse Lorentz transformation equations for coordinate differences are analogous:

$$\Delta t \equiv \gamma(\Delta t' - \beta \Delta x') \qquad (R6.13a)$$

$$\Delta x \equiv \gamma(\beta \Delta t' - \Delta x') \qquad (R6.13b)$$

$$\Delta y = \Delta y' \qquad (R6.13c)$$

$$\Delta z = \Delta z' \qquad (R6.13d)$$

Exercise R6X.9: Using the same approach used to derive equation R6.12a, verify equations R6.12b, c, and d.

R6.8 TRANSFORMATIONS: VISUAL AND ANALYTICAL

The Lorentz transformation equations and two-observer diagrams are equivalent

I hope that you can see that the derivation on the previous page means that the inverse Lorentz transformation equations (or the "plain" Lorentz transformation equations) simply quantify more precisely what you could read from a two-observer spacetime diagram. I chose this method of deriving the Lorentz Transformation equations deliberately to drive home the point that the equations simply express *mathematically* exactly the same thing that a two-observer spacetime diagram expresses *visually*. The example on the next page illustrates how this works.

Problem: Consider an event that is observed in the Home Frame to occur at time $t = 4.2$ s and position $x = 7.0$ s. When and where does this event occur according to observers in an Other Frame that is moving with speed $\beta = 2/5$ with respect to the Home Frame?

EXAMPLE R6.1

Solution Figure R6.7 displays the solution using a two-observer spacetime diagram. Home Frame axes were constructed and scaled, and the event (here marked with an E) was plotted with respect to the Home Frame axes according to the coordinates given. Then the Other Frame's t' axis was drawn with slope 5/2 and the diagram x' axis was drawn with slope 2/5. The Other Frame's t' and diagram x' axes were calibrated with marks separated vertically and horizontally (respectively) by $\gamma(1 \text{ s}) = 1.09$ s. Finally, parallels were dropped from event E to the t' axis and the diagram x' axis, and the coordinates of E were read from the intersection of these parallels with the axes. We see that the coordinates of event E are about $t' \approx 1.5$ s and $x' \approx 5.7$ s.

Now let's *calculate* these coordinates using the Lorentz transformation equations. If $\beta = 2/5$, then $\gamma = [1-\beta^2]^{-1/2} = 1/\sqrt{1-4/5} \approx 1.09$, so:

$$t' = \gamma[t - \beta x] \approx 1.09[4.2 \text{ s} - (2/5)7.0 \text{ s}] \approx 1.5 \text{ s} \qquad \text{(R6.14a)}$$

$$x' = \gamma[-\beta t + x] \approx 1.09[-(2/5)(4.2 \text{ s}) + 7.0 \text{ s}] \approx 5.8 \text{ s} \qquad \text{(R6.14b)}$$

which are in substantial agreement with the results read from the diagram. (One should expect an uncertainty of about 3 to 5 percent in results read from even the most carefully constructed spacetime diagram.)

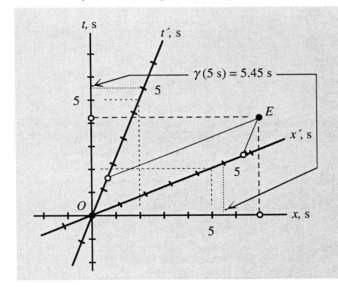

Figure R6.7: The two-observer diagram solving the question posed in this example. Event E has coordinates $t = 4.2$ s and $x = 7$ s in the Home Frame, and about $t' = 1.5$ s and $x' = 5.7$ s in the Other Frame.

KEY TO LINES:

——————	coordinate axes
- - - - - - -	indicate slope of same
– – – – – ·	parallels to t, x-axes
——————	parallels to t', x'-axes
· · · · · · · · ·	calibration lines

Exercise R6X.10: Determine (both graphically and analytically) the Other-Frame coordinates of an event with Home-Frame coordinates $t = 1.0$ s, $x = 4.0$ s, where the Home and Other frames are as described in example R6.1. (You can use the two-observer diagram in Figure R6.7 for the graphical solution.)

Exercise R6X.11: Determine (both graphically and analytically) the Home-Frame coordinates of an event whose Other-Frame coordinates are $t' = 4.0$ s and $x' = 2.0$ s, where the Home and Other frames are as described in example R6.1. (Again, you can use the two-observer diagram provided in Figure R6.7 for the graphical solution.)

SUMMARY

I. CONVENTIONS FOR COORDINATE TRANSFORMATIONS

    A. Corresponding axes of the two frames aligned (*standard orientation*)

    B. A single event serves as the origin event ($t = x = 0$) in *both* frames

    C. The Other Frame moves in the $+x$ direction relative to Home Frame

II. DRAWING A TWO-OBSERVER SPACETIME DIAGRAM

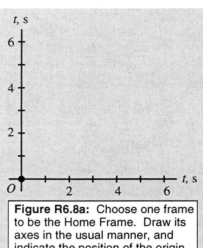

Figure R6.8a: Choose one frame to be the Home Frame. Draw its axes in the usual manner, and indicate the position of the origin event O. Calibrate the axes with some convenient scale.

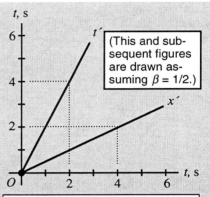

(This and subsequent figures are drawn assuming $\beta = 1/2$.)

Figure R6.8b: Draw the t' axis of the Other Frame from the origin event O with a slope $1/\beta$ (where β is the x-velocity of the Other Frame with respect to the Home Frame). Draw the diagram x' axis of the Other Frame with slope β.

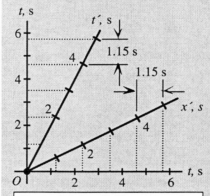

1.15 s

1.15 s

Figure R6.8c: Calibrate the t' axis with marks that are vertically separated $\Delta t = \gamma \, \Delta t'$, where $\Delta t'$ is the intended mark separation in the Other Frame (1 s in this case). Calibrate the diagram x' axis with marks having the same spacing. (When $\beta = 1/2$, $\gamma \approx 1.15$.)

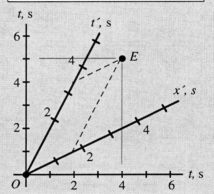

E

Figure R6.8d: Read the coordinates (in either frame) of any event E by dropping parallels from the event to the appropriate axes. (In this case, E has the coordinates $t \approx 5$ s, $x \approx 4$ s in the Home Frame and $t' \approx 3.4$ s, $x' = 1.7$ s in the Other Frame.)

II. THE LORENTZ TRANSFORMATION EQUATIONS (LTEs)

    A. The *direct* LTEs   The *inverse* LTEs

$$t' = \gamma(t - \beta x) \quad \text{(R6.11a)} \qquad t = \gamma(t' + \beta x') \quad \text{(R6.10a)}$$

$$x' = \gamma(-\beta t + x) \quad \text{(R6.11b)} \qquad x = \gamma(\beta t' + x') \quad \text{(R6.10b)}$$

$$y' = y \quad \text{(R6.11c)} \qquad y = y' \quad \text{(R6.10c)}$$

$$z' = z \quad \text{(R6.11d)} \qquad z = z' \quad \text{(R6.10d)}$$

    B. LTEs express mathematically what 2-observer diagrams display visually

    C. LTEs for coordinate *differences* have same form (replace t' by $\Delta t'$ etc.)

GLOSSARY

two-observer spacetime diagram: a spacetime diagram that displays the t and x coordinate axes for two observers in different inertial reference frames.

standard orientation: We say that two inertial reference frames are in standard orientation if their corresponding spatial axes point in the same directions in space and the motion of the frames is along the common x direction.

Home Frame, Other Frame: When two inertial reference frames are in standard orientation, we conventionally define the Other Frame so that this frame moves in the $+x$ direction with respect to the Home Frame. (Equivalently, the Home Frame is the frame that moves in the $-x$ direction relative to the Other Frame.) The coordinates of the Other Frame are conventionally written with **primes** (e.g. t', x').

(diagram) t' axis: the line on a spacetime diagram that connects all events that occur at $x' = 0$ (spatial origin) of a given inertial reference frame. This line is the worldline of the spatial origin of that frame in the spacetime diagram. (This description applies to the Home Frame t axis as well as the Other Frame t' axis: simply substitute t for t' and x for x' in the definition given above.)

diagram x' axis: the line on a spacetime diagram that connects all events that occur at $t' = 0$ (that is, that are sim-

ultaneous with the origin event) in a given inertial reference frame. This is to be sharply distinguished from the *spatial x' axis,* which is the line in physical space connecting all points in space having coordinates $y' = z' = 0$. (This description applies to the Home Frame diagram x axis as well as the Other Frame diagram x' axis: simply substitute t, x, y, z for t', x', y', z' in the definition given above.)

the (direct) Lorentz transformation equations (LTEs): the equations (equations R6.11) that describe mathematically how to compute the coordinates t', x', y', z' of an event in the Other Frame given that same event's coordinates t, x, y, z in the Home Frame. (These equations are named for the Dutch physicist H. A. Lorentz, who stated them in a paper published in 1904, the year before Einstein published the theory of relativity. Lorentz is not given credit for the theory of relativity, because he gave them a very different interpretation than Einstein did.)

the inverse Lorentz transformation equations: the equations (equations R6.10) that describe mathematically how to compute the coordinates t, x, y, z of an event in the Home Frame given that same event's coordinates t', x', y', z' in the Other Frame. (Note that these equations represent the inverse of the coordinate transformation described by the direct LTEs.)

TWO-MINUTE PROBLEMS

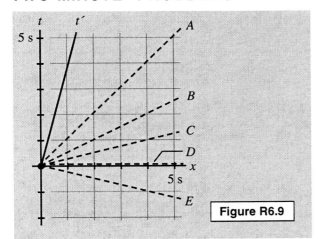

Figure R6.9

R6T.1 The Other Frame is moving with a speed of $\beta = 0.25$ in the $+x$ direction with respect to the Home Frame. The two-observer spacetime diagram in Figure R6.9 shows the diagram t and x axes of the Home Frame and the diagram t' axis of the Other Frame. Which of the choices in that figure best correspond to the diagram x' axis?

R6T.2 The Other Frame is moving with a speed of $\beta = 0.25$ in the $+x$ direction with respect to the Home Frame. The two-observer spacetime diagram in Figure R6.9 shows the diagram t and x axes of the Home Frame and the diagram t' axis of the Other Frame. Which of the choices in that figure would best correspond to the diagram x' axis if the Newtonian conception of time were true?

R6T.3 According to our conventional frame names, the Home Frame is our frame, the frame at rest (T or F).

R6T.4 Imagine that the marks on the Home Frame t axis in Figure R6.9 are 1.0 cm apart. What should be the *vertical* separation of the corresponding marks on the t' axis?

A. 0.94 cm	D. 1.03 cm
B. 0.97 cm	E. 1.07 cm
C. 1.0 cm	F. other

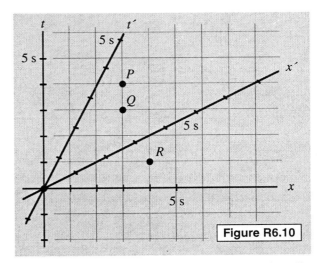

Figure R6.10

R6T.5 Figure R6.10 shows a two-observer spacetime diagram for an Other Frame that moves at a speed of 0.5 relative to the Home Frame. What are the coordinates of the event P in the Other Frame?

A. $t' = 3.4$ s, $x' = 2.6$ s	D. $t' = 3.7$ s, $x' = 3.4$ s
B. $t' = 5.2$ s, $x' = 2.6$ s	E. other (specify)
C. $t' = 2.9$ s, $x' = 1.2$ s	

R6T.6 Figure R6.10 shows a two-observer spacetime diagram for an Other Frame that moves at a speed of 0.5 relative to the Home Frame. What are the coordinates of the event Q in the Other Frame?

A. $t' = x' = 5.2$ s   D. $t' = x' = 1.7$ s
B. $t' = x' = 3.2$ s   E.   other (specify)
C. $t' = x' = 2.6$ s

R6T.7 Figure R6.10 shows a two-observer spacetime diagram for an Other Frame that moves at a speed of 0.5 relative to the Home Frame. What are the coordinates of the event R in the Other Frame?

A. $t' = 1.2$ s, $x' = 4.0$ s   D. $t' = 2.2$ s, $x' = 3.2$ s
B. $t' = 0.9$ s, $x' = 3.4$ s   E.   other (specify)
C. $t' = 6.5$ s, $x' = 1.7$ s

HOMEWORK PROBLEMS

BASIC SKILLS

Problems R6B.1 through R6B.6 all refer to the following situation. The spacetime diagram shown in Figure R6.11 shows the worldline of an alien spaceship fleeing at a speed of $\beta = 3/5$ in the $+x$ direction from space station DS9 after stealing some potentially destructive trilithium crystals. The departure of the ship from DS9 is event A. At event B, DS9 fires a phaser blast (which travels at the speed of light), hoping to disable the vessel. At event C, the fleeing spaceship drops a fuel tank behind, setting the tank at rest relative to DS9 while the spaceship continues on ahead of it (the tank now shields the ship from the point of view of DS9). At event D, the phaser blast hits and destroys the tank, leaving the ship unharmed.

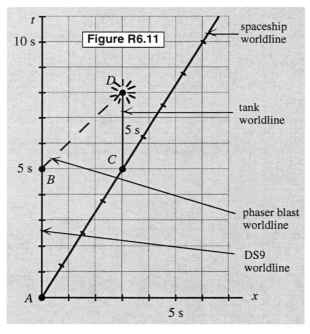

R6B.1 The t' axis of the spaceship frame is labeled on the diagram (this is just the worldline of the spaceship itself). This axis has also been calibrated. Check that the calibration is correct (explain how you checked this). On a copy of the diagram above, draw and calibrate the diagram x' axis for the spaceship frame.

R6B.2 When does the spaceship drop the tank according to its own clock? Explain how you arrived at your answer.

R6B.3 What is the approximate time of event D in the spaceship frame? (Do not use the Lorentz transformation equations: rather read the result from the diagram and explain how you arrived at your result.)

R6B.4 Calculate the time of event D in the spaceship's using the appropriate Lorentz transformation equation.

R6B.5 Which event, B or C, occurs first in DS9's frame (or are these events simultaneous)? Which occurs first in the spaceship frame?

R6B.6 Use the appropriate Lorentz transformation equation to compute the x' coordinate of the event D. Explain why the sign of your result makes sense.

R6B.7 (Do problem R6B.1 first.) Event Q is the explosion of a meteor as it collides with DS9's protective shield. According to measurements in the ship's frame, this event occurs at $t' = 3.0$ s, $x' = 2.0$ s. On the same copy of Figure R6.11 that you used to do problem R6B.1, draw and label this event on the spacetime diagram.

R6B.8 Use the appropriate inverse Lorentz transformation equations to compute the Home Frame coordinates of the event Q described in the previous problem.

SYNTHETIC

R6S.1 An event occurs at $t = 6.0$ s and $x = 4.0$ s in the Home Frame. When and where does this event occur in an Other Frame moving with $\beta = 0.50$ in the $+x$-direction with respect to the Home Frame? Answer this question using a two-observer spacetime diagram and check your work using the appropriate Lorentz Transformation equations.

R6S.2 An event occurs at $t = 1.5$ s and $x = 5.0$ s in the Home Frame. When and where does this event occur in an Other Frame moving with speed $\beta = 0.60 = 3/5$ in the $+x$-direction with respect to the Home Frame? Is the time order of this event and the origin event the same in both frames? Answer these questions using a two-observer spacetime diagram and check your work using the appropriate Lorentz transformation equations. [*Hint:* t' should come out to be *negative.*]

R6S.3 An Other Frame moves with speed $\beta = 0.60 = 3/5$ in the $+x$ direction with respect to the Home Frame. In the Other Frame, an event is measured to occur at time $t' = 3.0$ s and position $x' = 1.0$ s. When and where does this event occur as measured in the Home Frame? Answer this question using a two-observer spacetime diagram and check your work using the appropriate inverse Lorentz transformation equations.

R6S.4 An Other Frame moves with speed $\beta = 0.40 = 2/5$ in the $+x$ direction with respect to the Home Frame. In the Other Frame, an event is measured to occur at $t' = -1.5$ s and $x' = 5.0$ s. What are the Home-Frame coordinates of this event? Does this event occur before or after the origin event in the Home Frame? Answer these questions using a two-observer spacetime diagram and check your work using the inverse Lorentz transformation equations.

R6S.5 The Federation space cruiser *Execrable* is floating in Federation territory at rest relative to the border of Klingon space, which is 6.0 min away in the +*x* direction. Suddenly, a Klingon warship flies past the cruiser in the direction of the border at a speed $\beta = 3/5$. Call this event *A* and let it define time zero in both the Klingon and cruiser reference frames. At $t_B = 5.0$ min according to cruiser clocks, the Klingons emit a parting disrupter blast (event *B*) that travels at the speed of light back to the cruiser. The disrupter blast hits the cruiser and disables it (event *C*) and a bit later (according to cruiser radar measurements) the Klingons cross the border into Klingon territory (event *D*).
(a) Draw a two-observer spacetime diagram of the situation, taking the cruiser to define the Home Frame and the Klingon warship to define the Other Frame. Draw and label the worldlines of the cruiser, the Klingon territory boundary, the Klingon warship, and the disrupter blast. Draw and label events *A*, *B*, *C*, and *D* as points on your diagram.
(b) When does the disrupter blast hit and when do the Klingons pass into their own territory, according to clocks in the cruiser's frame? Answer by reading the times of these events directly from the diagram.
(c) The Klingon-Federation Treaty states that it is illegal for a Klingon ship in Federation territory to damage Federation property. When the case comes up in interstellar court, the Klingons claim that they are within the letter of the law: according to measurements made in their reference frame, the damage to the *Execrable* occurred *after* they had crossed back into Klingon territory: thus they were *not* in Federation territory at the time. Did event *C* (disrupter blast hits the *Execrable*) *really* happen after event *D* (Klingons cross the border) in the Klingon's frame? Answer this question using your two-observer diagram, and check your work with the Lorentz transformation equations.

R6S.6 Fred sits 65 ns west of the east end (and thus 35 ns east of the west end) of a 100 ns-long train station at rest on the Earth. Sally operates a reference frame in a train racing east across the countryside at a speed $\beta = 0.50$. At a certain time (call it $t' = 0$) Sally passes Fred. At that same instant, Fred flashes a strobe lamp (call this event *F*), which sends bursts of light both east and west. Alan, who is standing at the west end of the station, receives the west-going part of the flash (call this event *A*) and a bit later (according to clocks in the station) Ellen, who is standing at the east end of the station, receives the east-going flash (call this event *E*).
(a) When do events *A* and *E* occur in the station frame? Who sees the flash first (according to clocks in the station), Alan or Ellen?
(b) Draw a two-observer spacetime diagram of the situation, showing and labeling the worldlines of Sally, Fred, Alan, Ellen, and the two light flashes. Locate and label events *F*, *A*, and *E* as points on the diagram. Carefully draw and calibrate the t' and x' axes for Sally's train frame.
(c) When and where do events *A* and *E* occur in Sally's frame? Sally claims that Ellen sees the flash first in her frame. Is this true? Verify your assertions with calculations based on the Lorentz transformation equations.

RICH-CONTEXT

R6R.1 When we have two inertial frames in standard orientation, our convention in preparing a two-observer spacetime diagram is to choose the frame whose relative velocity is in the common +*x* direction to be the Other Frame in the diagram. What if we do it the other way around, that is choose the Other Frame to be moving in the −*x* direction with respect to the Home Frame? Go through the arguments presented in Sections R6.4 through 6.6 with this change in mind and then construct a complete and calibrated two-observer spacetime diagram for the case where the Other Frame moves with a speed of $\beta = 2/5$ in the −*x* direction with respect to the Home Frame. Describe why you chose to draw and calibrate the diagram as you did.

ADVANCED

R6A.1[*] We can derive the coordinate difference versions of the Lorentz transformations from scratch in the following way (which is similar to Einstein's own derivation). For the sake of argument, we will consider events that occur only along the spatial *x*-axis. First *assume* that the equations have to be linear; that is, they have the form

$$\Delta t' = A\Delta t + B\Delta x \qquad (R6.15a)$$

$$\Delta x' = C\Delta t + D\Delta x \qquad (R6.15b)$$

where *A*, *B*, *C*, and *D* are unknown constants that do not depend on the coordinates at all, but only on the relative orientation and velocity of the Home and Other reference frames. (It can be shown that only linear equations like these transform a constant-velocity worldline in the Home Frame into another constant-velocity worldline in the Other Frame. Since a free particle must be measured to move along a constant velocity worldline in all inertial frames, this is required of any reasonable transformation equation linking two inertial frames.) Then consider the following pairs of events.
(a) Consider events *E* and *F* that both occur at the spatial origin of the Other Frame, so that $\Delta x'_{EF} = 0$. If the Home Frame and Other Frame are in standard orientation, the spatial origin of the Other Frame moves with speed β in the +*x* direction with respect to the Home Frame, meaning that $\Delta x_{EF} / \Delta t_{EF} = \beta$. Use this to prove that the unknown constants *C* and *D* are related as follows: $C = -\beta D$.
(b) Imagine a light flash traveling in the +*x* direction that is emitted at event *G* and absorbed at event *H*. The velocity of this light flash has to be observed to be +1 in both frames: $\Delta x_{GH} / \Delta t_{GH} = \Delta x'_{GH} / \Delta t'_{GH} = +1$. Show that this implies that $C + D = A + B$.
(c) Imagine a different light flash emitted at event *J* and absorbed at event *K* that travels in the −*x* direction. The velocity of this light flash has to be observed to be −1 in both frames: $\Delta x_{JK} / \Delta t_{JK} = \Delta x'_{JK} / \Delta t'_{JK} = -1$. Show that this implies $C - D = -A + B$.
(d) The three equations from parts *a, b,* and *c* above, taken together, allow one to express three of the unknowns *A*, *B*, *C*, and *D* in terms of the fourth. Use these equations to find *B*, *C*, and *D* in terms of *A*.
(e) Finally, the spacetime interval Δs between two events calculated in *either* reference frame must have the same numerical value: we must have $\Delta t^2 - \Delta x^2 = \Delta t'^2 - \Delta x'^2$ (remember that we are only considering events along the *x*-axis here). Use this condition to fix the value of *A*, and thus all of the other constants. You should find that when you plug your results back into equation R6.15, you get the Lorentz transformation equations.

---

[*]Adapted from E. F. Taylor and J. A. Wheeler, *Spacetime Physics*, San Francisco: Freeman, 1966, p. 68.

ANSWERS TO EXERCISES

R6X.1 The train is the Home Frame in the first case and the Other Frame in the second case.

R6X.2 (see the answer for exercise R6X.4).

R6X.3 In the Other Frame, the light flash is measured to have a round-trip time of $2T$ by hypothesis and thus must have taken a time T for each leg of the trip. Since light has speed 1 in all frames, and the light-flash in this case travels up and down the spatial x' axis, the reflection event must have occurred along the spatial x' axis at a distance T from the origin, implying that $x' = T$ for the reflection event.

R6X.4 The diagram t' axis in this case should have a slope of rise/run = 5/4, and marks separated by $\Delta t' = 1.0$ s along the t' axis should have a vertical separation of $\Delta t = 5/3$ s = 1.67 s. The diagram x' axis would have a slope of 4/5 and the marks along the axis should have a horizontal separation of $\Delta x = 1.67$ s. See Figure R6.12.

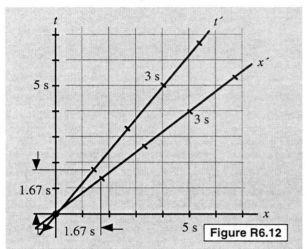

Figure R6.12

R6X.5 $t' \approx -0.9$ s, $x' \approx +2.2$ s.

R6X.6 $t = +2.8$ s, $x \approx +0.2$ s.

R6X.7 No! The events along the diagram x' axis of Figure R6.5 are by definition simultaneous in the Other Frame (they all occur at $t' = 0$ by definition), but these events are clearly *not* simultaneous in the Home Frame, since the line connecting these events is not horizontal (indeed events further to the right occur later in the Home Frame). Moreover, since *any* set of events simultaneous in the Other Frame must lie along lines *parallel* to the x' axis, and since such lines are not horizontal in a two-observer diagram based on the Home Frame, *no* set of events (with $y' = z' = 0$) that are simultaneous in the Other Frame will be simultaneous in the Home Frame.

R6X.8 To isolate the t', multiply equation R6.10b by β, and then subtract this equation from R6.10a, yielding

$$t - \beta x = \gamma(t' + \beta x - \beta^2 t' - \beta x) = \gamma(1 - \beta^2)t' \quad (R6.16)$$

Remember now that $\gamma \equiv [1 - \beta^2]^{-1/2}$, so $1 - \beta^2 = 1/\gamma^2$. Substituting in for the above and multiplying both sides by γ, we get:

$$\gamma(t - \beta x) = \gamma^2(1 - \beta^2)t' = t' \quad (R6.17)$$

which is equation R6.11a. The proof of equation R6.11b is entirely analogous.

R6X.9 We have

$$\Delta x' \equiv x'_B - x'_A = \gamma(-\beta t_B + x_B) - \gamma(-\beta t_A + x_A)$$
$$= \gamma(-\beta t_B + x_B + \beta t_A - x_A) = \gamma(-\beta[t_B - t_A] + [x_B - x_A])$$
$$= \gamma(-\beta \Delta t + \Delta x) \quad (R6.18)$$

The proof of equation R6.12c is even simpler:

$$\Delta y' \equiv y'_B - y'_A = y_B - y_A \equiv \Delta y \quad (R6.19)$$

The proof of equation R6.12d is analogous.

R6X.10 The Lorentz transformation equations imply that

$$t' = \gamma(t - \beta x) = 1.09(1.0\text{ s} - \tfrac{2}{5}4.0\text{ s}) = -0.66\text{ s} \quad (R6.20a)$$

$$x' = \gamma(-\beta t - x) = 1.09(-\tfrac{2}{5}1.0\text{ s} + 4.0\text{ s}) = 3.9\text{ s} \quad (R6.20b)$$

The graphical solution is shown in Figure R6.13 (event F).

R6X.11 By the inverse Lorentz transformation equations,

$$t = \gamma(t' + \beta x') = 1.09(4.0\text{ s} + \tfrac{2}{5}2.0\text{ s}) = 5.2\text{ s} \quad (R6.21a)$$

$$x = \gamma(\beta t' + x') = 1.09(\tfrac{2}{5}4.0\text{ s} + 2.0\text{ s}) = 3.9\text{ s} \quad (R6.21b)$$

The graphical solution is shown in Figure R6.13 (event G).

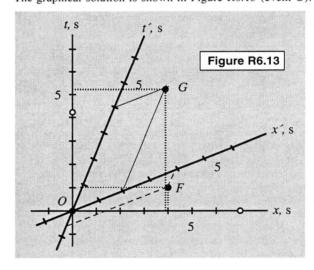

Figure R6.13

LORENTZ CONTRACTION

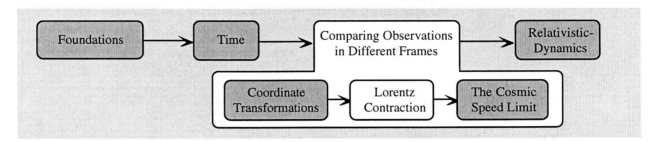

Physics is essentially an intuitive and concrete science. Mathematics is only a means for expressing the laws that govern phenomena.

Albert Einstein*

R7.1 OVERVIEW

Two-observer spacetime diagrams may be used to pictorially represent and solve (at least qualitatively) many problems and puzzles in relativity theory. Because such diagrams concisely and vividly express the relationships between inertial reference frames, solutions using such diagrams often prove clearer and more compelling than mathematical solutions. Even if we require the precision of a mathematical solution, a well-drawn spacetime diagram can speed us on the pursuit of an answer and help us qualitatively check the result.

In this chapter and the next, we will use two-observer spacetime diagrams (and their mathematical equivalent, the Lorentz transformation equations) to explore the meaning of some of the most peculiar aspects of special relativity. This chapter presents an extended discussion of the phenomenon of Lorentz contraction, including a detailed exploration of the kinds of apparent paradoxes that arise when one misunderstands the true nature of this contraction. The next chapter explains why nothing can go faster than light and explores how we can compute the velocity of an object in a given inertial frame knowing its velocity in another inertial frame. In both chapters, we will use two-observer spacetime diagrams to make the concepts more intuitive and concrete.

R7.2 *THE LENGTH OF AN OBJECT* discusses and carefully defines what we mean by the "length" of a moving object.

R7.3 *A TWO-OBSERVER DIAGRAM OF A STICK* shows how we can represent an extended object on a two-observer diagram and how such a diagram shows that the object's length is shorter in a frame where it is moving compared to its length in a frame where it is at rest.

R7.4 *WHAT CAUSES THE CONTRACTION?* makes it clear that this contraction is the direct consequence of the fact that observers in different inertial frames disagree about clock synchronization.

R7.5 *THE CONTRACTION IS FRAME-SYMMETRIC* discusses how Lorentz contraction is consistent with the principle of relativity.

R7.6 *THE BARN AND POLE PARADOX* uses two-observer diagrams to explore a classic apparant paradox of relativity theory.

R7.7 *OTHER WAYS TO DEFINE LENGTH* illustrates how reasonable alternative definitions of length also lead to Lorentz contraction.

---

*Quoted (by Maurice Solovine) in French (ed.), *Einstein: a Centenary Volume*, 1979, Cambridge, Mass.: Harvard University Press, 1979, p. 9.

R7.2 THE LENGTH OF A MOVING OBJECT

**How can we operationally
define the length of
something that is moving?**

The basic question that will concern us in this chapter can be stated simply as follows: what exactly do we mean by the length of a moving object?

As always, we need an *operational definition* of this word if it is to mean anything: that is, we need to describe exactly how the length of an object can be *measured* in a given inertial frame. In the particular inertial frame where the measuring stick is at rest, it is simple to compare the object to a stationary ruler. But the determination of an object's length in a frame in which it is observed to be moving presents difficulties that need to be handled carefully.

We have defined a reference frame to be an apparatus that measures the spacetime coordinates of *events*. Our first task in this problem (and indeed most problems in relativity theory) is to rephrase the problem in terms of *events*. In a given reference frame, how might we characterize the length of an object in terms of events?

Let us consider a concrete example. Imagine that we are trying to measure the length of a moving train in the reference frame of the ground. A clock lattice at rest on the ground records the passage of the train through it by describing the motion in terms of events. To be specific, imagine that a certain clock in the lattice records that the *back* end of the train passed at exactly 1:00:00 p.m. (call this event *O*). Another clock elsewhere in the lattice records that the *front* end of the train passed at exactly 1:00:00 p.m. (call this event *A*). Therefore, we can say that at exactly 1:00:00 p.m., the train lies between the location of the clock registering event *O* and the clock registering event *A*. It therefore makes sense to define the length of the train to be equal to the distance between those events as measured in the lattice.

With this image in mind, we will *define* the length of an object operationally as follows:

**Definition of the length of
a moving object**

The **length** of an object in a given inertial frame is defined to be the *distance* between any two *simultaneous events* that occur at the object's ends.

This expresses the definition of length in the language of events, enabling us to use the tools that we have been developing to describe the relationships between events to also talk about the *process* of measuring the length of an object.

R7.3 A TWO-OBSERVER DIAGRAM OF A STICK

**Definition of an object's
world-region**

Now, consider a measuring stick oriented along the spatial x direction and at rest in the Home Frame. How can we represent such an object on a spacetime diagram? In order to present the full reality of a measuring stick in spacetime, one must plot the worldline of each particle in the stick. Just as a point particle is represented on a spacetime diagram by a curve called a worldline, so a stick is represented by an infinite number of associated worldlines, which one might call a **world-region**. An example of a world-region is shown in Figure R7.1.

The definition of length given in the previous section yields the expected result when the object in question is at rest. Consider the 4-ns measuring stick of Figure R7.2, which is at rest in the Home Frame of the diagram. Events *O* and *A* lie at the ends of the measuring stick and are simultaneous in the Home Frame: both occur at $t = 0$ in that frame. According to our definition, then, the length of the measuring stick in the Home Frame is the distance between these two events, which, according to Figure R7.2, is simply 4 ns.

**Demonstration of Lorentz
contraction using a two-
observer diagram**

Now consider determining the length of this same measuring stick in an Other Frame that is moving with speed β in the $+x$ direction with respect to the Home Frame. An observer in that frame will observe the stick to move in the $-x$ direction with speed β. Figure R7.3 is a two-observer spacetime diagram showing the Home Frame and Other Frame axes superimposed on the world-region of the measuring stick. (For the sake of concreteness, the diagram is constructed assuming that the relative speed of the frames is $\beta = 2/5$.) In the Other Frame, it

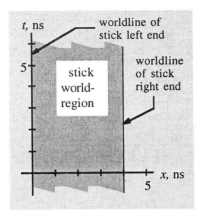

Figure R7.1: Part of the world-region of a 4-ns measuring stick at rest in the Home Frame with one end at $x = 0$ and the other end at $x = 4$ ns. Because it is at rest in the Home Frame, the worldlines of its endpoints are vertical lines, and the worldlines of all of the points in between fill in the region of spacetime shown in gray.

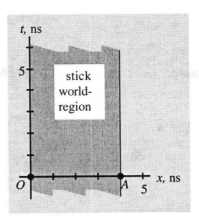

Figure R7.2: The two events O and A lie along the worldlines of the measuring stick's ends and also happen to occur at the same time in the Home Frame. The distance between these events (which is 4 ns in this case) is the measuring stick's length in the Home Frame by definition.

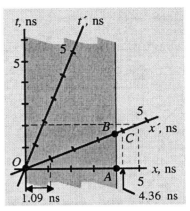

Figure R7.3: Events O and B lie along the worldlines of the measuring stick's ends and occur simultaneously (at $t' = 0$) in an Other Frame moving with $\beta = 2/5$ with respect to the Home Frame. According to the diagram, the distance between these events (which is the stick's length in the Other Frame) is ≈ 3.7 ns < 4 ns.

is not event A but B (as shown on the diagram) that is simultaneous with O and lies at the other end of the measuring stick (both O and B lie on the diagram x' axis, so both occur at $t' = 0$ in the Other Frame). This means that the length of the measuring stick as observed in the Other Frame is *defined* to be the distance between events O and B as measured in that frame.

But as the calibrated axes of the Other Frame show, the distance between O and B in that frame is *less* than 4 ns! We can see that this *must* be so as follows. Consider the 4-ns mark on the diagram x' axis (the event labeled C) on the space-time diagram. According to the standard method of calibrating diagram axes, this mark must be separated from the origin event by a horizontal displacement $\Delta x_{OC} = \Delta x'_{OC} = (1.09)(4 \text{ ns}) \approx 4.36$ ns. This means that event B must be closer to the origin event than the mark event C at $x' = 4.0$ ns, which in turn implies that $\Delta x_{OB}' < 4$ ns! So the right edge of the measuring stick, which is always exactly 4 ns from the spatial origin of the Home Frame, intersects the diagram x' axis at an event B that is *closer* to the origin event than the 4-ns mark on the diagram x' axis, implying that the stick is measured in the Other Frame to have a length of *less* than 4 ns. In fact, you can see that in the case shown, the stick will be determined to have a length of about 3.7 ns in the Other Frame.

We can also easily check this result with the help of the Lorentz transformation equations. In the Other Frame, the measuring stick's length L is *defined* to be the distance $\Delta x'$ between two *simultaneous* events that occur at the ends of the stick, that is, events for which $\Delta t' = 0$. Assuming we know that the length of the measuring stick in the Home Frame is $L_R = 4.0$ ns and that it is at rest in that frame, then the Home Frame distance between *any* pair of events that occur at the opposite ends of the measuring stick must be $\Delta x = L_R = 4.0$ ns (see Figure R7.3). One of the inverse Lorentz transformation equations for coordinate differences (equation R6.13b) says that:

$$\Delta x = \gamma(\beta\Delta t' - \Delta x') \tag{R7.1}$$

In the case at hand, we are looking for $L = \Delta x'$ knowing $\Delta x = L_R$ and $\Delta t' = 0$ for events that simultaneously mark out the ends of the measuring-stick in the Other Frame. Therefore, dropping the $\Delta t'$ term and solving for $\Delta x'$, we get

General formula for an object's length in a frame in which it is moving

$$L = \Delta x' = \frac{L_R}{\gamma} = L_R\sqrt{1-\beta^2} \qquad (R7.2)$$

Plugging in the relevant numbers in this case, we get:

$$L = (4.0 \text{ ns})\sqrt{1-(2/5)^2} = 3.7 \text{ ns} \qquad (R7.3)$$

in agreement with the result displayed in Figure R7.3.

We see that if we accept the definition of length given in Section R7.2 (and how *else* can we define the length of a moving object?), we are confronted with the fact that an object's length is a *frame-dependent* quantity: its value depends on which inertial frame one chooses to make the measurement. Equation R7.2 implies that the length of an object measured in a frame in which the object is moving will always be *smaller* than the value of its length in the frame in which it is at rest. This phenomenon is called **Lorentz contraction.**

Definition of an object's rest length

Equation R7.2 can be used in general to compute the magnitude of the measured contraction, as long as we remember that L_R (which we call the object's **rest length**) stands for the length of the stick measured in the frame in which it is at rest, and L stands for the contracted length of the stick measured in an inertial frame that moves with speed β with respect to the stick's rest frame.

Exercise R7X.1: By drawing appropriate axes on the diagram, estimate the length of the measuring stick shown in Figure R7.3 when it is observed in a frame that is moving with $\beta = 4/5$ relative to the Home Frame.

Exercise R7X.2: Use equation R7.2 to check the answer that you found for the previous exercise.

R7.4 WHAT CAUSES THE CONTRACTION?

Lorentz contraction has its origin in problems of clock synchronization

The discussion above shows that this contraction effect has nothing to do with some effect of motion that physically compresses a moving object (as, for example, an elastic object like a balloon would be compressed if it were forced to move rapidly through water). The physical reality of the measuring stick (as represented by its world-region on the spacetime diagram) actually *remains the same*, no matter what reference frame one uses to describe it. The fundamental reason why observers in different inertial frames will measure the same object to have different lengths is that the observers disagree about clock synchronization, and therefore disagree about which events mark out the ends of the object "at the same time". For example, observers in the Home Frame of Figure R7.3 use events O and A, while observers in the Other Frame use events O and B. We see then that the phenomenon of Lorentz contraction has its origin in the problem of clock synchronization!

A geometric analogy

Nonetheless, the idea that the same object can be measured to have different lengths in different inertial frames may be hard to accept. Yet we are not at all surprised by the analogous behavior of geometric objects on a two-dimensional plane. Let me illustrate. Imagine that we want to determine the east-west width of a road running in a roughly northerly direction on the earth's surface. Two different surveyors set up differently oriented coordinate systems and make this measurement. Is it surprising that they get different results (see Figure R7.4)?

The east-west width of the road shown in Figure R7.4 is seen to be greater in the primed coordinate system than in the unprimed system. Has the road magically expanded for the surveyor who laid out the primed coordinate system? Hardly! The physical reality of the road does not change just because we change the coordinate system in which we measure it. But because the two surveyors cannot agree on which two points that lie along the sides of the road also lie on

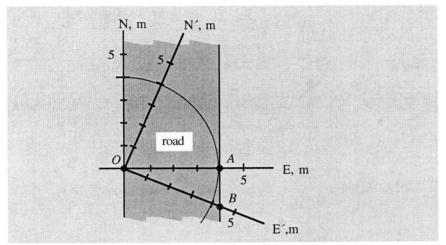

Figure R7.4: Points *O* and *A* span the east-west width of the road in the Home coordinate system, while points *O* and *B* span the same in the Other coordinate system. The circle shown connects all points that lie 4 m from the origin. From the picture, it is clear that the road has a greater east-west width in the Other coordinate system than in the Home system. Does this mean that the road has magically expanded for the surveyors in the Other coordinate system?

an east-west line, they will measure the east-west width of the road to have different values.

We do not find this problematic or even unexpected. Now, we should say that if you are going to measure the "true" width of the road, you should measure it using a coordinate system in which the road runs parallel to the y axis, so that the x axis is *perpendicular* to the road. In that special coordinate system, the width of the road will have its "true" value (which is *shorter* than the value of the same measured in any secondary coordinate system).

Similarly, we might say that to measure an object's "true" length in spacetime, we should measure its length in the inertial frame in which it is at rest. This "true length" (sometimes called the object's **proper length**) will be *longer* than the value measured in any other inertial frame. For clarity's sake, let us always refer to this length as the object's **rest length**.

The analogy between a road's "true width" and an object's rest length.

Exercise R7X.3: Find a formula for the east-west width of a road W in terms of its perpendicular width $W_\perp$ and the slope S of the E' axis in the Home coordinate system. Compare with equation R7.2.

R7.5 THE CONTRACTION IS FRAME-SYMMETRIC

But, you might ask, does not this Lorentz contraction effect violate the principle of relativity? We have seen that an object at rest in the Home Frame is measured to have a shorter length in the Other Frame. Does this not imply that there is a physically measurable distinction between the two frames, a distinction that would violate the requirement that all inertial frames be equivalent when it comes to the laws of physics?

The principle of relativity does *not* require that measurements of a specific object or of a set of events have the same values in all reference frames. What the principle *does* require is that if we do exactly the same *physical experiment* in two different inertial reference frames, we will get exactly the same result (otherwise, the laws of physics that predict the outcome of the experiment will be seen to be different in the different frames). Now, we have seen that if we take a measuring stick that is at rest in the Home Frame and 4 ns long in that frame and measure its length in the Other Frame, we will find it to be Lorentz contracted to 3.7 ns in length. The principle of relativity *does* require that if we perform the *same* experiment in the Home Frame, we should get the *same* result: that is, if we take a 4.0 ns measuring stick at rest in the Other Frame and measure its length in a Home Frame moving at a speed of $\beta = 2/5$ with respect to the Other Frame, we should find the stick to be Lorentz contracted to 3.7 ns.

Does Lorentz contraction provide a way of distinguishing a rest frame from a moving frame?

The principle requires that identical experiments yield identical results

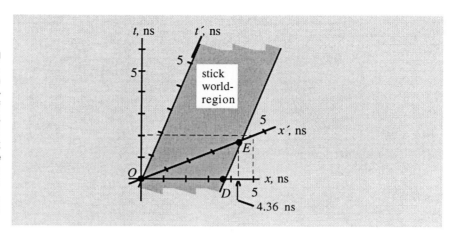

Figure R7.5: This measuring stick has a rest length of 4.0 ns, because events O and E, which occur simultaneously (in the Other Frame) and at opposite ends of the measuring stick, are 4.0 ns apart in this frame. Events O and D at opposite ends of the stick and simultaneously in the Home Frame, so the distance between these events is defined to be the length of the stick in that frame. We can see from the diagram that this length is about 3.7 ns.

Figure R7.5 shows that this is indeed so. The worldlines of the ends of a measuring stick that is at rest in the Other Frame will be parallel to the t' axis, as shown. Events O and D mark out the two ends of the measuring stick at time $t = 0$ in the Home Frame. The distance between these events (i.e. the length of the measuring stick in that frame) is seen to be about 3.7 ns, as expected.

Again we can also easily check this with the help of the Lorentz transformation equations. In the Home Frame, the length L of the measuring stick is *defined* to be the distance Δx between *simultaneous* events occurring at the ends of the stick, that is, events for which $\Delta t = 0$. Assuming that we know that the length of the measuring stick in the Other Frame is $L_R = 4.0$ ns and that it is at rest in that frame, then the distance between *any* pair of events that occur at the opposite ends of the measuring stick must be $\Delta x' = L_R = 4.0$ ns in that frame. One of the Lorentz transformation equations for coordinate differences (equation R6.12b) says that:

$$\Delta x' = \gamma(-\beta \Delta t + \Delta x) \tag{R7.4}$$

In the case at hand, we are looking for $L = \Delta x$ knowing that $\Delta x' = L_R$ and that $\Delta t = 0$ for the events in question. Therefore, dropping the Δt term in equation R7.4 and solving for Δx, we get

$$L = \Delta x = \frac{L_R}{\gamma} = L_R\sqrt{1 - \beta^2} = (4.0 \text{ ns})\sqrt{1 - (2/5)^2} = 3.7 \text{ ns} \tag{R7.5}$$

in agreement with the result displayed by Figure R7.5.

Lorentz contraction is frame-symmetric and thus consistent with the principle of relativity

In summary, we see that it doesn't matter whether the stick is at rest in the Home Frame or at rest in the Other Frame: if the stick is observed to have a length L_R in the frame in which it is at rest, it has a length $L = L_R[1 - \beta^2]^{1/2}$ in any frame that is moving with speed β relative to the stick's rest frame. If the stick is at rest in the Home Frame, it is observed to be contracted in the Other Frame. If it is at rest in the Other Frame, it is observed to be contracted in the Home Frame. This frame-symmetry of the Lorentz contraction phenomenon means that it *is* consistent with the principle of relativity.

R7.6 THE BARN AND POLE PARADOX

The predictions of the theory of relativity are sufficiently counterintuitive that it is easy (as a result of fuzzy thinking) to invent situations based on the ideas of relativity that at first appear to be paradoxical. We dealt with one of the most famous, the so-called *twin paradox*, in Chapter R5. In this section, we will examine another famous apparent paradox, generally known as the *barn and pole paradox*, that is based on a natural but mistaken understanding of the phenomenon of Lorentz contraction.

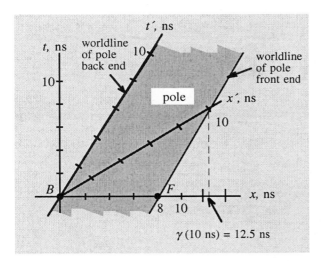

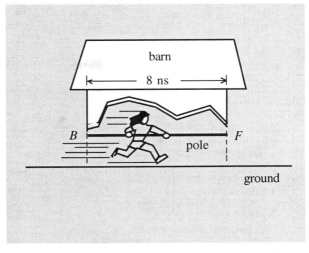

Figure R7.6: The world-region of a pole with a rest length of 10 ns being carried at a speed of 3/5 relative to the ground frame (the Home Frame in this diagram). Events *B* and *F* mark out the ends of the pole at $t = 0$ in the ground frame. The pole's length in the ground frame is thus the distance between these events, or about 8 ns according to the diagram.

Figure R7.7: A picture of the barn and pole problem as it would be observed in the ground frame. Events *F* (front of the pole passes through barn front door) and *B* (back of pole passes through barn back door) are simultaneous in the ground frame: we can define the coordinate time of these events to be $t = 0$. Note that at this instant, the pole is completely enclosed by the barn.

Consider the following problem. Imagine a pole carried by a pole-vaulter who is running along the ground at a speed $\beta = 3/5$. In the frame of the runner, the pole is at rest (of course): let us assume that it has a rest length of 10 ns. An observer on the ground is moving with speed β with respect to the rest frame of the pole and so will measure the pole to be Lorentz contracted to a length of only $L = L_R[1 - \beta^2]^{1/2} = (10 \text{ ns})[1 - 9/25]^{1/2} = (10 \text{ ns})[16/25]^{1/2} = (10 \text{ ns})(4/5) \approx$ 8 ns (see Figure R7.6). As the runner presses on, she runs through a barn that also happens to be 8 ns long as measured in the ground frame. Since both the pole and the barn are 8 ns in the ground frame, there is an instant of time in that frame in which *the pole is entirely enclosed by the barn*.

But now look at the situation from the perspective of the runner. In her frame, the pole is at rest and has its normal length of 10 ns. She sees the *barn* to be moving relative to her at a speed of 3/5, and so it is the *barn* that is Lorentz-contracted to 4/5 of its ground-frame length, that is, to $(4/5)(8 \text{ ns}) = (32/5)$ ns = 6.4 ns. Thus the paradox: *how can a barn that is 6.4 ns long ever enclose a 10-ns pole?*

This apparent paradox results from a naïve application of the idea that "moving objects are contracted" without really understanding *why* objects are measured to be contracted and exactly how the length of a moving object is measured. We will see that the apparent paradox is resolved if we carefully consider the precise meaning of the words in the paradox above.

The first step in resolving this problem (and virtually every other problem in special relativity) is to rephrase the problem in terms of *events*. Let us call the arrival of the front end of the pole at the front end of the barn event *F*. Call the arrival of the back end of the pole at the back of the barn event *B*. To say that there is an instant at which the barn encloses the pole is to say that events *F* and *B* are simultaneous in the ground frame (see Figure R7.7).

For the sake of argument, let us agree to use event *B* as the origin of both space and time in both frames (that is, *B* occurs at $x = 0$ and $t = 0$ in the ground frame and $x' = 0$ and $t' = 0$ in the runner's frame). The statement that *F* and *B* are simultaneous in the ground frame then means that event *F* also occurs at $t = 0$ in the ground frame. But when does event *F* occur in the runner's frame?

Description of the barn and pole problem

Restating the problem in terms of events

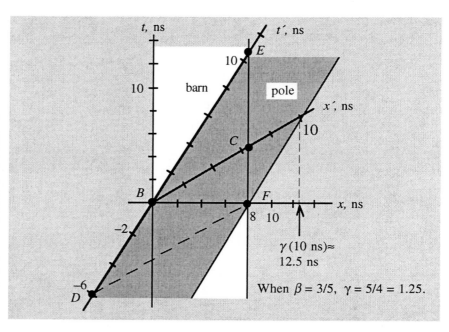

Figure R7.8: Graphical solution to the barn and pole paradox. Events B and C mark the end of the barns at $t' = 0$ in the runner's frame. These events are roughly 6.4 ns apart according to the diagram, so the barn is indeed about 6.4 ns long as measured in the runner's frame. But note that events B and F are not simultaneous in the runner's frame. Indeed, event F occurs at the same time as event D, or about 6 ns before event B (note that the line connecting events F and D is parallel to the x' axis).

Figure R7.8 shows a two-observer spacetime diagram for this problem. I have chosen the ground frame to be the Home Frame of the diagram. I have also taken the ground observer's description of the events to be truthful: events B and F *do* occur simultaneously in the ground frame and the pole is enclosed by the barn at time $t = 0$ in the ground frame. Notice also that the diagram *does* support the runner's assertion that the barn is 6.4 ns long in her frame: events B and C are simultaneous in the runner's frame and lie at the ends of the barn, so the distance between them is the length of the barn in that frame (by definition). The diagram shows that this length is indeed about 6.4 ns.

Solution to the paradox

So what is the solution to the paradox? The diagram shows that *the runner never observes the pole to be enclosed by the barn*. Event F is *not* simultaneous with event B in the runner's frame: rather F is simultaneous with event D (note that the line connecting F and D is parallel to the x' axis). This means that event F (front of pole reaches front of barn) occurs about 6 ns *before* event B (back of pole reaches back of barn) in the frame of the runner. At the same time as event F occurs in the runner's frame (i.e. at $t' = -6$ ns), you can see from the diagram that the pole's back end is still sticking out behind the barn. When event B finally occurs (at $t' = 0$), the pole's front end is sticking out in front of the barn. (Remember that all events occuring "at the same time" as a given event in the runner's frame lie on a line parallel to the diagram x' axis.)

Check using the Lorentz transformation equations

We can verify that event F occurs before B in the runner's frame using the Lorentz transformation equations. In the Home Frame, the coordinate differences between events F and B are $\Delta t_{BF} = 0$ and $\Delta x_{BF} \equiv x_F - x_B = 8$ ns $- 0 = 8$ ns. (The factor $\gamma = 1/[1 - \beta^2]^{1/2} = 5/4$ here.) Therefore, in the runner's frame,

$$\Delta t'_{BF} = \gamma[\Delta t_{BF} - \beta \Delta x_{BF}] = \tfrac{5}{4}[0 - \tfrac{3}{5}(8 \text{ ns})] = -\tfrac{3}{4}(8 \text{ ns}) = -6 \text{ ns} \qquad (R7.6)$$

Since $\Delta t'_{BF} = t'_F - t'_B$ and $t'_B = 0$, we have $t'_F = -6$ ns, implying that event F occurs about 6 ns before B in the runner's frame, as we read from the diagram.

To the runner, everything looks exactly as if a 10-ns pole is being carried through a 6.4-ns barn

Now let us think about this for a minute. If *you* were the runner and you were told that you were about to run a 10-ns pole through a 6.4-ns barn, what would you *expect* to see? First you would see the front end of your pole reach the front end of the barn (event F). At this time, your 10-ns pole would stick out 3.6 ns behind the rear of the 6.4-ns barn. After the barn moves backwards relative to you another 3.6 ns, the back end of your pole will coincide with the back end of the barn (event B), at which time the front of the pole sticks out 3.6 ns in *front* of the barn (see Figure R7.9).

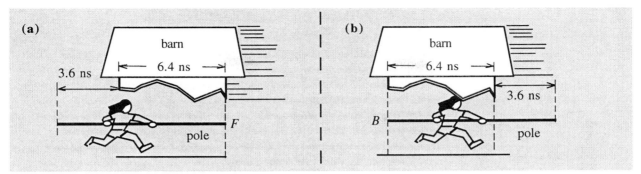

Figure R7.9: (a) The view from the runner's frame. Event F occurs first, at which time the pole sticks out about 3.6 ns behind the barn. (b) Event B occurs next, at which time the pole stick 3.6 ns in front of the barn. The time between events F and B is the time that it takes the barn to move a distance of 3.6 ns at its speed of $\beta = 3/5$ relative to the runners frame.

How long before event B should event F occur? The time between these events should be the time required for the barn to move backwards a distance of 3.6 ns at a speed of $\beta = 3/5$ (in the runner's frame), or:

$$\Delta t = \Delta x/\beta = (3.6 \text{ ns})/(3/5) = (3.6 \text{ ns})(5/3) = 6 \text{ ns} \qquad (R7.7)$$

which is the time between the events indicated on spacetime diagram in Figure R7.8. In fact, you should go over that diagram very carefully and convince yourself that the description given above is indeed exactly what the runner will observe in her reference frame.

The point is that nothing strange or weird happens in either frame. In the barn frame, observed events are consistent with the interpretation that an 8-ns pole is being carried through an 8-ns barn. In the runner's frame, the time relationship between the same events is, on the other hand, consistent with the interpretation that a 10-ns pole is being carried through a 6.4-ns barn: we do not see anything like "a 10-ns pole enclosed by a 6.4-ns barn". The apparent paradox in the problem as it was stated is based on an unstated and erroneous assumption that if events F and B were simultaneous (that is, the pole is enclosed in the barn) in the ground frame, the events will *also* be simultaneous in the runner's frame. However, when we remember that the coordinate time measured between two events will *not* in general be the same in different frames, the paradox dissolves. Excepting the phenomenon of Lorentz contraction itself, *nothing* unusual is seen to happen in either frame.

People have invented a number of apparent paradoxes analogous to the barn and pole paradox (see the homework problems for examples). Such paradoxes almost always involve a hidden assumption that two events that are simultaneous in a given inertial reference frame are simultaneous in all reference frames. We are taken in by the "paradox" because our intuitive belief in the absolute nature of simultaneity is so natural that we hardly notice when it is assumed. But special relativity teaches us that this assumption is *not* true: because observers in different inertial frames do *not* observe clocks in other frames to be synchronized, they will disagree about whether two given events are simultaneous. Moreover, because we have defined the *length* of a moving object in a given frame in terms of simultaneous events in that frame, it follows that different observers will disagree about that length as well. The frame-dependence of simultaneity, and the phenomenon of Lorentz contraction are bound together, and indeed fail to make sense without each other (as these paradoxes show).

Similar "paradoxes" hinge on the same error about simultaneous events

Exercise R7X.4: Using Figure R7.8, describe how you could verify that at the time of event F in the runner's frame, the pole's back end is about 3.6 ns of distance behind the barn's back door.

Exercise R7X.5: Use the Lorentz transformation equations to verify that at the time of event F in the runner's frame, the pole's back end is about 3.6 ns of distance behind the barn's back door.

R7.7 OTHER WAYS TO DEFINE LENGTH

Alternative definitions of length

We have seen that if we define the length of a moving object as the distance between simultaneous events occuring at its ends, we get a frame-dependent (Lorentz contracted) answer. Are there other ways that we might define a moving object's length? If so, do these yield different results than our original definition?

An example of such an alternative definition

The answers to these questions are as follows. Yes, there are other logically reasonable ways of defining the length of a moving object, but these definitions, if they are logically reasonable, yield the *same* numerical result for the object's length as the definition involving synchronized events presented in section R7.2.

For example, consider again a moving train. Instead of defining its length to be the distance between simultaneous events at its ends, we might define its length L in our frame to be the total time Δt that the train takes to pass a given point in our frame times its speed β in our frame:

$$L \equiv \beta \, \Delta t \tag{R7.8}$$

The value of $\beta \, \Delta t$ should yield the distance that the train moves as it passes the point, which is a reasonable definition of its length.

This definition yields the same result as the original

This definition, however, yields exactly the same (Lorentz contracted) result as our original definition. To see this, let us apply this formula to determine the length in the runner's frame of the barn described in the last section. Event B is the event of the barn's back end passing the point $x' = 0$ (that is, the diagram t' axis) in the runner's frame, while event E is the event of the barn's front end passing this point. You can see from Figure R7.8 that it takes the barn roughly $\Delta t' \approx 10.6$ ns to pass the point $x' = 0$ in the runner's frame. Since the barn is traveling backwards at a speed of $\beta = 3/5$ in the runner's frame, the barn's length according to our new definition must be

$$L \approx \tfrac{3}{5}(10.6 \text{ ns}) = 6.36 \text{ ns} \approx 6.4 \text{ ns} \tag{R7.9}$$

which is roughly the same (contracted) result we found before.

We can (as usual) use the Lorentz contraction formula to calculate the exact length according to this definition. Both events B and E occur at $x' = 0$ in the runner's frame by definition, so $\Delta x' = 0$ for these events. Since these events occur at opposite ends of the barn, they are separated by $\Delta x = 8.0$ ns in the barn's frame. One of the inverse Lorentz transformation equations tells us that:

$$\Delta x = \gamma(\beta \Delta t' + \Delta x'), \quad \text{so (since } \Delta x' = 0), \tag{R7.10a}$$

$$\Delta t' = \frac{\Delta x}{\gamma \beta} = \frac{8 \text{ ns}}{\frac{5}{4}\frac{3}{5}} = \frac{4}{3}(8 \text{ ns}) = \frac{32}{3} \text{ ns} = 10.67 \text{ ns} \tag{R7.10b}$$

According to equation R7.8, the length of the barn in the runner's frame is thus

$$L = \beta \Delta t = \frac{3}{5}\left(\frac{32}{3} \text{ ns}\right) = \frac{32}{5} \text{ ns} = 6.4 \text{ ns} \tag{R7.11}$$

which is exactly the same as the result we found before.

... as do other definitions

This is just one example of an alternative definition of length (see Problem R7A.1 for discussion of another). *All* known reasonable definitions of the length of a moving object yield the same result as equation R7.2: no matter how you compute it, the length of an object determined in a frame where it is moving is Lorentz contracted from its rest length by the factor $[1 - \beta^2]^{1/2}$.

Exercise R7X.6: Using equation R7.8, find the length of the runner's pole in the ground frame (a) by reading Δt from Figure R7.8, and (b) by computing Δt with the help of an appropriate Lorentz transformation equation.

SUMMARY

I. LENGTH OF A MOVING OBJECT
   A. We define the *length* of a moving object in a given frame to be *the distance between simultaneous events ocurring at its ends* in that frame.
   B. This provides a precise and operational definition of an object's length

II. TWO-OBSERVER DIAGRAM OF A MOVING OBJECT
   A. An object's *world-region* = worldlines of all particles in the object
      1. looks like a two-dimensional plane on a two-observer diagram
      2. has edges which are worldlines of the object's ends
   B. We can use a two-observer diagram to find an object's length in a frame by locating the two events on the diagram that occur simultaneously in that frame and at the edges of the object's world region
   C. The diagram shows that the length found this way is shorter than the object's length in its rest frame: this is *Lorentz contraction*
   D. We can verify this result using the Lorentz transformation equations
      1. Consider simultaneous events marking out the object's ends in the frame (call it the Other Frame) where we want to find its length
         a) We know that $\Delta t' = 0$ between the events in the Other Frame
         b) We know that $\Delta x = $ *rest length* L_R in the object's rest frame
         c) A Lorentz equation then gives $L = \Delta x'$ in terms of $\Delta t'$ and Δx
      2. The quite general result is $L = L_R[1 - \beta^2]^{1/2}$ (R7.2)

III. WHAT CAUSES THE CONTRACTION?
   A. Since observers in different frames disagree about clock synchronization
      1. They disagree about what events at object's ends are simultaneous
      2. They disagree about the object's length as a result
   B. Geometric analogy
      1. The east-west width of a road depends on orientation of one's coordinate system (even though physical reality of road does not)
      2. Similarly, an object's projection on a frame's spatial axis (length) is frame-dependent, even though its four-dimensional reality is not

IV. CONSISTENCY WITH RELATIVITY PRINCIPLE
   A. It might *seem* that this contraction contradicts the principle of relativity
      1. An object, after all, is contracted in one frame but not in another
      2. Doesn't this allow us to distinguish physically the two frames?
   B. But the principle of relativity only requires that the *same experiment* performed in different inertial frames yield the *same result*
      1. Objects at rest in frame *A* are contracted in frame *B and vice versa*
      2. This *symmetry* ensures consistency with the principle of relativity

V. BARN AND POLE PARADOX
   A. Statement of the paradox: runner carries a pole (rest length 10 ns) through a barn (rest length 8 ns) at a speed of $\beta = 3/5$ relative to barn
      1. In the ground frame, pole is 8 ns long, and therefore there is an instant where the pole fits inside the barn
      2. In the runner's frame, though, the barn is 6.4 ns long and the pole is 10 ns long.
      3. How can a 10-ns pole fit in a 6.4-ns barn?
   B. Solution of the paradox:
      1. "Fits inside" means event *B* of pole's back end entering barn is simultaneous with event *F* of pole's front end leaving the barn
      2. But *B* and *F* are *not* simultaneous in runner's frame (*F* occurs first)!
      3. So runner never sees the barn enclose the pole: there is no paradox
   C. Other apparent paradoxes can be created that analogously depend on a hidden assumption that events simultaneous in one frame are so in all

VI. OTHER DEFINITIONS OF LENGTH
   A. One can devise alternative definitions of a moving object's length
   B. But reasonable definitions are consistent with equation R7.2.

GLOSSARY

length (of a moving object in a given inertial frame) L: the distance (measured in that frame) between two events that occur simultaneously (in that frame) at opposite ends of the object.

rest length L_R: the length of an object measured in the frame in which it is at rest. (Since the ends of an object are not going anywhere in the object's rest frame, the events that mark out the object's ends do not *necessarily* have to be simultaneous in the rest frame to accurately mark out the object's length in that frame.)

proper length: another term for rest length.

Lorentz contraction: the term describing the fact that an object's length is always observed to be *smaller* in a frame where the object is moving than in a frame where the object is at rest: we say that a moving object length in the direction of motion is *Lorentz contracted*. The equation linking the object's rest length L_R with its length L observed in a frame where it is moving at a speed β is given by $L = L_R[1 - \beta^2]^{1/2}$.

TWO-MINUTE PROBLEMS

R7T.1 A moving object's length in a given frame is defined to be the distance between two events that occur at opposite ends of the object and that are simultaneous in that frame. *Why* is it crucial that the events we use to define a moving object's length be *simultaneous*?
A. This is purely conventional: there is no other reason.
B. This choice makes it easier to use the Lorentz transformation equations to find the length.
C. If the events are *not* constrained to be simultaneous, then the length is poorly defined: its value would depend on the time interval between the events.
D. If the events are simultaneous, then the length will be a frame-independent quantity.
E. other (specify).

R7T.2 Since the ends of an object do not move in its rest frame, the events used to mark out an object's length in that frame do not *have* to be simultaneous: the distance between them is the object's rest length whether they are simultaneous or not (T or F).

R7T.3 An object of rest length L_R moving at half the speed of light will have a length equal to
A. $\frac{1}{2} L_R$ C. $[\frac{1}{2}]^{1/2} L_R$ E. $\frac{1}{4} L_R$
B. $\frac{3}{4} L_R$ D. $0.87 L_R$ F. other (specify)

R7T.4 An object is at rest in the Home Frame. Imagine an Other Frame moving at a speed of $\beta = 4/5$ with respect to the Home Frame. The object's length in the Other Frame is measured to be 15 ns. What is its length as observed in the Home Frame?
A. 15 ns   C. 9 ns   E. 25 ns
B. 12 ns   D. 19 ns   F. other (specify)

R7T.5 The most important reason that an object is observed to be shorter in a frame where it is moving than in a frame where it is at rest is that
A. the force of motion strongly compresses an object that is moving at relativistic speeds.
B. "simultaneity" is a frame-dependent concept
C. the measuring sticks used by the moving observer are Lorentz contracted
D. the clocks used by the moving observer run slower

R7T.6 In the pole and barn problem, the barn never actually encloses the pole in the ground frame (T or F).

R7T.7 We can define the length of a moving object to be its speed times the time that it takes to pass a given point (T or F).

HOMEWORK PROBLEMS

BASIC SKILLS

R7B.1 How fast would an object have to be moving in a given frame if its measured length in that frame is half its rest length?

R7B.2 How fast would an object have to be moving in a given frame if its measured length in that frame is to be significantly different from its rest length? (Assume that you can measure the object's length to 1 part in 10,000, that is, to four significant figures.)

R7B.3 An Other Frame moves with a speed of 0.80 relative to the Home Frame. An object at rest in the Home Frame has a length of 30 ns. What is the object's length in the Other Frame?

R7B.4 An Other Frame moves with a speed of 0.80 relative to the Home Frame. An object at rest in the Other Frame has a length of 30 ns as measured in the Home Frame. What is the object's length in the Other Frame?

R7B.5 Imagine that an object with a rest length of 10 ns is at rest in a frame that is moving wtih a speed of $\beta = 0.50$

relative to the Home Frame. Draw a two-observer spacetime diagram of this situation and use it to determine the length of the object in the Home Frame. Check your result using equation R7.2.

R7B.6 Imagine that an object with a rest length of 5 ns is at rest in the Home Frame. The Other Frame is moving wtih a speed of $\beta = 0.50$ relative to the Home Frame. Draw a two-observer spacetime diagram of this situation and use it to determine the length of the object in the Other Frame. Check your result using equation R7.2.

R7B.7 An observer at rest with respect to the sun measures the diameter of the earth (in the direction of its motion) as it swings by in its orbit. How many centimeters shorter is this diameter in this frame than its rest diameter of 12,760 km? [*Hint:* use the binomial approximation.]

R7B.8 About how many femtometers shorter than its rest length is the length of a car measured in the ground frame if the car is traveling at 30 m/s (66 mi/hr) in that frame? Assume for the sake of argument that the car's rest length is 5.0 m. Remember that 1 fm = 10^{-15} m ≈ approximate size of an atomic nucleus.

SYNTHETIC

R7S.1 Imagine an alien spaceship traveling so fast that it crosses our galaxy (whose rest diameter is 100,000 ly) in only 100 y of spaceship time. Observers at rest in the galaxy would say that this is possible because the ship's speed β is so close to 1 that the proper time it measures between its entry into and departure from the galaxy is much shorter than the galaxy-frame coordinate time ($\approx 100,000$ y) between those events. But how does this look to the aliens? To them, their clocks are running normally, but the galaxy, which moves backward relative to them at speed $\beta \approx 1$ is Lorentz contracted to a bit less than 100 ly across: *this* is what makes it possible for the whole galaxy to fly by them in only 100 y. Find the exact value of the speed β that the aliens must have to cross the galaxy in 100 y. Then find the diameter of the galaxy in the aliens' frame, and verify that it is possible for a galaxy moving at speed β with this diameter to pass the aliens' ship completely in 100 y.

R7S.2 In the experiment described in problem R4S.6, particles travel at $v = 0.866$ between detectors 2.08 km apart. This takes 8.0 μs as measured by laboratory clocks. Since the half-life of the particles involved is 2.00 μs, we might naively expect only about 1/16 of the particles to survive the trip. But it was shown in that problem that the particles' clocks only measure 4.00 μ s for the trip between the detectors, and thus about 1/4 of the particles survive.

But now consider how this all looks to an observer traveling with one of the particles. In the particle's frame, the laboratory and the detectors appear to be moving past at a speed of 0.866. In 4.00 μs (as measured by the particle's clock), the laboratory will only move by a distance of 1.04 km at that speed, so the particles will only see *half* the distance between the detectors go by. But laboratory observers claim that by the time that the particles' clock read 4.00 μs, they have covered the *full* distance between the detectors. Is this not a paradox?

Resolve the apparent paradox by considering the phenomenon of Lorentz contraction. How far apart are the detectors in the particle frame? How does this resolve the paradox? [*Hint*: See problem R7S.1 for a similar situation.]

R7S.3 *A useful approximation.* Consider a speed β that is very close to the speed of light: $\beta = 1 - \delta$, where δ is a very small number. Use the binomial approximation to show that under these circumstances $1/\gamma = [1 - \beta^2]^{1/2} \approx [2\delta]^{1/2}$. How accurate is this approximation when $\beta = 0.9$? 0.99?

R7S.4 How fast would you have to be moving relative to our Milky Way galaxy so that the galaxy (whose rest diameter is 100,000 ly) is only 3.65 light-days across in your reference frame (enabling you to cross it in about 3.65 days according to your clock). Express your answer in the form $\beta = 1 - \delta$. [*Hint*: see the previous problem.]

R7S.5 Imagine a cube 30 cm on a side. About how fast would this cube have to be moving relative to you if in your frame it as thin as a sheet of paper in the direction of its motion? [*Hint*: you may find the approximation discussed in problem R7S.3 useful. Also, can you think of an easy way to estimate the thickness of a sheet of paper?]

R7S.6 As discussed in section R4.4, muons created in the upper atmosphere are sometimes able to reach the earth's surface. Imagine that one such muon travels the 60 km from

the upper atmosphere to the ground (in the earth's frame) in one muon half-life of 1.52 μs (in the muon's frame). How thick is that part of the earth's atmosphere from the muon's creation point to the ground in the *muon's* frame?

R7S.7 We can derive equation R7.2 using the metric equation as follows. An object with rest length L_R moving with a speed β passes a clock at rest in your inertial frame. Let event F be the object's front end passing that clock, and let event B be the object's rear end passing that clock.

(a) Argue that in the object's frame, the coordinate time between these events is equal to L_R/β.

(b) What is the *distance* between these events in the object's frame?

(c) Let's define the length of the object in *your* reference frame to be the distance that the object travels in the time that it takes to pass by your clock, that is, $L = \beta \Delta t$, where Δt is the time measured between events F and B by your clock. Use the metric equation and the information in parts (*a*) and (*b*) above to arrive at equation R7.2. [*Hint*: your clock is present at both events.]

R7S.8 Prove mathematically that the alternative definition of length given in section R7.7 *always* yields the same result as equation R7.2 as follows. Consider an object of rest length L_R at rest in a frame that we can choose to call the Other Frame. Let β be the speed with which the Other Frame (and thus the object) is moving with respect to the Home Frame. Let Δt be the Home-Frame time between the events of the object's front end passing a certain point in the Home Frame and its rear end passing the same point. Since these events occur at the same place in the Home Frame, $\Delta x = 0$ between these events in that frame. But since these events occur at opposite ends of the object, the distance between them in the Other Frame is $\Delta x' = L_R$. Use an appropriate Lorentz transformation equation to determine Δt in terms of Δx, $\Delta x'$, and β, and then use the result to prove that $L \equiv \beta \Delta t = L_R[1 - \beta^2]^{1/2}$.

R7S.9 *Transformation of angles.* Consider a meterstick at rest in a given inertial frame (make this the Other Frame) oriented in such a way that it makes an angle of θ' with respect to the x' direction in that frame. In the Home Frame, the Other Frame is observed to move with a velocity of β in the $+x$ direction.

(a) Keeping in mind that the distances measured *parallel* to the line of relative motion are observed to be Lorentz contracted in the Home Frame while distances measured perpendicular to the line of motion are not, show that the angle θ that this meterstick will be observed to make with the x direction in the Home Frame is given by the expression:

$$\theta = \tan^{-1}\left(\frac{\tan\theta'}{\sqrt{1-\beta^2}}\right) \qquad (R7.12)$$

(b) What would the length of the meterstick be as measured in the Home Frame?

(c) Assume that the meterstick makes an angle of 30° with the x' direction in the Other Frame. How fast would that frame have to be moving with respect to the Home Frame for the meterstick to be observed in the Home Frame to make an angle of 45° with the x direction?

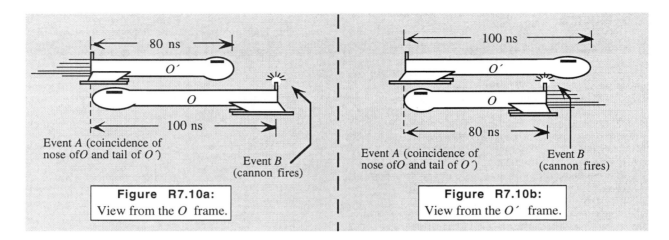

Figure R7.10a:
View from the O frame.

Figure R7.10b:
View from the O' frame.

RICH-CONTEXT

R7R.1 *The spacewars paradox.** * Two spacecraft of equal rest length $L_R = 100$ ns pass very close to each other as they travel in opposite directions at a relative speed of $\beta = 3/5$. The captain of ship O has a laser cannon at the tail of her ship. She intends to fire the cannon at the instant that her bow is lined up with the tail of ship O'. Since ship O' is Lorentz contracted to 80 ns in O's reference frame, she expects the laser burst to miss the other by 20 ns, as shown in Figure R7.10a (she intends the shot to be "across the bow"). However, to the observer in ship O', it is ship O that is contracted to 80 ns. Therefore, the observer on O' concludes that if the captain of O carries out her intention, the laser burst will strike ship O' about 20 ns *behind* the bow, with disastrous consequences (Figure R7.10b).

Assume that the captain of O carries out her intentions exactly as described, according to measurements in her own frame, and analyze what *really* happens as follows:

(a) Construct a carefully calibrated two-observer spacetime diagram of the situation described. Define event A to be the coincidence of the bow of ship O and the tail of ship O', and event B to be the firing of the laser cannon. Choose A to define the origin event in both frames, and locate B according to the description of O's intentions above. When and where does this event occur as measured in the O' frame, according to the diagram? (You may assume that the ships pass each other so closely that the travel time of the laser burst between the ships is negligible.)

(b) Verify the coordinates of B using the Lorentz transformation equations.

(c) Write a short paragraph describing whether the cannon burst really hits or not, according to the results you found above. Discuss the hidden assumption in the statement of the apparent paradox, and point out how one of the drawings in Figure R7.10 is misleading.

R7R.2 *The bullet-hole paradox.** ** Two guns are mounted a distance of 40 ns apart on the embankment beside some railroad tracks. The barrels of the guns project outward toward the track so that they almost brush a speeding express train as it passes by. The train moves with a speed of $\beta =$

3/5 with respect to the ground. Suppose the two guns fire simultaneously (as measured in the ground frame), leaving two bullet holes in the train.

(a) Let event R be the firing of the rear gun and event F the firing of the front gun. These events occur 40 ns apart and at the same time in the ground frame. Draw a carefully constructed two-observer diagram of the situation, taking the ground frame to be the Home Frame, and taking R to be the origin event. Be sure to show and label the axes of the ground and train frames, the worldlines of the guns, the worldlines of the bullet-holes that they produce, and the events R and F on your diagram.

(b) Argue using your diagram that the bullet hole worldlines are about 50 ns apart as measured in the train frame. Verify this by using the Lorentz transformation equations to show that the events R and F occur 50 ns apart in the train frame.

(c) In the ground frame, the guns are 40 ns apart. In the train frame, the guns are moving by at a speed of $\beta = 3/5$, and the distance between them will be measured to be Lorentz contracted to less than 40 ns. Show using the Lorentz contraction formula that the guns are in fact 32 ns apart in the train frame. Describe how this same result can be read from your spacetime diagram.

(d) Doesn't this lead to a contradiction? How can two guns that are 32 ns apart in the train frame fire simultaneously and yet leave bullet holes 50 ns apart in the train frame? Write a paragraph in which you carefully describe the logical flaw in the description of the "contradiction" given in the last sentence [*Hint*: focus on the word "simultaneously"]. Describe what *really* is observed to happen in the train frame, and thus how it is perfectly natural for guns that are 32 ns apart to make holes 50 ns apart.

R7R.3 *The space cadets paradox.† * A very long measuring stick is placed at rest in empty space in an inertial frame we'll call the "stick frame". A spaceship of rest length L_R travels along the measuring stick at a speed $\beta = 4/5$ relative to it. Two space cadets P and Q are each equipped with knives and synchronized watches and are stationed at rest on the ship frame in the ends of the spaceship. At a prearranged time, each cadet simultaneously reaches through a porthole and slices through the measuring stick.

---

*Adapted from E.F. Taylor and J.A. Wheeler, *Spacetime Physics,* San Francisco: Freeman, 1966, pp. 70-71.

**Adapted from B.M. Casper and R.J. Noer, *Revolutions in Physics,* New York: Norton, 1972, pp. 363-364.

---

†Thanks to W. F. Titus of Carleton College.

(a) How long is the spaceship according to the cadets?

(b) How long is the spaceship according to observers along the measuring stick (that is, observers at rest in the "stick frame")?

(c) Use the Lorentz transformation equations to show that observers along the measuring stick would conclude that the cut portion of the measuring stick has length $\frac{5}{3}L_R$.

(d) Since the cutting events occur simultaneously in the spaceship frame, they do *not* occur simultaneously in the stick frame. Use the Lorentz transformation equations to find the time separation of the two cutting events as viewed in the spaceship frame.

(e) Explain in a short paragraph how it is that two cadets that are only $\frac{3}{5}L_R$ apart (as measured in the stick frame) can cut a hunk of measuring stick $\frac{5}{3}L_R$ long if they really cut simultaneously according to their synchronized watches.

ADVANCED

R7A.1 *The radar method.* Imagine using the radar method to measure the length of an object moving at a speed β with respect to your own frame (the Other Frame). At a certain time (Event A) you send forth a light flash from a clock in your frame. This flash bounces off a mirror at the far end of the object (Event R), and then returns to your clock (Event B). If you time this all just right so that the near end of the object passes your clock (Event O) at exactly the time halfway between the emission event A and the reception event

B (as measured by that clock) then you know that events O and the reflection event R are simultaneous. This means that at that instant, the object lies exactly between the clock and the light flash as it bounces off the mirror. The length L of the object in your frame is thus equal (in SR units) to the time that it takes the light to come back from Event R, since light travels at a speed of 1 in all frames.

Now imagine viewing this measurement process from a Home Frame in which your frame is moving with a speed β in the $+x$ direction. The distance between the ends of the object in that frame is L_R. Draw a careful two-observer diagram of the situation as viewed by observers in the Home Frame (let O be the origin event in both frames). Argue that the coordinate distance between Events O and A in the Home Frame is $\Delta x = \beta \Delta t$, where Δt is the coordinate time measured between those events in the Home Frame. Also argue (using similar triangles on the diagram) that $\Delta t = L_R$. Then use the metric equation to relate the time measured between events O and A measured in *your* frame (which is equal to L) to the coordinate time Δt measured between the events in the Home Frame, and show that you end up with the same result as that given by the Lorentz contraction equation R7.2.

R7A.2 *Light clocks.* Consider a light clock as shown in Figure R4.1, except imagine the light clock to be laid on its side so that the light flash travels along the direction of motion of the clock. Show that the only way that this sideways light clock will measure the correct spacetime interval between the events A and B (as any decent clock should) is if the distance between its mirrors is Lorentz-contracted by the amount stated by Equation R7.2.

ANSWERS TO EXERCISES

R7X.1 When $\beta = 4/5$, $\gamma = [1 - 16/25]^{-1/2} = 5/3 = 1.67$. A redrawn version of Figure R7.3 would thus look like this:

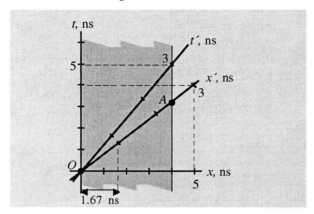

Events O and A occur simultaneously in the Other Frame and thus mark out the length of the stick in that frame. From the diagram, it looks like the stick is about 2.4 ns long in the Other Frame.

R7X.2 A 4-ns measuring stick moving at a speed $\beta = 4/5$ has a length of $L = L_R[1 - \beta^2]^{1/2} = (4\text{ ns})[1 - 16/25]^{1/2} = (4\text{ ns})(3/5) = 2.4$ ns.

R7X.3 Let the distance between points A and B in Figure R7.4 be D. Since the slope S of the E' axis is the rise over the run of that axis in the Home coordinate system, we have $S = -D/W_\perp$ implying that $D = -S(W_\perp)$. By the pythagorean theorem, then, the length of the road's projection on the E' axis is

$$W = \sqrt{W_\perp^2 + S^2 W_\perp^2} = W_\perp \sqrt{1 + S^2}$$

Note that except for the plus sign in the square root, this formula is quite similar in form to equation R7.2.

R7X.4 Event P shown on Figure R7.11 (a slightly modified version of Figure R7.8) occurs at the barn's back end at the same time as event F. To find out *where* this event occurs in the runner's frame, we draw a line parallel to the t' axis up to the x' axis, as shown. We see from this line that the back end of the barn is at $x' = 3.6$ ns at the time of event F, while the back end of the pole is (always) at $x' = 0$. Therefore the pole's back end is indeed 3.6 ns behind the barn's back end in the runner's frame at this time.

R7X.5 Event P locates the position of the barn's back end at the time of event F, and so occurs at $t'_P = -6$ ns in the runner's frame. The back end of the barn is always at $x_P = 0$ in the Home Frame. So, according to one of the inverse

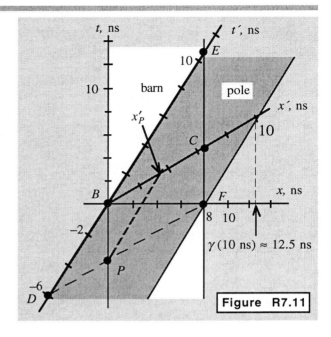

Figure R7.11

Lorentz transformation equations, we have

$$x_P = \gamma(\beta t'_P + x'_P) \qquad (R7.13)$$

$$\Rightarrow x'_P = \frac{x_P}{\gamma} - \beta t'_P = 0 - \tfrac{3}{5}(-6\text{ ns}) = 3.6\text{ ns} \qquad (R7.14)$$

Since the pole's back end is always at $x' = 0$, it is sticking out 3.6 ns behind the barn at this time.

R7X.6 (a) Figure R7.8 implies that it takes about 13 ns (the time between events F and E) in the Home Frame for the pole to pass the point $x = 8$ ns in the Home Frame. Since the pole has a speed of $\beta = 3/5$ in this frame, this implies that the pole has a length of $L = \beta \Delta t = (3/5)(13\text{ ns}) = 39/5\text{ ns} = 7.8$ ns. (b) Events F and E occur at the same position ($x = 8$ ns) in the Home Frame, so they are separated by $\Delta x = 0$ in that frame. Since these events occur at opposite ends of the pole in the runner's frame, they are separated by $\Delta x' = -10$ ns in that frame (*negative* because $\Delta x' \equiv x'_E - x'_F$ 0 ns – 10 ns = –10 ns). So using the Lorentz transformation equation $\Delta x' = \gamma(-\beta \Delta t + \Delta x)$, we find that

$$\Delta t = \frac{\Delta x}{\beta} - \frac{\Delta x'}{\gamma \beta} = 0 - \frac{-10\text{ ns}}{\frac{5}{4}\left(\frac{3}{5}\right)} = \frac{40}{3}\text{ ns} = 13.3\text{ ns} \quad (R7.15)$$

This means that $L = \beta \Delta t = \tfrac{3}{5}\left(\tfrac{40}{3}\text{ ns}\right) = 8$ ns exactly. The discrepancy between this answer and the answer for part (a) is a result of inevitable uncertainties that arise in reading the diagram: note that the answers are close (within 2.5%).

THE COSMIC SPEED LIMIT

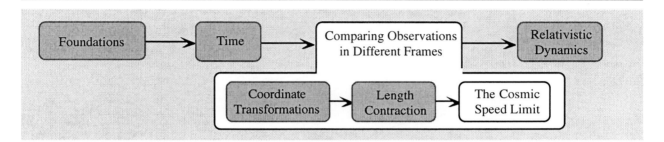

What I'm really interested in is whether God could have made the world in a different way; that is, whether the necessity of logical simplicity leaves any freedom at all.

Albert Einstein*

R8.1   OVERVIEW

One of the most fundamental and surprising consequences of the principle of relativity is that *nothing can go faster than the speed of light* (in a vacuum). In this chapter, we see (with the help of some two-observer diagrams) that making the concept of causality consistent with the principle of relativity implies that not only can no *object* travel faster than light, it is not even possible for a *message* to travel faster than light! The speed of light thus represents a true "cosmic speed limit" for any kind of physical influence.

This discussion also provides an appropriate context for discussing the Einstein velocity transformation equations that will replace the galilean velocity transformation equations (equations R1.3), since the latter allow for the possibility of faster-than-light speeds. The Einstein velocity transformation equations provide important background for the next two chapters.

Here is an overview of the sections in this chapter:

R8.2   *CAUSALITY AND RELATIVITY* shows how requiring that causality be consistent with the principle of relativity implies that nothing (not even a message) can travel faster than light in any inertial frame.

R8.3   *TIMELIKE, LIGHTLIKE, AND SPACELIKE INTERVALS* discusses how the spacetime interval between a pair of arbitrarily chosen events will always fit into one of *three* possible categories.

R8.4   *THE CAUSAL STRUCTURE OF SPACETIME* explores how these categories are related to whether one event can cause the other or not.

R8.5   *THE EINSTEIN VELOCITY TRANSFORMATION* demonstrates how we can use spacetime diagrams or the Lorentz transformation equations to compute an object's velocity in one inertial frame knowing its velocity in another.

---

*Quoted in A. P. French (ed.), *Einstein: A Centenary Volume,* Cambridge, Mass.: Harvard, 1979, p. 128.

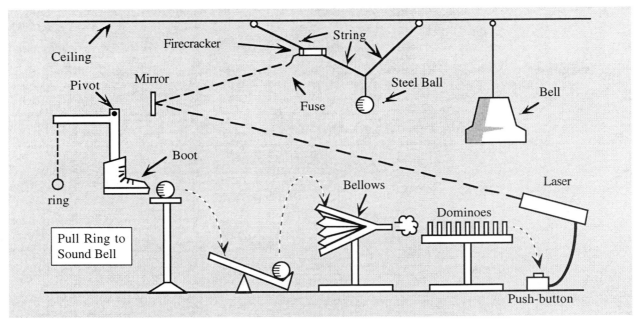

Figure R8.1: Some causal connections.

R8.2   CAUSALITY AND RELATIVITY

"Nothing can go faster than the speed of light." This statement is a well-known consequence of special relativity. But why *must* this statement be true? Are there any loopholes that might make faster-than-light travel possible?

In sections R4.3 and R5.4, we saw how the metric equation and the proper time equation fail if we apply them to a clock moving faster than light: both equations imply that the time registered between two events by such a clock would be an imaginary number, which is absurd. In both cases, this absurdity results from the violation of the $\Delta t^2 > \Delta d^2$ restriction necessary for the derivation of the metric equation. Thus neither equation really says anything useful about what a clock traveling at faster than light would measure.

What is causality?

In this section, we will see that there is a deeper problem traveling faster than light: *it violates causality*. What do I mean by "causality"? In physics (and more broadly, in daily life), we know that certain events *cause* other events to happen (see Figure R8.1). For example, even couch potatoes know that if you press the appropriate button on the remote control, the TV channel will change. Causally connected events *must* happen in a certain order in time: the event being caused following the event that causes it (for example, we would be deeply disturbed if the TV channel changed just *before* we pressed the remote control button!).

Consider two distinct events (call them P and Q respectively) such that event P causes event Q, or more precisely, Q happens as a direct consequence of the reception of some kind of information that P has occurred. This information can be transmitted from P to Q in any number of ways: via some mechanical effect (such as the movement of an object or the propagation of a sound wave), via a light flash, via an electrical signal, via a radio message, etc. Basically, the information can be carried by *any* object or effect that can move from place to place and is detectable.

Let's consider the TV remote control again as a specific example. Imagine that you press a button on your TV remote control handset (event P). The information that the button has been pressed is sent to the TV set in some manner, and in response, the TV set changes channels (event Q). Keep this basic example in mind as we go through the argument that follows.

Why faster-than-light causal influences are absurd

Now let us pretend that the **causal influence** that connects event P to event Q *can* flow between them at a constant speed v_{ci} *faster* than the speed of

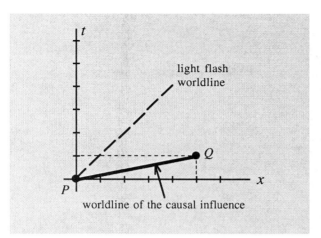

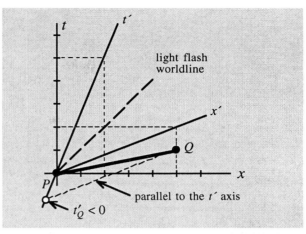

Figure R8.2: Imagine that events P and Q are connected by a hypothetical causal influence traveling with a speed v_{ci} faster than the speed of light. (In the drawing above, I have assumed for the sake of concreteness that the causal influence travels in the Home Frame at 5 times the speed of light.)

Figure R8.3: This two-observer spacetime diagram shows the same situation as Figure R8.2, but with added axes for an Other Frame moving at $\beta = 2/5$ with respect to the Home Frame. Note that in the Other Frame, event Q occurs *before* event P.

light as measured in your inertial frame, which we will call the Home Frame. (Perhaps the TV manufacturer has found some way to convey a signal from the remote to the TV using "Z waves" that travel faster than light.) We will show that this leads to a logical absurdity. Choose event P to be the origin event in that frame and choose the spatial x axis of the frame so that both events P and Q lie along it. (We can always do this: it is just a matter of choosing the origin and orientation of our reference frame. Choosing the frame to be oriented this way is just a matter of convenience).

Figure R8.2 shows a spacetime diagram (drawn by an observer in the Home Frame) of a pair of events P and Q fitting the description above. Note that if the causal influence flows from P to Q faster than the speed of light, its worldline on the diagram will have a slope $1/v_{ci} < 1$, that is, *less* than the slope of the worldline of a light flash leaving event P at the same time (which is also shown on the diagram for reference).

Now consider Figure R8.3. In this two-observer spacetime diagram, I have drawn the t' and x' axes for an Other Frame that travels with a speed $\beta = 2/5$ relative to the Home Frame. Note that according to section R6.5, the slope of the diagram x' axis in such a diagram is β. Note also that since the slope of the causal influence worldline is $1/v_{ci} < 1$, it is *always* possible to find a value of β such that $1/v_{ci} < \beta < 1$, meaning that it is always possible to find a reference frame moving slower than the speed of light relative to the Home Frame whose x' axis lies *between* the light-flash worldline and the causal influence worldline, as shown. In such a frame, event Q will be measured to occur *before* event P, as one can see by reading the time coordinates of these events from the diagram.

Thus in such an Other Frame, event P is observed to occur *after* event Q does. But this is absurd: event P is supposed to *cause* event Q. How can an event be measured to occur before its cause? This is not merely a semantic issue, nor is it mere appearance. According to any and every physical measurement that one might make in the Other Frame, event Q will really be observed to occur *before* its "cause" P.

To vividly illustrate the absurdity, consider our TV remote example. If the signal could go from your remote control to the TV faster than light, in certain inertial reference frames, you would observe the TV set to change channels *before* the button was pushed. If this were to happen in your reference frame, you would consider this a violation of the laws of physics (presuming your TV set was not broken). But the laws of physics are supposed to hold in *every* inertial

Faster-than-light influences imply reversal of cause and effect in some frames

Figure R8.4: Assume that the speed v_{ci} of the causal influence satisfies the restriction $v_{ci} < 1$ in the Home Frame. Then consider *any* Other Frame whose speed β relative to the Home Frame satisfies the same restriction: $\beta < 1$. Since the Other Frame's x′ axis has slope β, it is less than 1 and thus less than the slope $1/v_{ci}$ of the worldline of the causal influence. This means that event Q can never be *below* the x′ axis, which in turn implies that Q will occur after P in *every* inertial reference frame.

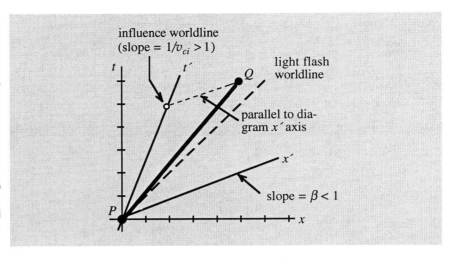

reference frame. Therefore this observed inversion of cause and effect violates the principle of relativity!

We have only three options at this point. We can reject the principle of relativity and start over at square one. We can radically modify our conception of causality in a way that is yet unknown. Or we can reject the assumption that got us into this trouble in the first place: namely, that a causal influence can flow from P to Q faster than light ($v_{ci} > 1$).

The latter option is clearly the least drastic. If information can only flow from P to Q with a speed $v_{ci} \leq 1$ in the Home Frame, then the worldline of the causal influence connecting event P to event Q will have a slope $1/v_{ci} > 1$. Any Other Frame must travel with $\beta < 1$, by this hypothesis (since the parts of the reference frame, like any material object, could in principle be the agent of a causal influence). Therefore, the slope β of the Other Frame's diagram x′ axis on a spacetime diagram must always be less than the slope $1/v_{ci}$ of the causal connection worldline connecting P and Q, and thus Q will occur after P in *every* Other inertial reference frame (Figure R8.4).

So, if the speed of reference frames and causal influences is limited to some $v_{ci} < 1$, then effects will occur *after* their causes in every inertial reference frame, which is necessary if the idea of causality is to be consistent with the principle of relativity.*

Consistency of causality and relativity thus implies the cosmic speed limit

> **THEOREM: The Cosmic Speed Limit:** In order for causality (that is, the idea that one event can *cause* another event to happen) to be consistent with the principle of relativity, information (that is, *any* effect representing a causal connection between two events) *cannot* travel between two events with a speed v_{ci} greater than that of light.

Since anything movable and detectable can carry information (that is, cause things to happen), this consequence of the principle of relativity applies not only to all physical objects (waves, particles, and macroscopic objects) but indeed to *any* trick or means of conveying a message that exists or might be imagined (e.g., instantaneous changes in a gravitational field, telepathy, magic, whatever).

---

*At the most basic physical level, the physical law that defines the temporal order of cause and effect is the *second law of thermodynamics*, which requires that the entropy of the universe always increase (or at least remain the same) during a physical process. This law thus implies that events in certain physical processes can occur in one temporal order but cannot occur in the reverse order. Therefore, if the second law of thermodynamics is to be true in all inertial frames (as required by the principle of relativity), then the temporal order of all events that might be linked by that law must be preserved in all inertial frames. "Cause and effect" is thus really a colloquial way to talk about the invariant temporal order imposed on events by the second law.

So, with a straightforward argument using two-observer spacetime diagrams, we have proved the existence of a cosmic speed limit, an idea having profound physical and philosophical implications. As usual, this prediction is amply supported by experiment. No particle, object, or signal of any kind has ever been definitely observed to travel at faster than the speed of light in a vacuum. Science fiction fans and space travel buffs who hope for the discovery of faster-than-light travel may hope in vain: both the argument (based as it is on the firmly accepted and fundamental ideas of the principle of relativity and the physical reality of causality) and the experimental evidence present a pretty ironclad case for this cosmic speed limit.*

Exercise R8X.1: Imagine that a causal influence moves between events P and Q at 3 times the speed of light relative to the Home Frame. How fast would an Other Frame have to move relative to the Home Frame for event Q to occur *before* event P in the Other Frame?

R8.3 TIMELIKE, LIGHTLIKE, and SPACELIKE INTERVALS

We are now in a position to understand more fully the true physical nature of the spacetime interval between *any* two events in spacetime. In Section R4.3, we saw that for two events whose coordinate differences in a given inertial reference frame are Δt, Δx, Δy, and Δz, the quantity $\Delta s^2 = \Delta t^2 - \Delta x^2 - \Delta y^2 - \Delta z^2$ has a frame-independent value whose value is equal to the time registered by an inertial clock present at both events. But to make the proof of the metric equation (equation R4.5) work, we had to assume that $\Delta d = [\Delta x^2 + \Delta y^2 + \Delta z^2]^{1/2}$ was *smaller* than Δt so that there was more than sufficient time for a light flash to travel from one event to the other along the length of the light clock. The purpose of this section is to investigate the meaning of the spacetime interval when $\Delta d > \Delta t$, that is, when this condition is violated.

We have exploited the analogy between spacetime geometry and euclidian plane geometry extensively in the last few chapters. We have noted, though, that the negative signs in the metric equation (which do not appear in the corresponding pythagorean relation) lead to some subtle differences between spacetime geometry and euclidian geometry. Yet another one of these differences is the following. In euclidian geometry the square distance Δd^2 between two points on a plane is necessarily positive:

Δs^2 **between two arbitrary events can be positive, negative or zero**

$$\Delta d^2 = \Delta x^2 + \Delta y^2 \geq 0 \qquad (R8.1)$$

But taken at face value, the metric equation allows the squared spacetime interval between two events to be positive, zero, or negative, depending on the relative sizes of the coordinate separations Δd and Δt between those events:

$$\Delta s^2 = \Delta t^2 - \Delta d^2$$

Therefore,

$$\text{if } \Delta d > \Delta t, \text{ then } \Delta s^2 < 0! \qquad (R8.2)$$

---

*This does not mean that interstellar travel is out of the question. Remember that the ship time measured in a spaceship traveling close to the speed of light (relative to the galaxy) is much shorter than the coordinate time we would measure (at rest in the galaxy). Therefore, a trip to distant stars can be made as short as desired for the *passengers* by simply constraining the ship's speed to be sufficiently close to the speed of light. But (at least if special relativity is true) there appears to be no way to make a trip of 1000 ly in our galaxy in less than 1000 y *in the frame of the galaxy*, no matter how short this might seem to the passengers. This does put some severe limits on the possibilities of interstellar commerce! We will examine other difficulties associated with interstellar travel in chapter R10.

We see that while there is only *one* kind of distance between two points on a plane, the possible spacetime intervals between two events in spacetime fall into *three* distinct categories depending on the sign of Δs^2. These categories are:

The three categories for the spacetime interval

If $\Delta s^2 > 0$, we say that the interval between the events is **timelike.**
If $\Delta s^2 = 0$, we say that the interval between the events is **lightlike.**
If $\Delta s^2 < 0$, we say that the interval between the events is **spacelike.**

The reasons for these names will become clear shortly.

The peculiar category here is the *spacelike* category — there is nothing corresponding to it in ordinary plane geometry (where the squared distance between two events is always positive). What does it mean for two events to have a *spacelike* spacetime interval between them?

Spacelike spacetime intervals exist, but cannot be measured with a clock

First of all, note that events separated by spacelike spacetime intervals certainly do exist. Consider, for example, the case of two events that are measured in a certain inertial frame to occur at the same *time* but at different *locations*. Since the time separation between these events is zero in that reference frame, we have $\Delta s^2 = 0 - \Delta d^2 = -\Delta d^2 < 0$, so the interval between these events is necessarily spacelike. Therefore, the spacelike interval classification is needed if we are to be able to categorize the spacetime interval between arbitrarily chosen events.

As we have already discussed, the squared spacetime interval between two events Δs^2 that appears in the metric equation $\Delta s^2 = \Delta t^2 - \Delta d^2$ has been linked with the frame-independent time measured by an inertial clock present at both events *only* in the case that $\Delta t^2 > \Delta d^2$. For two events for which $\Delta t^2 < \Delta d^2$, it is not clear how one can directly measure the squared spacetime interval between the events at all. For example, for an inertial clock to be present at both events where $\Delta d > \Delta t$, it would have to travel at a speed $v > 1$ in that frame. We have just seen that this is impossible; thus a spacelike spacetime interval *cannot* be measured by a clock or anything else that travels between the events. Since the proof of the metric equation given in section R4.3 does not handle the case of spacelike intervals, it is not even obvious that the squared spacetime interval $\Delta s^2 = \Delta t^2 - \Delta d^2$ is frame-independent when it is less than zero.

Δs^2 is frame-independent even when it is negative

In fact, the squared spacetime interval Δs^2 *does* have a frame-independent value, no matter what its sign is. This can easily be demonstrated by using the Lorentz transformation equations for coordinate differences given by equations R6.12. The argument goes like this. Let Δt, Δx, Δy, Δz be the coordinate separations of two events measured in the Home Frame, and let $\Delta t'$, $\Delta x'$, $\Delta y'$, $\Delta z'$ be the coordinate separations of the same two events measured in an Other Frame moving with speed β in the $+x$ direction with respect to the Home Frame. Then, equations R6.12 imply that:

$$
\begin{aligned}
(\Delta t')^2 &- (\Delta x')^2 - (\Delta y')^2 - (\Delta z')^2 \\
&= [\gamma(\Delta t - \beta\,\Delta x)]^2 - [\gamma(-\beta\Delta t + \Delta x)]^2 - \Delta y^2 - \Delta z^2 \\
&= \gamma^2(\Delta t^2 - 2\beta\Delta t\Delta x + \beta^2\Delta x^2) - \gamma^2(\beta^2\Delta t^2 - 2\beta\Delta t\Delta x + \Delta x^2) - \Delta y^2 - \Delta z^2 \\
&= \gamma^2(\Delta t^2 + \beta^2\Delta x^2 - \beta^2\Delta t^2 - \Delta x^2) - \Delta y^2 - \Delta z^2 \\
&= \gamma^2(1 - \beta^2)(\Delta t^2 - \Delta x^2) - \Delta y^2 - \Delta z^2 \\
&= \Delta t^2 - \Delta x^2 - \Delta y^2 - \Delta z^2
\end{aligned}
\tag{R8.3}
$$

where in the last step, I used $\gamma \equiv 1/\sqrt{1 - \beta^2}$. The sign of $\Delta s^2 = \Delta t^2 - \Delta d^2$ is irrelevant to this derivation, so we will find that the squared interval Δs^2 has the same frame-independent value in *every* inertial reference frame, whether Δs^2 is spacelike, timelike, or lightlike.

How can we measure the value of the spacetime interval between two events separated by a spacelike interval? We cannot use a clock, as we have noted already. In fact, we measure a spacelike spacetime interval with a *ruler*, as we will shortly see.

Let us define the **spacetime separation** $\Delta\sigma$ of two events this way:

The spacetime separation

$$\Delta\sigma^2 \equiv \Delta d^2 - \Delta t^2 = -\Delta s^2 \qquad (R8.4)$$

The spacetime separation, so defined, is conveniently real whenever the interval between the events is spacelike. Now note that *if* we can find an inertial reference frame where the events are simultaneous ($\Delta t = 0$), we have:

$$\Delta\sigma^2 = \Delta d^2 \quad \Rightarrow \quad \Delta\sigma = \Delta d \quad \text{(in a frame where } \Delta t = 0) \qquad (R8.5)$$

Now, I claim that we can *always* find a frame in which $\Delta t = 0$ if the events are separated by a spacelike interval. This can be seen as follows. Imagine that two events occur with coordinate differences Δt and Δd ($> \Delta t$) as measured in the Home Frame. Reorient and reposition the axes of the Home Frame so that the events in question both occur along the spatial x axis, with the later event located in the +x-direction relative to the earlier event. (This can be done without loss of generality: we are always free to choose the orientation of our coordinate system to be whatever we find convenient.) Once this is done, $\Delta d = \Delta x$ in the Home Frame.

Now, consider an Other Frame in standard orientation with respect to the Home Frame and traveling in the +x direction with speed β with respect to the Home Frame. According to equation R6.12a, the time-coordinate difference between these events in the Other Frame is:

$$\Delta t' = \gamma(\Delta t - \beta\Delta x) \qquad (R8.6)$$

These events will be simultaneous in the Other Frame (that is, $\Delta t'$ will equal zero) if and only if the relative speed of the frames is chosen to be $\beta = \Delta t/\Delta x = \Delta t/\Delta d$. This relative speed β will be less than 1 since $\Delta d > \Delta t$ for our events by hypothesis. In short, given *any* pair of events that are separated by a spacelike interval in some inertial frame (which we are calling the Home Frame), it is possible to find an Other inertial frame moving with speed $\beta < 1$ with respect to the Home Frame in which observers will find the two events to be simultaneous (see Figure R8.5).

In short, if the spacetime interval between two events is *spacelike*, then:

1. It is possible to find an inertial frame where these events are observed to occur at the *same time*.

2. $\Delta\sigma$ is the *distance* between the events in that special frame. We can measure this with a ruler stretched between the events in that frame.

3. If observers in any other inertial frame use equation R8.4 to *calculate* $\Delta\sigma$, they will get the same value measured directly in the special frame.

These statements are directly analogous to statements that can be made about events separated by a timelike spacetime interval. If the spacetime interval between two events is *timelike*, then:

1. It is possible to find an inertial frame in which these events occur at the *same place* (this is the frame of the inertial clock that is present at both events).

2. Δs is the *time* between the events in this special frame. We can measure this with a clock present at both events and at rest in this frame.

3. If observers in any other inertial frame use the ordinary metric equation to calculate Δs, they will get at the same value measured directly in the special frame.

Thus there is a fundamental symmetry between spacelike and timelike spacetime intervals, a symmetry that arises because both reflect the same underlying physi-

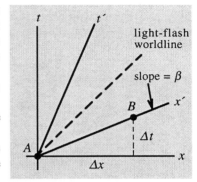

Figure R8.5: Given any pair of events A and B separated by a spacelike interval ($\Delta x > \Delta t$) in the Home Frame, we can find an Other Frame where the two events are simultaneous. The speed of this Other Frame simply must have the right value so that the diagram x' axis can connect both points. Since this axis has slope β, this means that β must equal $\Delta t/\Delta x$, where Δt and Δx are the coordinate separations of the events in the Home Frame.

How to measure a spacelike spacetime interval

Comparison with measuring a timelike interval

cal truth: it is possible to describe the separation of *any* two events in space and time with a frame-independent quantity Δs^2 (which we will call the **squared spacetime interval**) analogous to the *squared distance* between two points in plane geometry. It is simply a peculiarity of the geometry of spacetime that the quantity in spacetime that corresponds to ordinary (unsquared) distance on the plane comes in three distinct flavors (the spacetime *interval* Δs if $\Delta s^2 > 0$ for the events, the spacetime *separation* $\Delta \sigma$ if $\Delta s^2 < 0$, and the lightlike interval $\Delta s = \Delta \sigma = 0$ when $\Delta s^2 = 0$) which are measured in different ways using different tools. But it is important to realize that these three quantities are only different aspects of the same basic frame-independent quantity Δs^2.

Why the categories of spacetime interval have the names that they do

We see that timelike intervals are directly measured with a *time*-measuring device (an inertial *clock* present at both events), while spacelike intervals are directly measured with a *space*-measuring device (a *ruler* stretched between the events in the particular inertial frame where Δt between the events is zero). This is why these interval classifications have the names *timelike* and *spacelike*: the names are intended to tell us whether we have to measure the interval with a clock (because the interval is *timelike*) or with a ruler (because it is *spacelike*). The lightlike interval classification stands between the other classifications. When the interval between two events is *lightlike*, we have $\Delta d = \Delta t$, which implies that these events could be connected by a flash of light.

Exercise R8X.2: Consider the events shown in the spacetime diagram to the right. Classify the spacetime interval between each *pair* of events as being timelike, spacelike, or lightlike.

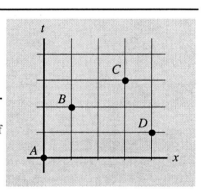

Exercise R8X.3: Imagine that event *B* happens 3.0 ns after and 5.0 ns east of event *A* in the Home Frame. In the Other Frame, the events happen at the same time. How fast is the Other Frame moving relative to the Home Frame? What is the distance between the events in that frame?

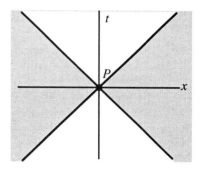

Figure R8.6: The frame independent regions of spacetime associated with the event *P*. The spacetime interval between *P* and any event in the white region is *timelike*, any event in the gray region is *spacelike*, and any event along the black diagonal lines is *lightlike*.

Understanding the causal structure of spacetime

R8.4 THE CAUSAL STRUCTURE OF SPACETIME

Now, *because* it is true that the value of the squared spacetime interval Δs^2 is frame-independent no matter what its sign, all inertial observers will agree as to whether the interval between a given pair of events is timelike, lightlike, or spacelike (since if they all agree on the *value* of Δs^2, they will surely all agree on its sign). This means that the spacetime around any event *P* can be divided up into the distinct regions shown in Figure R8.6, and every observer will agree about which events in spacetime belong to which region.

Because these regions can be defined in a frame-independent manner, it is plausible that they reflect something absolute and physical about the geometry of spacetime. In fact, *these regions distinguish those events that can be causally connected to P from those that cannot.* Remember that in section R8.2, we found that two events can be causally linked only if $\Delta d \leq \Delta t$ between them: otherwise the causal influence would have to travel between the events faster than the speed of light. This means that every event that can be causally linked with *P* must have a timelike (or perhaps lightlike) interval with respect to *P*: such events will lie in the white regions shown in Figure R8.6.

We can be more specific yet. Since the temporal order of events is preserved in all inertial frames if $\Delta d > \Delta t$ (see Figure R8.3 and the surrounding text), all events in the *upper* white region in Figure R8.6 will occur *after P* in every

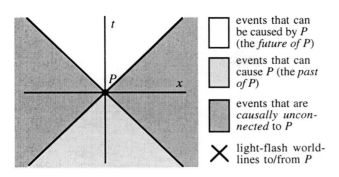

Figure R8.7: The causal structure of spacetime relative to the event *P*.

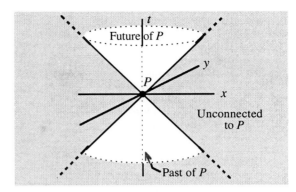

Figure R8.8: The *light cone* of *P* (shown on a spacetime diagram having two spatial dimensions).

frame (and thus could be caused by *P*), and all events in the lower white region of Figure R8.6 will occur *before P* in every frame (and thus could cause *P*). We refer to these regions as the *future* and *past* of *P* respectively.

Events whose spacetime interval with respect to *P* is spacelike ($\Delta d > \Delta t$) cannot influence *P* or be influenced by it. We say that these events (which inhabit the shaded region of Figure R8.6) are causally *unconnected* to event *P*.

With this in mind, we can relabel the regions in Figure R8.6 as shown in Figure R8.7. Remember that every observer agrees on the value of the spacetime interval between event *P* and any other event, so every observer agrees as to which event belongs in which classification. The structure illustrated is thus an intrinsic, frame-independent characteristic of the geometry of spacetime.

Now, the boundaries of the regions illustrated in Figure R8.7 are light-flash worldlines. If we consider two spatial dimensions instead of one, an omnidirectional light-flash is seen as an ever-expanding ring, like the ring of waves formed by the splash of a stone into a still pool of water. If we plot the growth of such a ring on a spacetime diagram, we get a cone. The boundaries between the three regions described are then two tip-to-tip cones, as shown in Figure R8.8. This boundary surface is often called the **light cone** for the given event *P*.

The light-cone associated with an event

To summarize, the point of this section is that the spacetime interval classifications, which are basic, frame-independent features of the geometry of spacetime, have in fact a deeply physical significance: the sign of the squared spacetime interval between two events unambiguously describes whether these events can be causally connected or not. The light cone shown in Figure R8.8 effectively illustrates this geometric feature of spacetime.

Exercise R8X.4: A meteor strikes the moon (event *A*), causing a large and vivid explosion. Exactly 0.47 s later (as measured in an inertial reference frame attached to the earth) the radio-telescope receiving signals from the moon goes on the fritz. Could these events be causally related? [*Hint:* The distance between the earth and the moon is roughly 384,000 km.]

R8.5 THE EINSTEIN VELOCITY TRANSFORMATION

In this section we turn our attention to the relativistic generalization of the galilean velocity transformation equations R1.3. Imagine a particle that is observed in the Other Frame to move along the spatial *x′* axis with a constant *x*-velocity v'_x. The Other Frame, in turn, is moving with a speed β in the positive *x* direction with respect to the Home Frame. What is the particle's *x*-velocity v_x as observed in the Home Frame?

Figure R8.9 shows how to construct a two-observer spacetime diagram that we can use to answer this question. After drawing both sets of coordinate axes,

Transforming velocities with a 2-observer diagram

Figure R8.9: We can use a two-observer diagram to find a particle's *x*-velocity in one frame knowing its *x*-velocity in another and the two frames' relative velocity. For example, if we know that the particle's Other Frame *x*-velocity is $v_x' = 3/5$ and that the Other Frame moves at $\beta = 3/5$ relative to the Home Frame, then we can construct an appropriate two-observer diagram for this β, draw the particle's worldline with a slope of 5/3 relative to the Other Frame axes, and read the slope of this line relative to the Home Frame axes (about 4.3/5 ≈ 0.86 in this case). If we knew the particle's Home Frame *x*-velocity, we could just reverse the process.

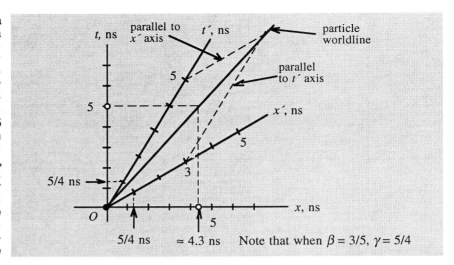

we simply draw the particle's worldline so that its slope in the Other Frame is $1/v_x'$. We can then find its *x*-velocity v_x in the Home Frame by taking the inverse slope of that line in the Home Frame, which we can do by picking an arbitrary "rise" (5 ns in Figure R8.9), determining the worldline's "run" for that rise, and then taking the inverse rise/run = run/rise. In the case shown in Figure R8.9, where $\beta = 3/5$ and $v_x' = 3/5$, we find that the value of v_x is about 0.86, and *not* $3/5 + 3/5 = 6/5$ that the galilean velocity transformation equations would predict.

How to derive the inverse Einstein velocity transformation equations

Now let us see if we can derive an exact equation that (like the diagram) allows us to find v_x in terms of v_x' and β. Imagine two infinitesimally separated events along the particle's worldline (which we will assume is moving along the spatial *x* axis). Let the coordinate differences between these events as measured in the Home frame be dt and dx. Let the coordinate differences between the same two events as measured in the Other Frame be dt' and dx'. The *x* component of the particle's velocity as it travels between these events is:

$$v_x \equiv \frac{dx}{dt} = \frac{\gamma(\beta dt' + dx')}{\gamma(dt' + \beta dx')} \tag{R8.7}$$

where I have used the difference version of the inverse Lorentz transformation equations (equations R6.13). Dividing the right side top and bottom by dt' and using $dx'/dt' \equiv v_x'$, we get the following relativistically exact equation:

$$v_x = \frac{\beta + v_x'}{1 + \beta v_x'} \tag{R8.8a}$$

In a similar fashion, you can show that the *y* and *z* components of the particle's Home Frame velocity are:

$$v_y = \frac{v_y'\sqrt{1-\beta^2}}{1+\beta v_x'}, \qquad v_z = \frac{v_z'\sqrt{1-\beta^2}}{1+\beta v_x'} \tag{R8.8b,c}$$

Exercise R8X.5: Verify equation R8.8b.

An example application

As an example of the use of equation R8.8a, consider the particular problem illustrated by Figure R8.9, where we have $v_x' = \beta = 3/5$. The final speed of the particle in the Home Frame (according to equation R8.8a) is:

$$v_x = \frac{3/5 + 3/5}{1 + (3/5)(3/5)} = \frac{6/5}{34/25} = \frac{30}{34} \approx 0.88 \tag{R8.9}$$

This is close to the result that we read from Figure R8.9.

We call equations R8.8 the **inverse Einstein velocity transformation equations**: they express algebraically what a two-observer diagram like Figure R8.9 expresses graphically. Note that the result is different from what the *galilean* velocity transformation predicts: solving equation R1.3a for v_x yields

These equations reduce to the galilean equations at low speeds...

$$v_x = \beta + v'_x \quad \text{(from the Galilean velocity transformation)} \quad \text{(R8.10)}$$

Note that when the velocities β and v'_x are very small, the factor $\beta v'_x$ that appears in the denominator of Equation R8.8 becomes *very* small compared to one. In this limit, then equation R8.8a reduces to the galilean equation R8.10:

$$v_x = \frac{\beta + v'_x}{1 + \beta v'_x} \approx \frac{\beta + v'_x}{1} = \beta + v'_x \quad \text{(in the low-velocity limit)} \quad \text{(R8.11)}$$

The same kind of argument applies to the other two component equations as well. The Galilean transformation equations are therefore reasonably accurate for everyday velocities, but only represent an *approximation* to the true velocity transformation law expressed by equations R8.8.

Equation R8.8 never yields a Home Frame x-velocity that exceeds the speed of light: even if both β and $v'_x = 1$ (their maximum possible value), then

...and are consistent with the cosmic speed limit and the invariant speed of light

$$v_x = \frac{1+1}{1+1\cdot 1} = \frac{2}{2} = 1 \quad \text{(R8.12)}$$

Moreover, equation R8.8a (unlike the galilean equation R1.3a) is consistent with the idea that the speed of light is equal to 1 in all frames: if the x-velocity of a light flash in the Other Frame is $v'_x = 1$, its speed in the Home Frame will be

$$v_x = \frac{\beta + 1}{1 + \beta \cdot 1} = \frac{\beta + 1}{1 + \beta} = 1 \quad \text{(R8.13)}$$

independent of the value of β.

In short, the Inverse Einstein velocity transformation equations (equations R8.8) provide the answer to the question that we raised in chapter R2 about how the galilean velocity transformation equations can be modified to be consistent with the principle of relativity. Equations R8.8 reduce to the galilean transformation equations at low velocities (where the galilean transformation is known by experiment to be very accurate), but at relativistic velocities, they are consistent with both the assertion that nothing can be measured to go faster than light and the assertion that light itself has the same speed in all inertial frames.

Equations R8.8 convert Other Frame velocity components v'_x, v'_y, v'_z to Home Frame components v_x, v_y, v_z. The (direct) **Einstein velocity transformation equations** transform the velocity components the other way:

The (direct) Einstein velocity transformation equations

$$v'_x = \frac{v_x - \beta}{1 - \beta v_x}, \quad v'_y = \frac{v_y \sqrt{1-\beta^2}}{1 - \beta v_x}, \quad v'_z = \frac{v_z \sqrt{1-\beta^2}}{1 - \beta v_x} \quad \text{(R8.14a,b,c)}$$

These equations can be derived either by solving equations R8.8 for the Other Frame components or by deriving them from the direct Lorentz transformation equations R6.12 in a manner similar to the way that we derived equation R8.8.

Exercise R8X.6: Verify the first component of equation R8.14 using the direct Lorentz transformation equations.

Exercise R8X.7: An object moves at 0.80 in the $+x$ direction as measured in the Home Frame. What is its x-velocity in an Other Frame that is moving at 0.60 in the $+x$ direction, also as measured in the Home Frame?

SUMMARY

I. CAUSALITY AND RELATIVITY
   A. The concept of causality
      1. A *causal influence* is any effect (particle, object, wave, or message) produced by one event that can cause another
      2. For causality to make sense, the temporal order of events must be preserved (the caused event cannot precede the event that causes it)
   B. The problem with faster-than-light travel is that it *violates causality*
      1. Imagine that P causes Q and that the causal influence moving from P to Q moves with a speed faster than light
      2. In such a case, we can always find a frame where Q occurs before P
      3. This is inconsistent with the principle of relativity, since it violates the concept of causality for an effect to precede its cause
   C. The only way to make relativity consistent with causality is to insist that *nothing* (not even a message) can travel faster than light

II. TIMELIKE, LIGHTLIKE, AND SPACELIKE INTERVALS
   A. The squared spacetime interval Δs^2 between two events can be negative
   B. This means that there are three distinct categories of spacetime interval:
      1. *timelike*, when $\Delta s^2 > 0$
      2. *lightlike*, when $\Delta s^2 = 0$
      3. *spacelike*, when $\Delta s^2 < 0$
   C. These categories are frame-independent, since the value of Δs^2 is
   D. The spacetime separation $\Delta\sigma \equiv [-\Delta s^2]^{1/2}$ is real for spacelike intervals
   E. How can we measure the spacetime interval between the two events?
      1. If Δs^2 is *timelike*, we can find a frame where the events occur at the same *place*: we then measure Δs with the frame clock there
      2. If Δs^2 is *spacelike*, we can find a frame where the events occur at the same *time*: we then measure $\Delta\sigma$ with a ruler in that frame

III. THE CAUSAL STRUCTURE OF SPACETIME
   A. Events separated by a spacelike interval *cannot* be causally connected, since the causal influence would have to travel faster than light
   B. The categories of spacetime interval are frame-independent
   C. For a given event P, then, *all* observers will agree which events have a
      1. timelike (or lightlike) interval with P and occur *after P* in all frames and so could be caused by P: these events are the *future of P*
      2. timelike (or lightlike) interval with P and occur *before P* in all frames and so could cause P: these events are the *past of P*
      3. spacelike interval with P and so must be *causally unrelated to P*
   D. In a spacetime diagram with two spatial axes, P's past and future look like cones whose points touch at P and whose surfaces are rings of light converging on or expanding from P: this structure is P's *light-cone*

IV. THE EINSTEIN VELOCITY TRANSFORMATION EQUATIONS
   A. Our task: to find a particle's velocity in one inertial frame knowing its velocity in another and the relative velocity of the two frames
   B. We can do this with a two-observer diagram as follows:
      1. Set up a calibrated two-observer diagram of both frames
      2. Draw the particle's worldline with the correct slope relative to the axes of the frame in which you know its velocity
      3. Measure that worldline's slope in the other frame
   C. The Einstein velocity transformation equations are:

$$\text{(direct)} \quad v'_x = \frac{v_x - \beta}{1 - \beta v_x}, \quad v'_y = \frac{v_y\sqrt{1-\beta^2}}{1-\beta v_x}, \quad v'_z = \frac{v_z\sqrt{1-\beta^2}}{1-\beta v_x} \qquad \text{(R8.14abc)}$$

$$\text{(inverse)} \quad v_x = \frac{\beta + v'_x}{1 + \beta v'_x}, \quad v_y = \frac{v'_y\sqrt{1-\beta^2}}{1+\beta v'_x}, \quad v_z = \frac{v'_z\sqrt{1-\beta^2}}{1+\beta v'_x} \qquad \text{(R8.8abc)}$$

GLOSSARY

causal influence: Any effect (particle, object, wave, or message) produced by one event that can cause another event to occur.

causally connected (events): a pair of events that are connected by a causal influence in such a way that one event causes the other.

temporal order: the order that two events occur in time in a given reference frame. For causality to make sense, the temporal order of causally connected events must be the same in all reference frames (an effect should never be observed to precede its cause).

cosmic speed limit: the speed of light (in a vacuum). The speed of light is the fastest that anything can travel because anything (even a message) traveling faster than light would violate causality.

squared spacetime interval Δs^2: the frame-independent quantity $\Delta s^2 = \Delta t^2 - \Delta x^2 - \Delta y^2 - \Delta z^2 = \Delta t^2 - \Delta d^2$. Depending on the two events in question, this quantity can be either positive, negative, or zero, but its value (and sign) are frame-independent independent of its sign.

timelike (spacetime interval): a spacetime interval between two events such that $\Delta s^2 > 0$. This interval can be measured by the clock present at both events in an inertial frame where the events occur at the same place.

lightlike (spacetime interval): a spacetime interval between two events such that $\Delta s^2 = 0$. If a light flash can connect the events, the interval between them is lightlike.

spacelike (spacetime interval): a spacetime interval between two events such that $\Delta s^2 < 0$. The spacetime separation (see below) corresponding to this interval can be measured by using a ruler to determine the distance between the events in an inertial reference frame where they happen at the same time.

spacetime separation $\Delta\sigma$: a way of expressing the magnitude of a spacetime interval between two events that is a real number when that spacetime interval is spacelike: $\Delta\sigma \equiv [-\Delta s^2]^{1/2}$.

past (of an event P): the set of all events having a timelike spacetime interval with P and occurring *before* P in all inertial frames. These events could conceivably cause P.

future (of an event P: the set of all events having a timelike spacetime interval with P and occurring *after* P in all inertial frames. These events could be caused by P.

light-cone (of an event P): the frame-independent structure of spacetime around P. When drawn on a two-observer spacetime diagram with two spatial axes, the past and future of P look like two infinite cones whose points touch at P. The boundaries of these cones are the set of events touched by rings of light that converge on or expand away from P. All observers will agree which events fall where in this structure.

Einstein velocity transformation equations: the set of equations that allow us to convert a particle's velocity in one inertial frame into its velocity in another (assuming that we know the relative velocity and orientation of the two frames. The **direct** transformation equations (equations R8.14) yield Other Frame velocity components in terms of Home Frame components; the **inverse** versions of the equations (equations R8.8) yield Home Frame velocity components in terms of Other Frame components.

TWO-MINUTE PROBLEMS

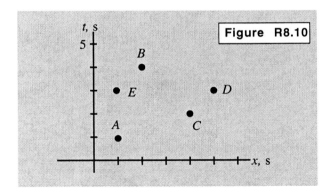

Figure R8.10

R8T.1 How would you classify the spacetime interval between each pair of events shown in Figure 8.10?
A. timelike   B. lightlike   C. spacelike

R8T.2 Which pairs of events in Figure R8.10 could be causally connected? Which could not? (For each pair, answer T if they could be causally connected, F if not.)

R8T.3 Imagine that event A is the origin event in the Home Frame and that event B occurs at $t = 1$ ns and $x = 10$ ns in that frame. What would be the minimum speed β that an Other Frame would have to have relative to the Home Frame if B occurs first in that frame?
A. 10   C. 0.60   E. 0.10
B. 1   D. 0.40   F. B can't occur first

R8T.4 Imagine that an explosion occurs at $x = 0$ in the Home Frame (event A). Light from the explosion is detected by a detector at position $x = -100$ ns (event B) and by a detector at position $x = +50$ ns (event C). Events B and C are causally connected (T or F).

R8T.5 A laser beam is emitted on earth (event A), bounces off a mirror placed on the moon by Apollo astronauts (event B) and then returns to a detector on earth (event C). The detector is 12 ns of distance from the laser.

(a) The spacetime interval between events A and B is
A. timelike   B. lightlike   C. spacelike
(b) The spacetime interval between events A and C is
A. timelike   B. lightlike   C. spacelike
(c) Events A and C are definitely causally connected (T/F).

R8T.6 If the spacetime interval between two events is timelike then the temporal order of the two events is the same in *every* inertial reference frame (T or F).

R8T.7 If the spacetime interval between two events A and B is spacelike and event A occurs before event B in some Home Frame, then it is *always* possible to find an Other Frame where the events occur in the other order (T or F).

R8T.8 An object moves with speed $v_x = +0.9$ in the Home Frame. In an Other Frame moving at $\beta = 0.60$ relative to the Home Frame, the object's x-velocity v'_x is
A. $v'_x = 1.5$ C. $0.9 < v'_x < 1$ E. $v'_x < 0.3$
B. $1 < v'_x < 1.5$ D. $0.3 < v'_x < 0.9$ F. $v'_x < 0$

HOMEWORK PROBLEMS

BASIC SKILLS

R8B.1 At 11:00:00 a.m. a boiler explodes in the basement of the Museum of Modern Art in New York City (call this event A). At 11:00:00.0003 a.m., a similar boiler explodes (call this event B) in the basement of a soup factory in Camden, NJ, a distance of 150 km from event A.

(a) Why is it impossible for the first event to have caused the second event?

(b) An alien spaceship cruising in the direction of Camden from New York measures the Camden event to occur at the same time as the New York event. What is the approximate speed of the spaceship relative to the earth?

R8B.2 Two balls are simultaneously ejected (event A) from the point $x = 0$ in some inertial frame. One rolls in the $+x$ direction with speed 0.80, and eventually hits a wall at x = 8.0 ns (event B). The other rolls in the $-x$ direction with speed 0.40, eventually hitting a wall at x = −8.0 ns (event C). Is the spacetime interval between B and C spacelike or timelike? Could these events be causally connected?

R8B.3 Derive equation R8.14a by solving equation R8.8a for v'_x.

R8B.4 An object moves with velocity $v'_x = 2/5$ in an inertial frame attached to a train, that in turn moves with velocity $\beta = 4/5$ in the $+x$ direction with respect to the ground. What is the object's velocity v_x with respect to the ground? Evaluate this by reading the velocity from a carefully constructed two-observer spacetime diagram. Check your answer using the appropriate Einstein velocity transformation equation.

R8B.5 Rocket A travels to the right, and rocket B travels to the left at speeds of 3/5 and 4/5 respectively, relative to the earth. What is the velocity of A measured by observers in rocket B? Answer by reading the velocity from a carefully constructed two-observer diagram. Check your answer using an appropriate Einstein velocity transformation.

R8B.6 Two trains approach each other from opposite directions along a linear stretch of track. Each has a speed of 3/4 relative to the ground. What is the speed of one train relative to the other? Answer this question using an appropriate Einstein velocity transformation equation.

R8B.7 Two cars travel in the same direction on the freeway. Car A travels at a speed of 0.90, while car B can only muster a speed of 0.60. What is the relative speed of the cars?

SYNTHETIC

R8S.1 Here is a quick argument that no material object can go faster than the speed of light. Consider an object traveling in the $+x$ direction with respect to some inertial frame (call this the Home Frame) at a speed $v > 1$ in that frame. Show using a two-observer spacetime diagram that it is possible to find an Other Frame moving in the $+x$ direction at a speed $\beta < 1$ with respect to the Home Frame in which the object's worldline lies along the diagram x' axis, and

find the value of β (in terms of v) that makes this happen. Why is it absurd for the worldline of any object to coincide with the diagram x' axis?

R8S.2 "Aly Carter stubs a toe on a brick on Earth. At the exact same instant, Knnnk Grblyx stubs a gnrrf on a zznkk on Alpha Centauri, which is 4.3 light-years from Earth." The theory of relativity teaches us that this statement needs some kind of qualification before it becomes meaningful. Describe the qualification and why it is necessary.*

R8S.3 Imagine spinning a laser at a speed of 100 rotations per second. How far away must you place a screen so that the spot of light on the screen produced by the laser beam sweeps along the screen at a speed faster than that of light? Would a spot speed greater than that of light violate the cosmic speed limit? [*Hint*: If you stand at one edge of the screen and a friend stands at the other, can you send a message to your friend using the sweeping spot? If so, how? If not, why not?]*

R8S.4 Starbase Alpha coasts though deep space at a speed of $\beta = 0.60$ in the $+x$ direction with respect to earth. Let the event of the starbase traveling by the earth define the origin event in both frames. Imagine that at $t = 8.0$ hrs, a giant accelerator on earth launches you toward the starbase at 10 times the speed of light, relative to the earth. After you get to the starbase, you use a similar accelerator to launch you back toward the earth at 10 times the speed of light, relative to the starbase. Using a carefully constructed (full-page) two-observer diagram, show that in such a case you will return to the earth before you left. (This is another way to illustrate the absurdity of faster-than-light travel.)

R8S.5 A flash of laser light is emitted by the earth (event A) and is absorbed on the Moon (event B). Is the spacetime interval between events A and B spacelike, lightlike or timelike? Now assume that the light flash is reflected at event B by something shiny on the moon and returns to earth, where it is absorbed at event C. Is the spacetime interval between B and C spacelike, lightlike, or timelike? What about the interval between events A and C? Support your answers by describing your reasoning.

R8S.6 A solar flare bursts through the surface of the sun at 12:05 p.m. GMT, as measured by an observer in an inertial frame attached to the sun. At 12:11 p.m., as measured by the same observer, the Macdonald family's radio fries a circuit board. Could these events be causally connected?

R8S.7 The first stage of a multi-stage rocket boosts the rocket to a speed of 0.1 relative to the ground before being jettisoned. The next stage boosts the rocket to a speed of 0.1 relative to the final speed of the first stage, and so on. How many stages does it take to boost the payload to a speed in excess of 0.95?

---

*Adapted from E. F. Taylor and J. A. Wheeler, *Spacetime Physics*, San Francisco: Freeman, 1966, p. 62.

R8S.8 Imagine that in the Home Frame, two particles of equal mass m are observed to move along the x axis with equal and opposite speeds $v = 0.60$. The particles collide and stick together, becoming one big particle which remains at rest in the Home Frame. Now imagine observing the same situation from the vantage point of an Other Frame that moves with speed $\beta = 0.60$ in the $+x$ direction with respect to the Home Frame. Find the velocities of all the particles as observed in the Other Frame using the appropriate Einstein velocity transformation equations. Check your results using a two-observer spacetime diagram of the situation.

R8S.9 (Do Problem R8S.8 first.) In the situation described in Problem R8S.8, show that while the momentum of the system is conserved in the Home Frame, it is *not* conserved in the Other Frame if momentum is defined as mass times velocity. (We'll deal with this problem in the next chapter.)

R8S.10 A train travels in the $+x$ direction with a speed of $\beta = 0.80$ with respect to the ground. At a certain time, two balls are ejected, one traveling in the $+x$ direction with x-velocity of $+0.60$ with respect to the train, and one traveling in the $-x$ direction with x-velocity of -0.40 with respect to the train. **(a)** What are the x-velocities of the balls with respect to the ground? **(b)** What is the x-velocity of the first ball with respect to the second? [*Hint:* The frames you will choose to be the Home and Other Frames for part (a) will not be the same as your choices for part (b).]

R8S.11 Show using the Einstein velocity transformation equations R8.8 that a particle traveling in any arbitrary direction at the speed of light will be measured to have the speed of light in all other inertial frames.

R8S.12 A particle moves with a speed of 4/5 in a direction 60° away from the spatial $+x'$ axis toward the spatial y' axis, as measured in a frame (the Other Frame) that is moving with speed $\beta = 0.50$ in the $+x$ direction of the Home Frame. What is the magnitude and direction of the particle's velocity in the Home Frame?

R8S.13 A train travels in the $+x$ direction with a speed of $\beta = 0.80$ with respect to the ground. At a certain time, two balls are ejected so that they travel with a speed of 0.60 (as measured in the train frame) in opposite directions *perpendicular* to the direction of motion of the train. **(a)** What are the speeds of the balls with respect to the ground? **(b)** What is the angle that the path of each ball makes with the x axis in the ground frame?

R8S.14 Show that when $\beta \ll 1$, the Lorentz transformation equations R6.11a and R6.11b reduce to the galilean transformation equations R1.2a and R1.2b. [*Discussion*: The problem is trivial except for equation R6.11a. In that equation, how can we justify dropping the βx term when we need to keep the $-\beta t$ term in R6.11b? Think about typical magnitudes of quantities in an everyday experiment.]

RICH-CONTEXT

R8R.1 It is the year 2048, and you are on the jury in a terrorism trial. The facts of the case are these. On June 12, 2047 at 2:25:06 p.m. GMT, the earth/Mars shuttle *Ares* exploded as it was being refueled in low earth orbit. (Fortunately, no passengers were aboard, and the refueling was handled by robots.) At 2:27:18 p.m., police videoCD a raid on a hotel room on Mars conducted on the basis of an unrelated anonymous tip. In the video, the defendant is shown with a radio control transmitter in hand. Forensic experts have testified that the *Ares* was blown up by remote control, and that the reconstructed receiver was consistent with the transmitter in the defendant's possession. Just before the explosion, a caller predicted the blast and took responsibility on behalf of the Arean Liberation Army; the defendant has known links to that organization. Phone records show that the defendant spoke with someone near the earth less than ten minutes before. Hall monitors in the hotel showed that the defendant entered the hotel room at 2:23:12 p.m., and was not carrying the transmitter at that time. The defendant has taken the Fifth Amendment and has offered no defense other than a plea of not guilty. A fragment of the trial transcript follows.

Prosecutor: The time shown at the bottom of the video sequence taken of the raid, is that from a clock internal to the camera?

Police witness: No, I am told that that time is computed from signals originating from the master clock on earth that is part of the Solar System Positioning System (SSPS) that defines a solar-system-wide inertial frame fixed on the sun. According to the manual (*pulls out the manual*), "The signal from the earth master clock is suitably corrected in the camera for the motions of the earth and Mars and the light travel time from the earth, so that the time displayed is exactly as if it were from clock at the camera's location, at rest in the solar system frame, and synchronized with the earth-based master clock." We do this deliberately so as to be able to correlate events on a solar-system-wide basis.

Prosecutor: There is no chance that *this* time (*freezes video display*), which shows the police yanking the device from defendant here at exactly 2:27:20 p.m. GMT, is in error?

Police witness: No, the camera was checked two days previously as part of a normal maintenance program.

Prosecutor: We have been told that the *Ares* blew up at exactly 2:25:06 p.m. GMT. Was that time determined using the SSPS also?

Police witness: Yes.

Prosecutor: You have testified that the hall monitors show the defendent entering the room at exactly 2:23:12 p.m. This time is also determined using the SPSS?

Police witness: Yes.

Prosecutor: So, the defendant was alone in the room at the time that the Ares exploded.

Police witness: Yes, in the SPSS frame.

Prosecutor: So this videoCD shows you capturing the defendant red-handed just after blowing up the *Ares,* with the incriminating transmitter still in hand...

Defense: Objection, your Honor!

Judge: Sustained.

Guilty or not guilty? Write a paragraph justifying your reasoning very carefully.

R8R.2 A spaceship travels at a speed of $\beta = 0.90$ along a straight-line path that passes 300 km from a small asteroid. Exactly 1.0 ms (in the asteroid frame) in time before reaching the point of closest approach, the ship fires a photon torpedo which travels at the speed of light. This torpedo is fired perpendicular to the ship's direction of travel (as measured in the ship's frame) on the side closest to the asteroid. Will this torpedo hit the asteroid? If not, does it pass the asteroid on the near side or far side (relative to the ship)? Carefully explain your reasoning.

ADVANCED

R8A.1 Imagine that in its own reference frame, an object emits light uniformly in all directions. Imagine also that this object moves with a speed β in the $+x$ direction with respect to the Home Frame. Show that the half of the light that is emitted anywhere in the forward hemisphere in the object's own frame is in the Home Frame observed to be concentrated in a cone that makes an angle of

$$\phi = \sin^{-1}\frac{1}{\gamma} \qquad (R8.15)$$

with respect to the x axis. Show that if $\beta = 0.99$, the angle where half the object's light is concentrated is only 8.1°. (This forward concentration of the radiation emitted by a moving object is called the *headlight effect*.)

R8A.2 Consider a very long pair of scissors. If you close the scissor blades fast enough, you might imagine that you could cause the *intersection* of the scissor blades (i.e. the point where they cut the paper) to travel from the near end of the scissors to the far end at a speed faster than that of light, without causing any *material part* of the scissors to exceed the speed of light. Argue that (1) this intersection can indeed travel faster than the speed of light in principle, but that (2) if the scissors are originally at open and at rest and you decide to send a *message* to a person at the other end of your scissors by suddenly closing them, you will find that the intersection (and thus the message) *cannot* travel faster than the speed of light. [*Hint*: The information that the handles have begun to close must travel through the metal from the handles to the blades and then down the blades to cause the intersection to move forward. What effect carries this information? With what speed does this information travel?]*

---

*See M. A. Rothman, "Things that Go Faster than Light," *Sci. Am.* **203**: 142, July 1960.

ANSWERS TO EXERCISES

R8X.1 Let us take event P to be the origin event in the Home Frame. Now, consider Figure R8.3. For event Q to occur below the x' axis in the Other Frame, the x' axis must have a slope greater than that of the worldline of the causal influence connecting events P and Q. If the causal influence moves at a speed of 3, then its slope on a two-observer diagram like Figure R8.3 will be 1/3. The slope of the Other Frame x' axis must be therefore greater than 1/3. Since the slope of this axis is equal to β, the speed at which the Other Frame moves with respect to the Home Frame, the speed of the Other Frame must be greater than 1/3.

R8X.2 The spacetime interval between A and B is timelike, between A and C is lightlike, and between A and D is spacelike. The interval between B and C is spacelike. The interval between D and B is spacelike, but the interval between D and C is timelike.

R8X.3 Let event A be the origin event in the Home Frame. If we look at Figure R8.5, we see that if A and B are to be simultaneous in the Other Frame, the x' axis in the Other Frame has to go through both A and B, and so has to have slope of 3/5 in this case (since B occurs 5 units to the right and 3 units above the origin in the two-observer diagram). Since the slope of this axis is equal to the speed β of the Other Frame with respect to the Home Frame, we see that this speed must be $\beta = 3/5$. Since the spacetime interval between the events must have the same value in all frames and since $\Delta t' = 0$ by definition in the Other Frame, the squared distance $\Delta d'^2$ between A and B in that frame is:

$$\Delta d'^2 = \Delta d'^2 - \Delta t'^2 = -\Delta s^2$$
$$= \Delta d^2 - \Delta t^2 = (5\text{ ns})^2 - (3\text{ ns})^2 = (25-9)\text{ ns}^2$$
$$= 16\text{ ns}^2 = (4\text{ ns})^2 \qquad (R8.16)$$

So $\Delta d' = 4$ ns.

R8X.4 The distance to the moon in seconds is

$$384{,}000\text{ km}\left(\frac{1\text{ s}}{300{,}000\text{ km}}\right) = 1.28\text{ s} \qquad (R8.17)$$

Since $\Delta d > \Delta t$ in this case, the spacetime interval between the events is spacelike. Thus the events cannot be causally connected in any way.

R8X.5 According to the inverse Lorentz transformation equations, we have:

$$v_y = \frac{dy}{dt} = \frac{dy'}{\gamma(dt' + \beta dx')} = \frac{dy'/dt'}{\gamma(1 + \beta[dx'/dt'])}$$
$$= \frac{v_y'}{\gamma(1 + \beta v_x')} = \frac{v_y'\sqrt{1-\beta^2}}{(1 + \beta v_x')} \qquad (R8.18)$$

R8X.6 According to the direct Lorentz transformation equations, we have:

$$v_x' = \frac{dx'}{dt'} = \frac{\gamma(-\beta dt + dx)}{\gamma(dt - \beta dx)} = \frac{-\beta dt + dx}{dt - \beta dx}$$
$$= \frac{-\beta + (dx/dt)}{1 - \beta(dx/dt)} = \frac{-\beta + v_x}{1 - \beta v_x} = \frac{v_x - \beta}{1 - \beta v_x} \qquad (R8.19)$$

R8X.7 Our aim here is to convert a velocity in the Home Frame to a velocity in the Other Frame, so we want to use the direct Einstein velocity transformation equations. The problem implies that $v_x = 0.80 = 4/5$ and $\beta = 0.60 = 3/5$, so according to equation R8.14a, we have

$$v_x' = \frac{v_x - \beta}{1 - \beta v_x} = \frac{4/5 - 3/5}{1 - \frac{3}{5}\frac{4}{5}} = \frac{1/5}{13/25} = \frac{5}{13} \qquad (R8.20)$$

which is about 0.38 (much larger than the $1/5 = 0.20$ that we would have expected from the galilean equations).

FOUR-MOMENTUM

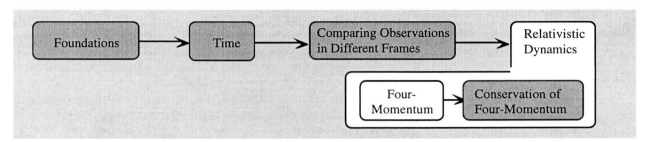

As soon as an equation seemed to him to be ugly, [Einstein] rather lost interest in it and could not understand why someone else was willing to spend much time on it. He was quite convinced that beauty was a guiding principle in the search for important results in theoretical physics.

H. Bondi*

R9.1 OVERVIEW

Up to this point, we have been studying **relativistic kinematics** (*kinematics* is the study of how the motion of objects is to be measured and described mathematically). But physicists are not only interested in *describing* motion: they are interested in explaining how objects interact and how the forces that they exert on each other *determine* their motion. The study of interactions between objects is called *dynamics*. In the remainder of this book, we will explore the basic principles of **relativistic dynamics**.

As we saw in unit *C*, the core of any theory of mechanics are the laws of conservation of momentum and energy. In this chapter, we will see how to make these laws consistent with the principle of relativity, combining both laws into a single law, which we call *conservation of four-momentum*. Chapter R10 then explores some of the implications of conservation of four-momentum.

Here is an overview of this chapter's sections.

R9.2 *A PLAN OF ACTION* provides an overview of how we make the law of conservation of momentum consistent with the principle of relativity.

R9.3 *CONSERVATION OF NEWTONIAN MOMENTUM IS NOT FRAME-INDEPENDENT* shows that the newtonian version of the law of conservation of momentum is inconsistent with the principle of relativity.

R9.4 *THE FOUR-MOMENTUM VECTOR* proposes a slight modification of the definition of momentum that reduces to the old definition at low speeds but is more natural in the context of relativity.

R9.5 *PROPERTIES OF FOUR-MOMENTUM* highlights some of the nice features of the four-momentum vector.

R9.6 *FOUR-MOMENTUM AND RELATIVITY* proves that a law of conservation of four-momentum *is* consistent with the principle of relativity.

R9.7 *FOUR-MOMENTUM'S TIME COMPONENT* describes how we can see that the conserved fourth component of the four-momentum vector is the relativistic generalization of the idea of energy.

R9.8 *THE SPATIAL PART OF FOUR-MOMENTUM* shows how the spatial part of a particle's four-momentum is linked to its mass and energy.

---

*Quoted in A. P. French, ed., *Einstein: A Centenary Volume,* Cambridge, Mass.: Harvard, 1979, p. 79.

R9.2 A PLAN OF ACTION

The laws of newtonian physics are not consistent with relativity

The basic principles of newtonian dynamics are expressed by Newton's famous three laws of motion. In section R1.7 (see also Problems R1S.6 through R1S.8), we saw that the laws of newtonian dynamics were consistent with the principle of relativity *if* the galilean velocity transformation equations (equations R1.2) are true. But as we saw in Chapter R8, the galilean velocity transformation equations are *not* true: they only represent the low-velocity limit of the relativistically correct Einstein velocity transformations (equation R8.14). *This means that the laws of newtonian dynamics are NOT generally consistent with the principle of relativity;* the laws of newtonian dynamics likewise represent only low-velocity approximations to the laws of *relativistic* dynamics, laws that are the same in *all* inertial frames (as the principle of relativity requires).

Well, what are these laws of relativistic dynamics, and how can we find them? We *could* address this question by searching for a relativistic generalization of Newton's second law, then Newton's third law, then the law of universal gravitation and so on. But it turns out that trying to do this is trickier than it looks, and the result is often ugly equations that are not really very illuminating.

To find a relativistic dynamics, we start with conservation of momentum

Things work much better if we instead start with the more basic law of *conservation of momentum* (which lies at the foundation of *any* theory of mechanics) and make this law consistent with the principle of relativity first. Not only is the correct adaptation of this law fairly easy to find, but it proves to be very illuminating and rich in implications and applications. Indeed, virtually everything that is useful to know about relativistic dynamics can be learned by a close examination of the law of conservation of momentum.

Overview of the argument to be found in this chapter

The basic argument in this chapter can be outlined as follows.

1. First, I will show you that conservation of newtonian momentum is *not* consistent with the principle of relativity: if an isolated system's total newtonian momentum is conserved in one inertial frame, it is *not* conserved in other frames. This means that we need to redefine momentum so that its conservation law *is* consistent with the principle of relativity.

2. I will then propose a natural relativistic generalization of the idea of momentum called *four-momentum*, which is a *four*-component vector having a time component as well as the usual *x*, *y*, and *z* components.

3. I will then show you that the law of conservation of *four*-momentum *is* consistent with the principle of relativity, and thus represents a reasonable relativistic realization of the law of conservation of momentum. But for this to be true, the *t* component of a system's total four-momentum must *also* be conserved along with its *x*, *y*, and *z* components. So the law of conservation of four-momentum not only makes the idea of conservation of momentum consistent with the principle of relativity, it tells us that something *else* is conserved as well.

4. This fourth conserved quantity turns out to be a relativistic version of the concept of *energy*. Thus the law of conservation of four-momentum actually *unifies* two of the great conservation laws discussed in unit *C*.

R9.3 CONSERVATION OF NEWTONIAN MOMENTUM IS NOT FRAME-INDEPENDENT

In this section, I will show you that the law of conservation of newtonian momentum is *not* consistent with the principle of relativity and thus cannot be a valid law of physics as stated. To illustrate the problem, it is sufficient to demonstrate a single instance of the inconsistency. For the sake of simplicity, I will illustrate the difficulty with the ordinary newtonian definition of momentum using a simple one-dimensional collision.

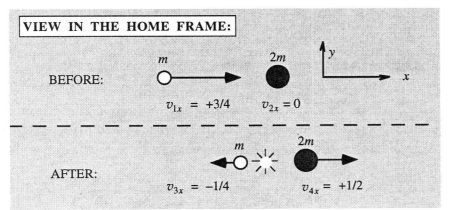

Figure R9.1: A hypothetical collision of two particles as observed in the Home Frame. The total newtonian momentum of this isolated system is conserved in this frame.

Figure R9.1 shows such a collision as observed in the Home Frame. In this frame, an object with mass m is moving in the $+x$ direction with an x-velocity $v_{1x} = +3/4$. It then strikes an object of mass $2m$ at rest ($v_{2x} = 0$). The lighter mass rebounds from the collision with an x-velocity of $v_{3x} = -1/4$, while the heavier object rebounds with an x-velocity of $v_{4x} = +1/2$. Consider the system to be isolated from external effects.

A hypothetical collision

The system's total newtonian x-momentum *is* conserved in the Home Frame in this case for the collision as described:

Newtonian momentum is conserved in the Home Frame for this collision

Total x-momentum before: $mv_{1x} + 2mv_{2x} = m(+\frac{3}{4}) + 2m(0) = +\frac{3}{4}m$ (R9.1a)

Total x-momentum after: $mv_{3x} + 2mv_{4x} = m(-\frac{1}{4}) + 2m(+\frac{1}{2}) = +\frac{3}{4}m$ (R9.1b)

Now consider how this collision looks when observed in an Other Frame that is moving with a speed $\beta = 3/4$ in the $+x$ direction. Since this frame essentially moves along with the lightweight particle, that particle appears to be at rest in the Other Frame: $v'_{1x} = 0$. Since the larger particle is at rest in the Home Frame, and the Home Frame is observed to be moving backward with respect to the Other Frame at a speed of 3/4, the x-velocity of the more massive object must also be $v'_{2x} = -3/4$ as well. The particles' final x-velocities are not so easy to intuit: we need to compute these velocities using the Einstein velocity transformation equation R8.14a:

How the collision looks in the Other Frame

$$v'_{3x} = \frac{v_{3x} - \beta}{1 - \beta v_{3x}} = \frac{-1/4 - 3/4}{1 - (3/4)(-1/4)} = -\frac{16}{19}$$ (R9.2a)

Similarly, you can show that

$$v'_{4x} = -\frac{2}{5}$$ (R9.2b)

Exercise R9X.1: Verify equation R9.2b.

Note that these *must* be the object's final velocities if the Einstein velocity transformation equations are true and the collision actually occurs as described in the Home Frame. In Other Frame, then, the collision is shown in Figure R9.2.

In this frame, though, the system's total x-momentum is *not* conserved:

Newtonian momentum is *not* conserved in the Other Frame

Total x-momentum before: $mv'_{1x} + 2mv'_{2x} = m(0) + 2m(-\frac{3}{4}) = -\frac{3}{2}m$ (R9.3a)

Total x-momentum after: $mv_{3x} + 2mv_{4x} = m(-\frac{2}{5}) + 2m(-\frac{16}{19}) = -\frac{156}{95}m$ (R9.3b)

We can see that in this frame, the x-component of the system's total momentum is somewhat larger after the collision than it was before the collision, since $156/95 > 3/2$. The law of conservation of newtonian momentum therefore

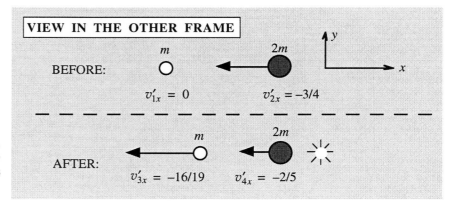

Figure R9.2: The same collision as observed in the Other Frame. Newtonian momentum is *not* conserved in this frame.

does *not* hold in the Other Frame, even though it did hold in the Home Frame. (Note that the law of conservation of momentum requires that *each* component of the system's total momentum be conserved separately, so a violation of the conservation of even *one* component, the *x*-component in this case, is a violation of the entire law.)

The principle of relativity requires that the laws of physics be the same in all inertial reference frames. The conclusion is inescapable: If the Einstein velocity transformation equations are true, then the law of conservation of newtonian momentum is *not* consistent with the principle of relativity.

The problem is the Einstein velocity transformation

Exercise R9X.2: It is important to understand that the root of the problem is the Einstein velocity transformation equations. Show that if the *galilean* velocity transformation equations (R1.3) were true (which they are *not*), newtonian momentum *would* be conserved in the Other Frame as well as the Home Frame.

R9.4 THE FOUR-MOMENTUM VECTOR

Review of the definition of newtonian momentum

In unit *C*, we defined an object's momentum $\vec{p}$ as *mass* times *velocity*:

$$\vec{p} \equiv m\vec{v} = m\frac{d\vec{r}}{dt} \tag{R9.4}$$

This is the *newtonian* definition of momentum, which we need to modify to make the law of conservation of momentum consistent with the principle of relativity. But *how* might we modify this definition? It helps to look at the newtonian definition very closely to try to understand its meaning.

The vector $d\vec{r}$ in equation R9.4 represents an infinitesimal displacement in space, which we divide by an infinitesimal time interval dt to get the object's velocity vector $\vec{v}$. The components of the infinitesimal displacement vector $d\vec{r}$ are $[dx, dy, dz]$, so the components of the newtonian momentum are:

$$p_x \equiv mv_x = m\frac{dx}{dt}, \quad p_y \equiv m\frac{dy}{dt}, \quad p_z = m\frac{dz}{dt} \tag{R9.5}$$

Notice that the momentum vector is *parallel* to the infinitesimal displacement $d\vec{r}$, and so will be tangent to the object's path through space (see Figure R9.3).

How we can revise this definition to make it more "relativistic"?

How can we arrive at a relativistic generalization of this process? In special relativity, space and time are considered to be equal parts of the unitary whole we call spacetime, so we describe the motion of an object not merely by describing its path through space but by describing its *worldline through spacetime*. The appropriate relativistic generalization of an "infinitesimal displacement in space" $d\vec{r}$ between two infinitesimally separated points on an object's path in space is a displacement $d\mathbf{R}$ in *spacetime* between two infinitesimally separated *events*

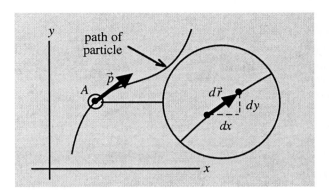

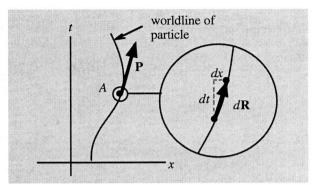

Figure R9.3: A graph showing the path of a particle through space. The particle's ordinary momentum $\vec{p}$ at point A is defined to be a vector parallel to the displacement $d\mathbf{r}$ that connects two infinitesimally separated points surrounding A.

Figure R9.4: A spacetime diagram showing the world-line of a particle through spacetime. The object's relativistic momentum **P** at event A is defined to be an arrow parallel to the displacement arrow $d\mathbf{R}$ that connects two infinitesimally separated events surrounding the event A. (The y and z dimensions are not shown here.)

on the object's *worldline* (see Figure R9.4). Note that the displacement $d\mathbf{R}$ in spacetime between two events is specified by *four* numbers:

$$d\mathbf{R} = [dt, dx, dy, dz] \qquad (R9.6)$$

Including the time-displacement dt on an equal footing with the spatial displacements dx, dy, dz makes the displacement $d\mathbf{R}$ a four-component vector that physicists call a **four-vector.** In this book, I will always use *boldface capital letters* (e.g. $d\mathbf{R}$, **P**, etc.) to represent such four-vectors.

Given the components $[dt, dx, dy, dz]$ of the displacement four-vector $d\mathbf{R}$ that stretches between two infinitesimally separated events on the worldline of our object, how do we define its relativistic momentum? By analogy with the newtonian momentum, we want to divide $d\mathbf{R}$ by a quantity that somehow represents the *time* between the two events, and then multiply by the object's mass. In newtonian mechanics, time is universal and absolute, so dividing by dt is unambiguous. The most important flaw in the definition of newtonian momentum from the *relativistic* viewpoint, however, is that time is *not* really universal and absolute, but depends on who does the observing. Why should time measured in one reference frame be chosen above time measured in any other frame?

Ah, but there *is* a special kind of time that one can measure between the events that has a frame-independent value and is uniquely related to the motion of the object in question: the infinitesimal proper time $d\tau$ between the events that would be measured by a clock traveling *with the object itself.* When you think about it, it makes a certain kind of sense to use the object's *own* time to characterize its momentum: only the object's own reference frame is uniquely and unambiguously linked to its motion.

Therefore our proposed relativistic generalization of an object's newtonian momentum $\vec{p}$ is the relativistic **four-momentum P**, defined as follows:

$$\mathbf{P} \equiv m\frac{d\mathbf{R}}{d\tau} \qquad (R9.7)$$

Definition of a particle's four-momentum vector

The four-momentum is thus a four-dimensional vector having components

$$[P_t, P_x, P_y, P_z] = [m\frac{dt}{d\tau}, m\frac{dx}{d\tau}, m\frac{dy}{d\tau}, m\frac{dz}{d\tau}] \qquad (R9.8)$$

Just as the newtonian momentum is a vector that is tangent to the object's *path* through space, the four-momentum (when drawn as an arrow on a spacetime diagram) is a vector tangent to the object's *worldline*, as shown in Figure R9.4.

Expressing the particle's four-momentum in terms of its mass and velocity

We can express the components of the four-momentum in a given inertial frame in terms of the object's ordinary velocity measured in that frame. Equation R5.5 tells us that the proper time between two infinitesimally separated events measured by a clock traveling between two events at a speed v in a given inertial frame is related to the coordinate time dt measured between those events by:

$$d\tau = \sqrt{1 - v^2}\, dt \tag{R9.9}$$

This means that

$$P_t \equiv m\frac{dt}{d\tau} = \frac{m}{\sqrt{1-v^2}}\frac{dt}{dt} = \frac{m}{\sqrt{1-v^2}} \tag{R9.10a}$$

$$P_x \equiv m\frac{dx}{d\tau} = \frac{m}{\sqrt{1-v^2}}\frac{dx}{dt} = \frac{mv_x}{\sqrt{1-v^2}} \tag{R9.10b}$$

$$P_y \equiv m\frac{dy}{d\tau} = \frac{m}{\sqrt{1-v^2}}\frac{dy}{dt} = \frac{mv_y}{\sqrt{1-v^2}} \tag{R9.10c}$$

$$P_z \equiv m\frac{dz}{d\tau} = \frac{m}{\sqrt{1-v^2}}\frac{dz}{dt} = \frac{mv_z}{\sqrt{1-v^2}} \tag{R9.10d}$$

These equations allow one to find the components of the four-momentum of an object in a given frame knowing the object's velocity vector $\vec{v}$ in that frame.

The low-velocity limit of the four-momentum components

When the speed v of an object becomes very small compared to the speed of light ($v \ll 1$), the square roots in the denominators in equations R9.10 become almost equal to 1, and we have:

$$P_t \approx m \tag{R9.11a}$$

$$P_x \approx mv_x \tag{R9.11b}$$

$$P_y \approx mv_y \tag{R9.11c}$$

$$P_z \approx mv_z \tag{R9.11d}$$

Thus in the limit where the velocity of an object is very small (as everyday velocities are), the spatial components of the four-momentum reduce to being the same as the corresponding components of the object's newtonian momentum.

Note also that since velocity in the SR unit system is unitless, all four components of an object's four-momentum have units of *mass* in SR units.

Exercise R9X.3: An object with a mass of 1. 0 kg moves with velocity of $[v_x, v_y, v_z] = [0,\ 4/5,\ 0]$ in the Home Frame. What are the components of its four-momentum in this frame? What are the components of its four-momentum in the frame where it is at rest?

R9.5 PROPERTIES OF FOUR-MOMENTUM

A particle's four-momentum vector is tangent to its worldline in spacetime...

Why define an object's relativistic four-momentum this way? The definition has several attractive features. One feature has already been mentioned: *on a spacetime diagram, the four-momentum is represented by an arrow tangent to the worldline of the object through spacetime*, just as the ordinary momentum vector is an arrow tangent to the path of the object through space.

...it puts space and time on an equal footing...

It is also nice that the definition of the four-momentum treats the time coordinate in the same manner as the spatial coordinates: all four coordinate displacements dt, dx, dy, dz appear on an equal footing in the definition of the four-momentum given by equations R9.8. We have already seen how it is important in relativity theory to treat time and space as being equal participants in the larger geometric whole that we call spacetime. The definition of four-momentum given above maintains this symmetry between the different spacetime coordinates.

All of this symmetry has a certain beauty about it which an intuitive physicist like Einstein might take as corroborating evidence that we are on the right track with this definition. But we will see that the most important feature of the four-momentum vector as defined is that it has a very simple transformation law: that is, given its components in one inertial frame, we can find its components in any other inertial frame in a straightforward manner.

...and has a very straightforward transformation law

The components of an object's four-momentum are *frame-dependent* quantities, because the values of the coordinate differences dt, dx, dy, dz that appear in the numerators of equations R9.8 are frame-dependent. The differential proper time $d\tau$ appearing in the denominator, on the other hand, is a *frame-independent* quantity. In this text, we will also consider the mass m of the object to be a *frame-independent* measure of the amount of "stuff" in the object.*

Let us imagine that we know the components $[P_t, P_x, P_y, P_z]$ of a given object's four-momentum in the Home Frame, and that we want to find the corresponding components in an Other Frame moving with speed β in the $+x$ direction with respect to the Home Frame. We can calculate the time component P_t' of the object's four-momentum in the Other Frame as follows:

$$P_t' = m\frac{dt'}{d\tau} = m\frac{\gamma(dt - \beta dx)}{d\tau} = \gamma m\frac{dt}{d\tau} - \gamma\beta m\frac{dx}{d\tau}$$
$$= \gamma P_t - \gamma\beta P_x = \gamma(P_t - \beta P_x) \qquad (R9.12a)$$

where I have used the Lorentz transformation (specifically equation R6.12a) to express dt' as measured in the Other Frame in terms of dt and dx as measured in the Home Frame. Similarly, you can show that the transformation equations for the four-momentum x-component is

$$P_x' = \gamma(-\beta P_t + P_x) \qquad (R9.12b)$$

We also have:

$$P_y' = m\frac{dy'}{d\tau} = m\frac{dy}{d\tau} = P_y \qquad (R9.12c)$$

$$P_z' = m\frac{dz'}{d\tau} = m\frac{dz}{d\tau} = P_z \qquad (R9.12d)$$

Exercise R9X.4: Verify that equation R9.12b is correct.

What is nice about these equations? Compare them with the Lorentz transformation equations given by equations R6.12. Equations R9.12 are the *same* as these Lorentz transformation equations except that the four-momentum components P_t, P_x, P_y, and P_z have been substituted for the coordinate displacement components Δt, Δx, Δy and Δz respectively. *Thus the components of the four-momentum transform from frame to frame according to the Lorentz transformation equations* just as coordinate differences do!

...which in fact have the same form as the Lorentz transformation equations

The transformation equations for the four-momentum come out so nicely because (1) the time coordinate appears on an equal footing with the spatial components in the definition of the four-momentum, (2) we have divided the displacement by the frame-independent differential proper time $d\tau$ instead of the frame-dependent differential coordinate time dt, and (3) we are considering the mass m to be a frame-independent quantity.

---

*You may have heard in another context that special relativity implies that the mass of an object depends on its velocity. This is an old-fashioned way of looking at mass that obscures some of the simplicity and beauty of relativity theory. See C.G. Adler, "Does Mass Really Depend on Velocity, Dad?", *Am. J. Phys.*, **55**(8), pp. 739-743, August 1987, for a careful and entertaining look at the problems with the old way of thinking about mass in relativity theory. Most modern treatments of relativity treat an object's mass as being frame-*independent*.

Formal definition of a four-vector quantity

In fact, the technical definition of a *four-vector* requires this kind of transformation law: physicists define a **four-vector** to be a physical quantity represented by a vector whose four components transform according to the Lorentz transformation equations (that is, just as the coordinate differences Δt, Δx, Δy, Δz do) when we go from one inertial reference frame to another.

The frame-independent four-magnitude of a four-vector

Now we know that although the coordinate differences Δt, Δx, Δy, Δz between two events are frame-*dependent* quantities, the spacetime interval Δs between the events given by:

$$\Delta s^2 = \Delta t^2 - \Delta x^2 - \Delta y^2 - \Delta z^2 \tag{R9.13}$$

has a frame-*independent* value. Similarly, we can define the frame-independent **four-magnitude** of a four-vector as follows: if a four-vector **A** has components $[A_t, A_x, A_y, A_z]$, then its squared four-magnitude is defined to be:

$$|\mathbf{A}|^2 \equiv A_t^2 - A_x^2 - A_y^2 - A_z^2 \tag{R9.14}$$

This is the relativistic analog to the definition (based on the pythagorean theorem) of the magnitude of an ordinary vector.

You can easily show that the four-magnitude of an object's four-momentum vector is equal to its frame-independent mass:

$$m = |\mathbf{P}| = \sqrt{P_t^2 - P_x^2 - P_y^2 - P_z^2} \tag{R9.15}$$

Exercise R9X.5: Verify that equation R9.15 is correct, using the fact that for infinitesimally separated events, there is no distinction between proper time and spacetime interval, so $d\tau = ds = [dt^2 - dx^2 - dy^2 - dz^2]^{1/2}$.

R9.6 FOUR-MOMENTUM AND RELATIVITY

We now have a suitable candidate for a relativistic generalization of the concept of momentum. The final step is to verify that a law of conservation of four-momentum is in fact consistent with the principle of relativity.

Proof that four-momentum is conserved in *all* inertial frames if it is in any one

Consider an arbitrary collision of two objects moving along the *x*-axis. The law of conservation of four-momentum says that:

$$\mathbf{P}_1 + \mathbf{P}_2 = \mathbf{P}_3 + \mathbf{P}_4 \tag{R9.16}$$

where $\mathbf{P}_1$ and $\mathbf{P}_2$ are the objects' four-momenta *before* the collision, and $\mathbf{P}_3$ and $\mathbf{P}_4$ are the objects' four-momenta *after*. We can usefully rewrite this as follows:

$$\mathbf{P}_1 + \mathbf{P}_2 - \mathbf{P}_3 - \mathbf{P}_4 = 0 \tag{R9.17}$$

which essentially says that the *difference* between the system's initial and final total momenta is zero. In component form, this last equation tells us that:

$$\begin{bmatrix} P_{1t} \\ P_{1x} \\ P_{1y} \\ P_{1z} \end{bmatrix} + \begin{bmatrix} P_{2t} \\ P_{2x} \\ P_{2y} \\ P_{2z} \end{bmatrix} - \begin{bmatrix} P_{3t} \\ P_{3x} \\ P_{3y} \\ P_{3z} \end{bmatrix} - \begin{bmatrix} P_{4t} \\ P_{4x} \\ P_{4y} \\ P_{4z} \end{bmatrix} = \begin{bmatrix} 0 \\ 0 \\ 0 \\ 0 \end{bmatrix} \quad \text{or} \quad \begin{matrix} P_{1t} + P_{2t} - P_{3t} - P_{4t} = 0 \\ P_{1x} + P_{2x} - P_{3x} - P_{4x} = 0 \\ P_{1y} + P_{2y} - P_{3y} - P_{4y} = 0 \\ P_{1z} + P_{2z} - P_{3z} - P_{4z} = 0 \end{matrix} \tag{R9.18}$$

When expressed in component form, the single equation R9.17 thus becomes a set of *four* equations, one for each of the four-momentum's four components. Each must be *independently* satisfied if four-momentum is to be conserved.

Let us assume that we have observed a collision in the Home Frame and we have determined that it satisfies the law of conservation of four-momentum in that frame. The principle of relativity requires that the same law apply in *every other* inertial reference frame, that is,

if $\mathbf{P}_1 + \mathbf{P}_2 - \mathbf{P}_3 - \mathbf{P}_4 = 0$ in the Home Frame

then $\mathbf{P}_1' + \mathbf{P}_2' - \mathbf{P}_3' - \mathbf{P}_4' = 0$ in any Other Frame   (R9.19)

If this statement is *not* true, our proposed relativistic generalization of the idea of momentum is not any better than newtonian momentum. If the statement *is* true, then the law of conservation of four-momentum represents at least a *possible* relativistic expression of the law of conservation of ordinary momentum.

We can in fact easily show that this is true for any collision as viewed in any Other inertial frame. Consider the x component of the conservation law in the Other Frame. According to the transformation law for the components of the four-momentum given by equation R9.12b:

$$P_{1x}' + P_{2x}' - P_{3x}' - P_{4x}' = \gamma(-\beta P_{1t} + P_{1x}) + \gamma(-\beta P_{2t} + P_{2x})$$
$$-\gamma(-\beta P_{3t} + P_{3x}) - \gamma(-\beta P_{4t} + P_{4x}) \qquad \text{(R9.20a)}$$

Collecting the terms on the right side of this equation that are multiplied by γ and those multiplied by $\gamma\beta$, we get:

$$P_{1x}' + P_{2x}' - P_{3x}' - P_{4x}' = -\gamma\beta(P_{1t} + P_{2t} - P_{3t} - P_{4t})$$
$$+\gamma(P_{1x} + P_{2x} - P_{3x} - P_{4x}) \qquad \text{(R9.20b)}$$

But if *both* the t and x components of the four-momentum are conserved in the Home Frame, then equations R9.18 tell us that the quantities in parentheses are equal to zero. This means that,

$$P_{1x}' + P_{2x}' - P_{3x}' - P_{4x}' = -\gamma\beta\,(0) + \gamma\,(0) = 0 \qquad \text{(R9.20c)}$$

So *if* both the t and x components of the system's total four-momentum are conserved in the Home Frame, then the x component of the system's total four-momentum will also be conserved in the Other Frame, as hoped.

Exercise R9X.6: In the same manner, verify that the t and y components of the four-momentum are conserved in the Other Frame if all components are conserved in the Home Frame.

What we have shown is that the law of conservation of four-momentum expressed by equation R9.17 is *consistent* with the principle of relativity in the sense that if it holds in one frame it holds in all. That does not make the law *true*: it simply makes it *possible*. But now let me argue for the *truth* of this law. (1) We know from a multitude of experiments at low velocities that *some* quantity that reduces to newtonian momentum at such velocities is conserved. (2) Conservation of *newtonian* momentum won't work: the law is inconsistent with the principle of relativity. (3) The hypothetical law of conservation of four-momentum *is* compatible with the principle of relativity. (4) The three spatial components of the four-momentum *do* reduce to the components of newtonian momentum at low velocities. (5) Therefore, if the law of conservation of four-momentum were true, it would both explain the low-velocity experimental data and maintain compatibility with the principle of relativity. Moreover, there must be some relativistically valid expression of the deep symmetry that gives rise to the principle of conservation of momentum. In the absence of compelling alternatives, it only makes *sense* to believe that it is the total four-momentum of a system that is conserved.

Of course, no matter how suggestive a theoretical argument might be, there is no substitute for direct experimental evidence. Since the 1950s, physicists have been using particle accelerators to create beams of subatomic particles

Thus conservation of four-momentum is consistent with the principle of relativity, but is it true?

Abundant experimental evidence suggests that it is

traveling at speeds very near the speed of light and colliding them with stationary targets or other particle beams. At such speeds, the distinction between newtonian momentum and four-momentum is very clear, and analysis of a typical experiment involves applying conservation of four-momentum to anywhere from thousands and to millions of particle collisions. The result is that conservation of four-momentum is implicitly tested thousands of times daily in the course of such research. In spite of this enormous wealth of data, no compelling evidence of a violation of the law of conservation of four-momentum has ever been seen.

R9.7 FOUR-MOMENTUM'S TIME COMPONENT

What is the interpretation of the fourth conserved quantity P_t?

Equations R9.20b and R9.20c make it clear that conservation of four-momentum is *only* consistent with the principle of relativity if all *four* components of the four-momentum (P_t as well as P_x, P_y, and P_z) are independently conserved. The three *spatial* components of an object's four-momentum correspond (at low velocities) to the three components of its newtonian momentum. What is the physical interpretation of the additional conserved quantity P_t?

Examination of meaning at low velocities suggests that P_t is related to energy

According to equation R9.10a, P_t for an object with mass m, as measured in a frame where the object moves with speed v, is given by the expression:

$$P_t = \frac{m}{\sqrt{1-v^2}} \qquad (R9.21)$$

We know that this reduces to the object's mass m at low velocities, but is not exactly equal to the mass. The binomial approximation (equation R5.17) says that when $x \ll 1$, $[1+x]^a \approx 1+ax$. Therefore, when $v \ll 1$

$$P_t = \frac{m}{\sqrt{1-v^2}} = m[1-v^2]^{-1/2} \approx m[1-(-\tfrac{1}{2})v^2] = m + \tfrac{1}{2}mv^2 \qquad (R9.22)$$

The first term here is the mass of the particle, and when v is zero, that is what P_t becomes. But when v is nonzero but still very small, we have an additional term in P_t that corresponds to the *kinetic energy* of the particle. If P_t is conserved in a collision at low velocities, what we are saying is that the sum of the particles' masses plus the sum of their kinetic energies is conserved. If the particles' masses remain unchanged in the collision, then conservation of P_t tells us that the kinetic energy of the particles is conserved.

Thus conservation of P_t is (at low velocities) basically the same as conservation of newtonian [kinetic] energy! As we have already generalized the concept of momentum, so now we will generalize the concept of energy. We *define* the component P_t of a particle's four-momentum to be that particle's *relativistic energy E*, and assert that it is this relativistic energy that is the fourth quantity that is conserved in an isolated system. So, the relativistic energy E of an object moving at a speed v as measured in a given inertial frame is

Definition of relativistic energy

$$E \equiv P_t = \frac{m}{\sqrt{1-v^2}} \qquad (R9.23)$$

Note that if the object's speed v is an appreciable fraction of the speed of light, equation R9.22 does not hold. An object's *relativistic kinetic energy* is defined (for all v) to be the difference between the object's total relativistic energy E and its mass-energy m:

Definition of relativistic kinetic energy

$$K \equiv E - m = \frac{m}{\sqrt{1-v^2}} - m = m\left(\frac{1}{\sqrt{1-v^2}} - 1\right) \qquad (R9.24)$$

The relativistic kinetic energy K becomes approximately equal to $\tfrac{1}{2}mv^2$ only for small values of v: in general, $K > \tfrac{1}{2}mv^2$.

In newtonian mechanics, we thought of conservation of energy and momentum as separate concepts. But just as special relativity binds space and time into a single geometry, so here it binds the laws of conservation of momentum and energy into a single statement: *the total four-momentum of an isolated system of particles is conserved.* Conservation of energy is impossible without conservation of momentum and vice versa: in the theory of relativity, energy and momentum are indissolvably bound together as parts of the same whole.

Note, however, that the relativistic energy of an object is not just the kinetic energy of that object (even at low velocities), but includes the *mass* of the object as well. The fact that $E = P_t$ is conserved does *not* imply that a system's total mass and its total kinetic energy are *separately* conserved: only that the *whole* (that is, the relativistic energy) is conserved. This implies that *processes that convert mass to kinetic energy, and vice versa, do not necessarily violate the law of conservation of four-momentum,* and therefore might exist. We will more fully explore this subject in the next chapter.

Equation R9.22 is expressed in SR units, where velocity is unitless and both kinetic energy and mass are measured in kilograms. If we want to to express a particle's relativistic energy in the SI unit of joules = kg·m²/s², we must multiply the energy in kilograms by two powers of the spacetime conversion factor $c = 2.998 \times 10^8$ m/s to get the units to come out right. Therefore, equation R9.22 in SI units would read:

$$E \approx mc^2 + \tfrac{1}{2}mv^2 \quad \text{when } v^2 \ll c^2 \quad \text{(SI units)} \qquad \text{(R9.25)}$$

In particular, when the particle is at rest, its relativistic energy in SI units is:

$$E_{rest} = mc^2 \qquad \text{(R9.26)}$$

This is the famous equation that has served as an icon representing both the essence of special relativity and also Einstein's achievement. This equation really is just a special case of the more general equation R9.23. Even so, it does focus our attention on the startling new idea implicit in R9.23: *an object at rest has relativistic energy simply by virtue of its mass*, and that this mass-energy is a part of the total energy conserved by interactions inside an isolated system.

Exercise R9X.7: A rock whose mass is 1.0 kg is moving in the $-z$ direction with a speed of 0.80. What is its relativistic energy E? Its relativistic kinetic energy K? (Express both results in kilograms and joules.)

R9.8 THE SPATIAL PART OF FOUR-MOMENTUM

Just as special relativity teaches us that time and space are but different aspects of spacetime, we now see that energy and momentum are but different aspects of four-momentum. The fact remains, however, that just as we experience time and space very differently, so we experience energy and momentum differently. It is often convenient, therefore, to split a particle's four-momentum into time and space components.

We have seen (equation R9.11) that at low velocities the spatial components of an object's four-momentum vector P_x, P_y, and P_z become approximately equal to the components of that object's newtonian momentum vector $\vec{p}$. Thus, they represent as close a relativistic analog to $\vec{p}$ that we have. We therefore call the three-dimensional vector $[P_x, P_y, P_z]$ the object's **relativistic three-momentum** (to distinguish it from its four-momentum). More often, we are interested in the simple vector magnitude of these three components, which we will call simply the particle's **relativistic momentum** p:

$$p \equiv \sqrt{P_x^{\,2} + P_y^{\,2} + P_z^{\,2}} \qquad \text{(R9.27)}$$

Conservation of four-momentum thus unifies newtonian conservation of energy and momentum

Processes that convert rest-energy (mass) to kinetic energy are possible

Converting SR units for energy into SI units

(The most famous equation of special relativity)

It is often helpful to split four-momentum into space and time components

Definition of relativistic momentum

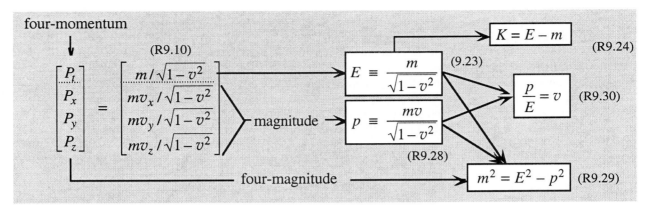

Figure R9.5: (Virtually) everything that you need to know about four-momentum.

The relativistic momentum p is thus the relativistic generalization of the *magnitude* of an object's newtonian momentum vector.

With the help of equations R9.10, we can express an object's relativistic momentum in terms of its mass m and speed v as follows:

$$p = \sqrt{\left(\frac{mv_x}{\sqrt{1-v^2}}\right)^2 + \left(\frac{mv_y}{\sqrt{1-v^2}}\right)^2 + \left(\frac{mv_z}{\sqrt{1-v^2}}\right)^2} = \frac{m\sqrt{v_x^2 + v_y^2 + v_z^2}}{\sqrt{1-v^2}} = \frac{mv}{\sqrt{1-v^2}} \quad \text{(R9.28)}$$

Note that p does indeed become approximately equal to the magnitude mv of the object's newtonian momentum when v is very much smaller than 1.

We can write equation R9.15, which shows how an object's frame-independent mass can be computed using the frame-dependent components of its four-momentum, in terms of E and p as follows:

$$m^2 = P_t^2 - (P_x^2 + P_y^2 + P_z^2) = E^2 - p^2 \quad \text{(R9.29)}$$

We can also use an object's relativistic energy E and relativistic momentum p in a given frame to determine the object's speed in that frame:

$$\frac{p}{E} = \frac{mv/\sqrt{1-v^2}}{m/\sqrt{1-v^2}} = v \quad \text{(R9.30)}$$

This relationship applies to each individual spatial component as well:

$$\frac{P_x}{E} = \frac{mv_x}{\sqrt{1-v^2}}\frac{\sqrt{1-v^2}}{m} = v_x; \quad \text{similarly}: \quad \frac{P_y}{E} = v_y, \quad \frac{P_z}{E} = v_z \quad \text{(R9.31)}$$

Indeed, the spatial components of the four-momentum can be thought of as expressing the rate at which relativistic energy is transported through space:

$$\begin{bmatrix} P_t \\ P_x \\ P_y \\ P_z \end{bmatrix} = \begin{bmatrix} m/\sqrt{1-v^2} \\ mv_x/\sqrt{1-v^2} \\ mv_y/\sqrt{1-v^2} \\ mv_z/\sqrt{1-v^2} \end{bmatrix} = \begin{bmatrix} E \\ Ev_x \\ Ev_y \\ Ev_z \end{bmatrix} \quad \text{(R9.32)}$$

Equations R9.23, R9.24, R9.28, R9.29, and R9.30 express relationships between the quantities $E, p, m, K,$ and v that are really helpful to know when working with the four-momentum: they are summarized in Figure R9.5.

Useful relationships between E, p, and m

Exercise R9X.8: Consider the rock described in Exercise R9X.7. Find its relativistic momentum p and write down its four-momentum vector.

I. OVERVIEW OF THE ARGUMENT   **SUMMARY**
  A. Path to relativistic dynamics is easiest if we look at momentum first
  B. Plan of action: we will see that
    1. conservation of newtonian momentum contradicts relativity
    2. four-momentum is a natural relativistic redefinition of momentum
    3. conservation of four-momentum is consistent with relativity
    4. the conserved fourth component of four-momentum is energy

II. NEWTONIAN MOMENTUM IS NOT CONSERVED IN ALL FRAMES
  A. Analyzing an example collision: If we construct the collision so that
     momentum is conserved in the Home Frame and then calculate veloci-
     ties in Other Frame using Einstein velocity transformation equations,
     we find that momentum is *not* conserved in the Other Frame.
  B. The problem is the Einstein velocity transformation (momentum would
     be conserved in the Other Frame if galilean equations were true).

III. THE FOUR-MOMENTUM
  A. We define a particle's newtonian momentum to be $\vec{p} \equiv m\vec{v} = m\,d\vec{r}/dt$
    1. $d\vec{r}$ is an infinitesimal displacement $[dx, dy, dz]$ in space
    2. This means that $\vec{p}$ is tangent to the particle's path through space
    3. We don't have to worry about who measures the time in the de-
       nominator, because time is universal and absolute
  B. We define a particle's *four-momentum* to be $\mathbf{P} = m\,d\mathbf{R}/d\tau$, a 4D vector
    1. $d\mathbf{R}$ is an infinitesimal four-displacement $[dt,dx,dy,dz]$ in spacetime
    2. This means that $\mathbf{P}$ is tangent to particle's worldline in spacetime
    3. The frame-independent time $d\tau$ is the proper time measured in the
       particle's own frame (a frame uniquely associated with the particle)
  C. Implication: $[P_t, P_x, P_y, P_z] = [1-v^2]^{-1/2}[m, mv_x, mv_y, mv_z]$ (R9.10)
  D. When $v \ll 1$, $[P_x, P_y, P_z] \approx [mv_x, mv_y, mv_z]$ (R9.11)

IV. THE PROPERTIES OF THE FOUR-MOMENTUM VECTOR
  A. The transformation law for $[P_t, P_x, P_y, P_z]$ is the same as the Lorentz
     transformation, with P_t substituted for Δt, P_x for Δx, and so on.
  B. The invariant mass m = four-magnitude of $\mathbf{P}$: $m^2 = P_t^2 - P_x^2 - P_y^2 - P_z^2$

V. FOUR-MOMENTUM AND RELATIVITY
  A. Because of the nice properties of the four-momentum transformation
     law, if four-momentum is conserved in one frame, it is conserved in all
  B. This makes it *possible* for conservation of four-momentum to be true
  C. Conservation of four-momentum of an isolated system *is* in fact true!
    1. It is the most natural generalization of conservation of momentum
    2. It appropriately reduces to newtonian momentum at low speeds
    3. Most importantly, it is amply supported by experiment

VI. THE TIME COMPONENT OF FOUR-MOMENTUM
  A. Conservation of four-momentum only works if P_t is also conserved
  B. In the low-speed limit, $P_t \approx m + \frac{1}{2}mv^2$, so conservation of P_t implies
     that the total particle mass + total kinetic energy of system is conserved
  C. Conservation of P_t is thus a generalization of conservation of energy
    1. Define $E \equiv P_t = m[1-v^2]^{1/2}$ = *relativistic energy*   (R9.23)
    2. Define $K \equiv E-m$ = *relativistic kinetic energy*   (R9.24)
  D. A particle has relativistic energy even when it is at rest: $E_{rest} = m$
    1. This mass-energy can be converted into other forms of energy
    2. In SI units, this equation reads $E_{rest} = mc^2$ (R9.26)

VII. THE SPATIAL PART OF FOUR-MOMENTUM
  A. We experience energy and momentum differently, so it is helpful
     sometimes to split the four-momentum vector into parts
  B. Define *relativistic momentum* $p \equiv [P_x^2 + P_y^2 + P_z^2]^{1/2}$ (R9.27)
  C. Figure R9.5 summarizes relationships between E, m, p, and v.

GLOSSARY

kinematics: the study of how the motion of objects is to be measured and described mathematically.

dynamics: the study of how the interactions between objects affect and determine their motion.

newtonian momentum $\vec{p}$: the three-dimensional momentum vector we defined in Unit C: $\vec{p} \equiv m\vec{v}$. This kind of momentum is not consistent with the principle of relativity, because if a collision conserves newtonian momentum in one inertial frame, it will not in another.

four-vector: a vector $\mathbf{A} = [A_t, A_x, A_y, A_z]$ with four components that (when one changes inertial frame) transform according to the Lorentz transformation equations, that is, like the components of the **four-displacement** four-vector $\Delta\mathbf{R} = [\Delta t, \Delta x, \Delta y, \Delta z]$. (We will always use bold capital letters for four-vectors in this text.)

four-momentum (of a particle) **P**: the four-vector defined by $\mathbf{P} \equiv m(d\mathbf{R}/d\tau)$, where m is the particle's invariant mass, $d\mathbf{R}$ is an infinitesimal four-displacement along the particle's worldline, and $d\tau$ is the proper time for that displacement measured along the particle's worldline. The spatial components $[P_x, P_y, P_z]$ of the four-momentum become equivalent to the components of newtonian momentum at low speeds, but conservation of four-momentum *is* consistent with the principle of relativity and in fact is amply supported by experiment.

four-magnitude (of a four-vector): the quantity found by subtracting the squares of the four-vector's spatial components from the square of its time component and taking the square root: $|\mathbf{A}| \equiv [A_t^2 - A_x^2 - A_y^2 - A_z^2]^{1/2}$. The four-magnitude of a four-displacement between two events is the spacetime interval between them. The four-magnitude of a particle's four-momentum is its frame-independent mass m.

relativistic energy (of a particle) E: the time component of the particle's four-momentum (which must be conserved along with the spatial components if the principle of relativity is to be consistent with conservation of four-momentum): $E \equiv P_t = m/[1 - v^2]^{1/2}$.

rest-energy (also called **mass-energy**): the relativistic energy $E_{rest} = m$ that a particle has when at rest.

relativistic kinetic energy K: the difference between a particle's relativistic energy E and its rest-energy: $K \equiv E - m$ (this is the part of the particle's relativistic that is due to its motion). At low speeds, $K \approx \frac{1}{2}mv^2$.

relativistic three-momentum: the spatial components of a particle's four-momentum vector. These components define a three-dimensional vector that reduces to the particle's newtonian momentum at low velocities.

relativistic momentum p: the magnitude of the spatial components of the particle's four-momentum vector: $p \equiv [P_x^2 + P_y^2 + P_z^2]^{1/2}$.

TWO-MINUTE PROBLEMS

R9T.1 A particle's newtonian x-momentum p_x is always *smaller* than the x component of its four-momentum P_x (T or F).

R9T.2 A particle's mass is always smaller than the time-component of its four-momentum. (T or F).

R9T.3 The absolute value of the x component of a particle's four-momentum vector is always smaller than its t component (T or F).

R9T.4 The squared magnitude of a four-vector could be negative (T or F). The squared magnitude of a particle's four-momentum could be negative (T or F).

R9T.5 Is a particle's relativistic kinetic energy always bigger than its newtonian kinetic energy (or does this depend on the particle's speed)?
A. $K > \frac{1}{2}mv^2$ B. $K < \frac{1}{2}mv^2$ C. depends on v

R9T.6 The components of a particle's four-momentum are the same in all inertial reference frames (T or F).

R9T.7 Imagine that a particle has a four-momentum vector whose components are $[P_t, P_x, P_y, P_z] = [5\text{ kg}, 3\text{ kg}, 0, 0]$. What is the mass of this particle?
A. 5 kg   C. 4 kg   E. $\sqrt{34}$
B. 8 kg   D. 3 kg   F. other (specify)

R9T.8 A dust particle has a rest energy (mass) of 1.0 μg. In joules, this rest energy is closer to
A. 10^{17} J   C. 10^8 J   E. 10^{-23}
B. 10^{11} J   D. 10^{-3} J   F. other (specify)

R9T.9 As a particle's speed approaches that of light, the difference between its relativistic momentum p and its relativistic energy E becomes small (compared to E) (T or F).

R9T.10 The mass of a particle is the same in all inertial reference frames (even though its speed is not) (T or F).

HOMEWORK PROBLEMS

BASIC SKILLS

R9B.1 A 2.0-kg object moves with a speed of 0.60 in the +x direction. Find the components of the object's four-momentum.

R9B.2 An alien spaceship with a mass of 12,000 kg is traveling in the solar-system frame at a speed of 0.80 in the $-z$ direction. Find the components of the spaceship's four-momentum vector.

R9B.3 A 12-kg rock moves with a velocity whose components $[v_x, v_y, v_z] = [4/13, -3/13, 0]$ in a certain frame. Find the components of its four-momentum in that frame.

R9B.4 Imagine that an object of mass 5.0 kg is observed in a certain inertial frame to have velocity components of of $v_x = -0.866$, $v_y = v_z = 0$. Evaluate the following in that reference frame: (a) the object's total energy E, (b) its relativistic momentum p, (c) the spatial components of its four-momentum, and (d) its relativistic kinetic energy K.

R9B.5 An object is observed in a certain frame to have a four-momentum of $[P_t, P_x, P_y, P_z] = [5.0\text{ kg}, 4.0\text{ kg}, 0, 0]$. (a) Find the object's x-velocity in this frame. (b) Find the object's mass. (c) Find its kinetic energy in this frame. (d) Find its relativistic momentum in this frame.

R9B.6 An object is observed in a certain frame to have a four-momentum of $[P_t, P_x, P_y, P_z] = [13$ kg, -12 kg, $0, 0]$. (a) Find the object's x-velocity in this frame. (b) Find the object's mass. (c) Find its kinetic energy.

R9B.7 A particle is observed in a certain inertial frame to have a four-momentum vector whose components are $[P_t, P_x, P_y, P_z] = [18$ kg, 9.0 kg, 15 kg, 1.0 kg]. (a) Find the object's velocity (vector). (b) Find the object's speed. (c) Find the object's mass. (d) Find the object's relativistic momentum p. (e) Find the object's kinetic energy.

R9B.8 A particle's four-momentum in a given inertial frame is $[P_t, P_x, P_y, P_z] = [5.0$ kg, 3.0 kg, $0, 0]$. What is its four-momentum in an inertial frame that moves in the $+x$ direction at a speed of 0.60 relative to the first frame?

R9B.9 A particle's four-momentum in a given inertial frame is $[P_t, P_x, P_y, P_z] = [5.0$ kg, -3.0 kg, $0, 0]$. What is its four-momentum in an inertial frame that moves in the $+x$ direction at a speed of 0.80 relative to the first frame?

SYNTHETIC

R9S.1 Verify equation R9.15 by squaring the definitions of the four-momentum components given in equations R9.10 and combining as required.

R9S.2 Prove that in the limit as $v \rightarrow 1$, $E \approx p$. What speed is required for these quantities to be equal to within 1%?

R9S.3 While solving a problem, friend claims that a particle's four-momentum vector is given by $[P_t, P_x, P_y, P_z] = [-0.10$ kg, $2/5, -1/5, 0]$. Even without knowing the particulars of the problem, there are at least three things wrong with this four-vector as stated. What are they?

R9S.4 Imagine that dust particle of mass 2.0 µg is traveling at a speed of 4/5 in the xy plane at an angle of 30° clockwise from the x axis in a certain inertial reference frame. Evaluate the following in that frame: (a) the particle's relativistic energy E, (b) its relativistic momentum p, (c) its three spatial four-momentum components, and (d) its kinetic energy K (in joules).

R9S.5 A particle's mass is 1.0 µg, its kinetic energy is 2.0 µg, and it is moving in the $+y$ direction. Find its four-momentum vector.

R9S.6 One can do a correct relativistic transformation of velocities using the four-momentum transformation law. Consider a 1.0-kg object moving at a speed of 3/5 in the $+x$ direction in the Home Frame. What are the components of its four-momentum in this frame? Using the Lorentz transformation equations, find the components of this object's four-momentum in an Other Frame moving at a speed of 4/5 in the $+x$ direction relative to the Home Frame. Then use equation R9.30 to find the object's speed in that Other Frame. Check your result with the Einstein velocity transformation equations.

R9S.7 If electrical energy can be sold at about $0.03 per 10^6 joules (the approximate current price in Southern California) compute how much your rest energy is worth in dollars. That is, find the amount of money that your survivors could put in your memorial fund if there was a way to convert your mass entirely into electrical energy. (It is probably a good thing that this is not easy to do.)

R9S.8 If electrical energy costs about $0.03 per 10^6 J (the approximate current price in Southern California) and you have $1.5 million at your disposal to spend on energy to convert to kinetic energy, about how fast can you make a 1.0-g object travel?

R9S.9 In a number of problems in this text, we have blithely spoken about trains traveling at significant fractions of the speed of light. If electrical energy costs about $0.03 per 10^6 J (the approximate current price in Southern California), what would it cost to accelerate an electric train with a mass of about 100,000 kg to a speed of 3/5?

R9S.10 At non-relativistic speeds ($v << 1$), a particle's kinetic energy is $K \approx \frac{1}{2}mv^2 = (mv)^2/2m \approx p^2/2m$, so we have $p \approx [2mK]^{1/2}$. Show that the exact relativistic expression for the particle's relativistic momentum p in terms of its relativistic kinetic energy K is

$$p = \sqrt{K(K+2m)} \qquad (R9.33)$$

and argue that at low speeds, this reduces to $p \approx [2mK]^{1/2}$.

RICH-CONTEXT

R9R.1 To compete with e-mail, imagine that the U.S. Postal Service now offers Super Express Mail, where a letter is sent to its destination at a speed of 0.999 using a special Letter Accelerator. Assume that a typical letter has a mass of about 25 g. What will be the minimum cost of the letter's stamp? If the letter misses its target and hits a nearby building, describe the consequences. [*Hint*: See problem R9S.8 for some useful information. It also may help you to know that a typical nuclear bomb releases on the order of magnitude of 5×10^{14} J of energy when it explodes.]

R9R.2 In this text we have blithely described people running at substantial fractions of the speed of light. Consider a runner that has somehow managed to accelerate to a speed of 3/5. Even assuming that this highly-trained athlete uses food energy very efficiently, describe the meal that the runner must have eaten before the race. (*Hint*: remember that one food calorie is 1000 physics calories, and each physics calorie is equivalent to the thermal energy required to raise the temperature of 1.0 g of water by 1°C = 4.186 J.)

R9R.3 A typical household might use about 2×10^{10} J of electrical energy per year. About one in every 5000 hydrogen atoms in a quantity of water is actually deuterium, and the fusion of two deuterium nuclei converts about 0.5% of the rest-energy of the deuterium nuclei to other forms of energy. Avogadro's number of hydrogen atoms has a mass of 1 g, the same number of deuterium atoms a mass of 2 g and the same number of oxygen atoms has a mass of 16 g. About how long could you run a typical household on the energy that would be produced by the fusion of the deuterium in one gallon of water?

ADVANCED

R9A.1 Prove that the four-magnitude of any four-vector is a frame-independent number. [*Hint*: What is the formal definition of a four-vector?]

R9A.2 Prove conclusively that a particle's relativistic kinetic energy $K \equiv E - m$ is always larger than $\frac{1}{2}mv^2$ (though the values are close for $v << 1$). [Hint: Both go to zero as v goes to zero, but you can show that the derivative of K with respect to v is always greater than the derivative of $\frac{1}{2}mv^2$ with respect to v. How does this help?]

ANSWERS TO EXERCISES

R9X.1 We have

$$v'_{4x} = \frac{v_{4x} - \beta}{1 - \beta v_{4x}} = \frac{+1/2 - 3/4}{1 - (1/2)(3/4)} = -\frac{1/4}{5/8} = -\frac{2}{5} \quad \text{(R9.34)}$$

R9X.2 If the galilean velocity transformations were true, then $v'_{1x} = 0$ and $v'_{1x} = -3/4$ as before, but

$$v'_{3x} = v_{3x} - \beta = -\frac{1}{4} - \frac{3}{4} = -1 \quad \text{(R9.35a)}$$

$$v'_{4x} = v_{4x} - \beta = +\frac{1}{2} - \frac{3}{4} = -\frac{1}{4} \quad \text{(R9.35b)}$$

The system's total momentum in the Other Frame before the collision is still $-3m/2$, but the total momentum after the collision is now

$$mv_{3x} + 2mv_{4x} = m(-1) + 2m(-\tfrac{1}{4}) = -\tfrac{3}{2}m \quad \text{(R9.36)}$$

also. So ordinary momentum would in fact be conserved if the galilean velocity transformation equations were valid.

R9X.3 If $v = 4/5$, then $[1-v^2]^{1/2} = [1-16/25]^{1/2} = 3/5$. So, according to equation R9.10, we have

$$\begin{bmatrix} P_t \\ P_x \\ P_y \\ P_z \end{bmatrix} = \frac{1}{\sqrt{1-v^2}} \begin{bmatrix} m \\ mv_x \\ mv_y \\ mv_z \end{bmatrix} = \frac{5}{3} \begin{bmatrix} m \\ 0 \\ \frac{4}{5}m \\ 0 \end{bmatrix} = \begin{bmatrix} \frac{5}{3} \text{ kg} \\ 0 \\ \frac{4}{3} \text{ kg} \\ 0 \end{bmatrix} \quad \text{(R9.37)}$$

In the frame where the object is at rest, $[1-v^2]^{1/2} = 1$, so

$$\begin{bmatrix} P_t \\ P_x \\ P_y \\ P_z \end{bmatrix} = \frac{1}{\sqrt{1-v^2}} \begin{bmatrix} m \\ mv_x \\ mv_y \\ mv_z \end{bmatrix} = \begin{bmatrix} m \\ 0 \\ 0 \\ 0 \end{bmatrix} = \begin{bmatrix} 1 \text{ kg} \\ 0 \\ 0 \\ 0 \end{bmatrix} \quad \text{(R9.38)}$$

R9X.4 Using the same basic approach outlined in equation R9.12a, we get

$$P_x' = m\frac{dx'}{d\tau} = m\frac{\gamma(-\beta dt + dx)}{d\tau} = -\gamma\beta m\frac{dt}{d\tau} + \gamma m\frac{dx}{d\tau}$$

$$= -\gamma\beta P_t + \gamma P_x = \gamma(-\beta P_t + P_x) \quad \text{(R9.39)}$$

R9X.5 Substituting the definition of the four-momentum components into the definition of the four-magnitude of the four-momentum we see that

$$|\mathbf{P}| \equiv \sqrt{P_t^2 - P_x^2 - P_y^2 - P_z^2}$$

$$= \sqrt{\left(m\frac{dt}{d\tau}\right)^2 - \left(m\frac{dx}{d\tau}\right)^2 - \left(m\frac{dy}{d\tau}\right)^2 - \left(m\frac{dz}{d\tau}\right)^2}$$

$$= m\frac{\sqrt{dt^2 - dx^2 - dy^2 - dz^2}}{d\tau} = m\frac{d\tau}{d\tau} = m \quad \text{(R9.40)}$$

(where in the next-to-last step, I used the provided hint).

R9X.6 We can prove conservation of P'_t as follows:

$$P'_{1t} + P'_{2t} - P'_{3t} - P'_{4t} = \gamma(P_{1t} - \beta P_{1t}) + \gamma(P_{2t} - \beta P_{2t})$$
$$\qquad -\gamma(P_{3t} - \beta P_{3x}) - \gamma(P_{4t} + \beta P_{4x})$$

$$= \gamma(P_{1t} + P_{2t} - P_{3t} - P_{4t}) - \gamma\beta(P_{1x} + P_{2x} - P_{3x} - P_{4x})$$

$$= \gamma(0) - \gamma\beta(0) = 0 \quad \text{(R9.41)}$$

since $P_{1t} + P_{2t} - P_{3t} - P_{4t} = 0$ and $P_{1x} + P_{2x} - P_{3x} - P_{4x} = 0$ if four-momentum is conserved in the Home Frame. Proving conservation of P'_y is even easier:

$$P'_{1y} + P'_{2y} - P'_{3y} - P'_{4y} = P_{1y} + P_{2y} - P_{3y} - P_{4y} = 0 \quad \text{(R9.42)}$$

R9X.7 According to equation R9.23, the rock's energy is

$$E = \frac{m}{\sqrt{1-v^2}} = \frac{1.0 \text{ kg}}{\sqrt{1-16/25}} = \frac{1.0 \text{ kg}}{\sqrt{9/25}} = \frac{5}{3} \text{ kg} \quad \text{(R9.43)}$$

Its kinetic energy is

$$K \equiv E - m = \frac{5}{3} \text{ kg} - 1.0 \text{ kg} = \frac{2}{3} \text{ kg} \quad \text{(R9.44)}$$

Converting to joules, we find that

$$E = \left(\frac{5}{3} \text{ kg}\right)\left(\frac{3.0 \times 10^8 \text{ m}}{1 \text{ s}}\right)^2 \left(\frac{1 \text{ J}}{1 \text{ kg} \cdot \text{m}^2/\text{s}^2}\right)$$

$$= 1.5 \times 10^{17} \text{ J} \quad \text{(R9.45)}$$

$$K = \left(\frac{2}{3} \text{ kg}\right)\left(\frac{3.0 \times 10^8 \text{ m}}{1 \text{ s}}\right)^2 \left(\frac{1 \text{ J}}{1 \text{ kg} \cdot \text{m}^2/\text{s}^2}\right)$$

$$= 6.0 \times 10^{16} \text{ J} \quad \text{(R9.46)}$$

For the sake of comparison, note that a typical nuclear bomb releases about 5×10^{14} J of energy when it explodes.

R9X.8 The rock's relativistic momentum is

$$p = \frac{mv}{\sqrt{1-v^2}} = \frac{(1.0 \text{ kg})(4/5)}{3/5} = \frac{4}{3} \text{ kg} \quad \text{(R9.47)}$$

Using equation R9.32, we see that the rock's four-momentum vector is

$$\begin{bmatrix} P_t \\ P_x \\ P_y \\ P_z \end{bmatrix} = \begin{bmatrix} E \\ Ev_x \\ Ev_y \\ Ev_z \end{bmatrix} = \begin{bmatrix} \frac{5}{3} \text{ kg} \\ 0 \\ 0 \\ \left(\frac{5}{3} \text{ kg}\right)\left(-\frac{4}{5}\right) \end{bmatrix} = \begin{bmatrix} \frac{5}{3} \text{ kg} \\ 0 \\ 0 \\ -\frac{4}{3} \text{ kg} \end{bmatrix} \quad \text{(R9.48)}$$

CONSERVATION OF FOUR-MOMENTUM

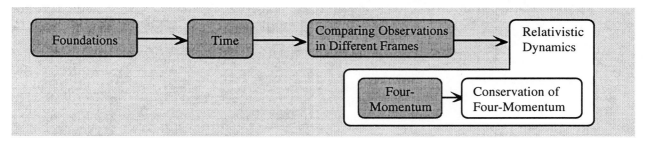

The Lord God is subtle, but not malicious.

Albert Einstein*

R10.1 OVERVIEW

In the last chapter, we saw that conservation of the total ordinary (Newtonian) momentum of a isolated system of objects is *inconsistent* with the principle of relativity, because of the complicated nature of the Einstein velocity transformation. On the other hand, we saw that conservation of the total four-momentum of an isolated system *is* consistent with the principle of relativity. Moreover, the four-momentum of an object reduces to the newtonian momentum in the low-velocity limit. Therefore, if anything like momentum is to be conserved, it is plausible that it is in fact four-momentum that is conserved, and this assertion is abundantly supported by experiment.

The purpose of this chapter is to explore some of the surprising consequences and experimental tests of this assumption. Here is an overview of the chapters sections.

R10.2 *ENERGY-MOMENTUM DIAGRAMS* describes how to construct a spacetime diagram of an object's four-momentum vector and explores what these diagrams can tell us.

R10.3 *WORKING CONSERVATION PROBLEMS* illustrates how we can analyze problems involving conservation of four-momentum both mathematically (using vector equations) and graphically (using energy-momentum diagrams).

R10.4 *THE MASS OF A SYSTEM OF PARTICLES* wrestles with the tricky question of what *mass* means in the context of relativity.

R10.5 *THE FOUR-MOMENTUM OF LIGHT* argues that a flash of light (since it carries energy) must have a four-momentum vector, and discusses what the form of this four-momentum vector must be.

R10.6 *APPLICATIONS TO PARTICLE PHYSICS* briefly examines one of the most important areas of physics where using special relativity is a genuinely practical necessity.

R10.7 *PARTING COMMENTS* discusses some places where the interested reader can look for more information about the theory of relativity.

*Quoted in A. P. French ed., Einstein: *A Centenary Volume,* Cambridge, Mass.: Harvard, 1979, p. 73.

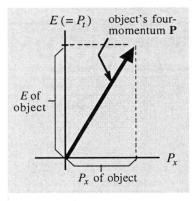

$E\,(=P_t)$ object's four-momentum **P**

E of object

P_x

P_x of object

Figure R10.1: An energy-momentum diagram displaying the four-momentum of an object moving in the $+x$ direction. The object's four-momentum is shown on the diagram as an arrow whose projections on the vertical and horizontal axes represent the values of the object's relativistic energy $E = P_t$ and its relativistic x-momentum P_x respectively.

R10.2   ENERGY-MOMENTUM DIAGRAMS

We can visually represent an object's four-momentum as an arrow on a special kind of spacetime diagram called an **energy-momentum diagram** (see Figure R10.1). We can do this conveniently only if the object is moving in the spatial x direction (so that $P_y = P_z = 0$ and $p = |P_x|$). We will assume this to be true in the rest of this chapter (unless otherwise specified).

Just as the direction of the arrow representing an object's ordinary momentum is tangent to its path through space, the direction of the arrow representing an object's four-momentum is tangent to its worldline in spacetime (because the object's four-momentum vector $\mathbf{P} = md\mathbf{R}/d\tau$ at any given point along its worldline is proportional to the object's differential displacement in spacetime $d\mathbf{R}$ along that worldline around that point: see Figure R10.2).

Since the inverse slope of an object's worldline at any instant is equal to its x-velocity at that instant, the inverse slope of the object's four-momentum arrow at a given time (i.e. run/rise = P_x / E) should also be equal to its x-velocity at that time if the two vectors are to be parallel. Equation R9.31 in the previous chapter says essentially the same thing:

$$\frac{P_x}{E} = \frac{mv_x}{\sqrt{1-v^2}}\frac{\sqrt{1-v^2}}{m} = v_x \qquad (R10.1)$$

The four-magnitude of an object's four-momentum is its mass m (see equation R9.15): this value is frame-independent and independent of the object's motion. But the *length* of the arrow that represents the object's four-momentum on an energy-momentum diagram *does* depend on the object's velocity: it is *not* pro-

Figure R10.2a: At any given time, the arrow that represents an object's four-momentum on an energy-momentum diagram points in a direction tangent to the object's worldline, because **P** is proportional to $d\mathbf{R}$.

Figure R10.2b: When an object is at rest (even at just an instant), its four-momentum arrow is vertical and its energy is equal to its mass (see equation R9.10a).

Figure R10.2c: When the object moves in the $-x$ direction, its x-momentum is negative (see equation R9.10b), but its energy remains positive.

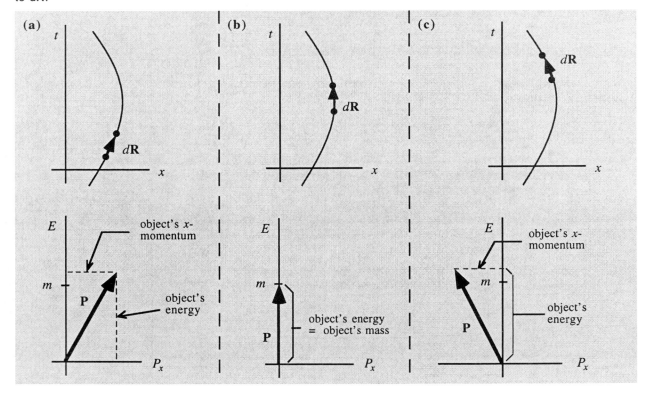

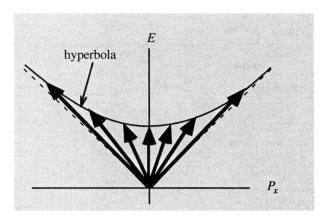

Figure R10.3: An energy-momentum diagram showing four-momentum arrows for a set of identical objects of mass m moving at different x-velocities in the Home Frame. The tips of all of these arrows lie on a hyperbola whose equation is $m^2 = E^2 - p^2$. Note that as the object's x-velocity approaches ± 1 (and thus p/E approaches 1), both p and E have to become very large if the difference of their squares is to remain fixed.

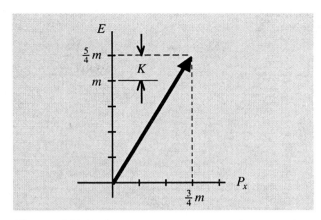

Figure R10.4: An energy-momentum diagram of an object of mass m traveling with an x-velocity $v_x = 3/5$. The arrow representing the object's four-momentum has a slope of 5/3 and (since $[1-v^2]^{1/2} = 4/5$ in this case) an energy of $E = m/[1-v^2]^{1/2} = 5m/4$. For the arrow to have the correct slope, we must have $P_x = 3m/4$. Note that the object's relativistic kinetic energy $K = E - m = m/4$ can be read directly from the diagram.

portional to the four-magnitude of the corresponding four-momentum. (This is analogous to the problem with the spacetime interval discussed in section R4.6.) In fact, according to equation R9.29, we have:

$$m^2 = E^2 - p^2 = E^2 - (P_x)^2$$

This means that the tips of the four-momentum arrows for objects of identical mass m traveling at different x-velocities (or the four-momentum arrows for a single accelerating object observed at different times) lie along curve on the diagram defined by the equation $m^2 = E^2 - p^2$. This curve is in fact a hyperbola, as shown in Figure R10.3.

If you know an object's x-velocity and its mass m, you can easily draw an energy-momentum diagram showing its four-momentum vector as follows:

Drawing the four-momentum for an object with known mass and speed

1. Set up your E and P_x axes.
2. Draw a line from the origin of those axes having the slope $1/v_x$.
3. Compute the value of $E = m/[1-v^2]^{1/2} = m/[1-v_x^2]^{1/2}$ for the object
4. Draw a horizontal line from this value on the E axis until it intercepts the line that you drew in step 2.
5. The arrow representing the object's four-momentum lies along the line drawn in step 2, with its tip at the intersection found in step 4.

We can easily read an object's relativistic kinetic energy $K = E - m$ directly from an energy-momentum diagram. For example, K for an object of mass m moving at a speed $v = 3/5$ is $m/4$, as shown in Figure R10.4. (Note that $m/4 \neq \frac{1}{2}m(3/5)^2$, but in fact is substantially larger!) Figures R10.3 and R10.4 together make it clear that as an object's speed v approaches 1 (the speed of light), both the object's total relativistic energy E and its kinetic energy K go to infinity. This means that *you would have to supply an infinite amount of energy to accelerate an object of non-zero mass to the speed of light.* (This is the most practical reason that no object can go faster than the speed of light: all the energy in the universe could not accelerate even a mote of dust to that speed!)

A practical reason why no object can travel at the speed of light or faster

Virtually all that you need to know to construct and interpret an energy-momentum diagram is summarized in Figure R10.5.

Exercise R10X.1: Check that $m/4 > \frac{1}{2}m(3/5)^2$, as claimed above.

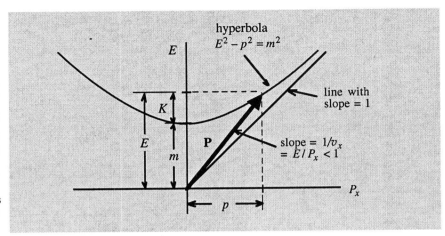

Figure R10.5: Virtually everything that you need to know about four-momentum diagrams. No matter what the x-velocity of an object of mass m might be, the tip of the arrow representing its four-momentum lies on the hyperbola $m^2 = E^2 - p^2$. The inverse slope of the arrow representing the four-momentum is equal to v_x, which always has a magnitude less than 1.

Exercise R10X.2: Draw an energy-momentum diagram of an object whose mass is 1.0 kg and which moves in the $-x$ direction at a speed of 4/5. Compute its energy E and then read its relativistic kinetic energy K and the x component of its four-momentum P_x from the diagram.

R10.3 WORKING CONSERVATION PROBLEMS

The law of conservation of four-momentum (like the law of conservation of ordinary momentum) is most useful when applied to an isolated system of objects undergoing some type of *collision* process (that is, a kind of sudden interaction between the objects in the system that may be strong and complicated but limited in time). In such a case, the system has a clearly defined state "before" and "after" the collision, making it easy to compute the total four-momentum in the system both before and after the collision. The law of conservation of four-momentum states that the system should have the *same* total four-momentum after the collision process as it had before.

What does this really mean mathematically? Since four-momentum is a (four-dimensional) vector quantity, conservation of four-momentum means that *each component of the system's total four-momentum is separately conserved.* For example, consider a system consisting of two objects, and let the objects' four-momenta before the collision be $\mathbf{P}_1$ and $\mathbf{P}_2$, and after the collision be $\mathbf{P}_3$ and $\mathbf{P}_4$. Conservation of four-momentum requires that:

Solving conservation problems algebraically

$$E_1 + E_2 = E_3 + E_4 \tag{R10.3a}$$

$$P_{1x} + P_{2x} = P_{3x} + P_{4x} \tag{R10.3b}$$

$$P_{1y} + P_{2y} = P_{3y} + P_{4y} \tag{R10.3c}$$

$$P_{1z} + P_{2z} = P_{3z} + P_{4z} \tag{R10.3d}$$

remembering that the time-component of a four-momentum vector (that is, the relativistic energy) is usually given the more evocative symbol E instead of P_t. Each one of equations R10.3 has to be *separately* true for four-momentum to be conserved.

As I said before, in this chapter we will mostly consider objects moving in only *one* dimension, which we can take to be the $\pm x$ direction. This allows us to ignore the four-momentum y and z components (which are always zero) and focus on the t and x components (equations R10.3a and R10.3b). Making this assumption simplifies the mathematics significantly, and there is not anything significant to be learned by not making this assumption.

Problem: Imagine that somewhere in deep space, a rock with mass $m_1 = 12$ kg is moving in the $+x$ direction with $v_{1x} = +4/5$ in some inertial frame. This rock then strikes another rock of mass $m_2 = 28$ kg at rest ($v_{2x} = 0$). Instead of instantly vaporizing into a cloud of gas (as any *real* rocks colliding at this speed would), pretend that the first rock simply bounces off the more massive rock and is subsequently observed to have an x-velocity $v_{3x} = -5/13$. What is the x-velocity v_{4x} of the larger rock after the collision?

EXAMPLE R10.1: Elastically Colliding Rocks

Solution The first step in solving this problem is to calculate the energy E_1 and the x-momentum P_{1x} of the smaller rock before the collision. Using the definitions of these four-momentum components, we find that:

$$E_1 \equiv \frac{m_1}{\sqrt{1 - v_{1x}^2}} = \frac{m_1}{\sqrt{1 - 16/25}} = \frac{m_1}{\sqrt{9/25}} = \frac{5}{3}(12\text{ kg}) = 20\text{ kg} \quad \text{(R10.4a)}$$

$$P_{1x} \equiv \frac{m_1 v_{1x}}{\sqrt{1 - v_{1x}^2}} = \frac{m_1(+4/5)}{3/5} = +\frac{4}{3}(12\text{ kg}) = +16\text{ kg} \quad \text{(R10.4b)}$$

Similarly, the larger rock's energy and x-momentum before the collision are:

$$E_2 \equiv \frac{m_2}{\sqrt{1 - v_{2x}^2}} = \frac{m_2}{\sqrt{1 - 0^2}} = m_2 = 28\text{ kg} \quad \text{(R10.5a)}$$

$$P_{2x} \equiv \frac{m_2 v_{2x}}{\sqrt{1 - v_{2x}^2}} = \frac{m_2(0)}{\sqrt{1 - 0^2}} = 0\text{ kg} \quad \text{(R10.5b)}$$

The smaller rock's energy and x-momentum *after* the collision are:

$$E_3 \equiv \frac{m_1}{\sqrt{1 - v_{3x}^2}} = \frac{m_1}{\sqrt{1 - (-5/13)^2}} = \frac{m_1}{\sqrt{144/169}} = \frac{13}{12}(12\text{ kg}) = 13\text{ kg} \quad \text{(R10.6a)}$$

$$P_{3x} \equiv \frac{m_1 v_{3x}}{\sqrt{1 - v_{3x}^2}} = \frac{m_1(-5/13)}{12/13} = -\frac{5}{12}(12\text{ kg}) = -5\text{ kg} \quad \text{(R10.6b)}$$

Conservation of four-momentum requires that the four-momentum vectors before the collision add up to the same value after the collision. Ignoring the y and z four-momentum components, this means that:

$$\begin{matrix} t \text{ component}: \\ x \text{ component}: \end{matrix} \quad \begin{bmatrix} E_1 \\ P_{1x} \end{bmatrix} + \begin{bmatrix} E_2 \\ P_{2x} \end{bmatrix} = \begin{bmatrix} E_3 \\ P_{3x} \end{bmatrix} + \begin{bmatrix} E_4 \\ P_{4x} \end{bmatrix}, \quad \text{implying that} \quad \text{(R10.7a)}$$

$$\begin{bmatrix} E_4 \\ P_{4x} \end{bmatrix} = \begin{bmatrix} E_1 \\ P_{1x} \end{bmatrix} + \begin{bmatrix} E_2 \\ P_{2x} \end{bmatrix} - \begin{bmatrix} E_3 \\ P_{3x} \end{bmatrix} = \begin{bmatrix} 20\text{ kg} \\ 16\text{ kg} \end{bmatrix} + \begin{bmatrix} 28\text{ kg} \\ 0 \end{bmatrix} - \begin{bmatrix} 13\text{ kg} \\ -5\text{ kg} \end{bmatrix} = \begin{bmatrix} 35\text{ kg} \\ 21\text{ kg} \end{bmatrix}$$
$$\text{(R10.7b)}$$

Knowing the energy and x-momentum of an object is sufficient information to determine both its energy and velocity. Using equation R9.29, we see that the larger rock's mass is still

$$m = \sqrt{E_4^2 - P_{4x}^2} = \sqrt{(35\text{ kg})^2 - (21\text{ kg})^2} = (7\text{ kg})\sqrt{5^2 - 3^2} = 28\text{ kg} \quad \text{(R10.8a)}$$

after the collision. According to equation R9.31, its final x-velocity is:

$$v_{4x} = \frac{P_{4x}}{E_4} = \frac{+21\text{ kg}}{35\text{ kg}} = +\frac{3}{5} \quad \text{(R10.8b)}$$

This completes the solution.

Exercise R10X.3: Show that the collision described in Example R10.1 does *not* conserve newtonian momentum.

EXAMPLE R10.2:
Solving the Rock Problem Graphically

Problem: Solve the rock collision problem discussed in the previous example using an energy-momentum diagram.

Solution Since the sum of four-momentum arrows is defined like the sum of ordinary vectors (we simply add the components), we can add four-momenta arrows on an energy-momentum diagram just as we would ordinary vector arrows (by putting the tail of one vector on the tip of the other while preserving their directions). Using this technique, we see in Figure R10.6a that in the rock example, the system's total four-momentum *before* the collision has components $E_T = 48$ kg, $P_{Tx} = 16$ kg. The two rocks' four-momentum arrows after the collision have to add up to the *same* total four-momentum arrow, and since we know the smaller rock's four-momentum after the collision, we can *construct* the larger rock's final four-momentum arrow $\mathbf{P}_4$ (Figure R10.6b). We can then read the components of this arrow right off the diagram, getting the same results as in equations R10.7. One can then use these results (as we did before) to compute that rock's mass and x-velocity.

Advantages and disadvantages of the graphical method

This kind of graphical approach to the problem is not usually much easier than the algebraic approach, but it does have some advantages: (1) It provides a more visual and concrete way of dealing with the problem, and may be helpful to you if you find the algebraic approach rather abstract. (2) When used in conjunction with the algebraic method, it serves as a useful check on the algebraic re-

Figure R10.6a: The four-momenta of the rocks *before* the collision. The vector sum of these four-momenta is represented by the arrow $\mathbf{P}_T$. Since the four-magnitudes of the individual four-momentum arrows (which equal the masses of the corresponding rocks) cannot be read directly from the diagram, I have adopted the expedient of attaching a "flag" to each four-momentum arrow that states its magnitude.

Figure R10.6b: The four-momenta of the rocks *after* the collision. The vector sum of these four-momenta is still $\mathbf{P}_T$ by four-momentum conservation. Since $\mathbf{P}_3$ is also known, it is possible to construct the unknown four-momentum $\mathbf{P}_4$, read its components from the diagram as shown, and use these to compute the corresponding rock's mass and x-velocity.

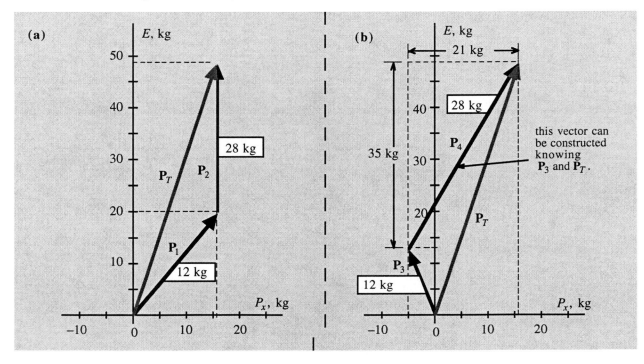

sults: it is harder to make errors using the graphical method. (3) In some cases, as we will see, simply *looking* at the diagram can yield qualitative information that is very difficult to get from the algebraic equations alone.

In short, the graphical method represents an alternative method for solving problems involving conservation of four-momentum that often complements the algebraic approach. Armed with both of these techniques, we are now ready to explore some of the strange and interesting consequences of the law of conservation of four-momentum.

R10.4 THE MASS OF A SYSTEM OF PARTICLES

As we have seen, the relativistic energy of an object is not simply equal to its kinetic energy (even at low velocities) but involves the mass of the object as well. The fact that $E = P_t$ is conserved by the internal interactions in an isolated system does not imply that the mass of an object and its kinetic energy are separately conserved, only that the sum of these two things are conserved. This implies that processes that convert mass to kinetic energy and vice versa do not necessarily violate the law of conservation of four-momentum and therefore may exist. Mass and kinetic energy are seen in the theory of special relativity to be simply two parts of the same whole (the relativistic energy). There is no reason to presuppose a barrier between these two manifestations of relativistic energy that would preclude the conversion of one into the other.

Conversion of rest-energy (mass) into other kinds of energy (or vice versa) is possible

In much of the remainder of this chapter, we will be considering a variety of examples of processes that do just that. We will begin with a simple example that illustrates a crucial thing that we need to understand about "mass" before we can go further: *the mass of a system is generally DIFFERENT than the sum of the masses of its parts.*

Consider the collision of two identical balls of putty with mass $m = 4$ kg which in some inertial frame are observed to have x-velocities of $v_{1x} = +3/5$ and $v_{2x} = -3/5$; that is, these putty balls are approaching each other with equal speeds. Imagine that when these putty balls collide, they stick together, as shown in Figure R10.7.

An example showing conversion of kinetic energy to mass

Note that before the collision, the x component of the system's total four-momentum is zero:

$$P_{1x} + P_{2x} = \frac{m(+3/5)}{\sqrt{1-(3/5)^2}} + \frac{m(-3/5)}{\sqrt{1-(3/5)^2}} = \frac{m(3/5-3/5)}{\sqrt{1-(3/5)^2}} = 0 \qquad (R10.9)$$

so conservation of four-momentum implies that the x-component of the final mass' four-momentum is zero as well, meaning that it must be at rest.

What of relativistic energy conservation in this case? A newtonian analysis of this collision would speak of the kinetic energy being converted into thermal energy in this inelastic collision. Such an analysis would also assert that the mass of the coalesced particle is $M = m + m = 2m$. But we have more constraints to consider in a relativistic solution to this problem. If the spatial components of the four-momentum are conserved in this collision, the time component must also be conserved, whether the collision is elastic or not. But how can we think of the relativistic energy being conserved in this case, since no mention has been made of thermal energy in the definition of the relativistic energy given in Chapter R9?

Figure R10.7: The inelastic collision of two balls of putty (each having mass $m = 4$ kg) as seen in the frame where they initially have equal speeds but opposite directions

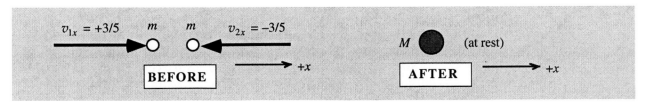

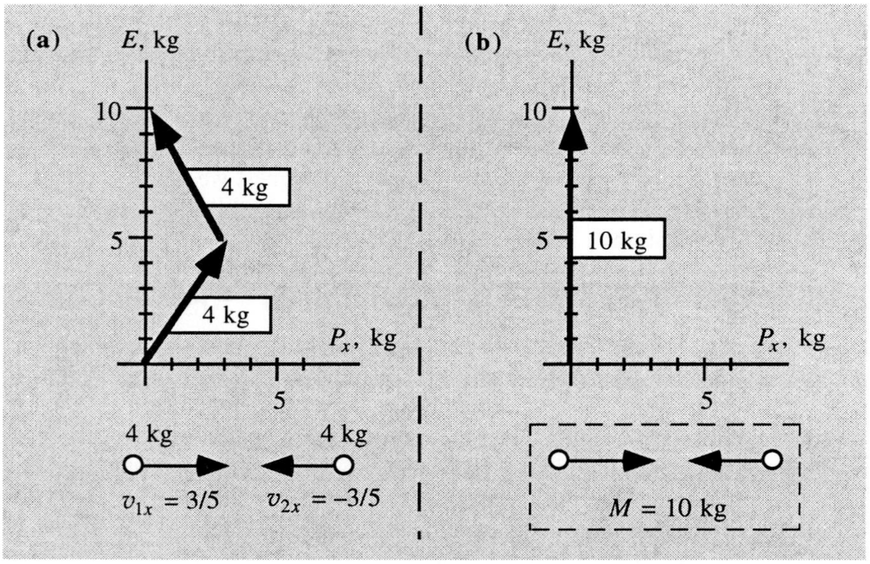

Figure R10.8:

(a) Putty balls before the collision, considered as two individual objects. Each has its own mass, energy, and x-momentum.

(b) Putty balls before the collision, considered as a single system. The system's x-momentum is zero, meaning that its total energy of 10 kg is the same as the system's mass.

The answer is direct and surprising. Since the final object is motionless, its relativistic energy is simply equal to its mass M. But by conservation of the time component of four-momentum, we have:

$$M = E_1 + E_2 = \frac{m}{\sqrt{1-(3/5)^2}} + \frac{m}{\sqrt{1-(3/5)^2}} = \frac{2m}{\sqrt{16/25}} = \frac{10}{4}m = 10 \text{ kg} \quad (R10.10)$$

which is *not* equal to $2m = 8$ kg! conservation of four-momentum thus requires that the final object have a *greater* mass than the sum of the masses that collided to form it!

We know from experience with collisions at low speeds that when two objects collide and stick together, their energy of motion gets converted to thermal energy: the final object is a little warmer than the original objects. (In this case, actually, the final object will be a *lot* warmer than the original objects, so much so that any *real* putty balls colliding at such speeds would vaporize instantly.) What equation R10.10 is telling us is that the final object *has* to be more massive than the original objects, and that the increased thermal energy is somehow correlated with this.

The mass of a system is not the same as the sum of the masses of its parts

But where does this extra mass actually reside? The final object has the same number of atoms as the original objects did. Does each atom gain some extra mass somehow? This seems absurd. The increased thermal energy in the final object means that its atoms will jostle around more vigorously. Can the motion of these atoms "have mass" in some sense? This seems crazy: *individual* particles have the same mass no matter how they move. *So where is this extra mass?*

There is only one fully self-consistent answer to this question: *the extra mass is a property of the system as a whole*: it does not reside in any of its parts.

This can be vividly illustrated as follows: consider the "system" consisting of the two balls of putty *before* they collide. If they are considered separate objects, the putty balls *each* have a mass m of 4 kg and an relativistic energy of 5 kg, and one has an x-momentum of –3 kg and the other +3 kg. On the other hand, if we consider the balls to constitute a single system, the system has a total x-momentum of zero, and a total energy of 10 kg, meaning that its mass $M \equiv [E_T^2 - p_T^2]^{1/2}$ is equal to 10 kg. (This is illustrated by Figures R10.8.) So we see that the thermal energy produced by the collision is *not* the source of this extra mass: the extra mass was present in the "system" *before* the collision, and remains the same after the collision.

So in some sense, mass is not "created" by the collision process at all: the collision simply *manifests* the mass of the *system* of two initial objects in the mass of a *single* final object. If we focus on the masses of the individual objects in the system before and after the collision, we think of mass being created. But if we focus on the *system* before and after the collision, we see that its mass remains the same.

It is possible to get unnecessarily hung up on the difference between the mass of a system and the masses of its parts. The reason this seems screwy is that we are *used* to treating mass as if it were additive: the mass of a jar of beans is the sum of the masses of the individual beans plus the mass of the container, right? This is true enough if the beans travel at low velocities. But if we had common experience with a jar full of beans that bang around inside the jar with speeds close to that of light, then we would be *used* to the idea that such a jar would have a different mass than the mass of the individual beans. Mass is simply *not* additive in the way that energy and *x*-momentum are.

There are actually many examples of things in the world where the whole is greater than the sum of its parts. The meaning of a poem is not the same as the sum of the meaning of the individual letters in its the words. The "life" of an organism cannot be localized in any of its parts. We simply need to start thinking about mass in the same way as we think about these things.

The best way to look at this is to think of the mass of a system of particles as *a property of the system as a whole* (that is, the magnitude of the system's total four-momentum vector) and something that simply doesn't have very much to do with the masses of its parts. The only self-consistent way to define the mass of a *system* is as the magnitude of the system's total four-momentum, and if this definition leads to the mass of a system being greater or less than the masses of its parts, well, that's the way it is!

A system's mass can't be localized: it is a property of the system as a whole

---

Exercise R10X.4: Let's look at the system described in Figure R10.8 in a frame moving with the left-hand ball. Use the Einstein velocity transformation to show that the other ball's *x*-velocity is $v'_{2x} = -15/17$. Find the *system's* four-momentum components E'_T and P'_{Tx} in this frame and show that the system's mass (found using $M' = [E'^2_T - P'^2_{Tx}]^{1/2}$) is still 10 kg. (A system's mass may not equal the sum of masses in the system, but it *is* frame-independent).

Exercise R10X.5: The molecules in a balloon at rest filled with air have an average kinetic energy of $K = 6.2 \times 10^{-21}$ J. If we convert this to kilograms, this is the additional energy that each molecule has (on the average) above its rest energy (which is $m \approx 2.4 \times 10^{-26}$ kg on the average). By about what fraction is the total mass of the air in a balloon more massive than the sum of the masses of the individual air molecules? Is this very significant?

R10.5 THE FOUR-MOMENTUM OF LIGHT

We all have experienced the fact that the light carries energy: we have felt sunlight warm our skin, or seen an electric motor powered by solar cells, or learned that plants convert the energy in sunlight into chemical energy. Since we have seen that energy is the time component of four-momentum, it follows that light should have an associated four-momentum vector. What does the four-momentum of light look like?

Previously, we have explored the four-momenta of objects (rocks or putty balls or the like) that could be considered to be *particles* that have a well-defined position in space and thus a well-defined worldline through spacetime. The analogous thing in the case of light would be a "flash" or "burst" of light energy that is similarly localized in space. We can consider a continuous beam of light to be composed of a sequence of closely spaced flashes, much as we might imagine a stream of water to be a sequence of closely spaced drops.

A light-flash as a "particle" of light

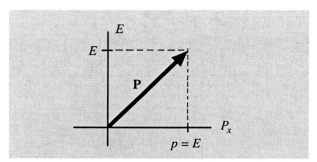

Figure R10.9: An energy-momentum diagram showing the four-momentum of a flash of light moving in the $+x$ direction. If the four-momentum is to be parallel to the flash's worldline, then it must be drawn with slope +1 on the energy-momentum diagram. This implies that a light-flash's relativistic momentum p must have the same value (in SR units) as its energy: $p = E$.

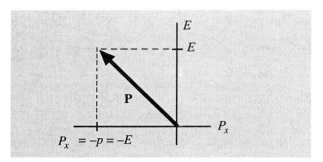

Figure R10.10: An energy-momentum diagram showing the four-momentum of a flash of light moving in the $-x$ direction. In this case, the flash's x-momentum is negative: $P_x = -p$, where p is equal to the *magnitude* of the flash's spatial momentum ($p = |P_x|$ in this case). Note that we still have $p = E$: this is a general relation for light independent of the flash's direction of travel.

A light-flash four-momentum vector has slope ±1

So what might the four-momentum of a flash of light look like? Arguably, the most basic feature of any object's four-momentum is that it is parallel to that object's worldline. If this is true for a flash of light, then it follows that the four-momentum vector for a flash of light must have a slope of ±1 on an energy-momentum diagram. The four-momentum vector of a flash with a given energy E moving in the $+x$ direction will thus look as shown in Figure R10.9.

You can see from this diagram that if the flash's four-momentum vector is to have such a slope, it must have a spatial relativistic momentum p that is equal to its relativistic energy E. This is in fact consistent with equation R9.30, which in the case of light tells us that:

The relativistic momentum of a light-flash is equal to its energy

$$\frac{p}{E} = v = 1 \qquad \Rightarrow \qquad p = E \qquad\qquad (R10.11)$$

One immediate implication of this important formula is that *light must carry momentum* (as well as energy). Light bouncing off a mirror will thus transfer momentum to the mirror (causing it to recoil) in much the same way that a ball bouncing off an object transfers momentum to the object and causes it to recoil. This has been experimentally verified,* and it is now known that the pressure exerted by light due to its momentum plays an important part in the evolution of stars and the early universe, and in a number of other astrophysical processes.

Another immediate consequence is that a "flash" of light has *zero* mass. We have defined the mass of an object in special relativity to be the invariant magnitude of its four-momentum. According to equation R10.11, the flash's mass is:

The mass of a light-flash is zero

$$m^2 = E^2 - p^2 = 0 \qquad\qquad (R10.12)$$

This is actually a good thing. If a flash of light were to have some *nonzero* mass m, then its relativistic energy $E = m/[1 - v^2]^{1/2}$ and relativistic momentum $p = mv/[1 - v^2]^{1/2}$ would both have to be infinite, since $v = 1$ for light, which makes the denominator zero in each expression. But since $m = 0$, these equations actually read $E = 0/0$ and $p = 0/0$. The ratio $0/0$ is technically *undefined* instead of being infinite, so instead of yielding absurdities, these equations simply don't tell us anything useful about the four-momentum of light.

If a light flash is moving in the $-x$ direction instead of the $+x$ direction, the slope of its four-momentum arrow on an energy-momentum diagram is -1 instead of $+1$, and its x-momentum is negative: $P_x = -p = -E$ (note that both p and E are positive by definition), as shown in Fig. R10.10.

*Maxwell's theory of electromagnetic waves also predicted (before relativity did) that light should carry momentum of this magnitude. Experiments performed in 1903 by Nichols and Hull in the United States and Lebedev in Russia confirmed this experimental prediction. See G. E. Henry, "Radiation Pressure", *Sci. Am.*, June 1957, p. 99.

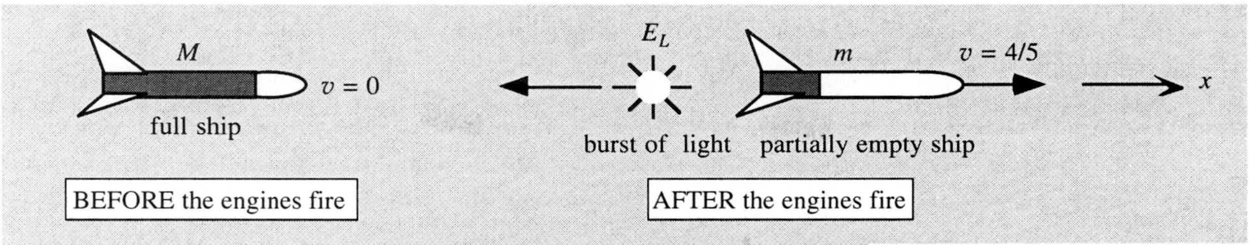

Figure R10.11: The situation discussed in Example R10.3.

EXAMPLE R10.3: A Matter-Antimatter Rocket

Problem: When antimatter is brought into contact with matter, they annihilate each other, converting their rest-energy entirely into light energy. A perfect rocket engine might mix antimatter with an equal amount of matter, and direct the resulting light in a tight beam out of the engine nozzle: no other kind of exhaust could possibly carry more momentum out the rear of the rocket per unit energy expended than light can. Imagine a rocket of original mass M = 90,000 kg sitting at rest in some frame in deep space (M includes the mass of the matter-antimatter fuel). Imagine that it fires its engines, emitting a burst of light having a total (unknown) energy E_L. If after doing this, the ship's final speed is v = 4/5, what is its final mass m? (See Figure R10.11.)

Solution The law of conservation of four-momentum tells us that the total four-momentum of an isolated system of interacting objects will be conserved. The system's initial four-momentum vector in this case is that of a mass M at rest, which has components $P_t = M$ and $P_x = P_y = P_z = 0$. After the engines have fired, the system consists of a light flash and the somewhat lighter ship. Let the ship's final direction of motion define the $+x$ direction, as shown in Figure R10.11. According to equation R10.11, the flash's relativistic momentum p_L will be equal to its energy E_L and since the flash is moving in the $-x$-direction, the light's spatial four-momentum components are $P_x = -p_L = -E_L$ and $P_y = P_z = 0$. We don't know the final ship mass m, but we do know that it is moving with v = 4/5 in the $+x$ direction, so by equations R9.10, we know that the ship's final four-momentum vector has components $P_t = m/[1-v^2]^{1/2} = m/[1-16/25]^{1/2} = m/[9/25]^{1/2} = 5m/3$, $P_x = +p = Ev = 4m/3$, $P_y = 0$, and $P_z = 0$. The law of conservation of four-momentum therefore implies that:

$$\begin{bmatrix} M \\ 0 \\ 0 \\ 0 \end{bmatrix} = \begin{bmatrix} E_L \\ -E_L \\ 0 \\ 0 \end{bmatrix} + \begin{bmatrix} \frac{5}{3}m \\ +\frac{4}{3}m \\ 0 \\ 0 \end{bmatrix} \Rightarrow \begin{matrix} M = E_L + \frac{5}{3}m \\ E_L = \frac{4}{3}m \\ 0 = 0 \\ 0 = 0 \end{matrix} \qquad \text{(R10.13)}$$

The bottom two equations don't tell us much, but the top two represent two equations in the unknowns m and E_L. Plugging the second into the first, we get

$$M = \tfrac{4}{3}m + \tfrac{5}{3}m = \tfrac{9}{3}m = 3m \quad \Rightarrow \quad m = \tfrac{1}{3}M = 30,000 \text{ kg} \quad \text{(R10.14)}$$

So even this perfect rocket has to use 60,000 kg of matter-antimatter fuel to boost the remaining 30,000 kg to a speed of 0.8.

Exercise R10X.6: Solve this problem using an energy-momentum diagram. (*Hint*: Since we do not know the light-flash's energy, we do not know how long to draw its four-momentum vector. But we know that its slope has to be −1, and that the slope of the rocket's final four-momentum vector has to have slope +4/5. Where do these lines intersect on the diagram?)

R10.6 APPLICATIONS TO PARTICLE PHYSICS

Particle physics as the most important practical application of relativity

In spite of our imaginative talk in this book about relativistic trains, spaceships, spaceships, runners and so on, special relativity has few genuine practical applications other than in the realm of elementary (subatomic) particle physics. Elementary particles (such as electrons, protons, neutrons, and so on) are light enough so that common processes can give them relativistic speeds. Virtually all of the experimental tests of relativity theory involve elementary particles.

Appropriate units for doing particle physics

The kilogram is an inappropriately large unit of mass or energy when one deals with elementary particles. Elementary particle physicists more commonly express the mass, energy, and momentum of such particles in terms of the energy unit of **electronvolts**, where 1 eV is the energy an electron gains by going through a one-volt battery. In terms of more common units,

$$1 \text{ eV} = 1.602 \times 10^{-19} \text{ J} = 1.782 \times 10^{-36} \text{ kg} \qquad (R10.15)$$

So, for example, an electron (whose mass is 0.511 MeV) moving at a speed of 4/5 has an energy $E = m/[1 - v^2]^{1/2} = \frac{5}{3}m = 0.852$ MeV, a kinetic energy of $K = E - m = 0.341$ MeV, and a relativistic momentum of $p = Ev = 0.682$ MeV.

The following is an example of how conservation of four-momentum can be applied to a very real problem in subatomic physics.

EXAMPLE R10.4:
Kaon Decay

Problem: The most stable version of the subatomic particle called the K^0 meson or *kaon* (which has a mass $M = 498$ MeV) decays with a half-life of about 36 ns to two identical π^0 mesons or *pions* (which have a mass $m = 135$ MeV). If the original kaon is at rest, what are the speeds of the pions after the decay?

Solution Let us number the pions 1 and 2, and choose the orientation of our reference frame so that the first pion moves in the $+x$ direction. Conservation of four-momentum then implies that

$$\begin{array}{c} \text{kaon four-} \\ \text{momentum} \end{array} = \begin{bmatrix} M \\ 0 \\ 0 \\ 0 \end{bmatrix} = \begin{bmatrix} E_1 \\ +p_1 \\ 0 \\ 0 \end{bmatrix} + \begin{bmatrix} E_2 \\ P_{2x} \\ P_{2y} \\ P_{2z} \end{bmatrix} = \begin{array}{c} \text{sum of pion} \\ \text{four-momenta} \end{array} \qquad (R10.16)$$

(Note that since the kaon is at rest, its spatial four-momentum components are zero and its energy is just its rest energy, which is its mass.) The bottom two lines of this equation tell us that $P_{2y} = P_{2z} = 0$, meaning that the second pion moves along the x axis. The second line tells us that $P_{2x} = -p_1$, which says that the second pion moves in the $-x$ direction with the same *magnitude* of relativistic momentum as the first: $p_2 = |P_{2x}| = p_1$. Since the pions have the same mass m, this means that the relativistic *energies* of the two pions are the same:

$$E_2 = \sqrt{m^2 + p_2^2} = \sqrt{m^2 + p_1^2} = E_1 \qquad (R10.17)$$

where the first step here follows from $m^2 = E^2 - p^2$ (equation R9.29). The first line of equation R10.16 then tells us that $M = 2E_1$ or $E_1 = \frac{1}{2}M = 249$ MeV. If we plug this into $m^2 = E^2 - p^2$, we can solve for p_1:

$$p_1 = \sqrt{E_1^2 - m^2} = \sqrt{(249 \text{ MeV})^2 - (135 \text{ MeV})^2} = 209 \text{ MeV} \qquad (R10.18)$$

Finally, we can find the pion speed using equation R9.30:

$$v_1 = \frac{p_1}{E_1} = \frac{209 \text{ MeV}}{249 \text{ MeV}} = 0.839, \qquad v_2 = \frac{p_2}{E_2} = \frac{p_1}{E_1} = v_1 \qquad (R10.19)$$

(Note that this process "converts" kaon mass-energy to pion kinetic energy.)

R10.7 PARTING COMMENTS

The principle of relativity is rich with fascinating implications, and this book has touched on just the most basic of these implications. I'd like to close with some suggestions as to where an interested reader can go from here.

An excellent and somewhat more advanced and detailed exploration of special relativity is E. F. Taylor and J. A. Wheeler's *Spacetime Physics*, 2/e, New York: Freeman, 1992. The *American Journal of Physics* (which is found in many college libraries and is written primarily for college physics professors) is a great place to look for articles on current issues in relativity theory. Look under "special relativity" in any one of the ten-year indexes of recent volumes for a list of such articles. (Many of these articles are accessible to students.)

The next step beyond special relativity is *general* relativity. A book that one can use when beginning a study of general relativity is G. F. R. Ellis and R. M. Williams, *Flat and Curved Spacetimes*, New York: Oxford, 1985.

More delights await: I encourage everyone to continue the exploration!

SUMMARY

I. ENERGY-MOMENTUM DIAGRAMS
   A. What is an energy-momentum diagram?
      1. It represents a particle's four-momentum as an arrow on a diagram whose vertical and horizontal components are E and P_x respectively
      2. The arrow's slope on the diagram is then $1/v_x$ (means the arrow is parallel to particle's worldline on a spacetime diagram)
      3. We use a "flag" on the arrow to indicate its four-magnitude (mass)
   B. See Figure R10.5 for a summary of how to read such a diagram

II. SOLVING CONSERVATION OF FOUR-MOMENTUM PROBLEMS
   A. Example of colliding rocks
   B. One can solve such problems either algebraically or with diagrams
      1. Diagrams are usually not really any easier to use than algebra
      2. They do offer a visual approach that can be a good check on algebra

III. THE MASS OF A SYSTEM OF PARTICLES
   A. Implications of mass defined as four-magnitude of four-momentum
      1. The mass of a particle or system is *frame-independent*
      2. However, mass is *not additive*: the mass of a system of particles is generally *greater* than the sum of the masses of the particles!
      3. This is because mass of a system whose center of mass is at rest is actually the sum of the *energies* of the particles in the system
   B. Conclusions drawn from an example of colliding putty balls of mass m
      1. Mass of final combined putty-ball is $M > 2m$ (so mass is created?)
      2. But *system* (as a whole) has *same* mass M even before collision!
   C. This extra mass does not reside anywhere that we can locate: it is rather a property of the system as a whole. (This is just something we have to accept about our definition of mass!)

IV. THE FOUR-MOMENTUM OF LIGHT
   A. A "flash" of light is the rough equivalent of a particle
   B. A light-flash carries energy, and so must have a four-momentum vector
   C. The four-momentum arrow must be parallel to the light's worldline, so:
      1. The slope of four-momentum arrow should be ± 1
      2. This means that $p = \pm E$
      3. This in turn means that the flash's mass $m = [E^2 - p^2]^{1/2} = 0$!
   D. Example: a matter-antimatter rocket

V. APPLICATIONS TO PARTICLE PHYSICS
   A. Most real applications and tests of relativity involve particle physics
   B. Particle physicists use the *electronvolt* as the unit of mass, energy and momentum (1 eV = 1.602×10^{-19} J = 1.782×10^{-36} kg).
   C. Example: Kaon decay

GLOSSARY

energy-momentum diagram: a diagram for illustrating four-momentum vectors of particles moving in one spatial dimension. A particle's four-momentum vector is represented on such a diagram as an arrow whose projection on the horizontal axis is the x component of the particle's four-momentum and whose projection on the vertical axis is the particle's relativistic energy. An energy-momentum diagram is to relativistic dynamics what a spacetime diagram is to relativistic kinematics.

electronvolt (eV): a unit of energy, equivalent to the energy gained by one electron as it moves through a one-volt battery. Particle physicists typically use the electronvolt in place of the kilogram for mass energy, and momentum, since the kilogram is an inappropriately large unit. (In the SR unit system, we can use any unit that we like for mass, energy, and momentum, as long as we use the *same* unit for all.) Conversion factors to other units are: 1 eV = 1.602×10^{-19} J = 1.782×10^{-36} kg.

TWO-MINUTE PROBLEMS

R10T.1 The length of the arrow representing an object's four-momentum on a energy-momentum diagram is proportional to the object's speed (T or F).

R10T.2 The slope of the arrow representing an object's four-momentum on an energy-momentum diagram is inversely proportional to the object's speed (T or F).

R10T.3 Which of the following processes is consistent with the law of conservation of four-momentum? (Answer C if it is consistent with the law; F if it violates it.)

(a) A particle moving eastward collides with and sticks to an identical particle at rest. The resulting single particle remains at rest but is more massive than the sum of the original particles' masses.

(b) Two identical particles with equal speeds, one moving east and one moving west, collide. After the collision, the same particles move north and south respectively with the same speeds that they had originally.

(c) Two electrons with equal speeds, one moving east and one moving west, collide. After the collision, the electrons move north and south with smaller speeds than they had originally. Nothing else is emitted.

(d) A spaceship of mass $2m$ originally at rest burns some matter-antimatter fuel until the ship's mass is m. The

light energy ejected from the ship in this process has total energy m as well.

(e) A particle of mass $2m$ at rest decays to two identical particles each of mass m that move in opposite directions away from the decay position at a speed 0.5.

R10T.4 A particle with a mass of 3.0 kg is accelerated to a speed of 0.80. The mass of this particle is now
A. greater than 3.0 kg   C. still 3.0 kg
B. less than 3.0 kg

R10T.5 A sealed cup of water is placed in a microwave oven. The water absorbs microwave energy, which causes its atoms to vibrate more vigorously, making the water warmer. In this process, the mass of the water in the cup
A. increases   B. decreases   C. does not change

R10T.6 In example R10.5.1, the spaceship engines convert 60,000 kg of matter-antimatter fuel into massless light. The mass of the total system (empty spaceship plus flash of light, considered as a unit) thus decreases (T or F).

R10T.7 In example R10.6.1, a kaon (whose mass is 498 MeV) decays to two pions (each with a mass of 135 MeV). Mass is being converted to energy in this process (T or F). The total mass of the system (considered as a whole) decreases in this process (T or F).

HOMEWORK PROBLEMS

BASIC SKILLS

R10B.1 Draw an energy-momentum diagram for an object with a mass of 12 kg moving in the $+x$ direction at a speed of 0.80. Estimate its kinetic energy from the graph.

R10B.2 Draw an energy-momentum diagram for an object with a mass of 5 kg moving in the $-x$ direction at a speed of 0.60. Estimate its kinetic energy from the graph.

R10B.3 A particle of mass m at rest decays into two identical particles, each with mass $\frac{1}{3}m$. Conservation of spatial momentum means that the product particles have to move off in opposite directions with the same speed. What is the kinetic energy of each particle?

R10B.4 A flash of light moves in the $+x$ direction. The flash has a total energy of 2.0×10^{-18} kg. What is this in joules? What is the x component of the flash's four-momentum vector (in kg)? What is this in kg·m/s?

R10B.5 Two balls of putty, each of mass m, move in opposite directions toward each other with speeds of 0.95. The balls stick together, forming a single motionless ball

of putty at rest. What is the mass of this ball of putty? (Express your answer as a multiple of m.)

R10B.6 A ball of putty with mass m moves in the $+x$ direction with speed $v = 4/5$. It hits another ball of putty of mass m at rest. The balls stick together after the collision, forming a single ball. What is the x component of this final ball's four-momentum? What is its relativistic energy? (Express both as multiples of m.) What is its x-velocity?

R10B.7 A spaceship with a mass m originally at rest burns matter-antimatter fuel, ejecting light energy in the $-x$ direction until the total energy of the light that it has emitted is $E_L = \frac{1}{3}m$. What is the total relativistic energy of the partially empty spaceship now? What is the x component of its four-momentum? (Express both answers as fractions of m.) What is the ship's final speed?

SYNTHETIC

R10S.1 A particle of mass m decays into two identical particles that move in opposite directions, each with a speed of 12/13. What is the mass of each of the product particles (expressed as a fraction of m)?

R10S.2 An object with a mass m sits at rest. A light-flash moving in the $+x$ direction with a total energy of $2m$ hits this object and is completely absorbed. What is the mass and the x-velocity of the object afterwards? *Solve this problem both algebraically and graphically.*

R10S.3 An object with mass $m_1 = 8$ kg traveling with an x-velocity of $v_{1x} = 15/17$ collides with an object with mass $m_2 = 12$ kg traveling with an x-velocity of $v_{2x} = -5/13$. After the collision, the 8-kg object is measured to have an x-velocity of $v_{3x} = -3/5$. **(a)** Find the relativistic energy and momentum of the other object, **(b)** find its x-velocity, and **(c)** show that it has the same mass as it started with. *Solve this problem both algebraically and graphically.*

R10S.4 A spaceship with rest mass m_0 is traveling with an x-velocity $v_{0x} = +4/5$ in the frame of the earth. It collides with a photon torpedo (an intense burst of light) moving in the $-x$ direction relative to the earth. Assume that the ship's shields totally absorb the photon torpedo.

(a) The oncoming torpedo is measured by terrified observers on the ship to have an energy of $0.75\, m_0$. What is the energy of the photon torpedo in the frame of the earth? [*Hint:* How do the components of four-momentum transform when we go from one inertial frame to another?]

(b) Use conservation of four-momentum to determine the final x–velocity (in the earth frame) and mass (in terms of m_0) of the damaged ship after it absorbs the torpedo. *Solve this part of the problem both graphically and algebraically.*

R10S.5 A spaceship of mass M is traveling through an uncharted region of deep space. Suddenly its sensors detect a black hole dead ahead. In a desperate attempt to stop the spaceship, the pilot fires the forward matter-antimatter engines. These engines convert the mass-energy of matter-antimatter fuel entirely into light, which is emitted in a tight beam in the direction of the ship's motion. If the spaceship's initial speed toward the black hole is $v = 4/5$, what fraction of its mass M must be converted into energy to bring the spaceship to rest with respect to the black hole? *Solve this problem both graphically and algebraically.* [*Hint:* Treat the emitted light as one big flash of light.]

R10S.6 *Traveling to the stars.* As discussed in section R10.6, the most efficient possible rocket engine would take matter and antimatter fuel, combine them in a controlled way, and focus the resulting photons into a tight beam traveling away from the stern of the spaceship. Imagine that you want to design a spaceship using such an engine that can boost a payload of mass $m = 25$ metric tons (25,000 kg) to a final cruising speed of 0.95. What does the ship's mass M at launch have to be? [*Hint:* The ship can essentially be considered to be a particle of mass M at rest that decays into a big flash of light and a smaller particle (the payload) of known mass m traveling at a known speed v. Use conservation of four-momentum to determine M.]

R10S.7 Consider a freely floating mirror placed initially at rest in a laser beam. Imagine the mirror to be oriented directly facing the beam so that it reflects the beam back the way it came. Each flash of light that rebounds from the mirror has undergone a change in its momentum as a result of the change in the direction of its velocity. This means that the mirror must recoil a bit from each rebound to conserve four-momentum. Use conservation of the spatial components of four-momentum to estimate how much power the laser beam would have to have to accelerate a perfect 1-g mirror at a rate of 1 cm/s². (You can assume that the mirror's momentum is essentially newtonian.) Express your final answer in watts (1 W = 1 J/s).

R10S.8 A π^- pion (mass 140 MeV) normally decays to a μ^- muon (mass 106 MeV) and a neutrino. The neutrino is a particle that is so light you can treat its mass as being essentially zero (like a flash of light). If the pion is at rest, find the speed of the emitted muon.

R10S.9 Quantum physics tells us that in certain circumstances, light can be considered a stream of massless particles called *photons*. Imagine that a photon with energy E_0 is traveling in the $+x$ direction and hits an electron of mass m at rest. The photon scatters from the electron and travels in the $-x$ direction after the collision. Find a formula for the final energy of the photon E in terms of E_0 and m. (Physicists call this process *Compton scattering*: the fact that the formula correctly describes the behavior of light scattering from electrons is one of the most important pieces of evidence supporting the photon model of light.)

RICH-CONTEXT

R10R.1 *Traveling to the stars II.* (It is recommended, though not essential, that you do problem R10S.6 first.) Consider the rocket design discussed in problem R10S.6. [The answer to that problem is $M = 6.25m$.]

(a) Assume that you can find astronauts who are willing to travel for up to 50 years (as measured by their watches) on a round trip to the stars. About how many light-years could the ship go out and return (assuming that the ship spends a negligible time accelerating). Is this very far compared to the galaxy as a whole?

(b) The takeoff mass calculated in Problem R10S.6 only included sufficient fuel to boost the payload to the cruising speed. For a complete round trip, one would have to carry enough fuel to boost the payload to the cruising speed, decelerate it to rest at the destination, boost it to cruising speed again for the return trip home, and decelerate it upon reaching earth. How much fuel is required for a complete round trip? Express your answer as a multiple of the payload mass m. [*Hint:* The answer is *not* four times the fuel required to boost the payload alone to the cruising speed!]

(c) Comment on the practicality of visiting the distant stars using a rocket which must carry its own fuel.

R10R.2 One method for getting around the difficulties discussed in problems R10S.6 and R10R.1 is to use light pressure to accelerate a payload (see problem R10S.7). Imagine that you attach a perfect mirror to the back of your payload, and then accelerate the payload by bouncing a powerful laser beam off the mirror. (This has the big advantage that you don't have to carry the mass of the fuel or the rocket engine!) The lasers producing the beam could be massive things powered by solar energy, so neither the size, mass, nor power of these driving lasers is a limitation (at least in principle). Imagine that you wish to accelerate a 2000-kg scientific payload outward from the earth's orbit around the sun at a rate of 1 m/s² (at this rate, it would take about a year to reach 10% of the speed of light). Assume that the payload has been already delivered at rest to a point far enough from the earth so that the earth's gravity is negligible (but *don't* ignore the gravity of the sun). How many watts of light would the driving laser have to produce?

ADVANCED

R10A.1 Rework the Compton scattering problem (problem R10S.9) to find the energy of the scattered photon if its trajectory after scattering from the electron makes an angle of θ with its original direction. (Not easy!)

ANSWERS TO EXERCISES

R10X.1 Doing the calculation, we find that

$$\tfrac{1}{2}m\left(\tfrac{3}{5}\right)^2 = \frac{9m}{50} = 0.18m < 0.25m \qquad (R10.20)$$

R10X.2 According to equation R9.23,

$$E = \frac{m}{\sqrt{1-v^2}} = \frac{1.0 \text{ kg}}{\sqrt{1-(4/5)^2}} = \frac{5}{3} \text{ kg} = 1.67 \text{ kg} \qquad (R10.21)$$

So to draw the arrow representing the object's four-momentum, we draw an arrow with a slope of $1/v = 5/4$ and with a vertical projection equal to 1.67 kg. The resulting energy-momentum diagram looks like this:

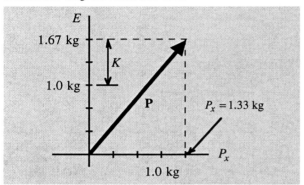

From this, we can see that $P_x = 1.33$ kg and $K = 0.67$ kg.

R10X.3 The system's total newtonian x-momentum *before* the collision is:

$$m_1 v_{1x} + m_2 v_{2x} = (12 \text{ kg}) \cdot \tfrac{4}{5} + (28 \text{ kg}) \cdot 0 = \tfrac{48}{5} \text{ kg} \qquad (R10.22)$$

After the collision, this quantity is

$$m_1 v_{3x} + m_2 v_{4x} = (12 \text{ kg})\left(-\tfrac{5}{13}\right) + (28 \text{ kg}) \cdot \tfrac{3}{5}$$

$$= -\frac{60}{13} \text{ kg} + \frac{84}{5} \text{ kg} = \frac{-300+1092}{65} \text{ kg}$$

$$= \frac{792}{65} \text{ kg} = \frac{60.92}{5} \text{ kg} \neq \frac{48}{5} \text{ kg} \qquad (R10.23)$$

The point is that conservation of four-momentum is different than conservation of newtonian momentum.

R10X.4 Let the Home Frame be the frame where the collision looks as shown in Figure R10.8. The Other Frame in question then moves relative to the Home Frame in the $+x$ direction at $\beta = 3/5$. According to equation R8.14a, then,

$$v'_{2x} = \frac{v_{2x} - \beta}{1 - \beta v_{2x}} = \frac{-3/5 - 3/5}{1 - (3/5)(-3/5)} = \frac{-6/5}{34/25}$$

$$= -\frac{30}{34} = -\frac{15}{17} \qquad (R10.24)$$

This means that

$$E'_2 = \frac{m}{\sqrt{1-v'^2_{2x}}} = \frac{m}{\sqrt{1-(-15/17)^2}} = \frac{m}{\sqrt{1-225/269}}$$

$$= \frac{m}{\sqrt{64/269}} = \frac{17}{8}m \qquad (R10.25)$$

$$P'_{2x} = E'_2 v'_{2x} = \left(\frac{17}{8}m\right)\left(-\frac{15}{17}\right) = -\frac{15}{8}m \qquad (R10.26)$$

The first ball is at rest in this frame, so $E'_1 = m$ and $P'_{1x} = 0$. The system's total four-momentum components thus are:

$$E'_T = E'_1 + E'_2 = m + \frac{17}{8}m = \frac{25}{8}m \qquad (R10.27a)$$

$$P'_{Tx} = P'_{1x} + P'_{2x} = 0 + \frac{15}{8}m = \frac{15}{8}m \qquad (R10.27b)$$

and its total mass is:

$$M' = \sqrt{E'^2_T - P'^2_{Tx}} = \frac{m}{8}\sqrt{25^2 - 15^2} = \frac{m}{8}\sqrt{625 - 225}$$

$$= \frac{m}{8}\sqrt{400} = \frac{20}{8}m = \frac{10}{4}m \qquad (R10.28)$$

Since $m = 4$ kg, $M' = 10$ kg $= M$, as claimed.

R10X.5 Converting the value of K given to kg, we get:

$$6.2 \times 10^{-21} \cancel{J}\left(\frac{1 \text{ kg} \cdot \cancel{m^2} \cancel{/s^2}}{1 \cancel{J}}\right)\left(\frac{1 \cancel{s}}{3.0 \times 10^8 \cancel{m}}\right)^2$$

$$= 6.9 \times 10^{-38} \text{ kg} \qquad (R10.29)$$

The total mass (that is, rest energy) of a system at rest is the sum of the energies of its constituent particles. If there are N molecules in the gas, the ratio of the gas's total mass to the sum of the masses of the molecules is:

$$\frac{N \cdot E}{N \cdot m} = \frac{N(m+K)}{N(m)} = 1 + \frac{K}{m} = 1 + \frac{6.9 \times 10^{-38}}{2.4 \times 10^{-26}}$$

$$= 1 + 2.9 \times 10^{-12} \qquad (R10.30)$$

So in this case, the system's mass is different than the sum of the masses of the molecules by only about 3 parts in a trillion. In nonrelativistic situations like this one, the idea that mass is additive (as we have always assumed before) is an excellent approximation.

R10X.6 Since we don't know either the light-flash's or the ship's final relativistic energy, we cannot immediately draw their four-momentum vectors on the diagram. But we do know that the slopes of these vectors is –1 and 4/5 respectively, and that the two vectors have to add up to the ship's original four-momentum vector, which (since the ship is initially at rest) is vertical. So sketch a line with slope 4/5 from the origin, and another with slope –1 down from the tip of the ship's original four-momentum vector, as shown in Figure R10.12a. Since the flash and ship's final vectors have to add to the ship's original four-momentum, the vectors have to lie on these lines and stretch to their intersection, as shown in Figure R10.12b. From the diagram, then, we can see that E and p for the ship after the engines fire are about $\tfrac{5}{9}M$ and $\tfrac{4}{9}M$ respectively and using $m = [E^2 - p^2]^{1/2}$, one can show that $m = \tfrac{1}{3}M$.

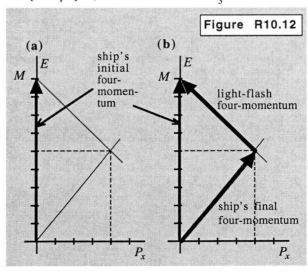

Figure R10.12

CONVERSION OF EQUATIONS TO SI UNITS

If you can't beat 'em, join 'em.

Anonymous

RA.1   WHY USE THE SR UNIT SYSTEM?

The equations of special relativity are greatly simplified when one uses SR units to measure distance, as we have seen. But the purpose of using SR units is not merely to simplify a few equations: using such units also vividly draws one's attention to the connections special relativity makes between quantities that were previously considered to be fundamentally distinct. For example, special relativity teaches us that energy, momentum, and mass are in fact different aspects of the same basic quantity, the four-momentum. It is not merely *convenient* to measure the time component E, the spatial components P_x, P_y, P_z, and the magnitude m of this four-vector in the same units: it is fundamentally *appropriate* as well. Similarly, the basic metaphor of spacetime geometry that lies at the root of both special and general relativity is obscured if one insists on using different units to measure time and distance.

SR units make relativistic relationships clearer

Nonetheless, this choice of units does lead to complications when one tries to apply the ideas presented in this book to practical situations, since practicing physicists in their everyday work still use traditional units to describe quantities. It is important to be able to use the simple and beautiful equations in this book in situations where the quantities in question are expressed in traditional units. Fortunately, it is straightforward to convert equations appearing in this text to equivalent equations involving quantities measured in SI units. The purpose of this appendix is to describe an easy method for doing this.

... but SI units are used in most practical applications

RA.2 CONVERSION OF BASIC QUANTITIES

The SR unit system as defined in Chapter R2 differs from the SI unit system only in the substitution of the *second* for the *meter* as the basic unit of distance. Mass and time thus have the same units in the SI and SR systems and need no conversion. The most important quantities that are affected by the shift in units as one changes systems are *distance*, *velocity*, *energy*, and *momentum*. We also should consider what happens to values of universal constants like c and Planck's constant h (we will treat h as an example of how we can handle such constants in general).

How to convert basic quantities between the SR and SI unit systems

To help keep things straight in what follows, let me denote quantities measured in SR units by with an "(SR)" subscript; for example, the speed of an object in SR units will be written in this appendix as $v_{(SR)}$, the energy of an object in the SR unit of joules will be written $E_{(SR)}$ and so on. Quantities without this subscript will be assumed to be measured in SI units.

In Chapter R2, we saw that the general rule for converting SI quantities to SR quantities was to multiply the SI quantity by the appropriate power of c that leads to the correct SR dimensions. Let us apply this rule to the quantities of interest listed above.

Distance in the SR system is measured in seconds. Distance in the SI system is measured in meters. To convert an SI distance x to an SR distance x_{SR}, we must divide x by one factor of c (in meters per second): $x_{(SR)} = x/c$. Energy has units of kilograms in the SR system: it has units of joules $= \mathrm{kg \cdot m^2/s^2}$ in the SI system. To convert from E (in joules) to $E_{(SR)}$ (in kilograms), we must divide E by two powers of c: $E_{(SR)} = E/c^2$. Planck's constant h has units of energy· time. In the SR system, energy is measured in kilograms instead of

Table A.1: SI EQUIVALENTS FOR SR QUANTITIES

Quantity	SR Symbol	SI equivalent
Time coordinate	$t_{(SR)}$	t
Spatial coordinate	$x_{(SR)}$	x/c
Speed (of an object)	$v_{(SR)}$	v/c
Speed (of a reference frame)	$\beta_{(SR)}$	β/c
Mass	$m_{(SR)}$	m
Momentum	$p_{(SR)}$	p/c
Energy	$E_{(SR)}$	E/c^2
Speed of light	1	c
Planck's constant	$h_{(SR)}$	h/c^2

joules, so again we have to divide the SI version of Planck's constant by two powers of c to get the correct SR units: that is, $h_{(SR)} = h/c^2$. Conversion equations involving velocity and momentum can be derived in a similar manner. The results are summarized in Table A.1.

RA.3 CONVERTING SR UNIT EQUATIONS TO SI UNIT EQUATIONS

To convert equations: take SR equation, substitute SI quantities from Table A.1

The trick for converting equations from the SR to the SI system is now very simple: you simply replace the SR quantities in an equation by the SI equivalents given in Table A.1. For example, consider the metric equation:

$$\Delta s^2_{(SR)} = \Delta t^2_{(SR)} - \Delta x^2_{(SR)} - \Delta y^2_{(SR)} - \Delta z^2_{(SR)} \tag{RA.1}$$

Both $\Delta s_{(SR)}$ and $\Delta t_{(SR)}$ have time units, and so have the same value in both systems. But Δx, Δy, Δz are measured in distance units in the SI system, and therefore $\Delta x_{(SR)} = \Delta x/c$, $\Delta y_{(SR)} = \Delta y/c$, and $\Delta z_{(SR)} = \Delta z/c$. The metric equation in SI units is thus:

$$\Delta s^2 = \Delta t^2 - \left(\frac{\Delta x}{c}\right)^2 - \left(\frac{\Delta y}{c}\right)^2 - \left(\frac{\Delta z}{c}\right)^2 \tag{RA.2}$$

As another example, in Unit Q we will study equations that give the energy of a light photon in terms of the frequency f or the wavelength λ of the light involved. In SI units, this equation is: $E_{(SR)} = h_{(SR)}f_{(SR)} = h_{(SR)}/\lambda_{(SR)}$. Both energy and Planck's constant gain a factor of c^{-2} when switching from SR to SI units, so this factor divides out in these equations above. The wavelength λ, on the other hand, has units of meters in the SI system but seconds in the SR system, so $\lambda_{(SR)} = \lambda/c$. The second equation thus becomes $E = hc/\lambda$ in SI units.

In some cases, equations can be made prettier by multiplying through by c^n

Table A.2 lists some of the important equations in the text and their SI equivalents. In many of the cases described there, the SI equations are simply found by substituting the SI-unit equivalents from Table A.1 for the SR-unit quantities in the equation from the text. However, in many cases, the SI-unit equations have been further simplified by dividing out common factors of c. For example, the SR-unit version of the equation giving the magnitude of the relativistic momentum of a particle in terms of its speed reads:

$$p_{(SR)} = \frac{m_{(SR)}v_{(SR)}}{\sqrt{1-[v_{(SR)}]^2}} \tag{RA.3}$$

Table A.2: SOME IMPORTANT EQUATIONS AND THEIR SI EQUIVALENTS

Equation	SR Version	SI equivalent
Metric	$\Delta s^2 = \Delta t^2 - \Delta x^2 - \Delta y^2 - \Delta z^2$	$\Delta s^2 = \Delta t^2 - \dfrac{\Delta x^2 + \Delta y^2 + \Delta z^2}{c^2}$
Proper Time	$d\tau = dt\sqrt{1-v^2}$	$d\tau = dt\sqrt{1-(v/c)^2}$
Lorentz transformations (*t* and *x*)	$\gamma \equiv 1/\sqrt{1-\beta^2}$ $t' = \gamma(t - \beta x)$ $x' = \gamma(-\beta t + x)$	$\gamma \equiv 1/\sqrt{1-(\beta/c)^2}$ $t' = \gamma(t - \beta x/c^2)$ $x' = \gamma(-\beta t + x)$
Lorentz contraction	$L = L_R\sqrt{1-v^2}$	$L = L_R\sqrt{1-(v/c)^2}$
Transformation for *x*-velocity	$v'_x = \dfrac{v_x - \beta}{1 - \beta v_x}$	$v'_x = \dfrac{v_x - \beta}{1 - \beta v_x/c^2}$
Energy in terms of speed	$E = \dfrac{m}{\sqrt{1-v^2}}$	$E = \dfrac{mc^2}{\sqrt{1-(v/c)^2}}$
Relativistic momentum	$p = \dfrac{mv}{\sqrt{1-v^2}}$	$p = \dfrac{mv}{\sqrt{1-(v/c)^2}}$
Mass in terms of *E, p*	$m^2 = E^2 - p^2$	$(mc^2)^2 = E^2 - (pc)^2$
Speed in terms of *E, p*	$v = \dfrac{p}{E}$	$\dfrac{v}{c} = \dfrac{pc}{E}$
Photon energy in terms of λ	$E = hf = \dfrac{h}{\lambda}$	$E = hf = \dfrac{hc}{\lambda}$

If we simply perform the substitutions called for in Table A.1, we get:

$$\frac{p}{c} = \frac{m(v/c)}{\sqrt{1-[v_{(SR)}]^2}} \qquad\qquad \text{(RA.4)}$$

The equation can be made prettier, however, by multiplying through by *c*:

$$p = \frac{mv}{\sqrt{1-(v/c)^2}} \qquad\qquad \text{(RA.5)}$$

This is the simplified equation given in Table A.2. Many of the equations in the right-hand column of the table have been simplified in this manner.

RA.4 THE MODIFIED SR SYSTEM

Most of the practical applications of special relativity are in nuclear and particle physics. Physicists in these fields typically focus on *energy* as the most important dynamic quantity, they usually modify the SR system by measuring energies, momenta, and masses in *energy* units (typically electronvolts) instead of the announced standard *mass* unit of the kilogram (see section R10.6). Let us call a unit system where four-momentum quantities are measured in units of energy the *modified SR system*. Note that in the SR equations dealing with four-momentum quantities (that is, the last five equations in Table A.2), it doesn't

Modified SR system uses energy units for *E, p*, and *m* instead of mass units.

really matter what units one uses to express the quantities m, p, and E as long as one uses the *same* units for these quantities. Note that mc^2, pc, and E all have SI units of energy, and thus are the quantities that most directly correspond to the quantities m, p, and E in the *modified* SR system.

In regard to the last equation on the table, if you use energy units instead of mass units to express quantities related to four-momentum, you should note that Planck's constant h (which has units of energy·time in both the SI system and the *modified* SR system) has the same *value* in both systems: $h_{(SR)} = h$, instead of the $h_{(SR)} = h/c^2$ in the unmodified SR system. Other constants involving mass or energy will also (of course) be different in the modified and unmodified SR systems.

Planck's constant is the same in the modified SR and SI unit systems

RA.5 EXERCISES FOR PRACTICE

Exercise RAX.1: Check that $p_{(SR)} = p/c$, as claimed in Table A.1.

Exercise RAX.2: Convert the equation describing the relativistic kinetic energy of a particle (equation R9.36 in the text) to its equivalent in SI units.

Exercise RAX.3: The spacetime separation $\Delta\sigma$ between two events is given by the equation:

$$\Delta\sigma^2_{(SR)} = \Delta d^2_{(SR)} - \Delta t^2_{(SR)} \tag{RA.5}$$

Since $\Delta\sigma$ is actually directly measured using a measuring stick as opposed to a clock, it would make sense to express its value in meters instead of seconds if one is going to use the SI unit system. With this in mind, what would be the equivalent of this equation expressed in terms of SI units?

Exercise RAX.4: What are the units of the universal gravitational constant $G_{(SR)}$ in the SR unit system? [*Hint*: The SI units of G can be inferred from Newton's law of universal gravitation: $F_g = Gm_1m_2/r^2$.] Derive an equation expressing $G_{(SR)}$ in terms of G in SI units.

THE RELATIVISTIC DOPPLER EFFECT

RB.1 INTRODUCTION TO THE DOPPLER EFFECT

An important application of the metric equation is the computation of the shift in the wavelength of light emitted by a relativistic moving source. You may already know that light emitted by a source moving with respect to an observer is measured by that observer to be red-shifted toward longer wavelengths (if the object is departing from the observer) or blue-shifted toward shorter wavelengths (if the object is approaching the observer). This shift in wavelength is called a **Doppler shift** and the general effect the **Doppler effect** (after Christian Johann Doppler, the 19th-century physicist who first described the effect for light). This effect has numerous and important applications in astrophysics and biophysics (as well as many other fields), and forms the basis of such technologies as Doppler weather radars (that can detect and study tornadoes and other forms of severe weather) and the radar guns that police use to detect speeders.

Introduction to the concept of the Doppler effect

In this appendix, we will examine this effect in some detail using the tools and concepts we have developed through chapter R5. In section RB.2, we will use a simple model of the emission/detection process and a spacetime diagram to find a formula for the magnitude of the shift in wavelength. Section RB.3 looks at an example application, and section RB.4 explores the nonrelativistic limit of our formula. Finally, section RB.5 looks at the slightly different situation involved in Doppler-shift radar.

Overview of the appendix

(This appendix follows an approach to the Doppler shift formula suggested as an exercise by E. F. Taylor and J. A. Wheeler in *Spacetime Physics,* 2/e, San Francisco: Freeman, 1992, p. 82.)

RB.2 DERIVING THE DOPPLER SHIFT FORMULA

To simplify matters, let us consider a source that moves directly toward or away from the observer in question, and let us take the x axis of the observer's frame (the Home Frame) to coincide with the line connecting the source and the observer. Let us also assume that the observer is located at $x = 0$ in that frame.

Some basic assumptions

First consider a clock that emits brief flashes of light (we will generalize this to continuous light waves shortly). Let the event of the emission of any one flash be event A, and the emission of the next flash be event B. Since the clock is present at both events, it measures a proper time between these flashes. If the time between flashes happens also to be so short that the clock follows an essentially straight worldline between the events, then the relationship between the proper time $d\tau_{AB}$ measured in the emitting clock's frame and the coordinate time dt_{AB} measured in the observer's frame is given by equation R5.5:

A simplified model

$$d\tau_{AB} = \sqrt{1 - v^2}\, dt_{AB} = \sqrt{1 - v_x^2}\, dt_{AB} \qquad \text{(RB.1)}$$

where v is the emitting clock's speed as measured in the observer's frame. (The last step follows because if the emitting clock is moving directly toward or away from the observer, it is moving along the x axis, so $v = |v_x|$.) Therefore,

$$dt_{AB} = \frac{d\tau_{AB}}{\sqrt{1 - v_x^2}} \qquad \text{(RB.2)}$$

Implication of relativistic time dilation in this case

Now, dt_{AB} is the time our observer would measure between the *emission* of the flashes. But how much time dt_R passes between the observer's *reception* of

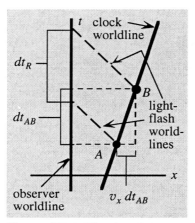

Figure RB.1: The time between the reception of the flashes dt_R is not the same as the coordinate time dt_{AB} between their emission because the light from flash event B has to travel an extra distance $v_x \, dt_{AB}$ to get back to the observer compared to the flash traveling from event A.

Different flashes take different times to return to the observer

The link to wavelength of a continuous light wave

The relativistic Doppler shift formula

those flashes? The times dt_{AB} and dt_R are not necessarily the same! Since both flashes travel at a speed of 1 back to the observer, the time (in the observer's frame) that it takes a flash to get from its emission event back to the observer is equal to the *distance* the emission event is from the origin (as measured in the observer's frame). If the emitting clock were at rest in the observer's frame, then these distances would be the same for both flashes, and therefore the time between reception would be the same as the time between emission: $dt_R = dt_{AB}$. But if the source is moving relative to the observer, then the two events will *not* happen at the same place in the observer's frame, meaning that the light-travel-times for the two flashes will not be the same, implying that $dt_R \neq dt_{AB}$.

Exactly how should we correct for this effect? We can answer this question fairly easily with the help of a spacetime diagram. Figure RB.1 shows the worldlines of the light flashes in question as they travel back to the observer from a clock that happens to be moving in the $+x$ direction. In the time dt_{AB} between the emission events (as measured in the observer's frame), the emitting clock moves a distance $v_x \, dt_{AB}$ away from the observer. This means (since the speed of light is 1 in the observer's frame) that it takes $v_x \, dt_{AB}$ *more* time for the second flash to make it back to the observer than it took the first flash. Therefore, the time between the observer's reception of the flashes is simply the time between their emission dt_{AB} (as measured in the observer's frame) plus the extra light-travel time $v_x \, dt_{AB}$ required for the second flash to reach the observer:

$$dt_R = dt_{AB} + v_x \, dt_{AB} = dt_{AB}(1+v_x) \qquad \text{(RB.3)}$$

Combining this with the result given by equation RB.2, we get:

$$dt_R = \frac{d\tau_{AB}}{\sqrt{1-v_x^2}}(1+v_x) = d\tau_{AB}\frac{\sqrt{1+v_x}\sqrt{1+v_x}}{\sqrt{1+v_x}\sqrt{1-v_x}} = d\tau_{AB}\sqrt{\frac{1+v_x}{1-v_x}} \qquad \text{(RB.4)}$$

Now what has all this to do with with the wavelength of a continuous beam of light waves? Consider! Each crest of a continuous light wave moves at the speed of light, just as a flash of light would. Therefore, for the purposes of this calculation, a wave crest is analogous to a light flash, and there is a direct analogy between a sequence of light flashes and a continuous series of light-wave crests. Therefore equation RB.4 should also apply to light *waves* if we interpret $d\tau_{AB}$ as the time between emission of light-wave crests in the emitter's frame and dt_R as the time between the reception of light-wave crests in the observer's frame.

Moreover, the **wavelength** λ of a light wave is defined to be the distance between successive crests in the wave. Since the crests also move at a speed of 1, this means that the distance λ between crests is equal to the time dt that it takes two successive crests to pass a given point in space (or emerge from the emitter): $\lambda = dt$. Plugging this into equation RB.4, we find that

$$\frac{\lambda_R}{\lambda_E} = \sqrt{\frac{1+v_x}{1-v_x}} \qquad \text{(RB.5)}$$

where λ_R is the wavelength of the light in the observer's frame, and λ_E is its wavelength as measured in the emitter's frame.

Equation RB.5 is the **relativistic Doppler shift formula**. Though Figure RB.1 (and the argument following) assumes that the emitter is moving *away from* the observer ($v_x > 0$), the formula also applies if the emitter is moving *toward* the observer ($v_x < 0$).

Exercise RBX.1: Verify the claim that RB.5 is correct even when $v_x < 0$.

Note also that if $v_x > 0$, then $\lambda_R > \lambda_E$, meaning that the received light has a longer (*red-shifted*) wavelength compared to its wavelength observed in the emitter frame. On the other hand, if $v_x < 0$, then $\lambda_R > \lambda_E$: the received light has a shorter (*blue-shifted*) wavelength than the wavelength observed in the emitter frame. This coincides with what you have probably heard before.

Exercise RBX.2: We have assumed in this derivation that the time between emission events (or successive crests of the light wave) is small compared with the time required for significant changes in the emitter's motion (so that it can be assumed to follow an approximately straight worldline during the interval in question). Is this approximation likely to be valid in the case of light waves (which have a wavelength ≈ 600 nm)? Justify your answer.

RB.3 APPLICATIONS IN ASTRONOMY

Since excited atoms emit light having a characteristic set of wavelengths (in their own frame), equation RB.5 is commonly used by astronomers to compute the radial velocity of astrophysical objects relative to the earth. This equation technically only applies to an emitter that we know is moving directly toward or away from an observer (a somewhat more complicated formula applies when the emitter has a tangential velocity as well), but it is a useful approximation in most cases (since tangential velocities are rarely large enough to matter much). The following is a typical example of such an astronomical application.

A standard application of this formula in astronomy

Problem: Light from excited atoms in a certain quasar is received by observers on the earth. The wavelength of a certain spectral line of this light is measured by those observers to be 1.12 times longer than it would be if the atoms were at rest in the laboratory (that is, the light has been *redshifted* by about 12 percent). What is the quasar's speed relative to the earth (assuming that it is moving directly away from the earth)?

An example calculation

Solution We are told that $\lambda_R / \lambda_E = 1.12$. Equation RB.5 then implies that

$$\frac{\lambda_R}{\lambda_E} = \sqrt{\frac{1+v_x}{1-v_x}} = 1.12 \qquad (RB.6)$$

To solve this for v_x, let us define $u \equiv \lambda_R / \lambda_E = 1.12$ and square both sides of equation RB.6. We get:

$$u^2 = \frac{1+v_x}{1-v_x} \quad \Rightarrow \quad (1-v_x)u^2 = 1+v_x$$

$$\Rightarrow \quad u^2 - u^2 v_x = 1 + v_x$$

$$\Rightarrow \quad u^2 - 1 = v_x + u^2 v_x = (u^2 + 1)v_x$$

$$\Rightarrow \quad v_x = \frac{u^2 - 1}{u^2 + 1} = \frac{(1.12)^2 - 1}{(1.12)^2 + 1} = 0.11 \qquad (RB.7)$$

The quasar's speed relative to the earth is thus 11 percent of the speed of light.

Exercise RBX.3: How should we correct equation RB.5 if the emitter does not move directly toward or away from the observer? Assume that we still choose the observer's x axis to go through the emitter's position at the time it emits the light flashes we observe. (*Hints:* Where did we assume in section RB.2 that the motion was along the x axis? Argue that the emitter's motion in the y or z direction during a small time interval will not significantly affect the distance between the emitter and the observer.)

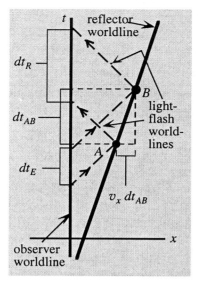

Figure RB.2: A spacetime diagram showing the relationship between the time dt_E between two light flashes omitted by an observer and the time dt_R between their reception after being reflected by a moving object at events A and B.

Doppler shift formula when the emitter and observer are in the same frame but waves are reflected from an moving object

RB.4 THE NONRELATIVISTIC LIMIT

The derivation of the relativistic Doppler-shift formula given by equation RB.5 actually combines two effects: (1) the relativistic distinction between the emitter's proper time and the observer's coordinate time between successive pulses (see equation RB.2), and (2) the delay of successive received pulses due to the changing separation between emitter and observer (see equation RB.3). The first effect arises only in the theory of relativity, the latter would apply even if time were absolute (as long as light moves with a speed of roughly 1 in the observer's frame). We might therefore suspect that when $v_x \ll 1$, we can ignore the relativistic effect in comparison to the other, so that equation RB.5 becomes

$$dt_R = (1+v_x)dt_{AB} \approx (1+v_x)d\tau_{AB} \quad \Rightarrow \quad \frac{\lambda_R}{\lambda_E} \approx 1+v_x \quad \text{(for } v_x \ll 1) \quad \text{(RB.8)}$$

Exercise RBX.4: Verify that equation RB.8 is indeed correct by using the binomial approximation to rewrite both the numerator and denominator of equation RB.5 in the limit that $v_x \ll 1$.

RB.5 DOPPLER RADAR

Doppler radar (used by weather observers and police) involves a somewhat different situation. In this case, the emitter and observer are typically in the same frame, and the emitted waves are reflected by an object moving relative to both. You can use the spacetime diagram shown in Figure RB.2 (and an argument analogous to that given in section RB.2) to show that in this situation:

$$\frac{\lambda_R}{\lambda_E} = \frac{1+v_x}{1-v_x} \quad \text{(RB.9)}$$

Exercise RBX.5: Verify this using Figure RB.2. [*Hint:* Note that all of the times shown on the diagram are coordinate times measured in the observer's frame. In this case, the time between events A and B measured by a clock traveling with the reflector is irrelevant.]

HOMEWORK PROBLEMS

BASIC SKILLS

RBB.1 A spaceship moves directly away from the earth at a speed of 0.5. By what factor is the spaceship's taillight redshifted?

RBB.2 The hydrogen fusion flare from an alien ship's engine is detected from earth. If the light emitted from the hydrogen atoms is observed to be blueshifted by 35 percent compared to normal, how rapidly is the ship approaching?

SYNTHETIC / RICH-CONTEXT

RBS.1 (Adapted from Taylor and Wheeler, *Spacetime Physics*, 2/e, p. 263-264.) A physicist brought to court for running a red light argues that the light *looked* green and thus must have been Doppler shifted. The judge changes the charge to speeding and fines the physicist a penny for every mile per hour the physicist was traveling over the speed limit of 45 mi/h. What was the fine (approximately)? [*Hints:* Red light has a wavelength of ≈ 650 nm; green light has a wavelength of ≈ 530 nm. 2.2 mi/h = 1.0 m/s.]

ANSWERS TO EXERCISES

RBX.1 If the emitter is approaching, the time between reception events is $dt_R = dt_{AB} - |v_x|dt_{AB} = dt_{AB} + v_x dt_{AB}$, where the last step follows because $v_x = -|v_x|$ here. The rest of the derivation follows as before.

RBX.2 If the distance between visible light crests is about 600 nm, the time (in SI units) between crest emission events will be the time that it takes the first crest to travel 600 nm from the emitter at the speed of light, or about $(6.0 \times 10^{-7}$ m$) / (3.0 \times 10^8$ m/s$) = 2.0 \times 10^{-15}$ s. It is hard to imagine something accelerating so violently that its motion would change much in such a time interval!

RBX.3 The corrected equation is

$$\frac{\lambda_R}{\lambda_E} = \frac{1+v_x}{\sqrt{1-v^2}} \quad \text{(RB.10)}$$

RBX.4 The binomial approximation tells us that:

$$(1+v_x)^{1/2} \approx 1 + \tfrac{1}{2}v_x \quad \text{and} \quad (1-v_x)^{-1/2} \approx 1 + \tfrac{1}{2}v_x \quad \text{(RB.11)}$$

in the limit that $v_x \ll 1$. Multiplying these factors together and dropping the v_x^2 term (which will be *very* small), we get equation RB.8.

RBX.5 Note that $dt_{AB} = dt_E + v_x dt_{AB}$. Combine this with equation RB.3 to get equation RB.9.

INDEX TO UNIT *R*